T0138655

Enhancing LAN Performance

Fourth Edition

OTHER AUERBACH PUBLICATIONS

The ABCs of IP Addressing
Gilbert Held
ISBN: 0-8493-1144-6

The ABCs of LDAP: How to Install, Run, and Administer LDAP Services
Reinhard Voglmaier
ISBN: 0-8493-1346-5

The ABCs of TCP/IP
Gilbert Held
ISBN: 0-8493-1463-1

Building an Information Security Awareness Program
Mark B. Desman
ISBN: 0-8493-0116-5

Building a Wireless Office
Gilbert Held
ISBN: 0-8493-1271-X

The Complete Book of Middleware
Judith Myerson
ISBN: 0-8493-1272-8

Computer Telephony Integration, 2nd Edition
William A. Yarberry, Jr.
ISBN: 0-8493-1438-0

Electronic Bill Presentment and Payment
Kornel Terplan
ISBN: 0-8493-1452-6

Information Security Architecture
Jan Killmeyer Tudor
ISBN: 0-8493-9988-2

Information Security Management Handbook, 5th Edition
Harold F. Tipton and Micki Krause, Editors
ISBN: 0-8493-1997-8

The Complete Project Management Office Handbook
Gerald M. Hill
ISBN: 0-8493-2173-5

ISO 9000:2000 for Software and Systems Providers
Robert Bamford and William Deibler, III
ISBN: 0-8493-2063-1

Information Technology for Manufacturing: Reducing Costs and Expanding Capabilities
Kevin Aki, John Clemons, and Mark Cubine
ISBN: 1-57444-359-3

Information Security Policies, Procedures, and Standards: Guidelines for Effective Information Security Management
Thomas R. Peltier
ISBN: 0-8493-1137-3

Information Security Risk Analysis
Thomas R. Peltier
ISBN: 0-8493-0880-1

Interpreting the CMMI: A Process Improvement Approach
Margaret Kulpa and Kurt Johnson
ISBN: 0-8493-1654-5

IS Management Handbook, 8th Edition
Carol V. Brown and Heikki Topi
ISBN: 0-8493-1595-6

Managing a Network Vulnerability Assessment
Thomas R. Peltier and Justin Peltier
ISBN: 0-8493-1270-1

A Practical Guide to Security Engineering and Information Assurance
Debra Herrmann
ISBN: 0-8493-1163-2

The Privacy Papers: Managing Technology and Consumers, Employee, and Legislative Action
Rebecca Herold
ISBN: 0-8493-1248-5

Securing and Controlling Cisco Routers
Peter T. Davis
ISBN: 0-8493-1290-6

Six Sigma Software Development
Christine B. Tayntor
ISBN: 0-8493-1193-4

Software Engineering Measurement
John Munson
ISBN: 0-8493-1502-6

A Technical Guide to IPSec Virtual Private Networks
James S. Tiller
ISBN: 0-8493-0876-3

Telecommunications Cost Management
Brian DiMarsico, Thomas Phelps IV, and William A. Yarberry, Jr.
ISBN: 0-8493-1101-2

AUERBACH PUBLICATIONS
www.auerbach-publications.com
To Order Call: 1-800-272-7737 • Fax: 1-800-374-3401
E-mail: orders@crcpress.com

Enhancing LAN Performance

Fourth Edition

Gilbert Held

AUERBACH PUBLICATIONS

A CRC Press Company

Boca Raton   London   New York   Washington, D.C.

Library of Congress Cataloging-in-Publication Data

Held, Gilbert, 1943–
    Enhancing LAN performance / Gilbert Held.—4th ed.
        p.   cm.
    Includes bibliographical references and index.
    ISBN 0-8493-1942-0 (alk. paper)
    1. Local area networks (Computer networks)—Evaluation. I. Title.

TK5105.7.H4383 2004
004.6′8—dc22
                                         2003063686
                                            CIP

Visit the Auerbach Publications Web site at www.auerbach-publications.com

© 2004 by CRC Press LLC
Auerbach is an imprint of CRC Press LLC

No claim to original U.S. Government works
International Standard Book Number 0-8493-1942-0
Library of Congress Card Number 2003063686
Printed in the United States of America 1 2 3 4 5 6 7 8 9 0
Printed on acid-free paper

Table of Contents

Preface

Local area network (LAN) performance at many organizations is a topic as frequently discussed as the weather. However, unlike the weather, for which our options of control are extremely limited, we have a significant ability to control the performance of LANs.

As I began to revise this book, I returned to my original outline several times to think about the issues I face as a network manager. Some of those issues include responsibility for establishing new LANs as well as expanding existing networks and providing the communications capability for users on different networks to communicate with one another or access a number of mainframe applications residing on different computers. As a network manager with a fixed budget, there are numerous economic-related problems I need to consider. For example, when interconnecting two LANs via a wide area network (WAN), I need to determine an optimum transmission line rate. If the line rate selected does not provide sufficient bandwidth, then user productivity will suffer. If the bandwidth exceeds what users require, my organization will be paying for wasted resources. Thus, selecting an appropriate line rate to interconnect geographically separated LANs represents both a technical and financial issue. Another common issue facing network managers and LAN administrators occurs when considering whether or not to use multiport devices or dual devices for reliability. In addition, network managers and LAN administrators commonly are tasked with estimating network traffic for networks they plan to install but for which no prior traffic estimate exists. Other frequently performed tasks include estimating the effect of network configuration changes on the performance of Ethernet and Token Ring networks and understanding how to design switch-based networks to prevent data traffic bottlenecks. These and other issues can be considered to represent a core set of operational issues you will want to answer to ensure that your networks not only meet the requirements of your user community but, in addition, are not overconfigured. Concerning the latter, as sure as the sun rises in the East, you will never hear an end user complain that network performance is too good. Thus, you will more than likely never be told that you overconfigured your network or transmission facilities used to interconnect networks, although doing so can result in a considerable expenditure of funds beyond those necessary. Once you realize this, you must also recognize that in an era of budgetary constraints, it is just as important not to oversize your network components and transmission facilities as it is not to undersize those components and transmission facilities.

In presenting various LAN performance issues, I have also attempted to provide you with the tools to answer those issues based upon your specific networking requirements. To accomplish this goal, mathematical models of different LAN performance issues are developed throughout this book — models that you can use to determine answers to your specific networking requirements. And because the execution of some models is tedious and time consuming, I also developed several QBASIC programs and Excel spreadsheet models that you can use to facilitate your computations.

Because a book must be finite in length, there are probably some issues I have overlooked or, due to space constraints, have not covered. If there is a particular issue you would like me to work on, please feel free to contact me and I will do my best to answer your questions. Perhaps your questions, as well as the answers to those questions, will result in their inclusion in a fifth edition of this book, which will allow future readers to gain from your experiences. As a professional author, I value your comments and encourage you to write me through my publisher or you can contact me directly via e-mail at gil_held@yahoo.com.

Acknowledgments

In several books I have alluded to the fact that the development of a book is a team effort, and this book is certainly no exception.

As the author, I am directly responsible for the contents of this book. However, the many processes involved from its acquisition through its production require the skills and efforts of many individuals. Thus, I would be remiss if I did not take the time to acknowledge those individuals who certainly contributed to the development and production of this book.

As an old-fashioned writer, I like to work with pen and paper and use my notebook computer for those really labor-intensive operations, such as developing programs whose execution saves hours or days of hand-held calculator effort. In addition, the use of pen and paper provides me with the ability to easily modify drawings, which is especially convenient when encountering turbulence at 30,000 feet or when the notebook "battery low" warning light illuminates. While it is easy for me to use pen and paper to develop a manuscript, it truly takes a special talent to turn that draft manuscript into a professional manuscript complete with camera-ready illustrations. Once again, I am indebted to Linda Hayes for her fine effort in preparing the manuscript for submission.

Once a manuscript is submitted for production, a burden is removed from the author and placed upon the publisher. Thus, I would be remiss if I did not acknowledge the fine effort of CRC Press in bringing this new edition into print. Concerning CRC Press, my hat is once more tipped in acknowledgment to Rich O'Hanleyof Auerbach Publications for backing another book written by me.

Last, but certainly not least, the time spent writing a book places a considerable burden upon family life. Thus, my gratitude to my wife Beverly, whose cooperation and understanding during the many evenings and weekends I worked on this book are truly appreciated.

Gilbert Held
Macon, Georgia

Chapter 1
LAN Performance Issues

This introductory chapter focuses attention on a core set of local area network (LAN) performance issues. In doing so, it discusses why such issues are important for inter- and intra-network communications in the form of questions that we will want to answer when planning or expanding a network. Although we leave it to future chapters in this book to answer questions raised in this chapter, our discussion of performance issues serves a dual purpose. First, it makes us aware of the many factors that affect the performance of individual networking devices, as well as the networks to which they are connected. Second, it makes us aware of the fact that performance can involve the trade-off of many operating characteristics. This means that in some instances the modification of the operating characteristics of a networking device to enhance its performance may require adjustments to other features of that device and other networking devices and transmission facilities. Thus, we note that LAN performance issues in many instances involve a detailed relationship between different network components, as well as the transmission facilities used to provide a connection between separate networks.

1.1 Network Basics

Readers of this book are presumed to have a degree of familiarity with the basic operation and utilization of Ethernet, Token Ring, and ATM networks. Thus, this book was written neither as an introductory text on local area networks nor on local area networking concepts. However, because Ethernet, Token Ring, and ATM network performance requires a degree of knowledge concerning the format of the frames and their composition, Chapter 2 in this book reviews both areas.

The remainder of this chapter reviews the material in succeeding chapters with respect to the performance issues they raise. Thus, Sections 1.2 through 1.13 in this chapter can be considered previews to Chapters 2 through 13, respectively.

1.2   Ethernet, Token Ring and ATM Frame and Cell Operations

Material in Chapter 2 is presented to provide readers with a review of LAN dataflow operations. The key to understanding many performance-related issues is a detailed knowledge of the frame and cell format used on different types of LANs — material that is presented in Chapter 2.

Chapter 2 focuses attention on the fields of Ethernet and Token Ring frames, to include a discussion of Fast and Gigabit Ethernet. This will provide us with information necessary to understand the relationship between the overhead of a frame and the length of its information field. Doing so will assist us in understanding the effect of the frame length upon the efficiency of transmission on different types of LANs. Once the preceding is accomplished, we turn our attention to ATM and examine the overhead of the ATM cell and its effect on the transmission efficiency of ATM-based networks. Thus, the primary focus of Chapter 2 is to provide readers with information that can be used in later chapters to answer many LAN performance-related questions. Answers to such questions will allow us to note techniques that can be used to adjust the length of LAN frames and enhance their information transfer capability, which can result in an improvement in the efficiency of transmission over the network. Other questions we will tackle in later chapters that are related to the material presented in Chapter 2 include how to determine the effect of the frame length on bridge and router operations, as well as on their buffer memory requirements.

1.3   Estimating Network Traffic

If we already have a network in existence, there are a large number of tools we can use to determine network traffic. Once this is done, we can use the results obtained from traffic monitoring to predict the effect of a network expansion or use such information to estimate the traffic on a similar type network that is anticipated to be established. However, what can you do to estimate traffic if your organization plans to install its first local area network or a network in which the user community will significantly differ from the users of an existing corporate network? When those situations occur, you have no baseline from which you can project network traffic — a situation that can result in a significant degree of a trial-and-error unless you have a reasonable mechanism to follow to estimate network traffic.

Chapter 3 focuses on methods you can use to estimate inter- and intra-network traffic. After discussing the need for developing a realistic traffic measurement technique, this chapter focuses on the use of a traffic estimation worksheet that can facilitate the network traffic estimation process. This is followed by examples of the use of the worksheet to estimate the traffic load that will be placed on a network. In addition, this chapter examines how you can use the results obtained from the use of a traffic estimation worksheet to predict future network traffic growth, as well as how to analyze the potential effect of such growth on your existing or planned LAN. Once the traffic estimation process has been reviewed, it is used to illustrate how you can use this data to subdivide a network via the use of a local bridge or router to improve network performance. Thus, this chapter provides information concerning the traffic estimation process as well as illustrates its use to improve the performance level of a network.

1.4 Understanding and Applying Waiting Line Analysis

What is the effect on transmission between LANs when dataflow must cross a pair of remote bridges or routers? The answer to this question can be quite complex and is based on the use of waiting line analysis, which is an alternative term to the more popular expression of "queuing theory."

Chapter 4 investigates the application of waiting line analysis to network traffic that must use remote bridges, switches, or routers to reach their destination. After reviewing some of the terms associated with queuing theory, we will apply its use to answer some key questions associated with the use of remote bridges, switches, and routers. Those questions include: What is an optimum line operating rate for those devices? What is the effect of using single or multiple port devices? And what is the effect of altering the memory capacity of a bridge, switch, or router on its servicing capacity.

Commencing in Chapter 4 we begin to use a series of programs developed using Microsoft Corporation's QuickBASIC compiler and its Excel electronic spreadsheet program to facilitate performing a series of repetitive and tedious computations. The selection of QuickBASIC was based on the fact that it is very similar to Qbasic, which was included in MS-DOS version 5.0 and later versions of that operating system. In addition, readers with earlier versions of DOS can easily modify the QuickBASIC programs presented in this book to operate with the commonly available BASICA or GW-BASIC interpreters. Similarly, Excel represents the most popular electronic spreadsheet program currently in use. Through the creation of Excel templates, it becomes a relatively simple process for readers to modify such templates to tailor them to one or more specific operational requirements. Thus, most readers should be able to use the programs and templates presented in this book without additional cost.

To facilitate the use of the programs contained in this book, you can access them from the following Web site: http://www.crcpress.com/ e_products/downloads/default.asp. At that Web address you will find three series of files you can download. One series of files has the extension .BAS and contains the source version of the QuickBASIC programs. If you have a QuickBASIC or QBasic compiler, you can easily modify those programs to reflect your specific networking environment and then compile and execute the modified program. With a little additional effort you can also use a BASICA or GW-BASIC interpreter to execute the programs presented in this book. For those readers who desire to execute programs without modification, a directly executable version of each program can be downloaded. Those programs have the same filename as the source language versions of programs presented in this book but have the extension .EXE. While you cannot modify those programs that are directly executable, many of those programs operate based upon a variable input, which allows you to adjust the use of those programs to your particular networking environment. A third series of programs you can download consist of Excel templates. The filename of each template is the same as that used in this book to facilitate their use.

1.5   Sizing Communications Equipment and Line Facilities

During the 1920s, a field of mathematics was developed to assist telephone companies in determining the number of long-distance trunks they should install between their offices to provide subscribers with a predefined capability to make long-distance calls. This field of mathematics is referred to as traffic sizing and is considered to represent a classical application of mathematics.

If we fast-forward to the present time, we find that a key area of concern of Internet service providers (ISPs), network managers, and LAN administrators is to determine how many ports or channels are required on LAN access controllers. A similar question involves determining the number of channels or ports required on a Windows-based server supporting remote access services. For both questions we can use traffic sizing to determine the number of channels or ports, modems, and access lines required to support a given subscriber base, employees that work from home, or customers who access an organization's network. Thus, Chapter 5 focuses attention on the methodology and terminology associated with sizing communications equipment and line facilities. Through the information presented Chapter 5, you can learn how to use the scientific approach to determine the level of support required to provide dial-user access to a network in an economical manner.

1.6   Determining Availability Levels

Depending on the activities performed by your organization, you may be required to incorporate a degree of redundancy into your network structure. To do so you can simply acquire additional pairs of remote bridges or routers and connect them through the use of separate transmission facilities. As an alternative to duplicating certain network components, you can also consider the use of multiport bridges and routers, the cost of which is considerably less than separate devices. However, what is the difference in the level of availability provided by the use of dual port devices versus the use of separate devices? The answer to this question, as well as a detailed examination of the concept of availability, are the focus of Chapter 6.

Chapter 6 explains how mean time before failure (MTBF) and mean time to repair (MTTR) information — usually available from vendor product specification sheets — is used to determine both component and system availability levels. Concerning the latter, a portion of Chapter 6 illustrates how the availability level of a complex network can be reduced to a series of simple computations. Chapter 6 also includes the use of BASIC language programs and Excel templates to facilitate tedious computations and provides you with the ability to compute the availability level of devices and transmission facilities connected in series or in parallel. These programs and templates also serve as a mechanism to compute the availability level of a mixed topology network, or you can even use the information in this chapter to compare and contrast redundant and nonredundant computer hardware configurations. Using these programs, templates, or the calculation methods described in Chapter 6, you can obtain the information necessary to determine whether or not the cost of one network configuration versus another is worthwhile with respect to the additional level of network availability obtained through the use of different communications configurations.

1.7   Ethernet Network Performance

Just how fast can frames flow on an Ethernet network? While the preceding question might appear to be taken from a technically oriented game show, in actuality the answer to this question has a considerable bearing on the performance level of bridges and routers prior to those devices becoming possible network bottlenecks.

Chapter 7 focuses attention on the Carrier Sense Multiple Access with Collision Detection (CSMA/CD) network access protocol. By closely examining this protocol, we can determine the maximum frame rate that can be supported on a 10 Mbps, 100 Mbps, and even 1 Gbps Ethernet networks based upon different frame lengths. This, in turn, provides us with the ability to determine if the performance level of a bridge or router listed by a manufacturer is an appropriate decision criterion for equipment acquisition. That is, if the performance level of a device is greater than a certain frame forwarding rate, which represents the maximum frame rate that can be supported on an Ethernet network, the ability of a bridge, switch, or router to transfer frames beyond that rate is superfluous if the device only supports one communications circuit. Thus, the ability of one vendor's bridge or router to forward frames at a faster rate than another vendor's product may not be applicable to consider when evaluating competitive products.

Once the Ethernet frame rate is determined, Chapter 7 then presents an easy-to-use method to predict throughput between interconnected networks.

This method permits you to estimate the best-case transfer time to upload or download files across connected networks, as well as to project the average time required to perform those activities.

1.8   Token Ring Network Performance

The question previously asked concerning how fast frames can flow on an Ethernet network is also applicable to Token Ring networks. That is, if you can determine the flow of information on a Token Ring network, you can use this information to estimate the performance of the network as additional stations are added to the network. You can also use this information to determine the filtering and forwarding rates required by bridges, switches, and routers connected to a Token Ring network prior to those devices potentially becoming a bottleneck and congesting the flow of data between networks. Last, but not least, by determining the frame flow on a Token Ring network, you can use this information to develop a model to project network and inter-LAN transmission time. If the inter-LAN network is to be created or was created through the use of a WAN transmission facility, you can easily adjust the model to reflect different WAN operating rates. Then, you can determine an optimum WAN operating rate that will satisfy your organization's communications requirements without having to simply guess upon the selection of a WAN transmission facility or initiate an expensive trial-and-error process.

As might be expected from the previous paragraph, the initial focus of Chapter 8 is on the development of a model to reflect the flow of frames on a Token Ring network. Once this is accomplished, the model will be exercised to determine the frame carrying capacity of a Token Ring network under different operating conditions and network configurations.

The development of a Token Ring traffic model will require consideration of a large number of operating conditions and network configuration data. Some of the parameters that will have a bearing on the flow of frames on a Token Ring network include the number of stations on the network, the length of each lobe and the length of the ring, the average frame size, and the operating rate of the network. To facilitate our computations, we again turn to the BASIC programming language and develop several programs as well as spreadsheet models to facilitate our computations. Both the Token Ring program and spreadsheet model listings and results from executing each program are contained in this chapter. In addition, readers are referred to the use of a set of tables contained in a file at http://www.crcpress.com/ e_products/downloads/default.asp that can be used to reduce the Token Ring frame flow projection process to a simple table lookup operation.

Once the Token Ring model is developed and exercised, this information is used as a foundation for determining bridge, switch, and router performance requirements. In doing so, frame flow information is used to project a range of performance that network devices should support, as well as the effect of network changes on the frame flow on a Token Ring network.

1.9   ATM network performance

Although ATM is a connection-oriented network based on the use of switches, it has certain characteristics that affect its performance. For example, what happens when too many devices connected to an ATM switch initiate communications? Chapter 9 turns our attention to ATM network performance. However, to ensure readers have an appreciation for the characteristics of an ATM network, we first review those characteristics prior to developing models and exercising those models.

1.10   Working with Images

The old adage that "one picture is worth a thousand words" could be rewritten from the network manager's or LAN administrator's perspective as "transporting images can ruin network performance and eliminate server storage." Thus, advances in technology — to include methods for the transport and display of images — can carry a significant price tag in terms of their data storage requirements and use of network bandwidth when transported on a network. How do you minimize the effect of images on LAN performance? What techniques can be used to reduce their storage and transmission requirements? And how can you convert images to more effective formats? These are a few of the questions we must consider.

Chapter 10 focuses on the effect of images on network performance, to include their storage and transport requirements. After first examining the characteristics of images that define their data storage and transmission time, we then turn our attention to a variety of methods we can use to reduce their effect upon network performance. In doing so we investigate both methods to restructure networks as well as methods to restructure the manner by which images are stored and transported. This will provide us with knowledge of software- and hardware-based solutions we can consider to minimize the effect of images upon LAN performance. Because Web servers are connected to LANs and several Internet service providers (ISPs) now base their monthly charges on high-speed access lines, to include a data transfer fee, we will also examine the effect of Web-based images on an organization's budget. For a popular Web site, the ability to tailor the size of images can significantly reduce an organization's monthly ISP bill.

1.11   Using Intelligent Switches

Although LANs are considered by many to represent the most rapidly evolving area of communications technology, intelligent switches can be considered to represent the fastest growing segment of LAN technology.

In just a few years since the first edition of this book was published, intelligent switches have evolved from a curiosity into a multibillion dollar market. Accompanying this growth is the incorporation of a large number of features and operational considerations that make their effective use a challenge. How do you use switches effectively? What features can cause switches to become bottlenecks instead of improving network performance? How are switches best used in a network? These are important questions that must be answered to effectively use this networking device.

Chapter 11 focuses attention on the effective use of intelligent switches and answers those questions and more. We first review their basic operational characteristics, to include different methods used to perform switching and the advantages and disadvantages associated with each method. Next, we review the operational characteristics of different switch features to obtain an appreciation for their use in different network environments. In doing so we examine the use of switches in several network configurations to obtain an appreciation for how this important network device can be effectively used.

1.12   Monitoring Tools

Chapters 2 through 11 developed models and investigated the performance of different types of LANs based on a series of assumptions concerning LAN traffic. Chapter 12 focuses on how you can turn such assumptions into reality using different monitoring tools to obtain statistical information of key importance for considering techniques to enhance the performance of your organization's network.

In Chapter 12 focuses on the operation and utilization of two network monitoring tools. Both tools operate at layer 2 (data-link layer) and layer 3 (network layer) of the OSI Reference Model. As we discuss the use of these tools, we will examine many of their features that can be used to provide insight into network activity that can be used to enhance LAN performance.

1.13   Transmission Optimization

Network administrators and managers are always looking for methods that can increase the performance of their network. In doing so, they must examine and compare the use of equipment manufactured by different vendors and determine if the features of such equipment provide the capability to optimize the use of the bandwidth on a network or a WAN transmission facility. However, prior to examining the capability and functionality of local area networking equipment, it is important to understand the key techniques that can be used to optimize network and inter-network transmission. Thus, the purpose of Chapter 13 is to answer the following question: What are some of the key techniques available that can be used to optimize network and inter-network transmission?

Chapter 13 examines the features of bridges, switches, and routers developed by manufacturers to enhance transmission. Such features include the ability to filter frames, subdivide a queue into different areas to prioritize traffic, truncate frames, and use the switched network or the Internet to overcome short periods of private network congestion. Concerning the latter, the use of the switched network or the Internet as a supplement to the use of leased analog or digital transmission facilities to connect remote bridges or routers during peak periods of network activity provides you with the ability to economize upon your network design. That is, you can use the switched network or the Internet to satisfy peak transmission periods and size the operating rate of your organization's WAN transmission facility for average network traffic. Doing so may provide you with the ability to economize upon the cost of establishing or maintaining your organization's transmission facilities while maintaining or surpassing the transmission requirements of your organization.

Chapter 2
Ethernet, Token Ring, and ATM Frame and Cell Operations

The key to understanding local area network (LAN) performance issues is a detailed level of knowledge concerning the flow of data on a network. To understand how data flows on a LAN we must examine the method by which information is carried within a frame or cell and how different fields are used to provide such functions as routing, error detection, and other network functions. Thus, the purpose of this chapter is to obtain a detailed understanding of the composition of Ethernet and Token Ring frames and ATM cells, including their frame and cell fields and the function of each field within a frame or cell. This information will provide us with the ability to understand the overhead associated with different network frames and cells with respect to the field actually used to transport information. In addition, this information provides a review concerning how network access occurs, network addressing considerations, and similar information we must consider in attempting to determine problems that may occur when establishing or expanding a network or attempting to connect two previously independent networks. In examining LAN frame operations, we first focus attention on the frame format used on an Ethernet network and then examine the three types of transmission formats supported by a Token Ring network. Once the preceding is accomplished, we turn our attention to ATM, examining the composition of the ATM cell, obtaining an overview of ATM connectivity, and computing the overhead associated with the use of a cell-based technology.

2.1 Ethernet Frame Operations

In this section we first look at the composition of different types of Ethernet frames. In actuality, there is only one Ethernet frame, whereas the CSMA/CD (Carrier Sense Multiple Access with Collision Detection) frame format standardized by the IEEE is technically referred to as an 802.3 frame. However, in this book we collectively reference CSMA/CD operations as Ethernet and, when appropriate, indicate differences between

Ethernet and the IEEE 802.3 Ethernet-based CSMA/CD standard by a comparison of the two. One such area worthy of a comparison is the frame format, which differs between Ethernet and the IEEE 802.3 Ethernet-based CSMA/CD standard. Once we obtain an understanding of the composition of Ethernet and IEEE 802.3 frames, we will examine the function of fields within each frame and discuss the overhead of the frame with respect to its information transfer capability.

2.1.1 *Frame Composition*

Figure 2.1 illustrates the general frame composition of Ethernet and IEEE 802.3 frames. A third type of frame that I would be remiss if I did not mention is the Fast Ethernet, 100BASE-TX frame. That frame differs from the IEEE 802.3 frame through the addition of a byte at each end to mark the beginning and end of the frame. Because those bytes do not alter the composition of the frame, I first focus attention on the fields within Ethernet and IEEE 802.3 frames and then describe the bytes unique to Fast Ethernet. Once the preceding is accomplished, I will discuss two techniques used by Gigabit Ethernet to enhance transmission on that network/carrier extension and frame bursting.

In comparing the format of Ethernet and IEEE 802.3 frames, you will note that they slightly differ. An Ethernet frame contains an eight-byte preamble, while the IEEE 802.3 frame contains a seven-byte preamble followed by a one-byte start of frame delimiter field. A second difference between the composition of Ethernet and IEEE 802.3 frames concerns the two-byte Ethernet type field. That field is used by Ethernet to specify the protocol carried in the frame, enabling several protocols to be carried independently of one another. Under the IEEE 802.3 frame format, the type field was replaced by a two-byte length field that specifies the number of bytes that follow that field as data.

The differences between Ethernet and IEEE 802.3 frames, although minor, make the two technically incompatible with one another. Originally, this meant that a network must contain either all Ethernet-compatible network interface cards (NICs) or all IEEE 802.3-compatible NICs. During the late 1980s and early 1990s, software was developed that enabled multiple protocols to be simultaneously transmitted on a LAN, to include different versions of Ethernet. Such software represents multi-protocol drivers, which enables different types of frames to be supported by a common network adapter. Examples of multi-protocol drivers include the Open Data Interface (ODI) and the Network Data Interface Specification (NDIS). Today, the fact that the IEEE 802.3 frame format represents a standard resulted in most vendors now marketing 802.3-compliant hardware and software. Although a few vendors continue to manufacture Ethernet or dual functioning Ethernet/IEEE 802.3 hardware, such products

Ethernet

Preamble	Destination Address	Source Address	Type	Data	Frame Check Sequence
8 bytes	6 bytes	6 bytes	2 bytes	46–1500 bytes	4 bytes

IEEE 802.3

Preamble	Start of Frame Delimiter	Destination Address	Source Address	Length	Data	Frame Check Sequence
7 bytes	1 byte	2/6 bytes	2/6 bytes	2 bytes	46–1500 bytes	4 bytes

Figure 2.1   Ethernet and IEEE 802.3 Frame Formats

are primarily used to provide organizations with the ability to expand previously developed networks without requiring the wholesale replacement
of NICs. Although the IEEE 802.3 standard has essentially replaced Ethernet
due to their similarities and the fact that 802.3 was based on Ethernet, we
will consider both to be Ethernet. Now that we have an overview of the
structure of Ethernet and 802.3 frames, we can probe deeper and examine
the composition of each frame field. In doing so we will take advantage of
the similarity between Ethernet and IEEE 802.3 frames and examine the
fields of each frame on a composite basis, noting the differences between
the two when appropriate.

2.1.2   Preamble Field

The preamble field consists of eight (Ethernet) or seven (IEEE 802.3) bytes
of alternating 1 and 0 bits. The purpose of this field is to announce the
frame as well as enable all receivers on the network to synchronize themselves to the incoming frame. In addition, this field by itself under Ethernet
or in conjunction with the start of frame delimiter field under the IEEE 802.3
standard ensures there is a minimum spacing period of 9.6 milliseconds
(ms) between frames for error detection and recovery operations. As the
speed of Ethernet increases to 100 Mbps or to a Gigabit data rate, the minimum spacing correspondingly decreases. That is, at a 100 Mbps operating
rate, the minimum spacing is 0.96 ms between frames, while at a 1 Gbps
data rate the minimum spacing is reduced to 0.096 ms.

2.1.3   Start of Frame Delimiter Field

The start of frame delimiter field is only applicable to the IEEE 802.3
standard and can be viewed as a continuation of the preamble. In fact, the
composition of this field continues in the same manner as the format of
the preamble, with alternating 1 and 0 bits used for the first six bit positions of this one-byte field. The last two bit positions of this field are 11,
which breaks the synchronization pattern and alerts the receiver that
frame data follows.

Both the preamble field and the start of frame delimiter field are
removed by the controller when it places a received frame in its buffer.
Similarly, when a controller transmits a frame, it prefixes the frame with
those two fields if it is transmitting an IEEE 802.3 frame or a preamble field
if it is transmitting a true Ethernet frame.

The removal and addition of the preamble and start of delimiter fields
results in a bit of confusion concerning the minimum and maximum length
of an Ethernet frame. In some books and trade literature, the minimum and
maximum length of Ethernet frames are reduced by eight bytes to reflect
the fact that when manipulated within equipment there are no preamble
and start of frame delimiter fields. Other literature references minimum

and maximum length Ethernet frames to include the preamble and start of frame delimiter fields. In actuality, the differences in frame length references can be traced to the standardization process. When Ethernet was standardized by Digital Equipment Corporation, Intel, and Xerox (referred to as the DIX standard), the Version 2 specification defined a minimum frame length of 1526 bytes. That specification included all headers and trailer fields. When the IEEE subsequently standardized Ethernet as the IEEE 802.3 standard, the media access control (MAC) sublayer was only concerned with fields from the destination address through the cyclic redundancy check (CRC) carried in the four-byte frame check sequence field. Thus, the IEEE 802.3 standard recommends that the length of those fields together must range from a minimum of 64 to a maximum of 1518 bytes, which is equivalent to a minimum frame length of 72 bytes and a maximum frame length of 1526 bytes when you consider the eight bytes in the preamble and start of frame delimiter fields.

In this book we will base our Ethernet network utilization computations using minimum and maximum frame lengths of 72 and 1526 bytes, respectively. The reason for this usage is the fact that the preamble and start of frame delimiter fields always flow on a network wire and must be considered when examining Ethernet network performance.

2.1.4 *Destination Address Field*

The destination address identifies the recipient of the frame. Although this may appear to be a simple field, in actuality this field can vary between IEEE 802.3 and Ethernet frames with respect to field length. In addition, each field can consist of two or more subfields whose settings govern such network operations as the type of addressing used on the LAN and whether or not the frame is addressed to a specific station or to more than one station. To obtain an appreciation for the use of this field, let us examine how this field is used under the IEEE 802.3 standard as one of the two field formats applicable to Ethernet.

Figure 2.2 illustrates the composition of the source and destination address fields. As indicated, the two-byte source and destination address fields are only applicable to IEEE 802.3 networks, while the six-byte source and destination address fields are applicable to both Ethernet and IEEE 802.3 networks.

Although you can select either a two- or six-byte destination address field, when working with IEEE 802.3 equipment, all stations on the LAN must use the same addressing structure. Today, almost all 802.3 networks use six-byte addressing because the inclusion of a two-byte field option was primarily designed to accommodate early LANs that use 16-bit address fields.

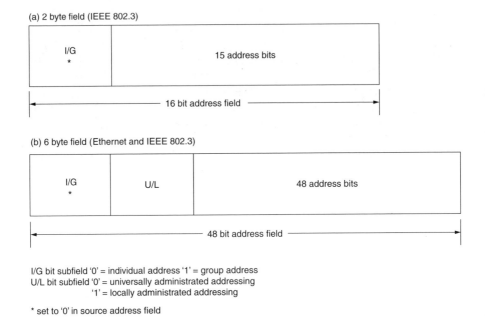

(a) 2 byte field (IEEE 802.3)

I/G *	15 address bits

← 16 bit address field →

(b) 6 byte field (Ethernet and IEEE 802.3)

I/G *	U/L	48 address bits

← 48 bit address field →

I/G bit subfield '0' = individual address '1' = group address
U/L bit subfield '0' = universally administrated addressing
'1' = locally administrated addressing

* set to '0' in source address field

Figure 2.2   Source and Destination Address Field Formats

2.1.4.1   I/G Subfield. The one-bit I/G subfield is set to 0 to indicate that the frame is destined to an individual station, while a setting of 1 indicates that the frame is addressed to more than one station. Here, the latter situation indicates a group address.

One special example of a group address is the assignment of all 1's to the address field. Here, the address, hex FFFFFFFFFFFF, which represents 48 bits all set to 1's, is recognized as a broadcast address and each station on the network will receive and accept frames with that destination address.

When a destination address specifies a single station, the address is referred to as a unicast address. A group address that defines multiple stations is known as a multicast address, while a group address that specifies all stations on the network is, as previously mentioned, referred to as a broadcast address.

2.1.4.2   U/L Subfield. The U/L subfield is only applicable to the six-byte destination address field. The setting of this field's bit position indicates whether the destination address is an address that was assigned by the IEEE (universally administered) or assigned by the organization via software (locally administered).

2.1.4.3   Universal versus Locally Administered Addressing. Each Ethernet network interface card (NIC) contains a unique address burned into its read-only memory (ROM) at the time of manufacture. To ensure this universally administered address is not duplicated, the IEEE assigns blocks of addresses to each manufacturer. Those addresses normally include a three-byte prefix that identifies the manufacturer and is assigned by the IEEE, as well as a three-byte suffix that is assigned by the adapter manufacturer to its NIC. For example, the prefix hex 02608C identifies an NIC manufactured by 3Com, while a prefix of hex 08002 identifies an NIC manufactured by Digital Equipment Corporation, the latter acquired by Compaq Computer, which in turn was acquired by Hewlett-Packard.

Although the use of universally administered addressing eliminates the potential for duplicate network addresses, it does not provide the flexibility obtainable from locally administered addressing. For example, under locally administered addressing, you can configure mainframe software to work with a predefined group of addresses via a gateway PC. Then, as you add new stations to your LAN, you simply use your installation program to assign a locally administered address to the NIC instead of using its universally administered address. As long as your mainframe computer has a pool of locally administered addresses which includes your recent assignment, you do not have to modify your mainframe communications software configuration. Because the modification of mainframe communications software typically requires a recompile and reload activity to be performed, doing so requires the attached network to become inoperative for a short period of time. As a large mainframe may service hundreds to thousands of users, such changes are normally performed late in the evening or on the weekend, making the changes for the use of locally administered addressing more responsive to users than the changes required when universally administered addressing is used.

2.1.5   Source Address Field

The source address field identifies the station that transmitted the frame. Similar to the destination address field, the source address can be either two or six bytes in length.

The two-byte source address is only supported under the IEEE 802.3 standard and requires the use of a two-byte destination address, with all stations on the network required to be set to two-byte addressing field use. The six-byte source address field is supported by both Ethernet and the IEEE 802.3 standard. When a six-byte address is used, the first three bytes represent the address assigned by the IEEE to the manufacturer for incorporation into each NIC's ROM. The vendor then normally assigns the last three bytes to each of its NICs.

2.1.6 Type Field

The two-byte type field is only applicable to the Ethernet frame. This field identifies the higher-level protocol contained in the data field. Thus, this field informs the receiving device how to interpret the data field.

Under Ethernet, multiple protocols can exist on the LAN at the same time and Xerox served as the custodian of Ethernet address ranges licensed to NIC manufacturers as well as defining the protocols supported by the assignment of type field values. Under the IEEE 802.3 standard, the type field was replaced by a length field that precludes compatibility between pure Ethernet and 802.3 frames.

2.1.7 Length Field

The two-byte length field is only applicable to the IEEE 802.3 standard and defines the number of bytes contained in the data field. Under both Ethernet and IEEE 802.3 standards, the minimum size frame must be 64 bytes in length from preamble through FCS (frame check sequence) fields. This minimum size frame was required to ensure that there was sufficient transmission time to enable Ethernet NICs to accurately detect collisions based on the maximum Ethernet cable length specified for a network and the time required for a frame to propagate the length of the cable. Based on the minimum frame length of 64 bytes and the possibility of using two-byte addressing fields, this means that each data field must be a minimum of 46 bytes in length.

When Ethernet was developed, an interesting problem that had to be considered was the effect of collisions on short frames. For example, if a station transmitted a short frame, it was possible that transmission could be completed prior to the first bit in the frame reaching its destination. If the destination station listened to the network prior to the arrival of the first bit and assumed it was OK to transmit, a collision would result. While collisions are a common occurrence on Ethernet networks, under the preceding short frame scenario the transmitting station would incorrectly conclude that the frame was correctly received. This conclusion would occur because upon sensing an increase in voltage from the collision, the receiver, because it is closest to the collision, generates a jam signal to warn all other stations on the LAN not to transmit. However, by the time the jam signal is received by the original transmitting station, it would have falsely concluded that the previous transmitted frame was correctly received.

Due to the preceding, all frames transmitted on an Ethernet network must have a minimum length that exceeds twice the propagation delay encountered on the medium. For the original 10 Mbps coaxial cable-based LAN that has a maximum length of 2500 meters, the minimum time defined by the IEEE is 51.2 microseconds (μs). That time corresponds to 64 bytes, because 64 bytes $* 8$ bits/byte $* (1.0 * 10^{-7})$ seconds/bit is 51.2 μs.

As the network speed increases, either the minimum frame length must increase or the maximum cable length must decrease. To provide scalability between different versions of Ethernet, frame size constraints were maintained when Fast Ethernet was developed. However, the maximum cable distance between any two stations was reduced to approximately 250 meters. When we discuss Gigabit Ethernet later in this section, we will also discuss two techniques used to make 1 Gbps operations more efficient so that a reasonable cabling distance can be supported.

2.1.8 Data Field

As previously discussed, the data field must be a minimum of 46 bytes in length to ensure that the frame is at least 64 bytes in length. This means that the transmission of one byte of information must be carried within a 46-byte data field and results in the padding of the remainder of the field if the information to be placed in the field is less than 46 bytes. Although some publications subdivide the data field to include a PAD subfield, the latter actually represents optional fill characters that are added to the information in the data field to ensure a length of 46 bytes. The maximum length of the data field is 1500 bytes, which results in the use of multiple frames to transport full screen images and almost all files transfers.

2.1.9 Frame Check Sequence Field

The frame check sequence (FCS) field is applicable to both Ethernet and the IEEE 802.3 standard and provides a mechanism for error detection. Each transmitter computes a cyclic redundancy check (CRC) that covers both address fields, the type/length field, and the data field. The transmitter then places the computed CRC in the four-byte FCS field.

The CRC is developed by treating the composition of the previously mentioned fields as one long binary number. The n bits to be covered by the CRC are considered to represent the coefficients of a polynomial $M(X)$ of degree $n-1$. Here, the first bit in the destination address field corresponds to the X^{n-1} term, while the last bit in the data field corresponds to the X^0 term. Next, $M(X)$ is multiplied by X^{32} and the result of that multiplication process is divided by the following polynomial:

$$G(X) = X^{32} + X^{26} + X^{23} + X^{22} + X^{16} + X^{12} + X^{11} + X^{10} + X^8 + X^7 + X^5 + X^4 + X^2 + X + 1$$

Readers should note that the term X^n represents the setting of a bit to a 1 in position n. Thus, part of the generating polynomial $X^5 + X^4 + X^2 + X^1$ represents the binary value 11011.

The result of the division produces a quotient and remainder. The quotient is discarded and the remainder becomes the CRC value placed in the four-byte FCS field. This 32-bit CRC reduces the probability of an undetected error to 1 bit in every 4.3 billion, or approximately 1 bit in $2^{32} - 1$ bits.

Once a frame reaches its destination, the receiver uses the same polynomial to perform the same operation on the received data. If the CRC computed by the receiver matches the CRC in the FCS field, the frame is accepted. Otherwise, the receiver discards the received frame as it is considered to have one or more bits in error. The receiver will also consider a received frame to be invalid and discard it under two additional conditions. Those conditions occur when the frame does not contain an integral number of bytes and when the length of the data field does not match the value contained in the length field. Concerning the latter condition, obviously it is only applicable to the 802.3 standard because an Ethernet frame uses a type field instead of a length field.

2.1.9.1   Fast Ethernet. As previously discussed in this section, the frame format of Fast Ethernet duplicates the IEEE 802.3 frame with the exception of the use of prefix and suffix bytes that surround the frame. The prefix bit is known as the Start of Stream Delimiter (SSD), while the suffix byte is known as the End of Stream Delimiter (ESD).

The SSD is used to align a received frame for subsequent decoding while the ESD is used as an indicator that data transmission terminated normally and a properly formed stream was transmitted. Figure 2.3 illustrates how the SSD and ESD bytes are used to "frame" the IEEE 802.3 frame. At the 100 Mbps operating rate of 100BASE-TX, the frames are known as streams, which accounts for the names of the two delimiters.

In comparing Fast Ethernet to Ethernet and IEEE 802.3 frame formats previously illustrated in Figure 2.1, you will note that other than the starting and ending stream delimiters, the Fast Ethernet frame duplicates the older frames. Another difference between the two is not shown, as it is not actually observable from a comparison of frames because this difference is associated with the time between frames. Ethernet and IEEE 802.3 frames are Manchester encoded and have an interframe gap of 9.6 µs between frames. In comparison, the Fast Ethernet 100BASE-TX frame is transmitted using 4B5B encoding, and idle codes are used to mark a 0.96-µs interframe gap. Both the SSD and ESD fields can be considered to fall within the interframe gap of Fast Ethernet frames. Thus, computations between Ethernet/IEEE 802.3 and Fast Ethernet becomes simplified as the latter has an operating rate ten times the former and an interframe gap one tenth the former.

2.1.9.2   Gigabit Ethernet. As previously discussed in this chapter, an increase in the speed of an Ethernet network must be accompanied by either an increase in the minimum frame length or a decrease in the maximum cable length. At a data rate of 1 Gbps, maintaining a minimum length frame of 64 bytes (72 when the preamble and start of frame delimiter fields are considered) would reduce the maximum network diameter to approximately 20 meters. While this distance might be suitable for connecting a

SSD 1 byte	Preamble 7 bytes	SFD 1 byte	Destination Address 6 bytes	Source Address 6 bytes	L/T 2 bytes	Data 46 to 1500 bytes	FAC 4 bytes	ESD

Figure 2.3 Fast Ethernet Frame

Legend:

SSD   Start of Stream Delimiter
SFD   Start of Frame Delimiter
L/T   Length (IEEE 802.3)/Type (Ethernet)
ESD   End of Stream Delimiter

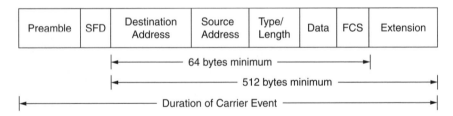

Figure 2.4   Gigabit Ethernet Frame Format with Carrier Extension

hub to a group of stations within close proximity of one another, it is not suitable to support horizontal wiring within a building where a 10-meter distance is allowed from a wall faceplate to the desktop. To enable Gigabit Ethernet to support a network diameter of up to 200 meters, a technique referred to as Carrier Extension was added to the technology.

2.1.9.3   Carrier Extension. Carrier Extension results in an extension of the Ethernet slot time from 64 bytes (512 bits) to a new value of 512 bytes (4096 bits). To accomplish this extension, frames less than 512 bytes in length are padded with special carrier extension symbols. Note that under Gigabit Ethernet, the minimum frame length of 64 bytes is not changed. All frames less than 64 bytes in length are first padded out to a minimum of 64 bytes. The carrier signal placed on the network is then extended to provide a minimum carrier length of 512 bytes.

The preceding discussion of frame length is based on the IEEE use of terminology and does not consider the eight bytes associated with the preamble and start of frame delimiter fields. Figure 2.4 illustrates the Gigabit Ethernet frame format, to include the location where non-data symbols are added. Note that the FCS is calculated only on the original, nonextended frame. At the receiver, the extension symbols are removed before the FCS value is checked. When we examine the performance of Gigabit Ethernet, we add eight bytes to the preceding values to account for the preamble and start of frame delimiter because both flow on a wire.

Carrier Extension is only applicable to half-duplex transmission. This is because full-duplex transmission uses the collision detection wire pair for transmission in the opposite direction since collisions cannot occur on a full-duplex connection. As we note later in this chapter, Carrier Extension can significantly degrade performance associated with short-packet transmission. In an attempt to offset short-packet performance, a second technique, referred to as Packet Bursting, is employed by Gigabit Ethernet.

2.1.9.4   Packet Bursting. Packet Bursting represents a Gigabit Ethernet technique developed in an attempt to compensate for performance degradation associated with Carrier Extension.

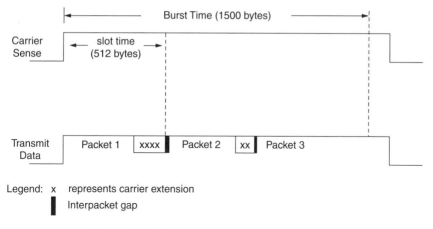

Figure 2.5   Gigabit Ethernet Packet Bursting

Under Packet Bursting, a station with more than one frame to transmit can transmit multiple frames if the first frame is successfully transmitted. If the first frame is less than 512 bytes in length, Carrier Extension is applied to that frame. Succeeding frames in the burst are limited to the length of the maximum frame length. That is, a burst can vary between a maximum of thirteen 64-byte frames to one 1518-byte frame.

Figure 2.5 illustrates the effect of Gigabit Packet Bursting. In this example, note that the first two packets transmitted were less than 512 bytes in length and were extended. Because Packet Bursting is controlled by a burst timer that expires after a duration of 1500 bytes, any packet being transmitted during the burst time will continue to completion. This is indicated by packet 3. Also note that an interframe or interpacket gap occurs between packets when Packet Bursting occurs. However, because transmission occurs at 1 Gbps, the gap between frames is reduced from 9.6 µs on a 10 Mbps Ethernet network to 0.096 µs.

2.1.10 Frame Overhead

As previously indicated in this section, each Ethernet frame consists of six fields (if we consider the preamble and start of frame delimiter as one field and do not consider the SSD and ESD fields, as they are considered to fall within the interframe gap), of which only one field actually transports information. That data field must contain a minimum of 46 bytes even if the frame is transporting a single character response to a client/server query. Thus, the overhead associated with an Ethernet frame depends on both the fixed length of the frame fields that do not carry information as well as the number of characters carried in the data field, which can vary from one to 1500 bytes.

If we assume six-byte addressing, which is applicable to almost all modern Ethernet networks, the number of fixed overhead bytes per frame is 26, consisting of eight preamble bytes, six destination and six source address bytes, two bytes for the type or length field, and four bytes for the FCS field.

A one-byte response carried in the data field must be padded by the addition of 45 fill characters when six-byte addressing is used. In this situation, the overhead required to carry a one-byte character is 26 + 45, or 71 bytes.

Now consider the situation in which you have 46 bytes of data to transmit. Here, the 46 bytes would not require the addition of pad characters because the frame length when using six-byte addressing would be 64 bytes (72 when considering the preamble and start of frame delimiter fields), which is the minimum frame length. Thus, 64 bytes of data would result in a frame overhead of 26 bytes.

Table 2.1 summarizes the overhead associated with transporting information in Ethernet frames as the number of bytes of information varies from one to the maximum 1500 bytes the frame can carry. As indicated in Table 2.1, the overhead associated with transporting information within an Ethernet frame can vary considerably, ranging from a high of 98.61 percent to a low of 1.7 percent when the maximum length data field is used to transport information.

2.1.10.1 Gigabit Ethernet Overhead. The previous computations did not take into consideration the overhead associated with frames transmitted on a Gigabit Ethernet network. As previously noted in this chapter,

Table 2.1 Ethernet Frame Overhead

Information Carried in Data Field (bytes)	Ratio of Bytes of Frame Overhead to Frame Length	Percent Overhead
1	71/72	98.61
10	62/72	86.11
20	52/72	72.22
30	42/72	58.33
45	27/72	37.50
46	26/72	36.11
64	26/90	28.89
128	26/154	16.88
256	26/282	9.22
512	26/538	4.83
1024	26/1050	2.48
1500	26/1526	1.70

packets less than 512 bytes in length (not including their eight-byte header) are extended in length through the use of carrier extension symbols. This means that a packet transporting a one-byte data character first is extended by the addition of 45 padding bytes and then further extended 448 carrier extension symbols. Thus, a Gigabit Ethernet frame transporting one data character contains 520 bytes, to include preamble and start of frame delimiter fields, of which 519 represent overhead.

To illustrate some additional overhead computations, let us assume a Gigabit Ethernet frame is transporting 64 bytes of data. In this case, there is no requirement for padding characters. However, because the frame must be 512 characters in length without considering the eight-byte header, this means there must be 430 carrier extension symbols appended to the frame (448 – 18). If you add the normal 26 overhead bytes to the 430 carrier extensions, you obtain a total overhead of 456 bytes.

Table 2.2 summarizes the overhead associated with transporting information in Gigabit Ethernet frames as the number of bytes of information varies from one to the maximum of 1500 that the frame can transport. The overhead entries in Table 2.2 indicate that the performance of Gigabit Ethernet can be significantly degraded by interactive transmission. Although Packet Bursting is designed to counter the effect of carrier extensions, in reality, interactive query-response applications will not benefit from Packet Bursting. This is because a short query is a one-time event, followed by a response and then perhaps another query, activity that Packet Bursting cannot enhance.

Table 2.2   Gigabit Ethernet Frame Overhead

Information Carried in Data Field (Bytes)	Ratio in Bytes Frame Overhead to Frame Length	Percent Overhead
1	519/520	99.81
10	510/520	98.07
20	500/520	96.15
30	490/520	94.23
40	480/520	92.31
45	475/520	91.35
46	474/520	91.12
64	456/520	87.69
128	392/520	75.38
256	264/520	51.56
384	136/520	26.15
512	26/538	4.83
1024	26/1050	2.48
1500	26/1526	1.70

One question you might have by now is: How can you use the overhead information presented in Tables 2.1 and 2.2 to your advantage for increasing network performance? The data contained in those tables can be extremely important for network performance if your organization is developing client/server applications. For example, assume your programming staff is developing screens to be displayed on a user's workstation in which the client enters information that is then transmitted to the server to initiate different activities. If there is a choice between generating a screen display that results in the transmission of a small number of characters to the server or generating a lesser number of screen displays and transmitting the fields of several screens at one time, the latter is preferable as it results in a lower overhead. This, in turn, will reduce the number of frames carried on the network. Because each version of Ethernet requires a fixed time gap between frames, reducing the number of frames increases the efficiency of dataflow. While altering the transmission of data carried by frames will probably not result in any noticeable increase in network performance if your network only has a handful of workstations, more notable results can be expected to be observed if your network has a large number of stations that perform client/server operations on a regular basis.

2.2 Token Ring Frame Formats

Three types of frame formats are supported on a Token Ring network: token, abort, and frame. The token format as illustrated in Figure 2.6 (a) is the mechanism by which access to the ring is passed from one computer attached to the network to another device connected to the network. Here, the token format consists of three bytes, of which the starting and ending delimiters are used to indicate the beginning and end of a token frame. The middle byte of a token frame is an access control byte. Three bits are used as a priority indicator, three bits are used as a reservation indicator, while one bit is used for the token bit, and another bit position functions as the monitor bit.

When the token bit is set to a binary 0, it indicates that the transmission is a token. When it is set to a binary 1, it indicates that data in the form of a frame is being transmitted.

The second Token Ring frame format signifies an abort token. In actuality, there is no token, because this format is indicated by a starting delimiter followed by an ending delimiter. The transmission of an abort token is used to abort a previous transmission. The format of an abort token is illustrated in Figure 2.6b.

The third type of Token Ring frame format occurs when a station seizes a free token. At that time the token format is converted into a frame that includes the addition of frame control, addressing data, an error detection

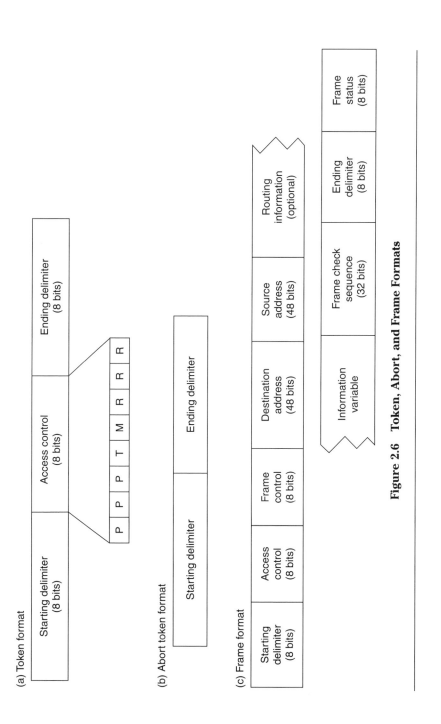

Figure 2.6 Token, Abort, and Frame Formats

field, and a frame status field. The format of a Token Ring frame is illustrated in Figure 2.6c.

2.2.1 Frame Composition

By examining each of the fields in the Token Ring frame, we can examine the token and abort token frames due to the commonality of fields between each frame. Note that, excluding the optional routing field, there are a total of 21 bytes of overhead associated with a Token Ring frame.

2.2.2 Starting/Ending Delimiters

The starting and ending delimiters mark the beginning and end of a token or frame. Each delimiter consists of a unique code pattern that identifies it to the network. To understand the composition of the starting and ending delimiter fields requires us to review the method by which data is represented on a Token Ring network using Differential Manchester encoding.

2.2.2.1 Differential Manchester Encoding.
Figure 2.7 illustrates the use of Differential Manchester encoding, comparing its operation to non-return to zero (NRZ) and conventional Manchester encoding.

In Figure 2.7 (a), NRZ coding illustrates the representation of data by holding a voltage low (–V) to represent a binary 0 and high (+V) to represent a binary 1. This method of signaling is called non-return to zero because there is no return to a 0 V position after each data bit is coded.

One problem associated with NRZ encoding is the fact that a long string of 0 or 1 bits does not result in a voltage change. Thus, to determine that bit m in a string of n bits of 0's or 1's is set to a 0 or 1 requires sampling at predefined bit times. This, in turn, requires each device on a network using NRZ encoding to have its own clocking circuitry.

To avoid the necessity of building clocking circuitry into devices requires a mechanism for encoded data to carry clocking information. One method by which encoded data carries clocking information is obtained from the use of Manchester encoding, which is illustrated in Figure 2.7b. In Manchester encoding, each data bit consists of a half-bit time signal at a low voltage (–V) and another half-bit time signal at the opposite positive voltage (V). Every binary 0 is represented by a half-bit time at a low voltage and the remaining half-bit time at a high voltage. Every binary 1 is represented by a half-bit time at a high voltage followed by a half-bit time at a low voltage. By changing the voltage for every binary digit, Manchester encoding ensures that the signal carries self-clocking information.

Figure 2.7c illustrates Differential Manchester encoding. The difference between Manchester encoding and Differential Manchester encoding occurs in the method by which binary 1's are encoded. In Differential

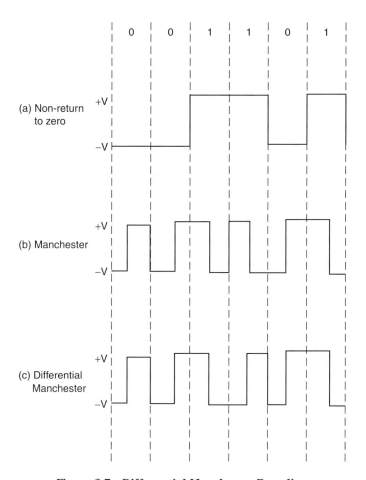

Figure 2.7   Differential Manchester Encoding

Manchester encoding, the direction of the signal's voltage transition changes whenever a binary 1 is transmitted, but remains the same for a binary 0. The IEEE 802.5 standard specifies the use of Differential Manchester encoding, and this encoding technique is used on Token Ring networks at the physical layer to transmit and detect four distinct symbols: a binary 0, a binary 1, and two non-data symbols.

2.2.2.2   Non-Data Symbols. Under Manchester and Differential Manchester encoding, there are two possible code violations that can occur. Each code violation produces what is known as a non-data symbol and is used in the Token Ring frame to denote starting and ending delimiters similar to the use of the flag in an HDLC (High-level Data-Link Control) frame. However, unlike the flag whose bit composition, 01111110, is uniquely maintained by

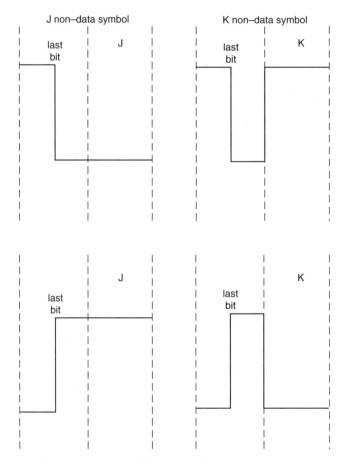

Figure 2.8   J and K Non-Data Symbol Composition

inserting a 0 bit after every sequence of five set bits and removing a 0 following every sequence of five set bits, Differential Manchester encoding maintains the uniqueness of frames by the use of non-data J and non-data K symbols. This eliminates the bit stuffing operations required by HDLC.

The two non-data symbols each consist of two half-bit times without a voltage change. The J symbol occurs when the voltage is the same as that of the last signal, while the K symbol occurs when the voltage becomes opposite of that of the last signal. Figure 2.8 illustrates the occurrence of the J and K non-data symbols based upon different last bit voltages. Readers will note in comparing Figure 2.8 to Figure 2.7c that the J and K non-data symbols are distinct code violations that cannot be mistaken for either a binary 0 or a binary 1.

Now that we have an understanding of the operation of Differential Manchester encoding and the composition of the J and K non-data symbols, we can focus our attention on the actual format of each frame delimiter.

The start delimiter field marks the beginning of a frame. The composition of this field is the bits and non-data symbols JK0JK000. The end delimiter field marks the end of a frame as well as denotes whether or not the frame is the last frame of a multiple frame sequence using a single token or if there are additional frames following this frame. The format of the end delimiter field is JK1JK1IE, where I is the intermediate frame bit. If I is set to 0, this indicates that it is the last frame transmitted by a station. If I is set to 1, this indicates that additional frames follow this frame. E is an error-detected bit. The E bit is initially set to 0 by the station transmitting a frame, token, or abort sequence. As the frame circulates the ring, each station checks the transmission for errors. Upon detection of a frame check sequence (FCS) error, inappropriate non-data symbol, illegal framing, or another type of error, the first station detecting the error will set the E bit to a value of 1. Because stations keep track of the number of times they set the E bit to a value of 1, it becomes possible to use this information as a guide to locating possible cable errors. For example, if one workstation accounted for a very large percentage of E bit settings in a 72-station network, there is a high degree of probability that there is a problem with the lobe cable to that workstation. The problem could be a crimped cable or a loose connector and represents a logical place to commence an investigation in an attempt to reduce E bit errors.

2.2.3   *Access Control Field*

The second field in both token and frame formats is the access control byte. As illustrated in Figure 2.6a, this byte consists of four subfields and serves as the controlling mechanism for gaining access to the network. When a free token circulates the network, the access control field represents one third of the length of the frame because it is prefixed by the start delimiter and suffixed by the end delimiter.

The lowest priority that can be specified by the priority bits in the access control byte is 0 (000), while the highest is seven (111), thus providing eight levels of priority. Table 2.3 lists the normal use of the priority bits in the access control field. Workstations have a default priority of three, while bridges have a default priority of four.

To reserve a token, a workstation inserts its priority level in the priority reservation subfield. Unless another station with a higher priority bumps the requesting station, the reservation will be honored and the requesting station will obtain the token. If the token bit is set to 1, this serves as an indication that a frame follows instead of the ending delimiter.

Table 2.3   Priority Bit Settings

Priority Bits	Priority
000	Normal user priority, MAC frames that do not require a token and response type MAC frames
001	Normal user priority
010	Normal user priority
011	Normal user priority and MAC frames that require tokens
100	Bridge
101	Reserved
110	Reserved
111	Specialized station management

A station that needs to transmit a frame at a given priority can use any available token that has a priority level equal to or less than the priority level of the frame to be transmitted. When a token of equal or lower priority is not available, the ring station can reserve a token of the required priority through the use of the reservation bits. In doing so, the station must follow two rules. First, if a passing token has a higher priority reservation than the reservation level desired by the workstation, the station will not alter the reservation field contents. Second, if the reservation bits have not been set or indicate a lower priority than that desired by the station, the station can now set the reservation bits to the required priority level.

Once a frame is removed by its originating station, the reservation bits in the header will be checked. If those bits have a non-zero value, the station must release a non-zero priority token, with the actual priority assigned based upon the priority used by the station for the recently transmitted frame, the reservation bit settings received upon the return of the frame, and any stored priority.

On occasion, the Token Ring protocol will result in the transmission of a new token by a station prior to that station having the ability to verify the settings of the access control field in a returned frame. When this situation arises, the token will be issued according to the priority and reservation bit settings in the access control field of the transmitted frame.

Figure 2.9 illustrates the operation of the priority (P) and reservation (R) bit fields in the access control field. In this example, preventing a high-priority station from monopolizing the network is illustrated by station A entering a priority-hold state. This occurs when a station originates a token at a higher priority than the last token it generated. Once in a priority-hold state, the station will issue tokens that will bring the priority level eventually down to zero as a mechanism to prevent a high-priority station from monopolizing the network.

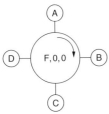

(a) Station A generates a frame using a non-priority token P,R = 0,0

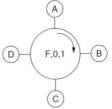

(b) Station B reserves a priority 1 in the reservation bits in the frame P,R = 0,1; Station A enters a priority-hold state.

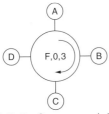

(c) Station C reserves a priority of 3, overriding B's reservation of 1; P, R = 0,3.

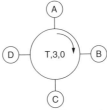

(d) Station A removes its frame and generates a token at reserved priority level 3, P, R = 3,0

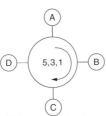

(e) Station B repeats priority token and makes a new reservation of priority level 1; P,R = 3,1.

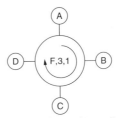

(f) Station C grabs token and transmits a frame with a priority of 3; P,R = 3,1.

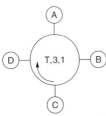

(g) Upon return of frame to Station C it is removed. Station C generates a token at the priority just used; P,R = 3,1.

Legend:

 = stations

(h) Station A in a priority-hold state grabs token and changes its priority to 1; P,R = 1,0. Station A stays in priority–hold state until priority reduced to 0.

Numeric outside station identifier indicates priority level.

Figure 2.9   Priority and Reservation Field Utilization

2.2.3.1 The Monitor Bit. The monitor bit is used to prevent a token with a priority exceeding zero or a frame from continuously circulating on the Token Ring. This bit is transmitted as a 0 in all tokens and frames, except for a device on the network that functions as an active monitor and thus obtains the capability to inspect and modify that bit. When a token or frame is examined by the active monitor, it will set the monitor bit to 1 if it was previously found to be set to 0. If a token or frame is found to have the monitor bit already set to 1, this indicates that the token or frame has already made at least one revolution around the ring and an error condition has occurred, usually caused by the failure of a station to remove its transmission from the ring or the failure of a high-priority station to seize a token. When the active monitor finds a monitor bit set to 1, it assumes an error condition has occurred. The active monitor then purges the token or frame and releases a new token onto the ring.

Now that we have an understanding of the role of the monitor bit in the access control field and the operation of the active monitor on that bit, let us focus our attention on the active monitor.

2.2.3.2 Active Monitor. The active monitor is the device that has the highest address on the network. All other stations on the network are considered standby monitors and watch the active monitor.

As previously explained, the function of the active monitor is to determine if a token or frame is continuously circulating the ring in error. To accomplish this, the active monitor sets the monitor count bit as a token or frame goes by. If a destination workstation fails or has its power turned off, the frame will circulate back to the active monitor, where it is then removed from the network. In the event the active monitor should fail or be turned off, the standby monitors watch the active monitor by looking for an active monitor frame. If one does not appear within seven seconds, the standby monitor that has the highest network address then takes over as the active monitor.

2.2.4 Frame Control Field

The frame control field informs a receiving device on the network of the type of frame that was transmitted and how it should be interpreted. Frames can be either Logical Link Control (LLC) or reference physical link functions according to the IEEE 802.5 Media Access Control (MAC) standard. A MAC frame carries network control information and responses, while an LLC frame carries data.

The eight-bit frame control field has the format FFZZZZZZ, where FF are frame definition bits. The top of Table 2.4 indicates the possible settings of the frame bits and the assignment of those settings. The ZZZZZZ bits convey MAC buffering information when the FF bits are set to 00. When the

Table 2.4   Frame Control Field Subfields

Frame Type Field

F bit settings	*Assignment*
00	MAC frame
01	LLC frame
10	Undefined (reserved for future use)
11	Undefined (reserved for future use)

Z bit settings	*Assignment[a]*
000	Normal buffering
001	Remove ring station
010	Beacon
011	Claim token
100	Ring purge
101	Active monitor present
110	Standby monitor present

[a] When F bits set to 00, Z bits are used to notify an adapter that the frame is to be expressed buffered.

FF bits are set to 01 to indicate an LLC frame, the ZZZZZZ bits are split into two fields, designated rrrYYY. Currently, the rrr bits are reserved for future use and are set to 000. The YYY bits indicate the priority of the LLC data. The lower portion of Table 2.4 indicates the value of the Z bits when used in MAC frames to notify a Token Ring adapter that the frame is to be expressed buffered.

2.2.5   Destination Address Field

Although the IEEE 802.5 standard is similar to Ethernet in that it supports both 16-bit and 48-bit address fields, IBM's implementation requires the use of 48-bit address fields and almost all Token Ring networks use six-byte address fields today. The destination address field is made up of five subfields, as illustrated in Figure 2.10. The first bit in the destination address identifies the destination as an individual station (bit set to 0) or as a group (bit set to 1) of one or more stations. The latter provides the capability for a message to be broadcast to a group of stations.

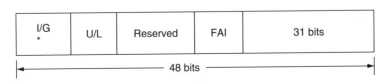

Figure 2.10   Destination Address Subfields

2.2.5.1 Universally Administered Address. Similar to Ethernet, the Token Ring universally administered address is a unique address permanently encoded into an adapter's ROM. Because it is placed into ROM, it is also known as a burned-in address. The IEEE assigns blocks of addresses to each vendor manufacturing Token Ring equipment, which ensures that Token Ring adapter cards manufactured by different vendors are uniquely defined. Some Token-Ring adapter manufacturers are assigned universal addresses that contain an organizationally unique identifier. This identifier consists of the first six hex digits of the adapter card address and is also referred to as the manufacturer identification. For example, cards manufactured by IBM will begin with the address hex X08005A or hex X10005A, whereas adapter cards manufactured by Texas Instruments will begin with the address hex X400014.

2.2.5.2 Locally Administered Address. A key problem with the use of universally administered addresses is the requirement to change software coding in a mainframe computer whenever a workstation connected to the mainframe via a gateway is added or removed from the network. To avoid constant software changes, locally administrated addressing can be used. This type of addressing temporarily overrides universally administrated addressing; however, the user is now responsible for ensuring the uniqueness of each address.

2.2.5.3 Functional Address Indicator. The functional address indicator subfield in the destination address identifies the function associated with the destination address, such as a bridge, active monitor, or configuration report server.

The functional address indicator indicates a functional address when it is set to 0 and the I/G bit position is set to a 1, the latter indicating a group address. This condition can only occur when the U/L bit position is also set to 1 and results in the ability to generate locally administered group addresses called functional addresses. Table 2.5 lists the functional addresses defined by the IEEE. Currently, 14 functional addresses have been defined, out of a total of 31 that are available for use, with the remaining addresses available for user definitions or reserved for future use.

2.2.5.4 Address Values. The range of addresses that can be used on a Token Ring primarily depends on the settings of the I/G, U/L, and FAI bit positions. When the I/G and U/L bit positions are set to 00, the manufacturer's universal address is used. When the I/G and U/L bits are set to 01, individual locally administered addresses are used in the defined range listed in Table 2.5. When all three bit positions are set, this situation indicates a group address within the range contained in Table 2.6. If the I/G and U/L bits are set to 11 but the FAI bit is set to 0, this indicates that the

Table 2.5   IEEE Token Ring Functional Addresses

Active Monitor	XC000 0000 0001
Ring Parameter Server	XC000 0000 0002
Network Server Heartbeat	XC000 0000 0004
Ring Error Monitor	XC000 0000 0008
Configuration Report Server	XC000 0000 0010
Synchronous Bandwidth Manager	XC000 0000 0020
Locate - Directory Server	XC000 0000 0040
NETBIOS	XC000 0000 0080
Bridge	XC000 0000 0100
IMPL Server	XC000 0000 0200
Ring Authorization Server	XC000 0000 0400
LAN Gateway	XC000 0000 0800
Ring Wiring Concentrator	XC000 0000 1000
LAN Manager	XC000 0000 2000
User-defined	XC000 0000 8000
	through hex XC000 4000 0000

Table 2.6   Token Ring Addresses

	Bit Settings			
	I/G	U/L	FAI	Address/Address Range
Individual, universally administered	0	0	0/1	Manufacturer's serial number
Individual, locally administered	0	1	0	X4000 0000 0000 to X4000 7FFF FFFF
Group address	1	1	1	XC000 8000 0000 to XC000 FFFF FFFF
Functional address	1	1	0	XC000 0000 0001 to XC000 0000 2000 (bit-sensitive)
All stations broadcast	1	1	1	XFFFF FFFF FFFF
Null address	0	0	0	X0000 0000 0000

address is a functional address. In this situation, the range of addresses is bit sensitive, permitting only those functional addresses previously listed in Table 2.5.

In addition to the previously mentioned addresses, there are two special destination address values that are defined. An address of all 1's (hex FFFFFFFFFFFF) identifies all stations as destination stations. If a null address is used in which all bits are set to 0 (hex 000000000000), the frame is not addressed to any workstation. In this situation, it can only be transmitted but not received, enabling you to test the ability of the active monitor to purge this type of frame from the network.

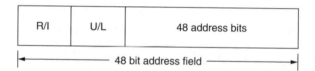

Figure 2.11   Source Address Field

2.2.6 Source Address Field

The source address field always represents an individual address that specifies the adapter card responsible for the transmission. The source address field consists of three major subfields, as illustrated in Figure 2.11. When locally administered addressing occurs, only 24 bits in the address field are used because the 22 manufacturer identification bit positions are not used.

The routing information bit identifier (R/I) identifies the fact that routing information is contained in an optional routing information field. This bit is set when a frame will be routed across a bridge using IBM's source routing technique.

2.2.7 Routing Information Field

The routing information field (RIF) is optional and is included in a frame when the RI bit of the source address field is set. Figure 2.12 illustrates the format of the optional routing information field. If this field is omitted, the frame cannot leave the ring it originated on under IBM's source routing bridging method. Under transparent bridging, the frame can be transmitted onto another ring. The routing information field is of variable length and contains a control subfield and one or more two-byte route designator fields when included in a frame, as the latter are required to control the flow of frames across one or more bridges.

The maximum length of the routing information field (RIF) supported by IBM is 18 bytes. Because each RIF must contain a two-byte routing control field, this leaves a maximum of 16 bytes available for use by up to eight route designators. As illustrated in Figure 2.12, each two-byte route designator consists of a 12-bit ring number and a four-bit bridge number. Thus, a maximum total of 16 bridges can be used to join any two rings in an Enterprise Token Ring network.

2.2.8 Information Field

The information field is used to contain Token Ring commands and responses as well as carry user data. The type of data carried by the information field depends on the F bit settings in the frame type field. If the F bits are set to 00, the information field carries Media Access Control (MAC)

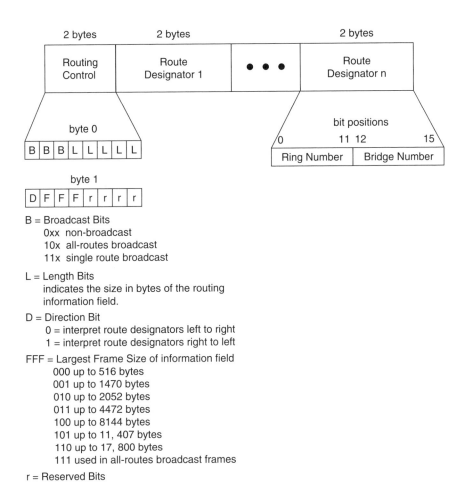

Figure 2.12 Routing Information Field

commands and responses that are used for network management operations. If the F bits are set to 01, the information field carries Logical Link Control (LLC) or user data. Such data can be in the form of portions of a file being transferred on the network or an electronic mail message being routed to another workstation on the network. The information field is of variable length and can be considered to represent the higher-level protocol enveloped in a Token Ring frame.

In the IBM implementation of the IEEE 802.5 Token Ring standard, the maximum length of the information field depends on the Token Ring adapter used and the operating rate of the network. Token Ring adapters with 64 K bytes of memory can handle up to 4.5 K bytes on a 4-Mbps network and up to 18 K bytes on a 16-Mbps network.

A = Address-Recognized Bits

C = Frame-Copied Bits

r = Reserved Bits

Figure 2.13   Frame Status Field

2.2.9   *Frame Check Sequence Field*

The frame check sequence (FCS) field contains four bytes that provide the mechanism for checking the accuracy of frames flowing on the network. The cyclic redundancy check data included in the FCS field covers the frame control, destination address, source address, routing information, and information fields. If an adapter computes a cyclic redundancy check that does not match the data contained in the frame check sequence field of a frame, the destination adapter discards the frame information and sets an error bit (E bit) indicator. This error bit indicator, as previously discussed, actually represents a ninth bit position of the ending delimiter and serves to inform the transmitting station that the data was received in error.

2.2.10   *Frame Status Field*

The frame status field serves as a mechanism to indicate the results of a frame's circulation around a ring to the station that initiated the frame. Figure 2.13 indicates the format of the frame status field. The frame status field contains three subfields that are duplicated for accuracy purposes because they reside outside of CRC checking. One field (A) is used to denote if an address was recognized, while a second field (C) indicates if the frame was copied at its destination. Each of these fields is one bit in length. The third field (rr), which is two bit positions in length, is currently reserved for future use.

2.3   **Frame Overhead**

Unlike Ethernet, which requires the use of fill characters to produce a minimum length frame of 64 bytes, there are no such restrictions on a Token Ring frame. Although this makes the computation of the Token Ring frame overhead more direct, this is only true when a frame does not contain a routing information field. If it does, then the length of that field, which can be up to 18 bytes, will affect the overhead of frames that traverse more than one Token Ring network.

If we focus our attention on frames limited to being carried on a single network, as indicated in Figure 2.6c, the overhead of a Token Ring frame is 21 bytes. This overhead is applicable to both 4- and 16-Mbps Token Ring networks.

Table 2.7 Token Ring Frame Overhead

Information Field (bytes)	Ratio of Frame Overhead to Total Bytes	Percent Overhead
1	21/22	95.45
32	21/53	39.62
64	21/85	24.71
128	21/149	14.09
256	21/277	7.58
512	21/533	3.94
1024	21/1045	2.01
2048	21/2069	1.01
4096	21/4117	0.51
4500	21/4521	0.46
8192	21/8213	0.26
16384	21/16405	0.13

Table 2.7 illustrates the overhead of Token Ring frames as the information field varies in length from 1 to 16,384 bytes. As previously noted, the maximum information field length is 4500 bytes for a 4-Mbps Token Ring network and 18,000 bytes for a 16-Mbps Token Ring network.

In examining the overhead associated with information fields whose lengths are under 512 bytes, we can express similar concerns to short Ethernet data fields with respect to network performance. That is, if your organization is in the process of developing client/server applications, network performance can be improved by developing client/server displays and transmitting a large grouping of information to the server rather than a series of short groups of data. Although there is no predefined time gap between Token Ring frames as there is with Ethernet frames, the lower operating rate of a 4-Mbps Token Ring frame increases the probability of poor performance with a lesser number of clients accessing a server and repeatedly transmitting short responses to server application program queries. Thus, you may be able to improve the performance of your Token Ring network, as well as extend its ability to service additional users without degrading network performance, by designing application programs to take advantage of the structure of network frames.

2.4 ATM and the ATM Cell

Asynchronous Transfer Mode (ATM) represents a switch-based, connection-oriented technology. In this section we obtain an overview of ATM, which will provide a foundation for examining the overhead associated with the use of ATM cells in this chapter as well as a reference for developing performance models in later chapters.

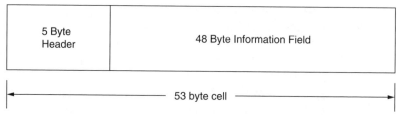

The ATM cell is of fixed length, consisting of a 48-byte information field and five-byte header.

Figure 2.14   The ATM Cell

2.4.1   The ATM Cell

ATM was developed as a transmission technology that can support both voice and data on a common network infrastructure. To accomplish this, ATM uses a fixed-size transmission unit known as a cell. The ATM cell is relatively short, containing a 48-byte information field and a 5-byte header. Figure 2.14 illustrates the basic composition of the ATM cell.

The selection of a relatively short 53-byte cell was based on the necessity to minimize the effect of data upon such time-dependent transmissions as voice and real-time video. For example, assume a variable frame length technology such as Ethernet or Token Ring is used. Then it becomes possible for a lengthy data transmission that fills a frame to its maximum length to gain access to a network between a sequence of digitized voice-filled frames. This action will delay the receipt of succeeding frames transporting digitized voice so that, upon their receipt, the converted voice sounds distorted by time. ATM is designed to eliminate such problems as cells are relatively short, thus resulting in cells transporting voice being able to arrive on a regular basis.

A second significant advantage associated with the use of fixed-length cells concerns the design of switching equipment. ATM logic can be developed as firmware embedded in hardware, enabling faster processing at a lower cost than if software was used to perform ATM operations.

In addition to its relatively short cell length facilitating the integration of voice and data, ATM provides three additional benefits. Those benefits are in the areas of scalability, transparency, and traffic classification.

ATM cells can be transported on LANs and WANs at a variety of operating rates. This enables different hardware, such as LAN and WAN switches, to support a common cell format, a feature lacking in other communications technologies. An ATM cell generated on a 25-Mbps LAN can be transported from the LAN via a T1 line at 1.544 Mbps to a central office. At that location, the cell might be switched onto a 2.4-Gbps SONET network for transmission on the communications carrier infrastructure, with the message maintained in the same series of 53-byte cells, with only the operating rate scaled for a particular transport mechanism.

Concerning transparency, the ATM cell is application transparent, enabling it to transport voice, data, images, and video. Due to its application transparency, ATM enables networks to be constructed to support any type of application or application mix instead of requiring organizations to establish separate networks for different applications.

2.4.2 Traffic Classification

Five classes of traffic are supported by ATM, to include one constant bit rate, three types of variable bit rates, and a user-definable class. As ATM standards were further developed, support for two traffic classes were merged together into a common ATM adaptation layer (AAL) protocol. Later in this section we discuss the role of the AAL and its support for different classes of traffic.

By associating such metrics as cell transit delay, cell loss ratio, and cell delay variation to a traffic class, it becomes possible to provide a guaranteed Quality of Service (QoS) on a demand basis. This enables a traffic management mechanism to adjust network performance during periods of unexpected congestion to favor traffic classes based upon the metrics associated with each class.

Quality of Service (QoS) is one of the key features of ATM; it enables the technology to provide a predefined level of support to different types of data streams. An endpoint requesting the setup of a connection through an ATM network can request a QoS from the network. Once granted, the endpoint will be assured that the network will provide the selected QoS for the life of the connection. The ATM Forum presently defines five traffic classes, which are summarized in Table 2.8. This table includes the type of each traffic class, a description of its intended use, and an example of its potential utilization.

As we probe further into ATM we will note that the only priority field within an ATM cell is used to indicate whether or not a cell can be dropped. Thus, the method used by an ATM network to provide a QoS is not priority based. Instead, it is based on a set of traffic parameters that define such metrics as the Peak Cell Rate (PCR), Cell Delay Variation Tolerance (CDVT), Sustainable Cell Rate (SCR), Burst Tolerance (BT), and Minimum Cell Rate (MCR). Only some of these metrics are applicable for certain traffic classes. For example, only the Peak Cell Rate, which specifies how often data samples are transmitted, and the Cell Delay Variation Tolerance (CDVT), which determines the amount of displacement of a signal from its intended location, are applicable for constant bit rate (CBR) traffic. Later in

Table 2.8   ATM Traffic Classes

Traffic Class	Description
Continuous bit rate (CBR)	Constant bit traffic with a fixed timing relationship between data samples, such as an emulated voice circuit
Variable bit rate – real-time (VBR/RT)	Variable bit rate traffic that has a fixed timing relationship between data samples, such as compressed video
Variable bit rate – non-real-time (VBR/NRT)	Variable bit rate traffic that has no timing relationship between data samples but for which a guarantee of a QoS is required, such as Frame Relay
Available bit rate (ABR)	Variable data transmission that has no timing relationship and can be handled on a best-effort basis, such as electronic mail
Unspecified bit rate (UBR)	A class of traffic for which there is no service guarantee; the user can transmit any amount of data up to a specified maximum but the network does not guarantee delay or a cell loss rate

this section we examine the relationship between ATM adaptation layers, traffic classes, and traffic definition metrics.

2.4.3   The ATM Protocol Stack

Similar to other networking architectures, ATM is a layered protocol. The ATM protocol stack is illustrated in Figure 2.15 and consists of three layers: the ATM adaptation layer (AAL), the ATM layer, and the physical layer. Both the AAL and the physical layer are subdivided into two sublayers. Although the ATM protocol stack consists of three layers, as we will shortly note, those layers are essentially equivalent to the first two layers of the ISO Reference Model. However, because ATM possesses many of the characteristics of a layer 3 or network layer protocol such as a hierarchical address space and a complex routing protocol, some people consider it to represent a network protocol.

2.5   The ATM Adaptation Layer

As illustrated in Figure 2.15, the ATM adaptation layer consists of two sublayers: a convergence sublayer and a segmentation and reassembly sublayer. The function of the AAL is to adapt higher-level data into formats compatible with ATM layer requirements. To accomplish this task, the ATM adaptation layer subdivides user information into segments suitable for encapsulation into the 48-byte information fields of cells. The actual adaptation process depends on the type of traffic to be transmitted, although all traffic winds up in similar cells. Currently, there are four

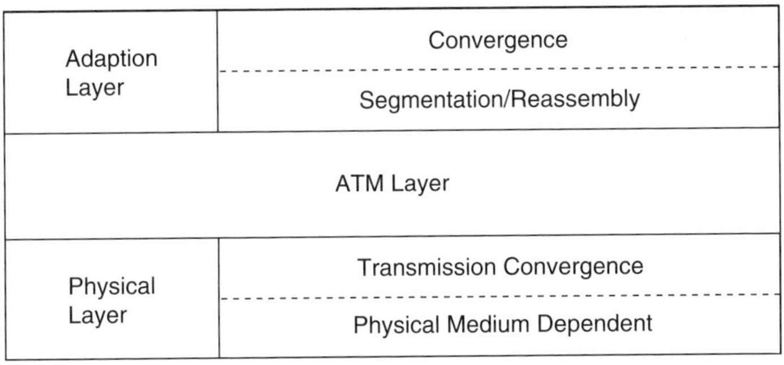

Adaption Layer	Convergence
	Segmentation/Reassembly
ATM Layer	
Physical Layer	Transmission Convergence
	Physical Medium Dependent

Figure 2.15   The ATM Protocol Stack

different AALs defined, referred to as AAL classes, which are described later in this section.

When receiving information, the ATM adaptation layer performs a reverse process. That is, it takes cells received from the network and reassembles them into a format the higher layers in the protocol stack understand. This process is known as reassembly. Thus, the segmentation and reassembly processes result in the name of the sublayer that performs those processes.

2.6   The ATM Layer

As illustrated in Figure 2.15, the ATM layer provides the interface between the AAL and the physical layer. The ATM layer is responsible for relaying cells both from the AAL to the physical layer and to the AAL from the physical layer. The actual method by which the ATM layer performs this function depends on its location within an ATM network. Because an ATM network consists of endpoints and switches, the ATM layer can reside at either location. Similarly, a physical layer is required at both ATM endpoints and ATM switches.

Because a switch examines the information within an ATM cell to make switching decisions, it does not perform any adaptation functions. Thus, the ATM switch operates at layers 1 and 2, while ATM endpoints operate at layers 1 through 3 of the ATM protocol stack as shown in Figure 2.16.

When the ATM layer resides at an endpoint, it will generate idle or "empty" cells whenever there is no data to send, a function not performed by a switch. Instead, in the switch, the ATM layer is concerned with facilitating switching functions, such as examining cell header information, which enables the switch to determine where each cell should be forwarded to. For both endpoints and switches, the ATM layer performs a variety of traffic management functions, to include buffering incoming and outgoing

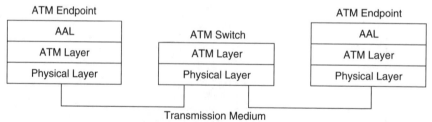

Transmission Medium

The ATM Adaption Layer is only required at endpoints within an ATM network.

Figure 2.16   The ATM Protocol Stack within a Network

cells as well as monitoring the transmission rate and conformance of transmission to service parameters that define a Quality of Service (QoS). At endpoints, the ATM layer also indicates to the AAL whether or not there was congestion during transmission, thus permitting higher layers to initiate congestion control.

2.7   The Physical Layer

Although Figure 2.15 and Figure 2.16 illustrate an ATM physical layer, a specific physical layer is not defined within the protocol stack. Instead, ATM uses the interfaces to existing physical layers defined in other protocols, which enables organizations to construct ATM networks on different types of physical interfaces and, in turn, connect to different types of media. Thus, the omission of a formal physical layer specification results in a significant degree of flexibility that enhances the capability of ATM to operate on LANs and WANs.

2.7.1   ATM Operation

As previously discussed, ATM represents a cell-switching technology that can operate at speeds ranging from T1's 1.544 Mbps to the gigabit-per-second rate of SONET. In doing so, the lack of a specific physical layer definition means that ATM can be used on many types of physical layers, which makes it a very versatile technology.

2.7.2   Components

ATM networks are constructed on the use of five main hardware components. Those components include ATM network interface cards, LAN switches, ATM routers, ATM WAN switches, and ATM service processors.

2.7.2.1   **ATM Network Interface Card.** An ATM network interface card (NIC) is used to connect a LAN-based workstation to an ATM LAN switch. The NIC converts data generated by the workstation into cells that are transmitted to the ATM LAN switch and converts cells received from the switch into a data format recognizable by the workstation.

2.7.2.2 LAN Switch. A LAN switch is a device used to provide inter-operability between older LANs, such as Ethernet, Token Ring, or FDDI, as well as from those networks to ATM. To provide connectivity to ATM, the LAN switch supports a minimum of two types of interfaces, with one being an ATM interface that enables the switch to be connected to an ATM switch that forms the backbone of the ATM infrastructure. The other interface or interfaces represent connections to older types of LANs.

The LAN switch functions as both a switch and protocol converter. Data received on one port destined to the ATM network is converted from frames to cells and transferred to the switch port providing a connection to the ATM switch. One of the key functions that must be performed by the switch in conjunction with the ATM switch it is connected to is a mapping between the MAC addresses used on a LAN switch and the virtual path/virtual channel (VP/VC) identifiers used by ATM. This mapping process is accomplished through a technology known as LAN Emulation (LANE), which is described in Chapter 9, Section 9.2.

Because one LAN switch port can be capable of servicing a LAN segment, the use of a switch can minimize an organization's investment in ATM NICs. Figure 2.17 illustrates the use of a LAN switch with a single ATM port to provide access to an ATM network for individual workstations connected directly to individual switch ports as well as a group of workstations on a LAN segment. Through the use of the LAN switch, an organization can selectively upgrade existing LANs to ATM while obtaining a connection to the ATM network.

2.7.2.3 ATM Router. An ATM router, or perhaps a more correct terminology, an ATM supportable router, is a router containing one or more ATM NICs. As such, it can provide a direct or indirect capability for LAN workstations to access an ATM network or for two ATM networks to be interconnected. For example, a network segment or individual workstations could be connected to a router, which in turn is connected to a LAN switch or directly to an ATM switch.

2.7.2.4 ATM Switch. An ATM switch is a multi-port device that forms the basic infrastructure for an ATM network. Unlike a LAN switch, an ATM switch only permits a single end station to be connected to each switch port. By interconnecting ATM switches, an ATM network can be constructed to span a building, city, country, or the globe.

The basic operation of an ATM switch is to route cells from an input port onto an appropriate output port. To accomplish this, the switch examines fields within each cell header and uses that information, in conjunction

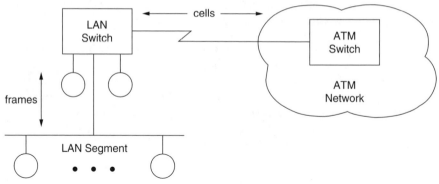

A LAN switch provides both a switching and protocol conversion function, allowing non-ATM devices to access an ATM network.

Legend:

⃝ workstations

Figure 2.17   Using a LAN Switch

Table 2.9   ATM Communications Operating Rates

Operating Rate (Mbps)	Transmission Media
25–51	Unshielded twisted pair category 3
100	Multi-mode fiber
155	Shielded twisted pair
622	Single-mode fiber

with table information maintained in the switch, to route cells. Later in this section we examine the composition of the ATM cell header in detail.

One of the key features of ATM switches reaching the market during the late 1990s was their rate adaptation capability, which in general is a function of the transmission media used to connect endpoints and to connect switches to other switches. Table 2.9 lists some of the communications rates associated with different transmission media.

2.7.2.5   ATM Service Processor. An ATM service processor is a computer operating software or firmware embedded in an ATM switch that performs services required for ATM network operations. For example, an ATM network address can have one of three formats, with one format similar to a telephone number. In comparison, the NIC in an IEEE 802 standardized LAN has a hardware (MAC) address burnt into the adapter. Stations on a LAN can register their addresses using the facilities of a LAN Emulation

Server (LES). That server would then act as a translator between the burnt-in LAN specific hardware addresses and ATM public or private network addresses that could considerably differ from the LAN addressing scheme. The LAN Emulation process, to include a description of the operation of the LES, is described in the LAN Emulation section in Chapter 9.

2.8   Network Interfaces

ATM supports two types of basic interfaces: the user-to-network interface (UNI) and the network-to-node interface (NNI).

2.8.1   User-to-Network Interface

The UNI represents the interface between an ATM switch and an ATM endpoint. Because the connection of a private network to a public network is also known as a UNI, the terms "public" and "private" UNI were used to differentiate between the two types of user-to network interfaces. That is, a private UNI references the connection between an endpoint and switch on an internal, private ATM network, such as an organization's ATM-based LAN. In comparison, a public UNI would reference the interface between either a customer's endpoint or switch and a public ATM network.

2.8.2   Network-to-Node Interface

The connection between an endpoint and switch is simpler than the connection between two switches. This results from the fact that switches communicate information concerning the utilization of their facilities as well as pass setup information required to support endpoint network requests.

The interface between switches is known as a network-to-node or network-to-network interface (NNI). Similar to the UNI, there are two types of NNIs. A private NNI describes the switch-to-switch interface on an internal network such as an organization's LAN. In comparison, a public NNI describes the interface between public ATM switches, such as those used by communications carriers. Figure 2.18 illustrates the four previously described ATM network interfaces.

2.9   The ATM Cell Header

The structure of the ATM cell is identical in both public and private ATM networks, with Figure 2.19 illustrating the fields within the five-byte cell header. As we will soon note, although the cell header fields are identical throughout an ATM network, the use of certain fields depends on the interface or the presence or absence of data being transmitted by an endpoint.

2.9.1   Generic Flow Control Field

The Generic Flow Control (GFC) field consists of the first four bits of the first byte of the ATM cell header. This field is used to control the flow of traffic

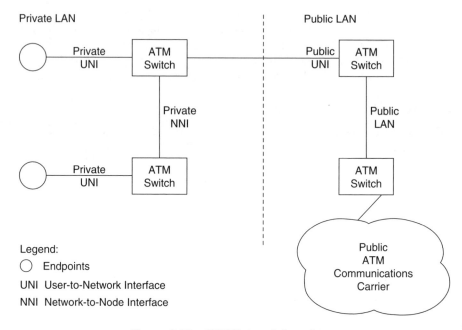

Figure 2.18   ATM Network Interfaces

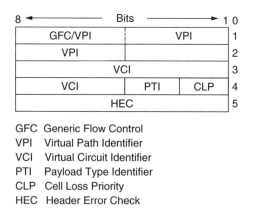

GFC Generic Flow Control
VPI   Virtual Path Identifier
VCI   Virtual Circuit Identifier
PTI   Payload Type Identifier
CLP Cell Loss Priority
HEC Header Error Check

Figure 2.19   The ATM Header

across the user-to-network interface (UNI) and is used only at the UNI. When cells are transmitted between switches, the four bits become an extension of the Virtual Path Identifier (VPI) field, permitting a larger VPI value to be carried in the cell header.

2.9.2   Virtual Path Identifier Field

The Virtual Path Identifier (VPI) identifies a path between two locations in an ATM network that provides transportation for a group of virtual channels, where a virtual channel represents a connection between two communicating ATM devices. When an endpoint has no data to transmit, the VPI field is set to all zeros to indicate an idle condition. As previously explained, when transmission occurs between switches, the GFC field is used to support an extended VPI value.

2.9.3   Virtual Channel Identifier Field

The Virtual Channel Identifier (VCI) can be considered to represent the second part of the two-level routing hierarchy used by ATM, where a group of virtual channels are used to form a virtual path.

Figure 2.20 illustrates the relationship between virtual paths and virtual channels. Here, the virtual channel represents a connection between two communicating ATM entities, such as an endpoint to a central office switch, or between two switches. The virtual channel (VC) can represent a single ATM link or a concatenation of two or more links, with communications on the channel occurring in cell sequence order at a predefined quality of service. In comparison, each virtual path (VP) represents a group of VCs transported between two points that can flow over one or more ATM links. Although VCs are associated with a VP, they are neither unbundled nor processed. Thus, the purpose of a VP is to provide a mechanism for bundling traffic routed toward the same destination. This technique enables switches to examine the VPI field within the cell header to make a decision concerning the relaying of the cell instead of having to examine the entire three-byte address formed by the VPI and the VCI. When an endpoint is in an idle condition, the VPI field is set to all zeros. Although the VCI field will also be set to all zeros to indicate the idle condition, other non-zero VCI values are reserved for use with a VPI zero value to indicate certain predefined conditions.

As noted later, all VPIs and VCIs have only local significance on a particular connection between an endpoint and a switch or between two switches. At each switch in an ATM network, VPIs and VCIs can be remapped to different VPIs and VCIs. The actual route through an ATM network is established by signaling packets that are transmitted on a "well-known virtual channel," VPI = 0, VCI = 5.

2.9.4   Payload Type Identifier Field

The Payload Type Identifier (PTI) field consists of three bits in the fourth byte of the cell header. This field is used to identify the type of information carried by the cell. Values 0 through 3 are reserved to identify various

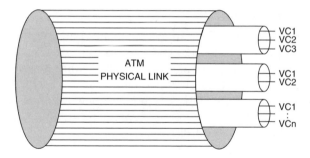

Figure 2.20   Relationship between Virtual Paths and Virtual Channels

types of user data, 4 and 5 denote management information, while 6 and 7 are reserved for future use.

2.9.5   Cell Loss Priority Field

The last bit in the fourth byte of the cell header represents the Cell Loss Priority (CLP) field. This bit is set by the AAL layer and used by the ATM layer throughout an ATM network as an indicator of the importance of the cell. If the CLP is set to 1, it indicates the cell can be discarded by a switch experiencing congestion. If the cell should not be discarded due to the necessity to support a predefined quality of service, the AAL layer will set the CLP bit to 0. The CLP bit can also be set by the ATM layer if a connection exceeds the quality-of-service level agreed to during the initial communications handshaking process when setup information is exchanged. For example, assume during the establishment of a VP/VC that the user and network agree upon the bandwidth and other QoS parameters. If the user's traffic violates the expected patterns, the CLP bit can be set to indicate that the cell is eligible for discarding.

2.9.6   Header Error Check Field

The last byte in the ATM cell header is the Header Error Check (HEC) field. The purpose of the HEC is to provide protection for the first four bytes of the cell header against the misdelivery of cells due to errors affecting the addresses within the header. To accomplish this, the HEC functions as an error detecting and correcting code. The HEC is capable of detecting all single and certain multiple bit errors as well as correcting single bit errors.

2.10   ATM Connections and Cell Switching

Having a basic understanding of the ATM cell header, to include the virtual path and virtual channel identifiers, we can turn our attention to the methods used to establish connections between endpoints as well as how connection identifiers are used for cell switching to route cells to their destination.

2.10.1 Connections

In comparison to most LANs that are connectionless, ATM is primarily a connection-oriented communications technology. This means that a connection must be established between two ATM endpoints prior to actual data being transmitted between the endpoints. The actual ATM connection can be established as a permanent virtual circuit (PVC) or as a switched virtual circuit (SVC).

A PVC can be considered similar to a leased line, with routing established for long-term use. Once a PVC is established, no further network intervention is required any time a user wishes to transfer data between endpoints connected via a PVC. In comparison, an SVC can be considered as being similar to a telephone call made on the switched telephone network. That is, the SVC requires network intervention to establish the path linking endpoints each time a SVC occurs.

Both PVCs and SVCs obtain the "V" as they represent virtual rather than permanent or dedicated connections. This means that through statistical multiplexing, an endpoint can receive calls from one or more distant endpoints.

2.10.2 Cell Switching

As previously mentioned, signaling packets are transmitted on the well-known virtual channel VPI = 0, VCI = 5 to set up a connection. That connection results in each switch allocating a VPI and VCI to route data between switches or from a switch to an endpoint. Because a switch can support numerous simultaneous connections as cells arrive, the switch examines the VIP and VCI fields in the cell header to determine the output port for relaying or transferring a cell. To determine the output port, the ATM switch first reads the incoming VPI, VCI, or both fields with the field read dependent upon the location of the switch in the network. Next, the switch will use the connection identifier information to perform a table lookup operation. That operation uses the current connection identifier as a match criterion to determine the output port the cell will be routed onto as well as a new connection identifier to be placed into the cell header. The new connection identifier is then used for routing between the next pair of switches or from a switch to an endpoint.

2.11 Types of Switches

There are two types of ATM switches, with the differences between each related to the type of header fields read for establishing cross-connections through the switch. A switch limited to reading and substituting VPI values is commonly referred to as a VP switch. This switch operates relatively fast. A switch that reads and substitutes both VPI and VCI values is commonly referred to as a virtual channel switch (VC switch). A VC switch

53

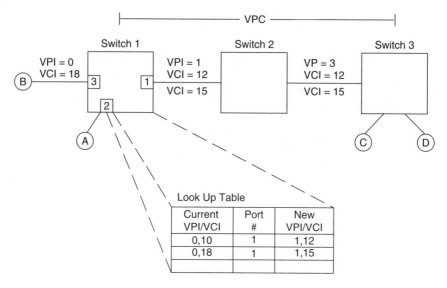

Figure 2.21   ATM Cell Switching Example

generally has a lower cell operating rate than a VP switch as it must examine additional information in each cell header. You can consider a VP switch as being similar to a central office switch, while a VC switch would be similar to end office switches.

2.12   Using Connection Identifiers

To illustrate the use of connection identifiers in cell switching, consider Figure 2.21, which illustrates a three-switch ATM network with four end-points. When switch 1 receives a cell from device A connected to port 2 with VPI = 0, VCI = 10, it uses the VPI and VCI values to perform a table lookup, assigning VPI = 1, VCI = 12 for the cell header and switching the cell onto port 1. Similarly, when switch 1 receives a cell on port 3 with VPI = 0, VCI = 18, its table lookup operation results in the assignment of VPI = 1, VCI = 15 to the cell's header and the forwarding of the cell onto port 1. If we assume switch 2 is a VP switch, it only reads and modifies the VP; thus, the VCIs are shown exiting the switch with the same values they had upon entering the switch. At switch 3, the VPI is broken down, with virtual chan-nels assigned to route cells to endpoints C and D that were carried in a common virtual path from switch 1 to switch 3.

The assignment of VPI and VCI values is an arbitrary process that considers those already in use, with the lookup tables being created when a connection is established through the network. Concerning that connec-tion, it results from an ATM endpoint requesting a connection setup via the

Table 2.10   Relationship of Traffic Classes, AAL Support, and Traffic Definition Metrics

	Traffic Classes				
	Constant Bit Rate	**Variable Bit Rate Real-Time**	**Variable Bit Rate Now Real-Time**	**Available Bit Rate**	**Unspecified Bit Rate**
ATM Adaption Layer	AAL 1	AAL 2	AAL 3/4, 5	AAL 3/4	Unspecified
Timing Relationahip Source Destination					
Bit Rate					
Traffic Definition Metrics	Specified	Specified	Specified	Specified	Unspecified
Cell Loss Ratio					
Cell Transfer Delay	Maximum Specified	Maximum	Mean Specified	Unspecified	Unspecified
Cell Delay Variation	Specified	Specified	Unspecified	Unspecified	Unspecified
Peak Cell Rate	Specified	Specified	Specified	Specified	Specified
Sustainable Cell Rate	N/A	Specified	Specified	N/A	N/A
Minimum Cell Rate	N/A	N/A	N/A	Specified	N/A

user–network interface through the use of a signaling protocol that contains an address within the cell. That address can be in one of three formats. One known as E.164 is the same as that used in public telephone networks, while the other two address formats include domain identifiers that allow address fields to be assigned by different organizations. The actual signaling method is based on the signaling protocol used in ISDN and enables a QoS to be negotiated and agreed to during the connection setup process. The QoS is based on metrics assigned to different traffic classes, permitting an endpoint to establish several virtual connections where each connection transports different types of data with different performance characteristics assigned to each connection. Table 2.10 summarizes the relationship between the five types of specified ATM traffic classes, the ATM Adaption Layer (AAL) that will support each class, the timing relationship between source and destination, and bit rate per traffic class, as well as summarizes seven metrics used to provide a QoS for each traffic class.

As previously indicated, ATM can be used as a desktop-to-desktop transport mechanism or can function as a backbone to connect existing IEEE 802 networks together and into an ATM infrastructure. Figure 2.21 illustrates an example of desktop-to-desktop or endpoint-to-endpoint ATM operation. In actuality, the cost of ATM adapters, as well as the considerable investment previously made in Ethernet, Token Ring, and FDDI infrastructures, precluded the widespread adoption of ATM to the desktop. However, the scalability of ATM resulted in the growing use of the technology as a backbone for interconnecting older LANs as well as providing for a migration strategy to ATM. Readers are referred to the LAN Emulation section in Chapter 9 for detailed information on how ATM is used as a backbone network.

2.13 Cell Overhead

As previously noted, the ATM cell consists of a 48-byte payload and five-byte header, resulting in a total cell length of 53 bytes. The overhead associated with transmission of data on an ATM network depends on the average quantity of data being transmitted. Under a best-case scenario, when a user has a multiple of exactly 48 bytes of data to transmit the cell overhead becomes (5/48) * 100, or approximately 9.43 percent. However, very rarely will anyone have a multiple of 48 bytes of information to transmit. Thus, let us examine the effect upon ATM overhead as we transmit different quantities of data.

Suppose you transmit a one-character message transported by an ATM cell. The overhead then becomes 52 bytes in a 53-byte cell, or 98.11 percent. Now suppose your message is 49 bytes in length, requiring two cells to transport the message. In this situation, the overhead decreases to [(5 + 52)/106] * 100, or 53.77 percent. Here, the first cell contains 52 bytes of overhead. Now let us examine a few additional data transfers occurring via ATM cells.

Assume you transmit a 97-byte message that fills the payload area of two cells and requires an additional byte in a third cell to transport the message. The overhead includes five bytes in each of the first two cells and 52 bytes in the third cell, for a total of 62 bytes for the 159 bytes in the three cells. This results in an overhead of (62/159) * 100, or 38.99 percent. Now assume our transmission increased to 193 bytes. With a 48-byte payload five ATM cells are now required, with the fifth cell also transporting one byte of information. Now the overhead is 72 bytes out of a total of 265 bytes, which is (72/265) * 100, or 27.16 percent.

Table 2.11 provides a summary of ATM cell overhead based upon a varying number of data bytes in a transmitted message. In examining the entries in Table 2.11, note that in addition to many common power of 2 message lengths, there are several that may appear curious as to why they were entered in the table. Those entries you may be curious about include message block lengths of 49, 145, 193, 433, 913, and 1393 bytes. Each of those entries represents an increasing message that has one more byte than necessary to fill a cell, resulting in an additional cell being required to transport the message. Note that the cell overhead diminishes, falling from 53.77 percent when a message consists of 49 bytes to 31.60 percent when a message consists of 145 bytes. As the length of the message continues to expand, our worst-case scenario results in a continuing decline in cell

Table 2.11   ATM Cell Overhead

Data Bytes per Message	Number of Cells	Overhead to Total Bytes	Cell Overhead
1	1	52/53	98.11
2	1	51/53	96.22
4	1	49/53	92.24
8	1	45/53	84.91
16	1	37/53	69.81
32	1	21/53	39.62
40	1	13/53	24.52
48	1	5/53	9.43
49	2	57/106	53.77
64	2	42/106	39.62
72	2	34/106	32.07
80	2	26/106	24.52
96	2	10/106	9.43
97	3	62/159	38.99
144	3	15/159	9.43
145	4	67/212	28.77
192	4	20/212	9.43
193	5	72/265	27.16
256	6	62/318	19.49
433	10	97/530	18.30
480	10	50/530	9.43
512	11	71/583	12.18
913	20	147/1060	13.87
1024	22	142/1166	12.17
1393	30	197/1590	12.39
1500	32	196/1696	11.56

overhead. That is, for a 193-byte message, the cell overhead falls to 27.17 percent, while a 433-byte message has a cell overhead of 18.30 percent and a 913-byte message has a cell overhead of 13.87 percent. This indicates that ATM is much more efficient for transporting files than interactive query data. Also note that for messages of 48, 96, and 480 bytes, which exactly fill one or more ATM cells, cell overhead is reduced to 9.43 percent. Thus, we can note from the overhead associated with different message lengths that ATM overhead will vary between a maximum of 98.11 percent and a minimum of 9.43 percent.

Chapter 3
Estimating Network Traffic

Although there are a large number of hardware and software products that can be used to obtain network utilization information, the use of those products obviously requires an existing network. If you are planning the installation of a new network, you cannot use a performance monitor to measure network utilization until the network is established. At that time you might notice a high level of utilization, requiring the network to be subdivided through the use of a local bridge or switching hub to provide a better level of performance to local area network (LAN) users. Thus, it is important to understand how you can estimate network traffic and use the results of that traffic estimation process. Doing so provides you with the ability to determine whether or not you should consider the subdivision of the network via the use of a local bridge, switching hub, or similar communications device to enhance the performance level of each network segment.

This chapter first focuses attention on developing a methodology to estimate network traffic on a local area network. We will develop a traffic estimation worksheet and use that worksheet to project the average and peak traffic that could be carried on a network. Next, we turn our attention to the typical average and peak utilization levels of Ethernet and Token Ring networks, discussing utilization levels that, when exceeded, may indicate a decision criterion for network subdivision. This will be followed by an example that will illustrate how the use of a local bridge can make performance on each part better than if a network was not subdivided.

3.1   The Network Traffic Estimation Process

Assuming you do not have access to monitoring equipment to analyze an existing LAN or that your network is in a planning stage, you can develop a reasonable estimate of traffic by considering the functions each network user performs. To facilitate the traffic estimation process, you can group a number of network users together into a "workstation class" category and perform your computations for a single workstation. Then you can multiply the results of that computation by the number of workstations grouped

Table 3.1   Traffic Estimation Worksheet

Workstation Class			Number of Stations		
Activity Performed	Message Size in Bytes	Number of Frames/Message	Frame Size in Bytes	Frequency /Hour	Resulting Bit Rate (bps)*
					Subtotal bps =

Total for all workstation class:

_____ = # stations _____ * subtotal bps _____ = _____

*Note:

$$\text{bit rate (bps)} = \frac{\text{frames/message} * \text{frame size} * 8 \text{ bits/byte} * \text{frequency/hour}}{3600 \text{ seconds/hour}}$$

into the specific workstation class to obtain an estimate of network traffic for a similar group of network users. You can then repeat this process for each workstation class you defined and add the traffic estimate for all workstation classes to obtain an estimate of the average traffic that will be carried on the entire network.

3.1.1   The Traffic Estimation Worksheet

As mentioned at the beginning of this chapter, you can expedite the traffic estimation process through the use of a worksheet. Table 3.1 illustrates the general format of a traffic estimation worksheet you can consider to facilitate your network traffic estimation process. Prior to illustrating how you can use the worksheet, let us first review the meaning of each entry in the worksheet.

3.1.2   Workstation Class

The workstation class identifies a specific category of LAN user. Normally you will use the occupational category of a group of persons for that entry. Typically, but not always, that entry reflects their average usage of the LAN. Examples of some common workstation classes include secretary, engineer, accountant, payroll clerk, application programmer, etc.

3.1.3   Number of Stations

The number of stations entry on the worksheet permits you to indicate the number of workstations that fall into a specific workstation class. Thus, you would normally have one worksheet for each defined workstation class.

3.1.4 Column Entries

Turning our attention to the column entries, you will note six specific column headings. The first column provides you with the ability to define the major activities performed by a workstation in the given class. Examples of major workstation activities include loading programs and data files residing on the network server, saving data files to the server, transmitting and receiving electronic mail, and directing print jobs to a network printer. Although the worksheet illustrated in Table 3.1 contains nine rows, you can add additional rows if you wish to define more than nine specific activities for a particular workstation class.

The Message Size column references the average number of bytes in a particular event performed by the defined activity. For example, suppose the transmission of electronic messages is expected to average 1800 characters. Thus, the message size in bytes would be entered as 1800.

Although several articles and technical manuals read by the author indicate the direct use of the message size, doing so results in a degree of inaccuracy. Although the use of a traffic estimation worksheet as its name implies results in an estimate of network traffic, we can reduce the degree of inaccuracy by considering the fact that Ethernet, Fast Ethernet, Token Ring, and other types of LAN frames have a degree of overhead. That degree of overhead can range in scope from a few percent for large message sizes to 30 to 50 percent or more for small-sized messages. The failure of the authors of those articles and technical manuals to consider the fact that a message must be encapsulated into one or more LAN frames and that each frame contains a number of fields that wrap around the encapsulated information results in their suggested computations having a built-in error. Thus, you must consider the number of frames used to carry a message as well as the frame size. Here, the latter includes the overhead fields that contain the preamble (Ethernet) or starting delimiter (Token Ring), source and destination addresses, and other frame information. As noted in Chapter 2, the overhead associated with Ethernet frames can vary from a low of 26 bytes when 38 or more bytes of information are carried in the data field to as many as 63 bytes when that field only carries one character of information. Under Gigabit Ethernet, up to 448 carrier extension symbols can be added to ensure that the minimum length of a frame is 520 bytes, to include the Preamble and Start of Frame Delimiter fields. This means that frame overhead when transmission occurs on Gigabit Ethernet will exceed that on Ethernet and Fast Ethernet until at least 494 data characters are carried in a frame. In comparison, a Token Ring frame that is not routed between rings has a fixed overhead of 21 bytes.

The fifth column contained in the traffic estimation worksheet is used to place your estimate of the frequency per hour in which the row activity is performed. Even if this activity is only performed once per day, such as the remote load of a diskless workstation, you can express the frequency on an hourly basis. For example, if you expect an activity to occur once a day and project the workstation user to work an eight-hour day, then the frequency per hour becomes 1/8, or 0.125.

The last column in the traffic estimation worksheet contains the resulting bit rate computed for the specific activity entered on the row. As indicated by the footnote at the bottom of the worksheet, the bit rate in bits per second (bps) is determined by the following equation:

$$\text{bit rate (bps)} = \frac{\text{frames/message} * \text{frame size} * 8 * \text{frequency/hour}}{3600 \text{ seconds/hour}}$$

Once you compute the resulting bit rate for each activity, you can sum the results of those computations to obtain the bit rate for all activities for one workstation in the class of workstations with which you are working. To complete your computation for the workstation class, you would then multiply the number of workstations in the class by the summed bit rate, as indicated in the lower portion of Table 3.1. Next, you would complete the traffic estimation process by computing a total bit rate for each remaining workstation class and then sum the total for each workstation class to obtain a network traffic estimate.

3.1.5 Developing a Network Traffic Estimate

Because the best way to illustrate the network traffic estimation process is by example, let us do so. In doing so, let us assume you want to install a Fast Ethernet LAN that will operate at 100 Mbps. Suppose this network is intended to support 87 design engineers; 30 technicians; 40 general support personnel in accounting, personnel, finance, sales, and marketing; 10 managers; and 10 secretaries. Thus, you would probably consider completing a series of five traffic estimation worksheets to cover each of the five general categories of users planned for the network. As an alternative, you might decide to complete separate traffic estimation worksheets for accounting, personnel, finance, sales, and marketing personnel, instead of grouping them into a general support personnel class of network user. If you do this, you would then be required to complete a total of nine traffic estimation worksheets instead of five.

3.1.6 Using the Traffic Estimation Worksheet

Table 3.2 illustrates the completion of a traffic estimation worksheet for the design engineer class of workstation users. In completing this worksheet, it was assumed that the average design engineer will perform a core set of seven LAN functions. Those functions are listed under the Activity Performed column in Table 3.2. The functions performed range in scope from loading a program that resides on a network server to loading and saving graphic

Table 3.2   Completed Traffic Estimation Worksheet

Workstation Class Engineers				Number of Stations	214

Activity Performed	Message Size in Bytes	Number of Frames/Message	Frame Size in Bytes	Frequency /Hour	Resulting Bit Rate (bps)*
1. Load graphic	512	350	1526	16	2373
2. Save graphic	1024	700	1526	8	2373
3. Send e-mail	1	1	1526	4	1
4. Receive e-mail	2	2	1526	4	3
5. Load program	1024	700	1526	3	890
				Subtotal bps =	5640

Total for all workstation class:

  <u>214</u> = # stations   214 * subtotal bps <u>5640</u> = <u>1206960</u>

*Note:

$$\text{bit rate (bps)} = \frac{\text{frames/message} * \text{frame size} * 8 \text{ bits/byte} * \text{frequency/hour}}{3600 \text{ seconds/hour}}$$

images, sending and receiving messages, and printing both graphic images and text data on a printer to be connected to the Fast Ethernet network.

3.1.6.1   Required Computations. To illustrate the computations used for the completion of the traffic estimation worksheet, let us consider the load program activity entry row. Here it was assumed that programs which occupy an average of 640 Kbytes of storage on the network server will be loaded four times each hour. Although this program loading frequency may appear high, many engineering programs actually consist of a series of overlays and the loading of one program could easily result in the loading of several modules each hour as the design engineer accesses different program features in performing the design effort.

If the size of the program or program module loaded into the workstation is 640 Kbytes, then the actual size of the program is 640 * 1024 bytes per K, or 655,360 bytes.

On an Ethernet network, the maximum length of the information field in a frame that contains the program data transported from the server to the workstation is 1500 bytes. Thus, 655,360 bytes in the program divided by 1500 bytes that can be carried in a frame results in 437 frames that will be required to transport the program. Although the information field is 1500 bytes, the actual frame size will be 1526 bytes because there are 26 overhead bytes in an Ethernet frame. Based on the preceding, the resulting bit rate attributed to the load program activity becomes:

$$\text{bit rate (bps)} = \frac{117 \text{ frames} * 1526 \text{ bytes/frame} * 8 \text{ bits/byte} * 4/\text{hour}}{60 \text{ sec/min} * 60 \text{ min/hour}}$$

If you anticipate installing a Token Ring network, you would consider a data field size ranging from a minimum of 1 byte to a maximum of 4500 bytes for a 4-Mbps Token Ring network and to a maximum of 1800 bytes for a 16-Mbps network. Because the overhead of a Token Ring network is fixed at 21 bytes, you would compute the number of frames required to transport each type of message. Next, you would add 21 bytes to the frame size and perform a computation similar to the one just illustrated for the load program activity for the design engineer workstation class using a Fast Ethernet network.

In performing the previous computation, readers will note that it was not precise because the number of frames was rounded to 437 and did not consider the fact that the last frame does not actually carry 1500 bytes. For file transfers, program loads, and print jobs, you can safely disregard the fact that the last frame used to carry an activity may have an information field whose length is less than 1500 bytes. This is because doing so results in a maximum divergence of 4 bps over an hour for the activity being computed for each occurrence of the activity. For example, 1500 bytes $*$ 8 bits/byte results in an Ethernet information field carrying a maximum of 12,000 bits, which when divided by 3600 seconds per hour is less than 4 bps. Thus, your activity projection would be off by a maximum of 16 bps, which is far less than 1 percent. Because you are estimating network traffic, a good rule of thumb to follow is to ignore the fact that the last frame's information field used to carry an activity may be partially filled unless the activity is performed more than 50 times per hour. The latter may represent the use of an application performed by clerical personnel entering batches of data concerning personnel file updates, corporate receipts and disbursements, and similar types of work.

If you look at the entries in Table 3.2 and take the time to perform your own computations, you will note that the frame size for the activities "send message," "receive message," and "print text data" precisely represent the amount of data transmitted for each activity. This is because the message size resulted in only one frame being required to support the indicated activity, which results in a precise frame length being used.

3.1.7 Network Printing Considerations

One item worthy of mention concerning the activity entries in Table 3.2 involves network printing. If your network infrastructure is designed so that file servers function as print servers as shown in the top portion of Figure 3.1, the computations shown for network printing are correct. However, many networks are constructed using separate print servers. When this occurs, a print job transmitted by a network user first flows from his or her workstation to the file server, where it is placed in a print queue. Then, the file server transmits the print job from the queue to the print

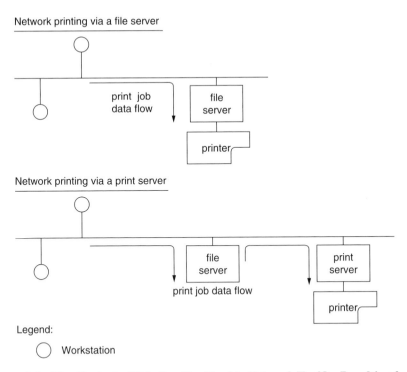

Network printing via a file server

print job
data flow

file
server

printer

Network printing via a print server

file
server

print
server

print job data flow

printer

Legend:

◯ Workstation

Figure 3.1   The Method of Printing Can Double Network Traffic, Resulting from the Execution of a Print Job

server as illustrated in the lower portion of Figure 3.1. Under this network printing configuration, the print job is transmitted twice, first from the workstation to the file server and then from the file server to the print server. If your network infrastructure will use separate print servers, you would then double the resulting bit rate for each print job computed in a traffic estimation worksheet.

To further illustrate the completion of the traffic estimation worksheet illustrated in Table 3.2, let us examine the load and save graphic image entries and the send and receive message activities. In addition, to further illustrate the computations involved in completing the worksheet, the resulting bit rate computations for each activity will also indicate the significant difference in the effect of graphic versus text information transfer on a LAN.

3.1.7.1 Graphic versus Text Transfer. Because the entries for loading and saving a graphic image are the same, you can compute one entry and use the resulting bit rate computation for each activity. Similarly, you can do the same for sending and receiving messages.

For each graphic image activity, let us assume the image consists of a file of 1024 Kbytes. Thus, the file size is 1024 * 1024 bytes per K, or 1,048,576 bytes. When carried by a 1500-byte Ethernet information field, this results in the use of 1,048,576 bytes/1500 bytes/frame, or 700 frames, to transport the graphic image. Because there are 26 overhead bytes in each frame, the actual frame length is 1526 bytes. Based on a frequency of 20 images loaded or saved per hour, each graphic image activity bit rate computation is as follows:

$$\text{bit rate (bps)} = \frac{700 \text{ frames} * 1526 \text{ bytes/frame} * 8 \text{ bits/byte} * 20/\text{hour}}{60 \text{ sec/min} * 60 \text{ min/hour}}$$

$$= 47.476$$

Now let us turn our attention to the send and receive message activities. For each activity, we assumed the message size is .5 K, or 512 bytes. Thus, the entire message can be transported by one Fast Ethernet frame that has a 1500-byte information field. Because there are 26 overhead bytes per Fast Ethernet frame, the frame size is 538 bytes. Based on a frequency of two messages sent or received per hour, each message activity's bit rate computation becomes:

$$\text{bit rate (bps)} = \frac{1 \text{ frame} * 538 \text{ bytes/frame} * 8 \text{ bits/byte} * 2/\text{hour}}{60 \text{ sec/min} * 60 \text{ min/hour}} = 3$$

In comparing the resulting bit rate of a graphic image activity to an electronic message activity, note the significant difference between the resulting bit rate of each activity. Here, each graphic image activity is in excess of 1500 times the resulting bit rate associated with a message. This comparison is performed by dividing the bit rate of 47,475 for 20 image operations per hour by 20 to obtain a per-image hourly bps rate of 2374. Performing a similar operation for a send or receive message results in a per-message hourly rate of 1.5. Then, the ratio of 2374 to 1.5 results in a value of 1582. Even if the message was doubled in size to 1024 bytes, the graphic image would have a bit rate approximately 800 times that of the message. If you consider the fact that a super VGA monitor color graphic image can easily exceed 1 Mbyte and that most electronic mail messages are relatively short, consisting of one or two paragraphs and typically less than 100 words, this explains why electronic mail has a negligible effect on LAN performance in comparison to the transmission of graphic images.

Returning to Table 3.2, note that the subtotal bps of 112,758 represents the average network traffic for one workstation used by a design engineer. Because there are 87 workstations used by design engineers, the total bit rate is 112,758 * 87, or 9,809,946 bps. Now that we have completed the traffic estimation worksheet for one workstation class, we would perform

Table 3.3 Projected Network Traffic by Workstation Class

Workstation Class	Bit Rate (bps)
Design engineer	9809946
Technicians	5422500
General support personnel	3238750
Managers	283920
Secretaries	1146750
Total estimated bit rate	**19901866**

similar computations for each of the remaining four workstation classes. To facilitate our analysis, let us assume that the results of the computations for the five workstation classes are as summarized in Table 3.3.

3.1.8   Network Utilization Considerations

In examining the projected network traffic summarized in Table 3.3, note that the total bit rate of 19.9 Mbps represents a projected utilization level of 19.9/100.0, or 19.9 percent, of the available network bandwidth. If you feel a projected 19.9 percent level of network utilization is low, you are correct in your assumption for both Ethernet and Token Ring networks. However, as the level of network utilization increases, the effect on network performance depends on the type of network. A Token Ring network's transmission capability depends on several variables, to include the number of stations on the network, the average length of frames transmitted on the network, and the total length of cable used to form the network.

Under certain variable relationships, the capability of a Token Ring network to transport data can be as low as one half of the network's operating rate. Although Chapter 8 contains specific information concerning the development and execution of a mathematical model to determine the information-carrying capacity of a Token Ring network, we can generalize the findings of that chapter by noting that, when possible, you should attempt to keep the utilization level of a Token Ring network to a maximum of 70 percent of its operating rate. Doing so will preclude the occurrence of excessive response times. For an Ethernet LAN to include Fast Ethernet, the utilization level should be kept to 40 to 50 percent of the network's operating rate. The rationale for an Ethernet LAN having a lower utilization level threshold than a Token Ring network is due to the difference in the access method used by each network. Ethernet access is not predictable and can result in collisions that require a random time delay during which no station on the network can transmit data. In comparison, network access on a Token Ring network is predictable because a station can only transmit when it is able to acquire a free token.

A second difference between the transmission capability of each network concerns the method of frame transmission used on each network. On an

Table 3.4 Network Growth Worksheet

Workstation Class	Estimated Bit Rate (bps)	Projected Growth Rate (%)	Projected Bit Rate (bps)
Design engineer	9809946	20	11771935
Technicians	5422500	0	5422500
General support personnel	3238750	0	3238750
Managers	283920	25	354900
Secretaries	1146750	5	1204087
Total projected bit rate			**21992172**

Ethernet network there is a minimum fixed delay period of time between frame transmissions. In comparison, transmission can occur on a Token Ring network as soon as a station acquires a free token. Readers are referred to Chapter 7 for specific information concerning the flow of data on an Ethernet LAN.

3.1.9 Planning for Network Growth

In addition to estimating traffic that will be carried by a network, it is equally important to consider network growth. Doing so permits you to determine if a network structure will be able to accommodate a buildup in workstation usage of the network and/or an increase in network users over a period of time.

To illustrate how you can consider network growth, let us assume your organization anticipates additional hiring that will increase the design engineering staff by 20 percent, management personnel by 25 percent, and the secretarial staff by 5 percent. To consider the potential effect of adding workstations to the network to accommodate the additional hiring, you could use a network growth worksheet similar to the one contained in Table 3.4. This worksheet was completed based upon the projected network traffic contained in Table 3.3 and the previously discussed projections for additional employees.

3.2 Network Modification

Previously, it was noted that the bit rate on the Fast Ethernet network was projected to be approximately 20 percent of the available network bandwidth. Based on the projected network growth, the bit rate is expected to increase to approximately 22 Mbps, which would be (22/100) * 100, or approximately 22 percent of the available network bandwidth. Thus, the relatively light level of network utilization is projected to slightly worsen over time if one network is used to provide a communications capability for both existing and anticipated employees. Now let us assume another series of computations resulted in a network utilization projection of 65 percent. This would be significantly higher than the 50 percent level of utilization on Ethernet where performance problems begin to be noticed. To alleviate potential problems associated with a high level of network utilization, one of the first modifications to a network infrastructure that you should consider is the installation of dual networks interconnected by a local bridge.

The use of a bridge to subdivide a network into two or more interconnected segments essentially doubles your effective bandwidth prior to considering inter-segment communications, a topic that is discussed in the next section of this chapter. Because the cost of a two-port bridge is usually considerably less expensive than an intelligent switch or router, from a cost perspective most network modification efforts begin by examining a network with respect to its subdivision into segments via a bridge.

3.2.1   *Network Subdivision Considerations*

In examining the entries in the completed traffic estimation worksheet contained in Table 3.2, you will note that the vast majority of network usage associated with workstations used by design engineers involves the loading of programs and graphic images as well as the saving and printing of graphic images. Thus, it appears that the requirement of design engineers to interact with other network users through the transmission and reception of electronic mail messages is relatively limited with respect to their total projected transmission on the LAN. Therefore, it appears you could safely place all design engineers on one Ethernet network, while all other network users could be placed on a second Ethernet network.

If we assume the growth in network utilization maintains a similar bit rate ratio between design engineers and other workstation classes, then from Table 3.4 the design engineers can be expected to account for (11.77 Mbps/21.99 Mbps) * 100, or approximately 54 percent of network traffic. Thus, if network utilization increased to 65 percent, splitting the network into two segments would result in one segment with a projected utilization of 65 * .54, or 35 percent, while the projected utilization on the other segment would be 65 * 46 percent, or 30 percent. While not a perfect subdivision, as per a popular movie staring Jack Nicholson and Helen Hunt, this may be "as good as it gets!"

Figure 3.2 illustrates the resulting subdivided Ethernet network in which it is assumed that all design engineers are placed on network segment A. This method of subdivision minimizes inter-LAN communications and reduces the forwarding rate the local bridge has to support.

As an alternative to placing all design engineers on network A, let us assume that you wish to consider network subdivision by placing half of

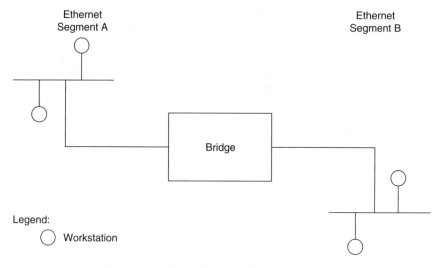

Figure 3.2   Resulting Subdivided Network

the employees on each network. Although this would more evenly balance the utilization level of each network, what would be the effect on inter-LAN communications? Unless you could distribute the programs and graphic images used by design engineers onto servers on each network, the design engineers on network B would require a significant amount of communications with the server located on network A. Although we did not analyze the activities of other classes of network users, we can safely assume that any subdivision in which a class of workstation users is subdivided onto two or more interconnected networks will result in a high level of inter-LAN communications unless the program's users access are located on servers on each network segment. Because the cost of a program license to operate on separate servers typically exceeds the cost of a program license to operate on one server, the additional cost associated with the separation or subdivision of users within a workstation class is normally not recommended. Thus, most organizations should consider the subdivision of network users based on the class of user.

3.2.2   Inter- versus Intra-Network Communications

One area that remains to be discussed concerning LAN traffic is the relationship between inter- and intra-network communications. This is especially important if your organization previously established separate LANs and now needs to interconnect those networks.

If you previously estimated traffic carried by separate networks or have access to monitoring equipment, you can estimate or determine the actual data flow on separate networks. However, what can you expect to occur when you connect two or more networks together?

Unless you use a poor design philosophy and require workstations on one network to access many applications on a server on a different network, the majority of transmissions will be local with respect to each LAN. In fact, the interconnection of separate networks usually results in traffic following according to what is commonly referred to as the 80/20 rule. That rule states that when separate networks are interconnected, intra-LAN communications will account for 80 percent or more of communications traffic while 20 percent or less of the traffic on a network will require the services of a bridge or router to flow between networks. The one exception to this is when organizations create a tiered network structure based on the use of LAN switches, which we will shortly discuss.

The effect of the 80/20 rule should be taken into consideration when estimating the potential effect on bandwidth resulting from the segmentation of a network. To illustrate the effect of the 80/20 rule, or a variation of the percentages of that rule to better fit your organization's operational requirements, consider Figure 3.3. This example illustrates the effect on the bandwidth of a segmented Token Ring network from inter-LAN communications, and its analysis is also applicable to each version of Ethernet. In this example, it was assumed that network A's initial utilization level was projected to be 50 percent, while network B's was projected to be 55 percent. It was also assumed that 80 percent of all traffic on each network segment would be local and remain on the segment from which it was placed on the network, while 20 percent of the traffic on each segment would be destined to a device on the other segment. This means that at an expected 50 percent utilization level, 0.50×0.20, or 10 percent of the utilization of network A will flow onto network B. Similarly, if network B has an expected utilization level of 55 percent, then 0.55×0.20, or 11 percent of the utilization of network B can be expected to flow onto network A. Because both networks are considered to represent the same type of Token Ring network, the inter-LAN communications result in an increase in the utilization of network A to 61 percent and an increase in the utilization of network B to 65 percent. Thus, it is extremely important to consider the effect of inter-LAN communications because such communications not only represent a consumption of bandwidth on the initial network on which a frame is placed but, in addition, a consumption of bandwidth for each network it is placed in.

As briefly mentioned at the beginning of this section, a key exception to the 80/20 rule concerning inter-LAN communications is when an organization uses switches to develop a tiered network topology. Figure 3.4 illustrates an example of a two-tiered network structure. In this example, note that two enterprise servers (ES) are connected to the 100-Mbps Ethernet switch at the top of the switch tier, while departmental servers

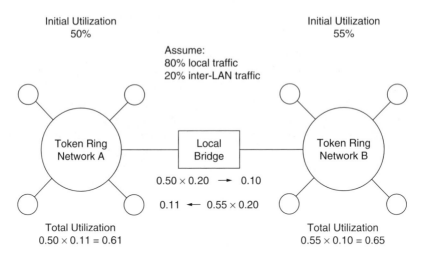

Figure 3.3   **The Effect on the Bandwidth of a Segmented Network Resulting from Inter-LAN Communications**

(DS) are connected to each of the 10-Mbps Ethernet switches at the bottom of the tier. Under this server arrangement, traffic flowing through each lower tier is probably very similar to the 80/20 rule, with only 20 percent of network traffic flowing beyond a local switch. Now suppose that instead of departmental servers being distributed throughout a building, the organization decided to place all servers in one controlled access area. In doing so let us assume that all servers were connected to the 100-Mbps Ethernet switch at the top of the tier shown in Figure 3.4. This would result in the creation of what is referred to as a *server farm*.

Although the creation of a server farm facilitates administrative operations and the physical security of servers, from a network perspective it results in all traffic from lower-tier switches flowing to the backbone switch that provides the connections to the servers in the server farm. Thus, instead of an 80/20 rule concerning inter-LAN communications, you obtain a 100/100 rule because all traffic from each station on the lower-tier switch must be forwarded to an upper-tier switch. In addition, if the upper-tier switch should fail or if the connection between switches becomes inoperative, a large number of employees can lose their ability to perform productive work. For these reasons, many switch vendors include a level of redundancy in their products and the connection between lower- and higher-tier switches occurs at a higher operating rate than the operating rate of the lower-tier switches. Despite a higher operating rate to connect switches, when too many stations on the lower-layer switch become active there can be delays in accessing the higher-tier switch. Readers are

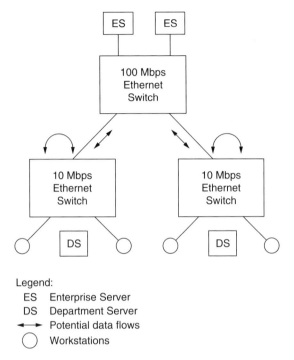

Figure 3.4 Data Flow on a Tiered Switch-Based Network Topology

referred to Chapter 11 for detailed information on the operation and utilization of LAN switches.

3.3 Automating Worksheet Computations

To provide readers with the ability to automate the traffic estimation process, a worksheet template was created for computing the projected activity
on an Ethernet network. This template was created using Microsoft's Excel
program and can be easily modified for Token Ring and Gigabit Ethernet.

Figure 3.5 illustrates the Traffic Estimation Worksheet template that is available at the indicated Web URL as a Microsoft Excel file named TRAFFIC.XLS in
the EXCEL directory. Note that the column labeled "Frame Size in Bytes" is
uniformly set to a value of 1526, which represents the maximum length
Ethernet frame. Because most activities that have a major effect on a
network, such as program loading, file transfers, and Web page surfing,
result in most of the frames used to transport the activity flowing as
maximum length frames, setting the frame length to 1526, while not fully
correct, will provide a very accurate estimate and is much simpler than
attempting to precisely estimate the length of each frame. In addition,

	A	B	C	D	F	H	J
1		**Traffic Estimation Worksheet**					
2							
3	Workstation class:					# of stations:	
4							
5		Activity Performed	Message Size in K Bytes	Number of Frames/Msg	Frame Size in Bytes	Frequency / Hour	Resulting Bit Rate (bps)*
6	1			0	1526		0
7	2			0	1526		0
8	3			0	1526		0
9	4			0	1526		0
10	5			0	1526		0
11	6			0	1526		0
12	7			0	1526		0
13	8			0	1526		0
14	9			0	1526		0
15	10			0	1526		0
16	11			0	1526		0
17	12			0	1526		0
18	13			0	1526		0
19	14			0	1526		0
20	15			0	1526		0
21							
22						Subtotal bps:	0
23							
24		* Note: bit rate (bps) = frames/message*frame size *8bits/byte * frequency/hour					
25							
26		Total for all workstations in class:					
27							
28		# of stations:	0	x subtotal bps	0	equals:	0
29							

Figure 3.5   The Traffic Estimation Worksheet Excel Template for Ethernet LANs

because we are estimating traffic, it is doubtful if we will ever approach 100 percent accuracy.

To complete the worksheet, you need to enter, at a minimum, the number of stations for a workstation class and for each activity performed the message size in Kbytes, the number of frames/message, and the frequency/hour for the activity. Figure 3.6 illustrates an example of a completed template for five activities performed by a presumed workstation class called Engineers. Note that by entering data for five activities the worksheet automatically computes the resulting bit rate for each activity, the subtotal bps rate for all activities, and the total bit rate for all workstations in the class, the latter placed in the box in the lower-right corner of the spreadsheet. The EXCEL template shown in Figure 3.6 is stored under the filename *trafficexample.xls* in the directory EXCEL at the Web URL that can be accessed by purchasers of this book.

Traffic Estimation Worksheet

	Workstation class: Engineers				# of stations:	214

	Activity Performed	Message Size in K Bytes	Number of Frames/Msg	Frame Size in Bytes	Frequency/ Hour	Resulting Bit Rate (bps)*
1	Load graphic	512	350	1526	16	2373
2	save graphic	1024	700	1526	8	2373
3	send email	1	1	1526	4	1
4	receive email	2	2	1526	4	3
5	load program	1024	700	1526	3	890
6			0	1526		0
7			0	1526		0
8			0	1526		0
9			0	1526		0
#			0	1526		0
#			0	1526		0
#			0	1526		0
#			0	1526		0
#			0	1526		0
#			0	1526		0
					Subtotal bps:	5640

* Note: bit rate (bps) = frames/message*frame size *8bits/byte * frequency/hour

Total for all workstations in class:

# of stations:	214	x subtotal bps	5640	equals:	1206960

Figure 3.6   An Example of a Completed Traffic Estimation Worksheet Excel Template

75

Chapter 4
Understanding and Applying Waiting Line Analysis

One of the more interesting areas of mathematics that many readers experience every day is waiting line analysis, also commonly referred to as queuing theory. Every time we approach a toll plaza, enter a fast food restaurant, and walk to position ourselves into a line or line up in a bank for service, we are in a waiting line. Over the past 30 years, a considerable amount of mathematical research has been performed that resulted in the development of a series of queuing systems that can be used to model different types of waiting lines. Fortunately for network personnel, this effort can also be applied to a variety of communication systems. For example, consider the operation of remote bridges and routers.

One of the major problems associated with the use of remote bridges and routers is the delay those devices introduce into linked networks. This delay results from the fact that a local area network (LAN) operating rate is normally an order of magnitude or higher than the wide area network (WAN) operating rate used to connect LANs via the use of remote bridges or routers. A second major problem associated with the use of remote bridges and routers concerns the selection of an appropriate amount of buffer memory for installation in each device. If too little memory is installed in such devices, the probability that memory will be filled when a frame arrives for forwarding increases. This, in turn, results in the inability of a bridge or router to service the frame, causing the originating network station to periodically regenerate the frame or a timeout to occur, which results in the termination of an existing communications session. Thus, an insufficient amount of buffer memory can result in both extended network delays as well as an increase in network traffic. The above problems are also applicable in modified form to LAN switches. If too much buffer memory is configured for switch ports, delays in the traversal of data could cause such real-time applications as voice and video to provide unacceptable results. In comparison, an insufficient amount of buffer memory would cause frames to be dropped. Because real-time voice transported over IP applications will not retransmit dropped packets, when too many are dropped, the receiving parties may think they are communicating with Bugs Bunny. Thus, packet loss and packet delay can be significant problems for VoIP (voice-over-IP) applications.

Through the use of queuing theory we can develop models to determine the delays associated with the use of remote bridges, switches, and routers. In addition, we can investigate the effect of modifying the operating rate of communications circuits used to interconnect those devices. Doing so will enable us to examine the effect of different communications circuit operating rates upon equipment delays, as well as to understand that beyond some operating rates, further increases in the operating rate of a communications circuit will have an insignificant effect on equipment and network performance.

Once we obtain an appreciation for the use of queuing theory to determine an acceptable operating rate for WAN transmission facilities linking LANs, we will examine a related problem. That problem involves the use of queuing theory to determine whether to use single or multiple communications circuits when connecting LANs with respect to their ability to service frames arriving at a remote bridge or router connected to single or multiple circuits. In examining this problem we will expand our knowledge of queuing theory to cover multiple channel, single-phase queuing systems, as such systems represent the flow of data through a remote bridge or router connected to multiple communications circuits. In concluding this chapter we turn our attention to the use of queuing theory to determine the minimum amount of buffer storage remote bridges and routers should contain to provide a predefined level of performance. In doing so we will develop a six-step approach readers can follow to select equipment with a sufficient amount of buffer storage to satisfy their specific organizational networking requirements.

4.1 Waiting Line Analysis

Queuing theory, the formal term for waiting line analysis, can be traced to the work of A.K. Erlang, a Danish mathematician. His pioneering work spanned several areas of mathematics, including the dimensioning or sizing of trunk lines to accommodate long-distance calls between telephone company exchanges. Readers are referred Chapter 5 for specific information concerning the application of Erlang's work conducted during the 1920s to the sizing of ports on modern LAN access devices. In this chapter we bypass Erlang's sizing work to concentrate on the analysis of waiting lines.

4.1.1 Basic Components

Figure 4.1 illustrates the basic components of a simple waiting line system. The input process can be considered the arrival of people, objects, or frames of data. The service facility performs some predefined operation on

Figure 4.1   Basic Components of a Simple Waiting Line System

arrivals, such as collecting tolls from passengers in cars arriving at a toll booth, or converting a LAN frame into an SDLC or HDLC frame by a remote bridge or router for transmission over a WAN transmission facility. If the arrival rate temporarily exceeds the service rate of the service facility, a waiting line known as a queue will form. If a waiting line never exists, this fact implies that the server is idle or an excessive service capacity exists.

The waiting line system illustrated in Figure 4.1 is more formally known as a single-channel, single-phase waiting line system. The term "single channel" refers to the fact that there is one waiting line, while the term "single phase" refers to the fact that the process performed by the service facility occurs once at one location. One toll booth on a highway or a single-port remote bridge or router connected to a local area network and a wide area network are two examples of single-channel, single-phase waiting line systems.

Figure 4.2 illustrates three additional types of waiting line systems. Here, the term "multiple channel" refers to the fact that arrivals are serviced by more than one service facility and results in multiple paths or channels to those service facilities. The term "multiple phase" references the fact that arriving entities are processed by multiple service facilities.

One example of a multiple-phase service facility would be a toll road in which drivers of automobiles are serviced by several series of toll booths. Any reader who drove on the Petersburg–Richmond, Virginia, turnpike during the 1980s is probably well aware of the large number of 25¢ toll booths you seemed to have encountered every few miles. Another example of a multiple phase would be the routing of data through a series of bridges and routers. Because the computations associated with multiple phase systems can become quite complex and we can analyze most networks on a point-to-point basis as a single phase system, we will primarily restrict our examination of queuing models to single phase systems in this chapter.

4.1.2   Assumptions

Queuing theory is similar to many other types of mathematical theory in that it is based on a series of assumptions. Those assumptions primarily focus on the distribution of arrivals and the time required to service each arrival.

If the arrival rate is stochastic (i.e., it varies in some random fashion over time), we need to further classify it through the use of a probability

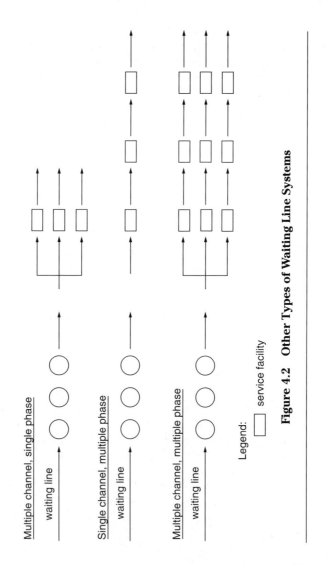

Figure 4.2   Other Types of Waiting Line Systems

distribution because arrivals can appear either singularly or in batches. A second method of categorizing the arrival rate occurs when arrivals occur at a fixed rate, with a fixed time between successive arrivals. This second type of arrival is referred to as deterministic. The Greek letter lambda (λ) is normally used to denote the arrival rate.

The time required to service arrivals is referred to as the service rate and can also be stochastic or deterministic. The Greek letter μ is normally used to represent the service rate.

Both the distribution of arrivals and the time to service them are normally represented as random variables. The most common distribution used to represent arrivals is the Poisson distribution, where:

$$P(n) = \frac{\lambda^n e^{-\lambda}}{n!}$$

where:
    P(n) = probability of n arrivals
    λ = mean arrival rate
    e   = 2.71828
    n!   = n factorial $n*(n-1)...3*2*1$

One of the more interesting features of the Poisson process concerns the relationship between the arrival rate and the time between arrivals. If the number of arrivals per unit time is Poisson distributed with a mean of λ, then the time between arrivals is distributed as a negative exponential probability distribution with a mean of $1/\lambda$. For example, if the mean arrival rate per 10-minute period is 3, then the mean time between arrivals is 10/3, or 3.3 minutes.

4.1.3 Queuing Classifications

The previously described relationship between Poisson arrival time and a negative exponential service rate is referred to as an M/M/1 queuing system. A queuing system format was developed by Kendall to provide a mechanism for classifying different types of queuing systems. The general format of Kendall's classification scheme is:

A/B/X/Y/Z

where:
    A specifies the inter-arrival time distribution
    B specifies the service time distribution
    X specifies the number of service channels
    Y specifies the system capacity
    Z specifies the queue discipline

The letter M used to describe a queuing system that has a Poisson arrival time, and a negative exponential service time denotes that the inter-arrival time and service time distributions are memory-less. When the system capacity and queue are considered to be infinite, the designators Y and Z are omitted. As we will note later in this chapter, as the level of utilization of a system increases, the difference between infinite and finite system capacity and queue length decreases. Because we often are primarily interested in determining the effect on a system under a high level of utilization, both infinite and finite models can provide satisfactory information.

4.1.4 Network Applications

Through the use of queuing theory or waiting time analysis, we can examine the effect of different WAN circuit operating rates. That is, we can examine the ability of remote bridges and routers to transfer data between LANs, and the effect of different levels of buffer memory on their ability to transfer data. In doing so we can obtain answers to such critical questions as: What is the average delay associated with the use of a remote bridge or router? What is the effect on those delays by increasing the operating rate of the WAN circuit? When does an increase in the wide area network circuit's operating rate result in an insignificant improvement in bridge or router performance? How much buffer memory should a remote bridge or router contain to avoid losing frames? To illustrate the application and value of queuing theory to network problems, let us look at an example of its use.

Let us assume you are planning to interconnect two geographically dispersed LANs through the use of a pair of routers or remote bridges as illustrated in Figure 4.3. In this example, a Token Ring network at one location will be connected to an Ethernet LAN at another location. Most routers and remote bridges support both RS-232 and V.35 interfaces, permitting the router or bridge to be connected to modems or higher-speed data service units (DSUs) that are used with digital transmission facilities. This opens a Pandora's box concerning the type of circuit to use to connect a pair of remote bridges, analog or digital, and the operating rate of the circuit. Fortunately, we can use queuing theory to determine an optimum line operating rate to interconnect the two LANs illustrated in Figure 4.3.

4.1.5 Deciding on a Queuing Model

In applying queuing theory to the network configuration illustrated in Figure 4.3, you would be correct in stating that it resembles a single-channel, multiple-phase waiting line system similar to the second example shown in Figure 4.2. However, prior to deciding on a queuing model to use, let us consider the delays associated with each phase of the network shown in Figure 4.3.

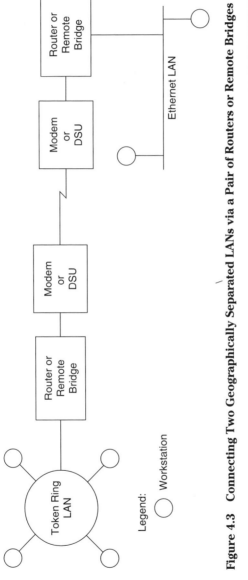

Figure 4.3   Connecting Two Geographically Separated LANs via a Pair of Routers or Remote Bridges

If data is routed from the Token Ring network to the Ethernet network, the primary delay occurs when a frame attempts to gain access to the router or bridge connected to the Token Ring LAN and use its encapsulation services to be placed onto the WAN. If the memory of the router or bridge is not full, the frame is placed into memory at the LAN's operating rate. After a delay based on the number of frames preceding that frame just placed in memory, it is transmitted bit by bit at the WAN operating rate, which is typically an order of magnitude lower than the LAN operating rate. If the memory of the router or bridge is full, the frame is discarded and the workstation that originated the frame must then retransmit it, further adding to the delay in the frame reaching its destination. At the Ethernet site, the frame is received on a bit-by-bit basis and the primary delay encountered is the time required to buffer the frame for placement on the Ethernet LAN.

Because multiple frames result in one following another, there is a degree of overlap between receiving frame n+1 and placing received frame n onto the network. In addition, because the WAN operating rate is but a fraction of the LAN operating rate, the delay associated with the destination router or bridge becomes primarily one of latency and is negligible with respect to the bridge at the transmit side of the interconnected network. Due to this we can simplify our computations by assuming that the second phase of the single-channel, multiple-phase model does not exist, thus reducing the network to a single-channel, single-phase model. Similarly, data flowing from the Ethernet to the Token Ring network has its primary delay attributable to the local router or bridge connected to the Ethernet network. Thus, dataflow in either direction can be analyzed using a single-channel, single-phase queuing model.

4.1.6   Applying Queuing Theory

Let us assume that based upon prior knowledge obtained from monitoring the transmission between locally interconnected LANs, you determined that approximately 10,000 frames per day can be expected to flow from one network to the other network. Let us also assume that the average length of each frame was determined to be 1250 bytes.

Based on the assumption that 10,000 frames will flow between each LAN, we must convert that frame rate into an arrival rate. In doing so let us further assume that each network is only active eight hours per day and both networks are in the same time zone. Thus, a transaction rate of 10,000 frames per eight-hour day is equivalent to an average arrival rate of $10,000/(8 * 60 * 60)$, or 0.347222 frames per second. In queuing theory, this average arrival rate (AR) is the average rate at which frames arrive at the service facility for forwarding across the WAN communications circuit.

Previously we said that through monitoring it was determined that the average frame length was 1250 bytes. Because a LAN frame must be converted into a WAN frame or packet for transmission over a WAN transmission facility, the resulting frame or packet will usually result in the addition of header and trailer information required by the protocol used to carry the LAN frame. Thus, the actual length of the WAN frame or packet will exceed the length of the LAN frame. For computational purposes, let us assume that 25 bytes are added to each LAN frame, resulting in the average transmission of 1275 bytes per frame.

Because the computation of an expected service time requires an operating rate, let us first assume that the WAN communications circuit illustrated in Figure 4.3 operates at 9600 bps. Then, the time required to transmit one 1275-byte frame or packet becomes 1275 bytes/frame * 8 bits/byte/9600 bps, or 1.0625 seconds. This time is more formally known as the expected service time and it represents the time required to transmit a frame whose average length is 1250 bytes on the LAN and 1275 bytes when converted for transmission over the WAN transmission facility. Given that the expected service time is 1.0625 seconds, we can easily compute the mean service rate (MSR). That rate is the rate at which frames entering the router or remote bridge destined for the other LAN are serviced and it is 1/1.0625, or 0.9411765 frames per second.

So far, we have computed two key queuing theory variables: the arrival rate and the mean service rate. Note that the service rate computation depended on the initial selection of a WAN circuit operating rate, which was initially selected as 9600 bps.

Figure 4.4 illustrates the results of our initial set of computations for one portion of our interconnected LANs. Because we assumed that 10,000 frames per eight-hour day flow in each direction, we can simply analyze one half of the interconnected network. This simplification is facilitated by the fact that we are also assuming that the average frame size flowing in each direction is the same or near equivalent. If this is not true, such as for internetwork communications restricted to network users on one LAN accessing a server on another network resulting in relatively short queries in one direction followed by long frames carrying responses to those queries, then our assumption would fall by the wayside. In this type of situation, you would analyze the traffic flow in each direction and select a line operating rate that meets your requirements for serving the worst-case transmission direction in terms of frame rate and frame size. However, if the traffic flow is even or near even in terms of frame rate and frame size, you can restrict your analysis to one direction. This is because full-duplex communications circuits operate at the same data rate in each direction; once you determine the required operating rate in one direction you have also determined the operating rate of the circuit.

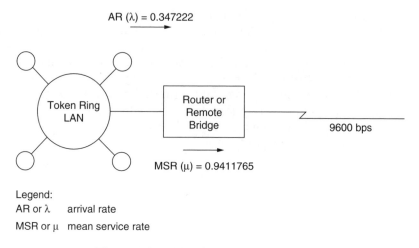

AR (λ) = 0.347222

Token Ring LAN

Router or Remote Bridge

9600 bps

MSR (μ) = 0.9411765

Legend:
AR or λ arrival rate
MSR or μ mean service rate

Figure 4.4   Initial Computational Results

4.1.7   Queuing Theory Designators

In examining Figure 4.4, note that queuing theory designators are indicated in parenthesis. Thus, in a queuing theory book, the average arrival rate of 0.347222 transactions or frames per second would be indicated by the expression $\lambda = 0.347222$. Similarly, the mean service rate in queuing theory books is designated by the symbol μ.

Although the mean service rate exceeds the average arrival rate, upon occasion the arrival rate will result in a burst of data that exceeds the capacity of the router or bridge to service frames. When this situation occurs, queues are created as the router or bridge accepts frames and places those frames it cannot immediately transmit into buffers or temporary storage areas. Through the use of queuing theory, we can examine the expected time for frames to flow through the router or bridge and adjust the circuit operating rate accordingly. In addition, we can use queuing theory to determine the amount of buffer memory a remote bridge or router should have to minimize the potential for the loss of frames to a specific probability.

As previously discussed, the use of remote bridges or routers can be considered to represent a single-channel, single-phase queuing model. For this model we will assume arrivals follow a Poisson distribution and a negative exponential distribution is associated with the service rate. In addition to the preceding, we will also make the following assumptions:

1. There is an infinite calling population.
2. There is an infinite queue.

3. Queuing is on a first-come, first-serve basis.
4. Over a prolonged period of time, the service rate exceeds the arrival rate ($\mu > \lambda$).

The use of the preceding assumptions results in the notation M/M/1 being used to classify this queuing system. Based on the preceding, the utilization of the service facility (p) is obtained by dividing the average arrival rate by the mean service rate. That is,

$$p = \frac{AR}{MSR} = \frac{0.347222}{0.9411765} = 0.3689$$

Thus, the use of a circuit operating at 9600 bps results in an average utilization level of approximately 37 percent. Readers should note that in queuing theory texts, the preceding equation will be replaced by $p = \lambda/\mu$, where λ is the symbol used for the average arrival rate, while μ is the symbol used for the mean service rate.

Because the utilization level of the service facility (router or remote bridge) is AR/MSR, the probability that there are no frames in the bridge, P_0, becomes:

$$P_0 = 1 - AR/MSR, \text{ or } 1 - \lambda/\mu$$

For the remote bridge connected to a 9600-bps circuit, we then obtain:

$$P_0 = 1 - .37 = 0.63$$

Thus, 63 percent of the time there will be no frames in the bridge's buffers awaiting transmission to the distant network.

4.1.8 Frame Determination

For a single-channel, single-phase system, the mean number of units expected to be in the system is equivalent to the average arrival rate divided by the difference between the mean service rate and the arrival rate. In queuing theory, the mean or expected number of units in a system is normally designated by the letter L. Thus,

$$L = \frac{AR}{MSR - AR} = \frac{\lambda}{\mu - \lambda}$$

Returning to our networking example, we can determine the mean or expected number of frames that will be in the system, including frames residing in the device's buffer area or flowing down the WAN transmission facility as follows:

$$L = \frac{0.347}{0.941 - 0.347} = 0.585$$

Thus, on the average, we can expect approximately six tenths of a frame to reside in the device's buffer and on the transmission line.

If we multiply the utilization of the service facility by the expected number of units in a system, we obtain the mean number of units in the queue or, in common English, the queue length. The queue length is denoted by Lq and thus becomes:

$$Lq = p*L = \frac{AR^2}{MSR(MSR - AR)} = \frac{\lambda^2}{\mu(\mu - \lambda)}$$

Again, returning to our network example, we obtain:

$$Lq = \frac{(0.347)^2}{0.941*(0.941 - 0.347)} = 0.216$$

Based on the preceding, we can expect, on average, 0.216 frames to be queued in the bridge or router for transmission when the operating rate of the WAN is 9600 bps and 10,000 frames per eight-hour day require remote bridging or routing to the opposite destination. Because we previously determined that there were 0.585 frames in the system, this means that the difference, (0.585 − 0.216) or 0.369 frames, is flowing on the transmission line at any particular point in time.

We can visualize the locations where frames are temporarily stored by examining Figure 4.5, which illustrates the relationship between L, Lq, and L − Lq. Here, Lq corresponds to the buffer memory of the device while L corresponds to the system consisting of the bridge or router and the transmission line. Thus, L −Lq then corresponds to the frames or portion of a frame flowing on the transmission line.

The preceding information also provides us with data concerning the average expected utilization of the WAN transmission facility. Because the

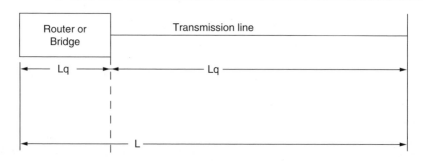

Figure 4.5   Temporary Frame Storage Relationship

frame length is 1275 bytes and 0.369 frames can be expected to be flowing on the circuit at any point in time, this means the line can be expected to hold 1275 bytes/frame * 0.369 frames, or 470.5 bytes. This is equivalent to 3764 bits on a line planned to operate at 9600 bps, or a circuit utilization level of approximately 39 percent.

4.1.9   Time Computations

In addition to computing information concerning the expected number of frames in queues and in the system, queuing theory provides us with the tools to determine the mean time in the system and the mean waiting time. In queuing theory, the mean waiting time is designated by the variable W, while the mean waiting time in the queue is designated by the variable Wq.

The mean time in the system, W, is:

$$W = \frac{1}{MSR - AR} = \frac{1}{\mu - \lambda}$$

For our bridged network example, the mean time a frame can be expected to reside in the system can be computed as follows:

$$W = \frac{1}{0.941 - 0.347} = 1.68 \text{ seconds}$$

By itself, this tells us that we can expect an average response time of approximately 1.7 seconds for frames that must be bridged or routed from one LAN to the other if our WAN transmission facility operates at 9600 bps. Whether this is good or bad depends on how you view a 1.7 second delay.

The next queuing item we will focus our attention on is the waiting time associated with a frame being queued. That time, Wq, is equivalent to the waiting time in the system multiplied by the utilization of the service facility. That is,

$$Wq = p * W = \frac{AR}{MSR} * \frac{1}{(MSR - AR)} = \frac{AR}{MSR(MSR - AR)}$$

In terms of queuing theory, Wq then becomes:

$$Wq = \frac{\lambda}{\mu(\mu - \lambda)}$$

Similar to the manner by which frame storage relationships were shown with respect to the bridge and transmission line, we can illustrate the relationship of waiting times. Figure 4.6 illustrates the relationship between W, Wq, and W − Wq with respect to the bridge and transmission line. Here, Wq

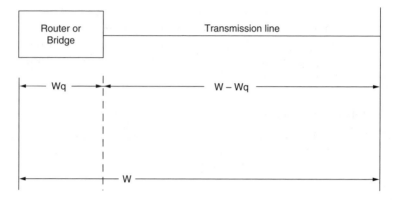

Figure 4.6   Waiting Time Relationship

corresponds to the waiting time for a frame to pass through the bridge or router, while W is the total frame waiting time to include the transit time through the device and across the transmission line. Thus, W – Wq corresponds to the time required for a frame to transit the transmission line.

Once again, let us return to our bridged network example. In doing so, we obtain:

$$Wq = \frac{0.347}{0.941 * (0.941 - 0.347)} = 0.621 \text{ seconds}$$

Note that we previously determined that a frame can be expected to reside for 1.68 seconds in our communications system, including queue waiting time and transmission time. Because we computed the queue waiting time as 0.621 seconds, the difference between the two, 1.68 – 0.621, or approximately 1.06 seconds, is the time required to transmit a frame over the 9600-bps WAN transmission facility.

Two of the more interesting relationships we should note are the variance of Lq and Wq as a function of utilization. As previously noted,

$$Lq = \frac{\lambda^2}{\mu(\mu - \lambda)} \quad \text{And} \quad Wq = \frac{\lambda}{\mu(\mu - \lambda)}$$

Because utilization (p) is the ratio of λ/μ, it is difficult to vary p and compute Lq and Wq. Instead, we can fix the arrival rate and vary the service rate to change the level of utilization. Doing so also enables us to compute the length of the queue (Lq) and the waiting time in the queue (Wq).

Figure 4.7 illustrates the display of a Microsoft Excel spreadsheet developed to compute Lq and Wq based upon the level of utilization for an

Queue Length and Waiting time vs Utilization

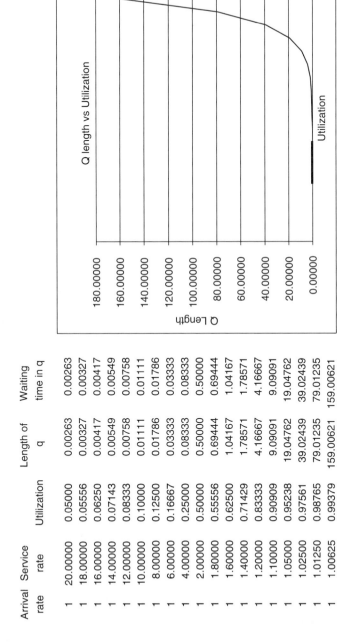

Arrival rate	Service rate	Utilization	Length of q	Waiting time in q
1	20.00000	0.05000	0.00263	0.00263
1	18.00000	0.05556	0.00327	0.00327
1	16.00000	0.06250	0.00417	0.00417
1	14.00000	0.07143	0.00549	0.00549
1	12.00000	0.08333	0.00758	0.00758
1	10.00000	0.10000	0.01111	0.01111
1	8.00000	0.12500	0.01786	0.01786
1	6.00000	0.16667	0.03333	0.03333
1	4.00000	0.25000	0.08333	0.08333
1	2.00000	0.50000	0.50000	0.50000
1	1.80000	0.55556	0.69444	0.69444
1	1.60000	0.62500	1.04167	1.04167
1	1.40000	0.71429	1.78571	1.78571
1	1.20000	0.83333	4.16667	4.16667
1	1.10000	0.90909	9.09091	9.09091
1	1.05000	0.95238	19.04762	19.04762
1	1.02500	0.97561	39.02439	39.02439
1	1.01250	0.98765	79.01235	79.01235
1	1.00625	0.99379	159.00621	159.00621

Figure 4.7 Queue Length and Waiting Time versus Utilization

91

M/M/1 queuing system. Note that by fixing the arrival rate at unity, Lq and Wq are equal. Also note that from both the graph and tabular data presented in Figure 4.7, as the level of utilization increases beyond 70 percent, the length of the queue as well as the waiting time in the queue begin to significantly increase. In fact, this example illustrates why an increase in the level of utilization beyond 70 percent can result in significant communications problems due to a queuing system buildup and expansion in waiting time. As we will note later in this chapter, we can compensate for the buildup in system utilization by adding a faster communications channel, in effect increasing the service rate, which lowers the level of utilization. Readers are referred to the file QLENUTIL in the directory Excel at the previously noted Web URL address, which contains the spreadsheet shown in Figure 4.7. You can alter the parameters in the spreadsheet to examine the effect on Lq and Wq based upon other arrival rates and service rates.

4.1.10 Frames in the System

The last queuing item we focus attention on in applying the M/M/1 model is determining the number of frames in the system. As previously noted, the utilization of the system is λ/μ. The probability of no units in an M/M/1 system is then $1 - \lambda/\mu$, which we defined as P_0. Thus, the probability that there are n units in the system becomes:

$$Pn = \frac{(\lambda)^n}{\mu}\left(1 - \frac{\lambda}{\mu}\right) = P_0\,\frac{(\lambda)^n}{\mu}$$

We can also determine the probability there are k or more units in the system as follows:

$$Pn > k = \frac{(\lambda)^k}{\mu}$$

Because $P_0 = 1 - P$ and $P = \lambda/\mu$, we can rewrite $P_{n>k}$ as follows:

$$P_{n>k} = P^k$$

Later in this chapter we will examine the effect of changes in the utilization level of a queuing system upon the probability of a specific number of frames in the system.

4.2 Determining an Optimum Line Operating Rate

Although we could recompute each of the previously computed variables based on different line operating rates, we can just as easily write a program to perform such tedious operations. Thus, let us do so.

4.2.1 Program QUEUE.BAS

Table 4.1 lists the statements of a BASIC language program appropriately named QUEUE.BAS. The execution of this program is shown in Table 4.2, which displays the values for eight queuing theory parameters based upon line speeds ranging from 4800 bps to 1.536 Mbps. The latter line speed represents the effective operating rate of a T1 circuit, because 8000 bps of the 1.544-Mbps operating rate of that circuit is used for framing and is not available for the actual transmission of data.

4.2.2 Utilization Level versus Line Speed

In examining the values of the queuing parameters listed in Table 4.2, let us focus attention on the utilization level, P, and the mean waiting time in the queue, Wq. At 4800 bps, note that the utilization level is approximately 74 percent, while the waiting time in the queue is almost six seconds! Clearly, linking the two LANs via remote bridges or routers operating at 4800 bps provides an unacceptable waiting time due to the high utilization level of the device.

As the line speed connecting the routers or remote bridges is increased, each device is able to service frames at a higher processing rate. Because the average arrival rate is fixed, increasing the line operating rate should lower the utilization level of the router or bridge as well as the time a frame resides in the queue. Our expectation is verified by the results of the execution of QUEUE.BAS shown in Table 4.2. Note that, as expected, both the utilization level and mean waiting time in the queue decrease as the line speed increases.

4.2.3 Spreadsheet Model

To facilitate queuing computations for those who prefer to work with spreadsheets, a queuing template was developed using Microsoft's Excel spreadsheet program. Figure 4.8 illustrates the screen display of the execution of the spreadsheet model. The actual spreadsheet template is stored on the file QUEUE1 in the directory Excel at the Web URL referenced in this book. Note that this model includes eight mini-charts that plot such computed variables as expected service time, mean service rate, utilization, probability of zero frames in the system, mean number of frames in the system and the queue, and mean waiting time in the system and in the queue. By focusing on either the tabular computational results or the charts, we can use the displayed information to determine an optimum operating rate. However, prior to doing so readers should note that similar to all Excel spreadsheet models, you can display cell formulas if you wish to examine the computations performed by this template.

4.2.4 Selecting an Operating Rate

At the beginning of this chapter, it was mentioned that queuing theory could be used to determine the operating rate of transmission lines for

Table 4.1   Program Listing of QUEUE.BAS

```
REM PROGRAM QUEUE.BAS

CLS

PRINT "Queuing Analysis Program - Single-Phase, Single-Channel Model"

REM AR=arrival rate

REM MSR=mean service rate

REM L=mean (expected) number of frames in system

REM Lq=mean number of frames in queue

REM W=mean time (s) in system

REM Wq=mean waiting time (s)

REM EST= expected service time

INPUT "Enter transactions/day"; transactions

INPUT "Enter average frame size in bytes"; avgframe

PRINT

hrsperday = 8

AR = transactions/(8 * 60 * 60)

DATA
9600,19200,56000,64000,128000,256000,384000,768000,1536000,1984000

FOR i = 1 TO 10

READ linespeed(i)

est(i) = avgframe * 8/linespeed(i)

msr(i) = 1/est(i)

utilization(i) = AR/msr(i)

prob0(i) = 1 - (AR/msr(i))

L(i) = AR/(msr(i) - AR)

Lq(i) = AR ^ 2/(msr(i) * (msr(i) - AR))

W(i) = 1/(msr(i) - AR)

Wq(i) = AR/(msr(i) * (msr(i) - AR))

NEXT i

PRINT "Line Speed  EST    MSR     Po         p         L        Lq
W         Wq"

FOR i = 1 TO 10

PRINT USING " #######  #.#### ###.## "; linespeed(i); est(i);
msr(i);

PRINT USING " #.#####.#####"; prob0(i); utilization(i);

PRINT USING "  #.#####  #.#####  #.#####   #.#####"; L(i); Lq(i);
W(i); Wq(i)

NEXT i
```

Table 4.1   Program Listing of QUEUE.BAS   (continued)

```
PRINT
PRINT "where:"
PRINT
PRINT " EST= expected service time  MSR = mean service rate"
PRINT " Po=probability of zero frames in the system  p = utilization"
PRINT " L= mean number of frames in system Lq = mean number in queue"
PRINT " W= mean waiting time in system  Wq = mean waiting time in
queue"
```

Table 4.2   Execution Results of Program QUEUE.BAS

Line Speed	EST	MSR	P_0	p	L	Lq	W	Wq
4800	2.1250	0.47	0.26215	0.73785	2.81457	2.07672	8.10596	5.98096
9600	1.0625	0.94	0.63108	0.36892	0.58459	0.21567	1.68363	0.62113
19200	0.5313	1.88	0.81554	0.18446	0.22618	0.04172	0.65141	0.12016
56000	0.1821	5.49	0.93676	0.06324	0.06751	0.00427	0.19444	0.01230
64000	0.1594	6.27	0.94466	0.05534	0.05858	0.00324	0.16871	0.00934
128000	0.0797	12.55	0.97233	0.02767	0.02846	0.00079	0.08196	0.00227
256000	0.0398	25.10	0.98617	0.01383	0.01403	0.00019	0.04040	0.00056
384000	0.0266	37.65	0.99078	0.00922	0.00931	0.00009	0.02681	0.00025
768000	0.0133	75.29	0.99539	0.00461	0.00463	0.00002	0.01334	0.00006
1536000	0.0066	150.59	0.99769	0.00231	0.00231	0.00001	0.00666	0.00002

where:

EST = expected service time; MSR = mean service rate;

P_0 = probability of zero frames in the system; p = utilization;

L = mean number of frames in system; Lq = mean number in queue;

W = mean waiting time in system; Wq = mean waiting time in queue.

linking remote bridges and routers. In actuality, such usage will not produce a "magic number." Instead, the use of queuing theory can provide a range of values from which you can make a logical decision. For example, returning to Table 4.2, a line operating rate of 4800 bps is clearly unacceptable. However, what can we say concerning an operating rate of 9600 bps, 19,200 bps, 56,000 bps, etc.?

To provide some "food for thought," consider the chart marked Utilization in Figure 4.8, which shows the utilization level of the device based on the ten line operating rates that were considered. Note that at a line operating rate above the 56 Kbps to 64 Kbps range, further reductions in the utilization level of the router or bridge and an increase in the probability of

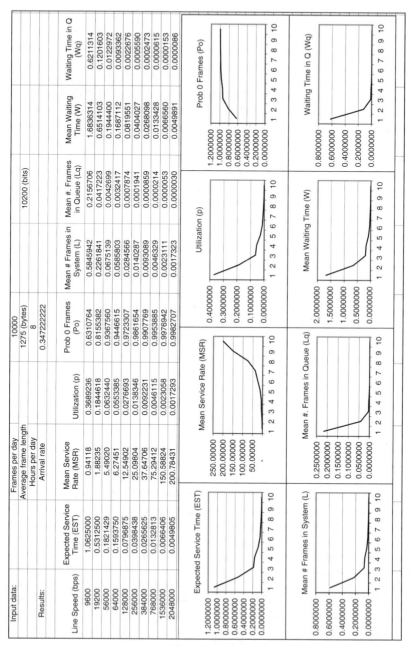

Input data:		Frames per day	10000			
		Average frame length	1275 (bytes)		10200 (bits)	
Results:		Hours per day	8			
		Arrival rate	0.347222222			
Line Speed (bps)	Expected Service Time (EST)	Mean Service Rate (MSR)	Utilization (p)	Prob 0 Frames (Po)	Mean # Frames in System (L)	Mean # Frames in Queue (Lq)	Mean Waiting Time (W)	Waiting Time in Q (Wq)
9600	1.0625000	0.94118	0.3689236	0.6310764	0.5845942	0.2156706	1.6836314	0.6211314
19200	0.5312500	1.88235	0.1844618	0.8155382	0.2261841	0.0417223	0.6514103	0.1201603
56000	0.1821429	5.49020	0.0632440	0.9367560	0.0675139	0.0042699	0.1944400	0.0122972
64000	0.1593750	6.27451	0.0553385	0.9446615	0.0585803	0.0032417	0.1687112	0.0093362
128000	0.0796875	12.54902	0.0276693	0.9723307	0.0284566	0.0007874	0.0819551	0.0022676
256000	0.0398438	25.09804	0.0138346	0.9861654	0.0140287	0.0001941	0.0404027	0.0005590
384000	0.0265625	37.64706	0.0092231	0.9907769	0.0093089	0.0000859	0.0268098	0.0002473
768000	0.0132813	75.29412	0.0046115	0.9953885	0.0046329	0.0000214	0.0133428	0.0000615
1536000	0.0066406	150.58824	0.0023058	0.9976942	0.0023111	0.0000053	0.0066560	0.0000153
2048000	0.0049805	200.78431	0.0017293	0.9982707	0.0017323	0.0000030	0.0049891	0.0000086

Figure 4.8 Spreadsheet Model Screen Display

zero frames in the system is essentially insignificant. Thus, you would more than likely restrict your line operating rate to a maximum of 56 to 64 Kbps in this example. To obtain a better grasp of the situation, from either Table 4.2 or Figure 4.8, note that raising the line operating rate from 64 Kbps to 128 Kbps only marginally decreases the waiting time in the queue from 0.009 seconds at 64 Kbps to 0.002 seconds at 128 Kbps. For an interactive application, the difference in the delay would not be noticeable. Thus, if you were fairly certain your application would not grow, you would probably install a digital leased line operating at 64 Kbps. Only if you anticipated further growth in transmission would you want to consider the installation of a higher speed and more costly leased line.

4.2.5 Summary

To correctly apply queuing theory to interconnecting LANs, you must first obtain knowledge about the number of transactions and the average frame size of each transaction that will flow to the other network. Once this is accomplished, you must estimate the growth in the average frame size to reflect the addition of header and trailer information required by the wide area protocol to carry your LAN frame. This then provides you with the ability to compute the average arrival rate of frames as well as the mean service rate of a remote bridge or router. Then, you can easily compute the additional queuing parameters previously discussed in this chapter and recalculate those parameters for different transmission line operating rates whose examination will enable you to select an appropriate operating rate to interconnect your LANs.

Prior to moving on to the next topic in this chapter, a few words about service time are in order. In our previous set of computations, we employed a single-channel, single-phase model based on a memory-less inter-arrival time and service time. This resulted in the model being based on the use of a negative exponential probability distribution for service time. As previously observed when we discussed the Kendall method of queuing notations, there are five basic queuing parameters that define the queuing system. Because the model we previously used was a single-channel, single-phase system and we assumed a first-in, first-out queuing method, we are basically left with considering variations in the arrival time and service time. Thus, let us focus on these two areas.

For a memory-less system, the use of a negative exponential distribution for inter-arrival time allows simple formulas to be developed to construct a queuing model. As an alternative, we could count arrivals in defined time intervals but the difference between the two over a period of time would not be significant if actual arrivals occur randomly. Because people operate computers in a random manner, this basically leaves us with the service time as a queuing system parameter to consider.

One variation in service time occurs when service time is fixed or deterministic. For Ethernet and Token Ring, a fixed service time would not be practical because frame lengths vary, resulting in a non-constant service time. However, for ATM whose cell length is fixed at 53 bytes, a deterministic service time would be more appropriate. Later in this book when we develop models to determine the performance of ATM, we will examine the use of a deterministic service time.

A second service time variation that warrants discussion occurs when the service time does not fit a negative exponential distribution but we can measure or estimate the mean service rate and its standard deviation. Then, the following set of equations would be used to model a single-channel, single-phase queuing system with Poisson arrivals and arbitrary service times:

Utilization: $P = \lambda/\mu$

Probability of no frames in the system:

$$P_0 = 1 - \frac{\lambda}{\mu}$$

Length of the queue: $\quad Lq = \dfrac{\lambda^2 6^2 + \left(\lambda/\mu\right)^2}{2\left(1 - \lambda/\mu\right)}$

Length of the system: $\quad L = Lq + \lambda/\mu$

Waiting time in queue: $\quad Wq = Lq/\lambda$

Waiting time in system: $\quad w = Wq + 1/\mu$

where: $6 =$ standard deviation.

Note that if we set the standard deviation to zero, we have a model that reflects constant service times. As we will note later in this book, we can consider this model and others as a mechanism to examine ATM.

4.3 Examining Single and Multiple Communications Circuits

One of the more common decisions facing a network designer is whether to use single or multiple communications circuits when connecting remote LANs via the use of bridges or routers. Obviously, from a reliability point of view, multiple circuits are preferable to the use of a single circuit. However, from a performance point of view, are two circuits, each with one half the transmission capacity of a single circuit, better than the use of a single transmission path? This is the question that will be examined in this section, while leaving an investigation of the gain in availability and reliability of multiple circuits over single circuits for Chapter 6.

4.3.1 Comparing the Use of Single- and Dual-Port Equipment

Figure 4.9 illustrates the use of single- and dual-port remote routers or bridges to connect an Ethernet LAN to a distant Token Ring LAN. Suppose the single-port devices are connected to data service units (DSUs) that operate at 19,200 bps, whereas the multi-port device is connected to two DSUs, each operating at 9600 bps. Although each pair of communications devices has access to an aggregate transmission capacity of 19200, does the use of single and dual transmission paths in which the single path operates at twice the rate of each dual transmission path provide an equivalent level of service? To answer this question, let us return to the use of queuing theory. In doing so, let us assume that the number of transactions estimated to flow between LANs is 21,600 per eight-hour day. Let us also assume that the average frame size, including communications framing for transmission, is 1200 bytes.

4.3.2 Single Circuit

As a review of our prior discussion of Kendall's notation, we can consider the single circuit to operate on a first-in, first-out basis. When we assume that the number of frames can approach infinity, this means we can consider the single circuit communications link illustrated at the top of Figure 4.9a to more formally represent what is known as an M/M/1 queuing system.

4.3.2.1 Notation. The notation M/M/1 is actually a shorthand abbreviation of the form A/B/C, which is used by queuing theorists to describe queuing problems. The letter used in the A position represents the statistical characteristics of the arrival rate of items to be serviced, such as customers approaching a teller or frames flowing to a bridge or router. A probability density function (pdf), such as the Poisson pdf, is typically used to describe a customer arrival rate. One of the most commonly used pdfs is the exponential pdf, which is denoted as M in queuing theory shorthand notation. The exponential pdf is defined as:

$$p(t) = \lambda e^{-\lambda t}$$

This pdf is equivalent to saying that arriving customers behave as if they are not aware of each other's existence (i.e., occur randomly). Thus, the arrival process is a process without memory and the shorthand abbreviation M used to denote an exponential arrival rate actually references the fact that the arrivals are "memory-less."

Readers should note that systems with an exponential inter-arrival distribution results in a Poisson arrival rate distribution. In fact, the probability that exactly n customers will arrive in a period of time t is given by the equation:

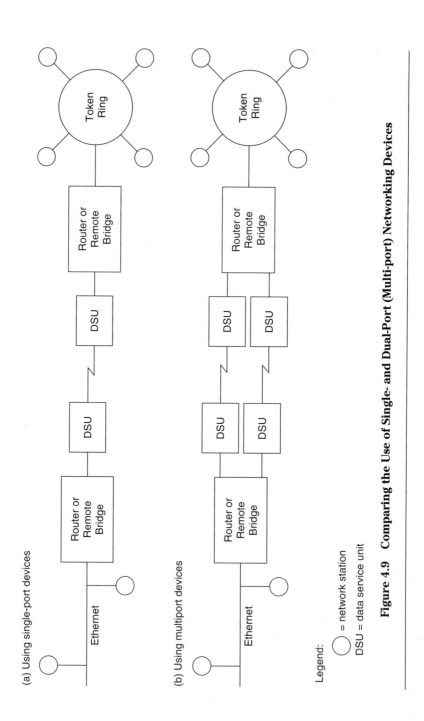

Figure 4.9   Comparing the Use of Single- and Dual-Port (Multi-port) Networking Devices

$$P(n, t) = \frac{\lambda t^n e^{-\lambda t}}{n!}$$

The above equation is the Poisson probability function. Thus, an exponential inter-arrival time distribution, which is memory-less and denoted in queuing shorthand notation by M, is generated by a Poisson process in which the arrival of any customer is independent of previous customers.

Returning to the A/B/C notation format used to describe a queuing problem, B represents the statistical characteristics of the server. A server that operates without regard to the length of a queue (e.g., does not get tired) has its behavior described by an exponential service time distribution. Thus, such servers are also "memory-less" and the letter M is used in position B to describe the characteristics of our server. Finally, the letter C in the queuing problem shorthand description format represents the number of servers. Thus, the numeric 1 was used in our shorthand queuing abbreviation for position C to complete our description of the queuing model in Figure 4.9a.

4.3.2.2 Computations. Based on 21,600 transactions occurring in an eight-hour day, the arrival rate becomes:

$$\lambda = \frac{21600}{8 * 60 * 60} = 0.75 \text{ per second}$$

Because it was assumed that the average frame size is 1200 bytes, the expected service time when the line operates at 19,200 bps becomes 1200 * 8/19200, or 0.5 seconds. Thus, the service rate becomes:

$$\mu = \frac{1}{\text{expected service time}} = \frac{1}{.5} = 2 \text{ per second}$$

The utilization of the server (p) is the arrival rate divided by the service rate. Thus,

$$p = \frac{\lambda}{\mu} = \frac{.75}{2} = 0.375$$

The probability that there are no frames in the system (P_0) is one minus the utilization. Thus,

$$P_0 = 1 - \frac{\lambda}{\mu} = 1 - 0.375 = 0.625$$

Let us continue and compute the mean number of frames expected in the system (L) and the mean length of the queue (Lq). Doing so, we obtain:

$$L = \frac{\lambda}{\mu - \lambda} = \frac{0.75}{2 - 0.75} = 0.6$$

$$Lq = \frac{\lambda^2}{\mu(\mu - \lambda)} = \frac{P^2}{1 - P} = \frac{(0.375)^2}{1 - 0.375} = 0.225$$

Thus, we can expect 0.6 frames to be in the system, while 0.225 frames, on the average, will be in the queue. Now let us focus attention on waiting times, the mean time waiting in the queue (Wq) and the mean time waiting in the system (W). Those two parameters are computed as follows:

$$Wq = \frac{\lambda}{\mu(\mu - \lambda)} = \frac{0.75}{2(2 - 0.75)} = 0.3 \text{ seconds}$$

$$W = \frac{1}{\mu - \lambda} = \frac{1}{2 - 0.75} = 0.8 \text{ seconds}$$

Note that the difference between the average waiting time in the system of 0.8 seconds and the average waiting time of 0.3 seconds in the queue is 0.5 seconds. That time is exactly the expected service time for a 1200-byte frame to be carried on a 19,200-bps transmission circuit. Now that the basic queuing-related performance elements for the single-path circuit have been computed, let us focus attention on the use of dual transmission circuits.

4.3.3   Dual Circuits

The dual transmission path illustrated in the lower portion of Figure 4.9 represents an M/M/2 queuing system in which the numeric indicates there are two servers or, in our example, two channels or circuits.

Although you will normally think of a server as a device with memory that enables queues to form, you can also treat each circuit as a server. In doing so, each router or remote bridge then provides the buffer memory for the formation of queues for service or placement onto each communications circuit. Here, the use of two channels or communications circuits can be considered to represent a queuing system that is more formerly referred to as a multiple-channel, single-phase queuing system.

   4.3.3.1   Computations. In computing the queuing parameters, note that the arrival rate of 0.75 frames per second remains the same. However, because each circuit now operates at 9600 bps, the expected service time is 1200 bytes * 8 bits/byte/9600 bytes, or 1 second. Thus, the service rate, μ, is 1/1, or 1 frame per second per transmission line.

   For a multiple-channel, single-phase system, utilization is computed as follows where s is the number of servers.

$$p = \frac{\lambda}{s\mu} = \frac{0.75}{2 * 1} = 0.375$$

So far, everything appears to be equivalent between a single transmission line and two lines in which each of the latter operate at one half the rate of the former.

In a multiple-channel, single-phase queuing system, the probability that there are no frames in the system (P_0) is determined using the following formula:

$$P_0 = \frac{1}{\displaystyle\sum_{n=0}^{s-1} \frac{(\lambda/\mu)^n}{n!} + \frac{(\lambda/\mu^s)}{s!(1 - \lambda/s\mu)}} = 0.375$$

where s represents the number of servers and n! and s! represent n and s factorial, where factorial n represents the value $mx(m - 1) * m - 2) * \ldots * 1$. The results of the computations for our two-server model to obtain the probability that there are no frames in the system are as follows:

$$P_0 = \frac{1}{1 + 0.75 + \dfrac{(0.75)^2}{2(1 - 0.75/2)}}$$

$$P_0 = \frac{1}{1 + 0.75 + .45} = \frac{1}{2.2} = 4.5$$

This means that there is a 45 percent probability that both servers do not contain any frames at any point in time.

Now that P_0 has been computed, we can use our prior computation in equations developed for multiple-channel, single-phase systems for other queuing parameters of interest. Those four parameters, Lq, L, W, and Wq are computed as follows:

$$Lq = \frac{P_0(\lambda/\mu)^2 p}{S!(1 - p)^2} = \frac{.45(0.75)^2 \times .375}{2(1 - .375)^2} = 0.1215$$

$$L = Lq + \frac{\lambda}{\mu} = 0.1215 + \frac{.75}{1} = 0.8715$$

$$Wq = \frac{Lq}{\lambda} = \frac{.1215}{.75} = 0.162$$

$$W = Wq + \frac{1}{\mu} = .162 + 1 = 1.162$$

Table 4.3   Comparing Single- and Dual-Path Queuing Values

Parameter	Single Path	Dual Path
Arrival rate	0.75	0.75
Service rate	2	1
Utilization	0.375	0.375
Probability of no frames in the system	0.625	0.45
Mean number of frames in system	0.6	0.87
Mean length of queue	0.225	0.12
Mean time in system	0.3	1.162
Mean waiting time	0.8	0.162

4.3.4   General Observations

So far, we have made a number of computations. Now let us compare our previous computations and use the comparison between single and dual server models to make some general observations. Table 4.3 compares the queuing computations for the single and dual communications paths illustrated in Figure 4.9.

In comparing the entries in Table 4.3 between the single and dual path scenarios, let us first focus attention on P_0, the probability that there is no frame in the system. Note that the single path has a higher probability that there is no frame in the system than the dual path. The reason for this can be explained by examining Figure 4.10, which indicates how transmission gaps can occur on two paths, each operating at a fraction of a single path.

Suppose a 2400-byte frame arrives at a server connected to a single 19,200-bps data circuit. As indicated in the upper portion of Figure 4.10, one 19,200-bps circuit could transmit the first 2400-byte frame in precisely one second. If a second frame shows up precisely one second later, the first frame would have been transmitted and the transmission of the second frame can then commence.

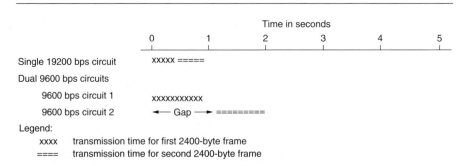

Figure 4.10   Transmission Gaps Commonly Occur on Multiple Circuits

If a second frame shows up just a fraction of a second after the first frame, the second frame will be queued for transmission. Then, once the first frame is transmitted, the second frame will immediately follow the first frame. In fact, the second frame can arrive at any time up to one second after the first frame without a transmission gap occurring. Now consider a similar situation in which two 2400-byte frames arrive one second apart at a bridge or router connected to two communications circuits. The first frame requires two seconds for transmission, while the second 9600-bps circuit is unoccupied for one second until the second frame arrives and is then transmitted on the second circuit because the first circuit is occupied. Because there is no way to split a frame between circuits, there is no way to fill the gap that occurred. The one-second gap illustrated at the lower portion of Figure 4.9 represents half the longest duration gap based on the previous assumptions. If a second frame arrived two seconds after the first, a two-second period of time would occur in which one circuit was not occupied. Similarly, if the second frame followed the first by 0.5 seconds, the gap would be reduced to a 0.5-second duration. As illustrated from this example, the use of two queuing systems, each with half the capacity of a single system will almost always have a lower level of performance due to the higher probability of occurrence of transmission gaps.

By comparing the single- and dual-path queuing values listed in Table 4.3, readers will note there are other significant differences between a single circuit operating at X bps and two circuits each operating at X/2 bps. For example, the mean number of frames in the system less the mean length of the queue tells us the mean number of frames on the circuit or circuits. Here, the use of a single path would result in 0.6 − 0.225, or 0.375 frames, while the dual path would have 0.87 0.12, or 0.75 frames. This means that the mean number of frames in a two-circuit system is twice the number of frames found in a single-circuit system — a situation we would intuitively expect.

Another area of difference between the single- and dual-circuit configurations concerns waiting times. Although the mean waiting time in the queue is less for a two-circuit configuration because it provides two paths for transmitting frames, its mean system time considerably exceeds that of a single-path system. What this tells us is that the use of multiple circuits provides a larger "moving storage" facility for frames than a single-circuit system; however, the end result is that although queuing time (Wq) is reduced, the total time in the system (W) is increased. Thus, discounting availability considerations, a choice between a single circuit operating at X bps and two circuits each operating at X/2 bps should be made in favor of the single circuit.

4.3.5 Program QUEUE2.BAS

To facilitate computations associated with two-channel, single-phase queuing systems, the program QUEUE.BAS was modified. The results of that modification provide queuing statistics for a two-channel, single-phase queuing system for line rates ranging from 4800 bps to 1.536 Mbps. This program modification was renamed QUEUE2.BAS and its statements are listed in Table 4.4. In addition to revising the program to compute two-channel, single-phase queuing system statistics, the program was also modified to accept daily transactions, operational hours per day, and an average frame size as user input.

Table 4.5 illustrates an example of the execution of QUEUE2.BAS. In this example, the program was executed using 21,600 transactions per eight-hour day, with an average frame size of 1200 bytes.

4.3.6 The Excel Model QUEUE2

To facilitate computations by those who prefer to use an electronic spread-sheet, another Microsoft Excel template was created. This template is stored in the file *QUEUE2* in the directory Excel at the Web URL previously mentioned in this book.

Figure 4.11 illustrates the display of the QUEUE2 model for a frame rate of 21,600 frames per day, where the average frame length is 1200 bytes. Note that similar to the previous queuing model created in this chapter, this model displays eight minicharts that provide a visual indication of different queuing system parameters as the line speed varies.

4.4 Buffer Memory Considerations

Most bridges and routers are modular devices whose feature selection list may contain more entries than a restaurant menu. Among the features from which you can normally select is a series of different memory modules that govern the buffer area in which frames can be queued when the frame arrival rate temporarily exceeds the service rate of the device.

Although the cost of memory has significantly declined over the past few years, a wild guess can still be costly from an operational perspective. Thus, we will conclude this chapter by examining how you can use queuing theory to make an educated estimate of the amount of buffer memory that should be installed in remote bridges and routers. It should also be mentioned that this section is applicable to LAN switches, because a related problem is the effect of buffer memory on delays through the switch.

4.4.1 Average Memory

Previously, we determined the mean length of the queue, denoted by Lq. By multiplying the value of Lq by the average frame size, you can determine the average amount of buffer memory that will be occupied. Unfortunately, this action results in the average amount of buffer memory required and means that half the time more memory will be required. Thus, to obtain a

Table 4.4   Program QUEUE2.BAS Program Listing

```
REM PROGRAM QUEUE2.BAS

CLS

PRINT "PROGRAM QUEUE2.BAS - STATISTICS FOR TWO CHANNEL SINGLE PHASE
QUEUE"

PRINT

REM AR=arrival rate

REM MSR=mean service rate

REM L=mean (expected) number of frames in system

REM Lq=mean number of frames in queue

REM W=mean time (s) in system

REM Wq=mean waiting time (s)

REM EST= expected service time

INPUT "Enter transactions per day      : "; transactions

INPUT "Enter operational hours per day : "; hrs

INPUT "Enter average frame size        : "; frame

AR = transactions/(hrs * 60 * 60)

DATA
4800,9600,19200,56000,64000,128000,256000,384000,768000,1536000

FOR I = 1 TO 10

READ linespeed(I)

est(I) = frame * 8/linespeed(I)

MSR(I) = 1/est(I)

UTILIZATION(I) = AR/(2 * MSR(I))

PROB0(I) = 1/(1 + (AR/MSR(I)) + (AR/MSR(I)) ^ 2/(2 * (1 - (AR/(2 *
MSR(I)))))))

Lq(I) = PROB0(I) * (AR/MSR(I)) ^ 2 * UTILIZATION(I)

Lq(I) = Lq(I)/(2 * (1 - UTILIZATION(I)) ^ 2)

L(I) = Lq(I) + AR/MSR(I)

Wq(I) = Lq(I)/AR

W(I) = Wq(I) + 1/MSR(I)

NEXT I

PRINT "Line Speed  EST    MSR     Po       p        L         Lq
W         Wq"

FOR I = 1 TO 10

PRINT USING " #######  #.#### ###.## "; linespeed(I); est(I);
MSR(I);

PRINT USING " #.#####  #.#####"; PROB0(I); UTILIZATION(I);

PRINT USING "  #.#####  #.#####  #.#####  #.#####"; L(I); Lq(I);
W(I); Wq(I)

NEXT I
```

107

Table 4.4   Program QUEUE2.BAS Program Listing   (continued)

```
PRINT
PRINT "where:"
PRINT
PRINT " EST= expected service time   MSR = mean service rate"
PRINT " Po=probability of zero frames in the system  p = utilization"
PRINT " L= mean number of frames in system Lq = mean number in queue"
PRINT " W= mean waiting time in system   Wq = mean waiting time in
queue"
```

Table 4.5   Execution of QUEUE2.BAS

```
PROGRAM QUEUE2.BAS - STATISTICS FOR TWO CHANNEL SINGLE PHASE QUEUE
Enter transactions per day      : ? 21600
Enter operational hours per day : ? 8
Enter average frame size        : ? 1200
```

Line Speed	EST	MSR	P_0	p	L	Lq	W	Wq
4800	2.0000	0.50	0.14286	0.75000	3.42857	1.92857	4.57143	2.57143
9600	1.0000	1.00	0.45455	0.37500	0.87273	0.12273	1.16364	0.16364
19200	0.5000	2.00	0.68421	0.18750	0.38866	0.01366	0.51822	0.01822
56000	0.1714	5.83	0.87919	0.06429	0.12910	0.00053	0.17214	0.00071
64000	0.1500	6.67	0.89349	0.05625	0.11286	0.00036	0.15048	0.00048
128000	0.0750	13.33	0.94529	0.02813	0.05629	0.00004	0.07506	0.00006
256000	0.0375	26.67	0.97227	0.01406	0.02813	0.00001	0.03751	0.00001
384000	0.0250	40.00	0.98142	0.00938	0.01875	0.00000	0.02500	0.00000
768000	0.0125	80.00	0.99067	0.00469	0.00938	0.00000	0.01250	0.00000
1536000	0.0063	160.00	0.99532	0.00234	0.00469	0.00000	0.00625	0.00000

```
where:
EST = expected service time; MSR = mean service rate;
P0 = probability of zero frames in the system; p = utilization;
L = mean number of frames in system; Lq = mean number in queue;
W = mean waiting time in system; Wq = mean waiting time in queue.
```

more meaningful mechanism to estimate buffer memory requirements, you must consider another method to determine the use of buffer memory. That method is obtained by computing the probability of the different numbers of frames in a queuing system.

4.4.2   Using Probability

The probability of n units (P_n) in a single-channel, single-server system is obtained from the following formula:

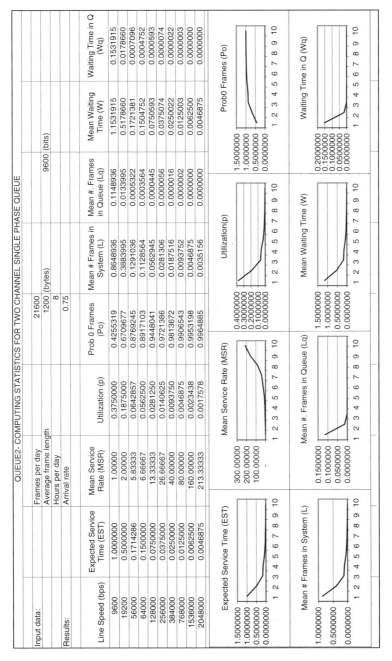

Line Speed (bps)	Expected Service Time (EST)	Mean Service Rate (MSR)	Utilization (p)	Prob 0 Frames (Po)	Mean # Frames in System (L)	Mean #. Frames in Queue (Lq)	Mean Waiting Time (W)	Waiting Time in Q (Wq)
9600	1.0000000	1.00000	0.3750000	0.4255319	0.8648936	0.1148936	1.1531915	0.1531915
19200	0.5000000	2.00000	0.1875000	0.6709677	0.3883995	0.0133995	0.5178660	0.0178660
56000	0.1714286	5.83333	0.0642857	0.8769245	0.1291036	0.0005322	0.1721381	0.0007096
64000	0.1500000	6.66667	0.0562500	0.8917103	0.1128564	0.0003564	0.1504752	0.0004752
128000	0.0750000	13.33333	0.0281250	0.9448041	0.0562945	0.0000445	0.0750593	0.0000593
256000	0.0375000	26.66667	0.0140625	0.9721386	0.0281306	0.0000056	0.0375074	0.0000074
384000	0.0250000	40.00000	0.0093750	0.9813672	0.0187516	0.0000016	0.0250022	0.0000022
768000	0.0125000	80.00000	0.0046875	0.9906543	0.0093752	0.0000002	0.0125003	0.0000003
1536000	0.0062500	160.00000	0.0023438	0.9953198	0.0046875	0.0000000	0.0062500	0.0000000
2048000	0.0046875	213.33333	0.0017578	0.9964885	0.0035156	0.0000000	0.0046875	0.0000000

QUEUE2- COMPUTING STATISTICS FOR TWO CHANNEL SINGLE PHASE QUEUE

Input data:
- Frames per day: 21600
- Average frame length: 1200 (bytes)
- Hours per day: 8
- Arrival rate: 0.75

Line Speed: 9600 (bits)

Figure 4.11   The Excel QUEUE2 Model

$$P_n = \left(\frac{\lambda}{\mu}\right)^n \left(1 - \frac{\lambda}{\mu}\right) = P^n (1 - P)$$

The probability of k or more units ($P_{n>k}$) in a single-channel, single-server system is given by the formula:

$$P_{n>k} = \left(\frac{\lambda}{\mu}\right)^k = P^k$$

To illustrate the use of the preceding formulas, let us return to our prior computations in which the utilization level was determined as 0.375. Table 4.6 lists the statements of a BASIC program labeled UNITS.BAS, which you will use to compute the value of P(N) and P(N>K) as N and K vary from 0 to 20 for a single-channel, single-server system. This program, which is stored on the file UNITS.BAS in the directory BASIC at the referenced Web URL was written to accept any server utilization level which provides you with the ability to use it to satisfy the computational requirements associated with a specific situation.

Table 4.7 illustrates the results obtained from the execution of the program UNITS.BAS with a server utilization level of 0.375, which is equivalent to 37.5 percent. In examining the data listed in Table 4.6, note the

Table 4.6 Program Listing of UNITS.BAS

```
REM PROGRAM UNITS.BAS TO COMPUTE PROBABILITY OF N UNITS IN SYSTEM
REM AND PROBABILITY OF K OR MORE UNITS IN SYSTEM
CLS
PRINT "PROGRAM TO COMPUTE PROBABILITY OF N UNITS AND K OR MORE UNITS
IN SYSTEM"
DIM P(20), K(20)
INPUT "Enter utilization level of server"; P
PRINT "PROBABILITY OF N UNITS     PROBABILITY K OR MORE UNITS"
PRINT "  N      P(N)                K         P(N>K) "
FOR N = 0 TO 20
P(N) = P ^ N * (1 - P)
K(N) = P ^ N
PRINT USING "### #.########          ###   #.########"; N; P(N);
N; K(N)
NEXT N
END
```

Table 4.7   Results Obtained from Executing Program UNITS.BAS with a Server Utilization Level of 0.375

PROGRAM TO COMPUTE PROBABILITY OF N UNITS AND K OR MORE UNITS IN SYSTEM

Enter utilization level of server?.375

PROBABILITY OF N UNITS		PROBABILITY K OR MORE UNITS	
N	P(N)	K	P(N>K)
0	0.62500000	0	1.00000000
1	0.23437500	1	0.37500000
2	0.08789063	2	0.14062500
3	0.03295898	3	0.05273438
4	0.01235962	4	0.01977539
5	0.00463486	5	0.00741577
6	0.00173807	6	0.00278091
7	0.00065178	7	0.00104284
8	0.00024442	8	0.00039107
9	0.00009166	9	0.00014665
10	0.00003437	10	0.00005499
11	0.00001289	11	0.00002062
12	0.00000483	12	0.00000773
13	0.00000181	13	0.00000290
14	0.00000068	14	0.00000109
15	0.00000025	15	0.00000041
16	0.00000010	16	0.00000015
17	0.00000004	17	0.00000006
18	0.00000001	18	0.00000002
19	0.00000001	19	0.00000001
20	0.00000000	20	0.00000000

relationship P(N) and P(N>K). That is, P(N) provides the probability for a specific number of units or, for our example, frames in a system, while P(N>K) provides the probability that there are K or more units in the system. Thus, there is a 62.5 percent probability that there are no frames in the system (P(N = 0)), while as expected there is a probability of unity that there are 0 or more frames in the system. Although you could use either column of probabilities as a decision criterion for determining the amount of buffer space you need in your bridge or router, as you will shortly note, the second column provides a more direct value.

In attempting to determine the size of the buffer space you require, the question you must answer is: How big should the buffer be to satisfy a predefined probability level of X percent? Then, once you define the probability level, you can answer the question. For example, assume you want a buffer size big enough to store 99.9 percent of the occurrences when the arrival rate exceeds the service rate. To accomplish this, you can directly use the second column listed in Table 4.7, in which the probability of K or more units was tabulated for K varying from 0 to 20. To obtain a level of 99.9 percent of the occurrences is equivalent to not being able to handle 0.1 percent of the occurrences, which would be displayed as 0.001 in the table in the second column of Table 4.7. Note that when K is 7, P(N>K) is 0.00104284, or slightly more than one tenth of 1 percent. Thus, you must select K equal to 8 to satisfy your requirement for handling 99.9 percent of the occurrences in which the frame arrival rate exceeds the service rate of the bridge or router. Thus, through the use of Table 4.7, you would want the bridge or router to be capable of storing or queuing up to eight frames. Because the frame length was defined as 1200 bytes, your memory storage requirement becomes 1200 bytes/frame * 8 frames, or 9600 bytes for this particular situation.

4.4.2.1 The Excel Model UNITS. Continuing our desire to develop Excel spreadsheet models when appropriate, Figure 4.12 shows the execution of the template stored in the Excel directory under the filename UNITS at the previously noted Web URL. This Excel template is a bit different from the Basic program of the same name. This difference results from the fact that the spreadsheet model requests the arrival rate and service rate to compute the level of utilization, providing a bit more flexibility. This additional flexibility results from the fact that you can override entering an arrival rate and service rate if you so desire and simply enter a utilization level in the appropriate cell position.

4.4.3 Six-Step Approach

The steps required to determine queuing storage requirements can be summarized as follows:

1. Determine the average frame arrival and average server service rates.
2. Determine the utilization level of the server.
3. Determine the level of service you want the server to provide with respect to storing or queuing frames for transmission when the frame arrival rate exceeds the server's service rate.
4. Determine the probability of K or more units in the system for a range of values.
5. Determine the probability that N>K, where K represents the level of service you want the server to provide and locate that value in the computed range of probabilities. Then, extract the value of K that represents the number of frames that must be queued.

6. Multiply the average or maximum frame length by the number of frames that must be queued. Note that multiplying by the average frame length results in obtaining the average buffer storage required for a given level of probability, while multiplying by the maximum frame length supported by your LAN results in obtaining a buffer storage value that will satisfy all situations for the predefined probability level.

4.4.4 Considering the Maximum Frame Size

Although the first five steps are relatively self-explanatory, the sixth step may be confusing to some readers. Thus, let us take a moment prior to proceeding and focus attention on the final step.

Previously you determined that your bridge or router should have 9600 bytes of buffer storage to queue 99.9 percent of the occurrences in which the frame arrival rate exceeds the server's service rate. In actuality, the prior computation was based on an average frame length of 1200 bytes. Thus, the amount of buffer storage you computed satisfies an average of 99.9 percent of the occurrences in which the frame arrival rate exceeds the server's service rate. If you wish to obtain a buffer storage value that fully satisfies your probability requirement, you must then use the maximum frame size supported by the LAN you are using or anticipate installing. For example, if you are using an Ethernet or IEEE 802.3 LAN, its maximum frame size is 1500 bytes (excluding overhead preamble and addressing and CRC bytes), while the use of a 4-Mbps or 16-Mbps Token Ring LAN would result in a maximum frame size of 4500 or 18,000 bytes, respectively.

4.4.4.1 Program QVU.BAS. To facilitate performing another set of calculations, the program QVU.BAS was developed. Table 4.8 lists the statements contained in this program that compute the buffer requirements for Ethernet and 4- and 16-Mbps Token Ring networks based on different server utilization levels ranging up to 99.0 percent. Readers can easily modify this program to obtain buffer requirements for other server utilization levels or to slightly expand frame sizes to better reflect the overhead associated with transmitting a frame using a specific WAN protocol.

Table 4.9 illustrates the results obtained from the execution of QVU.BAS. In examining the data in Table 4.9, note that the length of the queue in terms of frames is relatively small until the server's utilization level exceeds 70 percent. Thereafter, it rapidly increases and will approach infinity as the utilization level approaches 100 percent. Thus, you can use the data in Table 4.9 to determine if you really need to continue further and compute $P(N>K)$, or if you can simply estimate that at the level of server utilization the buffer requirements are so small that just about every bridge and router should have a sufficient amount of buffer memory. For example, suppose your server's utilization level was 80 percent and your

Table 4.8   Program Listing of QVU.BAS

```
REM PROGRAM QVU.BAS TO COMPARE QUEUE LENGTH VERSUS SERVER
UTILIZATION LEVEL

CLS

FRAME = 1500

LPRINT "ANALYSIS OF BUFFER STORAGE REQUIREMENTS"

LPRINT "MAXIMUM ETHERNET FRAME SIZE = 1500 BYTES"

LPRINT "MAXIMUM 4MBPS TOKEN-RING FRAME SIZE  = 4500 BYTES"

LPRINT "MAXIMUM 16MBPS TOKEN-RING FRAME SIZE =18000 BYTES"

LPRINT

LPRINT "UTILIZATION   LENGTH OF QUEUE      BUFFER REQUIREMENTS IN
BYTES"

LPRINT " PERCENT        IN FRAMES        ETHERNET    4MBPS T-R   16MBPS
T-R"

FOR P = 0! TO.9 STEP.1

LQ = P ^ 2/(1 - P)

B = INT(LQ * FRAME +.99)

T4 = INT(LQ * 4500 +.99)

T16 = INT(LQ * 18000 +.99)

LPRINT USING "###.##      ####.###       ########"; P * 100; LQ; B;

LPRINT USING "  ########  ########"; T4; T16

NEXT P

FOR P =.91 TO.99 STEP.01

LQ = P ^ 2/(1 - P)

B = INT(LQ * FRAME +.99)

T4 = INT(LQ * 4500 +.99)

T16 = INT(LQ * 18000 +.99)

LPRINT USING "###.##      ####.###       ########"; P * 100; LQ; B;

LPRINT USING "  ########  ########"; T4; T16

NEXT P

END
```

organization operates an Ethernet LAN. Table 4.9 indicates an average buffer storage requirement of 4800 bytes, infinitesimally small in comparison with the 32 or 64 Kbytes of buffer storage included in most remote bridges and routers. Thus, without further analysis to compute P(N>K), you could safely conclude that a 32-Kbyte buffer area should be sufficient for P(N > 99.9).

Table 4.9   Execution Results of Program QVU.BAS

ANALYSIS OF BUFFER STORAGE REQUIREMENTS

MAXIMUM ETHERNET FRAME SIZE = 1500 BYTES

MAXIMUM 4MBPS TOKEN-RING FRAME SIZE   = 4500 BYTES

MAXIMUM 16MBPS TOKEN-RING FRAME SIZE = 18000 BYTES

UTILIZATION PERCENT	LENGTH OF QUEUE IN FRAMES	BUFFER REQUIREMENTS IN BYTES		
		ETHERNET	4MBPS T-R	16MBPS T-R
0.00	0.000	0	0	0
10.00	0.011	17	50	200
20.00	0.050	75	225	900
30.00	0.129	193	579	2315
40.00	0.267	400	1200	4800
50.00	0.500	750	2250	9000
60.00	0.900	1350	4050	16200
70.00	1.633	2450	7350	29400
80.00	3.200	4800	14400	57601
91.00	9.201	13802	41406	165621
92.00	10.580	15870	47611	190441
93.00	12.356	18534	55601	222403
94.00	14.727	22090	66270	265080
95.00	18.050	27075	81225	324900
96.00	23.040	34560	103680	414720
97.00	31.363	47045	141135	564540
98.00	48.020	72030	216090	864359
99.00	98.009	147015	441043	1764171

4.4.4.2   The Excel Model QVU. The Excel template QVU, which provides a computation capability similar to the Basic program file with that name, is located in the directory Excel at the previously noted Web URL. Figure 4.13 illustrates an example of the execution of this spreadsheet model, to include the display of a graph that plots queue length versus the level of utilization. As we summarize this chapter in the next section, we will reference this plot and the first two columns of tabular data shown in the Excel model.

4.4.5   Summary

Although a variety of queuing concepts were examined in this chapter, it is most important to remember several concepts that govern the application

	A	B	C	D	E
1	**Probability of n frames in the system**				
2					
3	Arrival rate:	0.34722	Service rate:	0.9411765	
4					
5	Then, utilization becomes:		0.375	and Po is:	0.625
6					
7		n	Probability of n	Probability of n >k	
8		0	0.6250000000	1.0000000000	
9		1	0.2343750000	0.3750000000	
10		2	0.0878906250	0.1406250000	
11		3	0.0329589844	0.0527343750	
12		4	0.0123596191	0.0197753906	
13		5	0.0046348572	0.0074157715	
14		6	0.0017380714	0.0027809143	
15		7	0.0006517768	0.0010428429	
16		8	0.0002444163	0.0003910661	
17		9	0.0000916561	0.0001466498	
18		10	0.0000343710	0.0000549937	
19		11	0.0000128891	0.0000206226	
20		12	0.0000048334	0.0000077335	
21		13	0.0000018125	0.0000029001	
22		14	0.0000006797	0.0000010875	
23		15	0.0000002549	0.0000004078	
24		16	0.0000000956	0.0000001529	
25		17	0.0000000358	0.0000000573	
26		18	0.0000000134	0.0000000215	
27		19	0.0000000050	0.0000000081	
28		20	0.0000000019	0.0000000030	
29					

Figure 4.12   Execution of the Excel Template UNITS

of queuing theory to networking. One concept is that as the level of utilization of a server increases, its queue length increases. A second concept worth remembering is the fact that as the level of utilization for a single-server system exceeds 50 percent, queues become more observable to whatever process you are performing. A third concept worth noting is the fact that as the level of utilization of a server approaches 100 percent, the length of a queue dramatically begins to increase and will eventually approach infinity.

The first two columns in Figure 4.13 indicate in tabular form the queue length for different utilization levels of a single-phase, single-channel system. Note that at a 50 percent utilization level, the mean queue length is 0.5; however, at a 70 percent level of utilization, the queue length more than tripled. Also note that an increase in utilization from 70 to 80 percent results in a doubling of the mean queue length, while an increase in utilization from 80 to 91 percent results in the length of the queue nearly tripling. The minichart shown at the bottom of the Excel model presented in

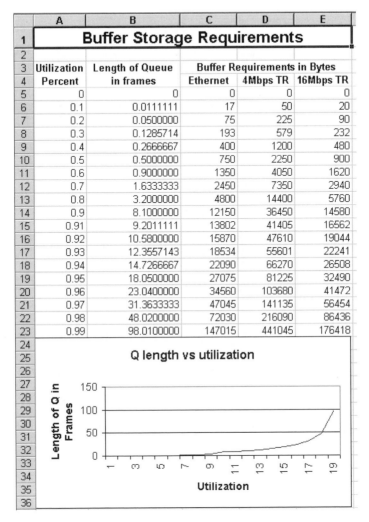

	A	B	C	D	E
1	**Buffer Storage Requirements**				
2					
3	Utilization	Length of Queue	Buffer Requirements in Bytes		
4	Percent	in frames	Ethernet	4Mbps TR	16Mbps TR
5	0	0	0	0	0
6	0.1	0.0111111	17	50	20
7	0.2	0.0500000	75	225	90
8	0.3	0.1285714	193	579	232
9	0.4	0.2666667	400	1200	480
10	0.5	0.5000000	750	2250	900
11	0.6	0.9000000	1350	4050	1620
12	0.7	1.6333333	2450	7350	2940
13	0.8	3.2000000	4800	14400	5760
14	0.9	8.1000000	12150	36450	14580
15	0.91	9.2011111	13802	41405	16562
16	0.92	10.5800000	15870	47610	19044
17	0.93	12.3557143	18534	55601	22241
18	0.94	14.7266667	22090	66270	26508
19	0.95	18.0500000	27075	81225	32490
20	0.96	23.0400000	34560	103680	41472
21	0.97	31.3633333	47045	141135	56454
22	0.98	48.0200000	72030	216090	86436
23	0.99	98.0100000	147015	441045	176418

Figure 4.13   Execution of the Excel Remplate QVU

Figure 4.13 graphically illustrates the same data. In examining Figure 4.13, it is important to remember that the mean queue length is directly related to the mean waiting time and explains why most network managers, analysts, and designers should consider modifying a network facility when its utilization level exceeds 50 percent.

Chapter 5
Sizing Communications Equipment and Line Facilities

Of the many problems associated with the acquisition of data communications networking devices, including LAN access controllers, multiplexers, and concentrators, one item often requiring resolution is the configuration or sizing of the device. The process of ensuring that the configuration of the selected device will provide a desired level of service is the foundation upon which the availability level of a network is built and, in may instances, is directly related to the number of dial-in lines connected to the device.

The appropriate sizing of local area network (LAN) access controllers is an important consideration for a large number of organizations. Because LAN access controllers can be used by Internet service providers (ISPs) as a mechanism to provide dial access to the Internet, they represent one of the most commonly employed data communications devices used by ISPs. Because it also enables government agencies, academia, and private organizations to provide dial-in access to their LANs, the LAN access controller also represents a popular communications product used by non-service providers. Although the term "LAN access controller" is commonly used by hardware manufacturers to denote a specialized product for enabling dial network users to access a LAN, another equivalent device that requires sizing is a "remote access server." Concerning the latter, remote access server support is included in the popular Windows NT and Windows 2000 operating systems as "remote access services" (RAS). If you install RAS on a Windows NT or Windows 2000 server to enable employees or customers to access your server or LAN, you can use the information in this chapter to determine the number of dial-in modems and access lines to connect to your server.

The failure to provide a level of access acceptable to network users can result in a multitude of problems. First, a user encountering a busy signal might become discouraged, take a break, or do something other than redial a telephone number of a network access port. Such action obviously will result in a loss of user productivity. If network usage is in response to customer inquiries, a failure to certify a customer purchase, return, reservation, or other action in a timely manner could result in the loss of customers to a competitor. This is similar to the situation where a long queue in front of a bank teller can result in the loss of customer accounts if the unacceptable level of service persists.

This chapter focuses attention on the application of telephone traffic formulas to the sizing of data communications equipment and line facilities. Although most telephone traffic formulas were developed during the 1920s,many are applicable to such common problems as determining the number of dial-in business and WATS lines required to service remote PC users, as well as the number of ports or channels that should be installed in communications equipment connected to the dial-in lines. To obtain an appreciation for the sizing process, we first examine several methods that can be used to size equipment and line facilities. This is followed by a detailed examination of the application of telephone traffic sizing formulas to data communications. More formally referred to as traffic dimensioning formulas, in this chapter we examine the application of the erlang B, erlang C, and Poisson formulas to data communications equipment and facility sizing problems.

5.1 Sizing Methods

There are many devices and line facilities that can be employed in a data communications network whose configuration or sizing problems are similar. Examples of line facilities include the number of dial-in local business and WATS lines required to be connected to telephone company rotaries, while examples of communications equipment sizing includes determining the number of channels on LAN access controllers, multiplexers, data concentrators, and port selectors.

5.1.1 Experimental Modeling

Basically, two methods can be used to configure the size of communications network devices. The first method, commonly known as *experimental modeling*, involves the selection of the device configuration based on a mixture of previous experience and intuition. Normally, the configuration selected is less than the base capacity plus expansion capacity of the device. This enables the size of the device to be adjusted or upgraded without a major equipment modification, if the initial sizing proved inaccurate. An example of experimental modeling is shown in Table 5.1.

Table 5.1   Experimental Modeling

Experimental modeling results in the adjustment of a network configuration based upon previous experience and gut intuition: (upper) initial configuration and (lower) adjusted configuration.

Power Supply	Central Logic	1	3	5	7	9	Empty Slots		
		2	4	6	8	10			

a

Power Supply	Central Logic	1	3	5	7	9	11	13	15
		2	4	6	8	10	12	14	16

b

A rack-mounted LAN access controller is shown in Table 5.1a. Initially, the controller was obtained with five dual-port adapters to support ten ports of simultaneous operation. Assuming the base unit can support eight dual-port adapters, if the network manager's previous experience or gut intuition proves wrong, the controller can be upgraded easily. This is shown in Table 5.1b where the addition of three dual-port adapters permits the controller to support 16 ports in its adjusted configuration.

Assuming each controller port is connected to a modem and business line, experimental modeling, while often representing a practical solution to equipment sizing, can also be expensive. For example, if your organization began with the configuration shown in Table 5.1b and adjusted the number of controller ports downward to that shown in Table 5.1a, you would incur some cost for the extra modems and business lines, even if the manufacturer of the LAN access controller was willing to take back the port adapters you did not actually need. Thus, while experimental modeling is better than simply guessing, it can also result in the expenditure of funds for unnecessary hardware and communications facilities.

5.1.2   *The Scientific Approach*

The second method that can be employed to size network components ignores experience and intuition. This method is based on acknowledgment of data traffic and the scientific application of mathematical formulas to traffic data. Hence, it is known as the scientific approach method of equipment sizing. While some of the mathematics involved in determining equipment sizing can become quite complex, a series of tables generated by the development of appropriate computer programs can be employed to reduce many sizing problems to one of a single table lookup process.

Although there are advantages and disadvantages to each method, the application of a scientific methodology to equipment sizing is a rigorously defined approach. Thus, there should be a much higher degree of confidence and accuracy of the configuration selected when this method is used. On the negative side, the use of a scientific method requires a firm knowledge or accurate estimate of the data traffic. Unfortunately, for some organizations, this may be difficult to obtain. In many cases, a combination of two techniques will provide an optimum situation. For such situations, sizing can be conducted using the scientific method, with the understanding that the configuration selected may require adjustment under the experimental modeling concept. In the remainder of this chapter, we focus attention on the application of the scientific methodology to equipment sizing problems.

5.2 Telephone Terminology Relationships

Most of the mathematics used for sizing data communications equipment evolved out of work originally performed to solve the sizing problems of telephone networks. From a discussion of a few basic telephone network terms and concepts, we will see the similarities between the sizing problems associated with data communications equipment and facilities and the structure of the telephone network. Building on this foundation, we will learn how to apply the mathematical formulas developed for telephone network sizing to data communications network configurations.

To study the relationship between telephone network communications component sizing problems, let us examine a portion of the telephone network and study the structure and calling problems of a small segment formed by two cities, each assumed to contain 1000 telephone subscribers.

5.2.1 Telephone Network Structure

The standard method of providing an interconnection between subscribers in a local area is to connect each subscriber's telephone to what is known as the local telephone company exchange. Other synonymous terms for the local telephone company exchange include the "local exchange" and "telephone company central office." When one subscriber dials another connected to the same exchange, the subscriber's call is switched to the called party number through the switching facilities of the local exchange. If we assume that each city has one local exchange, then all calls originating

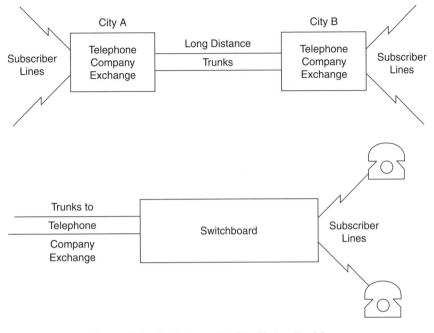

Figure 5.1   Telephone Traffic Sizing Problems

in that city and to a destination located within that city will be routed through one common exchange.

Because our network segment selected for analysis consists of two cities, we have two telephone company exchanges — one located in each city. To provide a path between cities for inter-city calling, a number of lines must be installed to link the exchanges in each city. The exchange in each city can then act as a switch, routing the local subscribers in each city to parties in the other city.

5.2.1.1   Trunks and Dimensioning. As shown in the top part of Figure 5.1, a majority of telephone traffic in the network segment consisting of the two cities will be among the subscribers of each city. Although there will be telephone traffic between the subscribers in each city, it normally will be considerably less than the amount of local traffic in each city. The path between the two cities connecting their telephone offices is known as a trunk.

One of the many problems in designing the telephone network is determining how many trunks should be installed between telephone company exchanges. A similar sizing problem occurs many times in each city at locations where private organizations desire to install switchboards. An example of the sizing problem with this type of equipment is illustrated in the lower portion of Figure 5.1. In effect, the switchboard functions as a small telephone exchange, routing calls carried over a number of trunks installed between the switchboard and the telephone company exchange to a larger number of subscriber lines connected to the switchboard. The determination of the number of trunks required to be installed between the telephone exchange and the switchboard is called *dimensioning* and is critical for the efficient operation of the facility. If insufficient trunks are available, company personnel will encounter an unacceptable number of busy signals when trying to place an outside telephone call. Once again, this will obviously affect productivity.

Returning to the inter-city calling problem, consider some of the problems that can occur in dimensioning the number of trunks between central offices located in the two cities. Assume that, based on a previously conducted study, it was determined that no more than 50 people would want to have simultaneous telephone conversations where the calling party was in one city and the called party in the other city. If 50 trunks were installed between cities and the number of inter-city callers never exceeded 50, at any moment the probability of a subscriber completing a call to the distant city would always be unity, always guaranteeing success. Although the service cost of providing 50 trunks is obviously more than providing a fewer number of trunks, no subscriber would encounter a busy signal.

Because some subscribers might postpone or choose not to place a long-distance call at a later time if a busy signal is encountered, a maximum level of service will produce a minimum level of lost revenue. If more than 50 subscribers tried to simultaneously call parties in the opposite city, some callers would encounter busy signals once all 50 trunks were in use. Under such circumstances, the level of service would be such that not all subscribers would be guaranteed access to the long distance trunks and the probability of making a long-distance call would be less than unity. Likewise, because the level of service is less than that required to provide all callers with access to the long-distance trunks, the service cost is less than the service cost associated with providing users with a probability of unity in accessing trunks. Similarly, as the probability of successfully accessing the long-distance trunk decreases, the amount of lost revenue or customer waiting costs will increase. Based on the preceding, a decision model factoring into consideration the level of service versus expected cost can be constructed as shown in Figure 5.2.

5.2.1.2   The Decision Model. For the decision model illustrated in Figure 5.2, suppose the optimum number of trunks required to link the two cities is 40. The subscriber line-to-trunk ratio for this case would be 1000 lines to 40 trunks, for a 25:1 ratio.

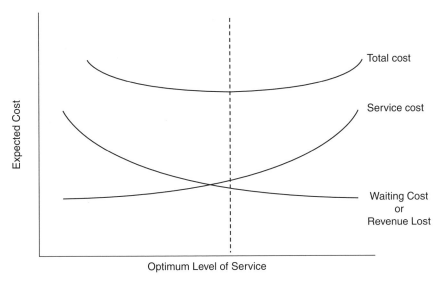

Figure 5.2   Using a Decision Model to Determine the Optimum Level of Service

To correctly dimension the optimum number of trunks linking the two cities requires an understanding of both economics and subscriber traffic. In dimensioning the number of trunks, a certain trade-off will result that relates the number of trunks or level of service to the cost of providing that service and the revenue lost by not having enough trunks to satisfy the condition when a maximum number of subscribers in one city dial subscribers in another. To determine the appropriate level of service, a decision model as illustrated in Figure 5.2 is required. Here, the probability of a subscriber successfully accessing a trunk corresponds to the level of service provided. As more trunks are added, the probability of access increases as does the cost of providing such access. Correspondingly, the waiting cost of the subscriber or the revenue loss to the telephone company decreases as the level of service increases, where the total cost represents the combination of service cost and waiting cost. The point where the cost is minimal represents the optimal number of trunks or level of service that should be provided to link the two cities.

From a LAN access perspective, a similar decision model can be constructed. However, instead of focusing on accessing trunks, our concern would be oriented toward providing access to a LAN via the switched telephone network. If the number of ports, modems, and business lines equals the number of employees or subscribers of the organization, nobody would experience a busy signal; however, the cost of providing this capacity level would be very high, and during a portion of the day, most of its capacity would more than likely be unused. As we reduce the number of ports, modems, and dial-in lines, the level of service decreases and eventually employee or subscriber waiting time results in either lost productivity or lost revenue. Thus, from a LAN access perspective, you would also seek to determine an optimum level of service.

5.3 Traffic Measurements

Telephone activity can be defined by the calling rate and the holding time, which is the duration of the call. The calling rate is the number of times a particular route or path is used per unit time period, while the holding time is the duration of the call on the route or path. Two other terms that warrant attention are the offered traffic and the carried traffic. The *offered traffic* is the volume of traffic routed to a particular telephone exchange during a predetermined time period, while the *carried traffic* is the volume of traffic actually transmitted through the exchange to its destination during a predetermined period of time.

5.3.1 The Busy Hour

The key factor required to dimension a traffic path is knowledge of the traffic intensity during the time period known as the busy hour (BH). Although traffic varies by day and time of day, and is generally random, it follows a certain consistency one can identify. In general, traffic peaks prior to lunch time and then rebuilds to a second daily peak in the afternoon. The busiest one-hour period of the day is known as the busy hour. It is the busy-hour traffic level that is employed in dimensioning telephone exchanges and transmission routes because one wants to size the exchange or route with respect to its busiest period.

It is important to note that the busy hour can vary considerably between organizations. For example, an Internet service provider (ISP) might experience its heaviest traffic between 7 and 8 p.m. once subscribers return home from work, digest their supper, and then attempt to go online. In comparison, a government agency would more than likely have its busy hour occur during the day.

Telephone traffic can be defined as the product of the calling rate per hour and the average holding time per call. This measurement can be expressed mathematically as:

$$T = C * D$$

where:
    C = calling rate per hour
    D = average duration per call

Using the above formula, traffic can be expressed in call-minutes (CM) or call-hours (CH), where a call-hour is the quantity represented by one or more calls having an aggregate duration of one hour.

If the calling rate during the busy hour of a particular day is 500 and the average duration of each call is 10 minutes, the traffic flow or intensity would be 500 * 10, or 5000 CM, which would be equivalent to 5000/60, or approximately 83.3 CH.

5.3.2 *Erlangs and Call-Seconds*

The preferred unit of measurement in telephone traffic analysis is the erlang, named after A.K. Erlang, a Danish mathematician. The erlang is a dimensionless unit in comparison to the previously discussed call-minutes and call-hours. It represents the occupancy of a circuit where one erlang of traffic intensity on one traffic circuit represents a continuous occupancy of that circuit.

A second term often used to represent traffic intensity is the call-second (CS). The quantity represented by 100 call-seconds is known as 1 CCS. Here, the first C represents the quantity 100 and comes from the French term "*cent.*" Assuming a one-hour unit interval, the previously discussed terms can be related to the erlang as follows:

$$1 \text{ erlang} = 60 \text{ call-minutes} = 36 \text{ CCS} = 3600 \text{ CS}$$

If a group of 20 trunks is measured and a call intensity of 10 erlangs determined over the group, then we would expect one half of all trunks to be busy at the time of measurement. Similarly, a traffic intensity of 600 CM or 360 CCS offered to the 20 trunks would warrant the same conclusion. Table 5.2 is a traffic conversion table that will facilitate the conversion of erlangs to CCS and vice versa. Because the use of many dimensioning tables is based on traffic intensity in erlangs or CCS, the conversion of such terms frequently is required in the process of sizing facilities.

To illustrate the applicability of traffic measurements to a typical communications network configuration, assume that your organization has a ten-position rotary connected to a LAN access controller. Further assume that you measured the number of calls and holding time per call during a one-hour period and determined the traffic distribution to be that illustrated in Figure 5.3. Note that the total holding time is 266 minutes (4.43 hours). Thus, the average traffic intensity during this one-hour period is 4.43/1, or 4.43 erlangs.

During the busy hour illustrated in Figure 5.3, a total of 45 calls resulted in a cumulative holding time of 266 minutes. Thus, the average holding time per call is 266/45, or 5.91 minutes, which is equivalent to 0.0985 hours. Multiplying the average holding time (0.0985 hours) per call by the number of calls (45) results in an average traffic intensity of 4.43 erlangs. Note that this tells us that if we know the average holding time and the number of calls, we can easily determine the traffic intensity. The previously noted relationship between the average traffic intensity (E) and the holding times

Table 5.2 Traffic Conversion Table

Dimension		Erlangs (intensity)	CCS
Minutes	Hours	Call-Hours (quantity)	(quantity)
12	0.2	0.2	6
24	0.4	0.4	12
36	0.6	0.6	18
48	0.8	0.8	24
60	1.0	1.0	36
120	2.0	2.0	72
180	3.0	3.0	108
240	4.0	4.0	144
300	5.0	5.0	180
360	6.0	6.0	210
420	7.0	7.0	252
480	8.0	8.0	288
540	9.0	9.0	324
600	10.0	10.0	360
900	15.0	15.0	540
1200	20.0	20.0	720
1500	25.0	25.0	900
1800	30.0	30.0	1080
2100	35.0	35.0	1260
2400	40.0	40.0	1440
2700	45.0	45.0	1620
3000	50.0	50.0	1800
6000	100.0	100.0	3600

on each rotary position (H_i) during some time period (T) can be expressed mathematically as follows:

$$E = \frac{\sum_{i=1}^{n} H_i}{T}$$

Substituting the data contained in Figure 5.3, we obtain for the one-hour period:

$$E = \frac{266}{1} = \text{call-minutes, or 4.43 CH}$$

The average call holding time or average call duration (D) can be expressed in terms of the total holding time ($\sum H_i$) and the number of calls (c) as:

$$D = \frac{\sum_{i=1}^{n} H_i}{C} = \frac{266}{45} = 5.91$$

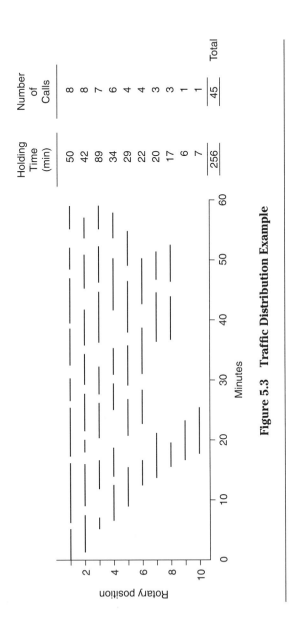

Holding Time (min)	Number of Calls
50	8
42	8
89	7
34	6
29	4
22	4
20	3
17	3
6	1
7	1
256	45
	Total

Figure 5.3   Traffic Distribution Example

Because $\Sigma H_i = C * D$ and, as previously noted, $E = \Sigma H_i/T$, we can express the traffic intensity (E) in terms of the number of calls, average call duration, and time period. Doing so, we obtain:

$$E = \frac{C \times D}{T}$$

Using the data contained in Figure 5.3, we can compute the traffic intensity in erlangs as follows using a call duration expressed in minutes:

$$E = \frac{45 \times 5.91}{60} = 4.43 \text{ erlangs}$$

To find the traffic intensity when call duration is expressed in hours, our substitution would become:

$$E = \frac{45 \times 5.91/60}{1} = 4.43 \text{ erlangs}$$

As indicated, knowledge of the average call duration and number of calls permits the computation of traffic intensity. Because many types of network management systems, as well as access controllers, multiplexers, and computer systems, collect statistics (to include the number of calls and call duration), it is often possible to obtain traffic intensity information. Even when you cannot obtain such information directly, it is often possible to obtain information indirectly. As an example, consider a ten-position rotary connected to modems that in turn are connected to ports on a LAN access controller. If the telephone company cannot provide the required information and your organization lacks monitoring equipment, the statistics you require may be obtainable from the access controller.

5.3.3 Grade of Service

One important concept in the dimensioning process is what is known as the *grade of service*. To understand this concept, let us return to our inter-city calling example illustrated in Figure 5.1, again assuming that 50 trunks are used to connect the telephone exchanges in each city. If a subscriber attempts to originate a call from one city to the other when all trunks are in use, that call is said to be blocked. Based on mathematical formulas, the probability of a call being blocked can be computed, given the traffic intensity and number of available trunks. The concept of determining the probability of blockage can be adapted easily to the sizing of data communications equipment.

From a logical analysis of traffic intensity, it follows that if a call is blocked, such blockage would occur during the busy hours because that is the period when the largest amount of activity occurs. Thus, telephone exchange capacity is engineered to service a portion of the busy hour traffic, the exact amount of service depending on economics as well as the political process of determining the level of service one desires to provide to customers.

You could over-dimension the route between cities and provide a trunk for every subscriber. This would ensure that a lost call could never occur and would be equivalent to providing a dial-in line for every terminal in a network. Because a 1:1 subscriber-to-trunk ratio is not economical and will result in most trunks being idle a large portion of the day, we can expect a lesser number of trunks between cities than subscribers. As the number of trunks decreases and the subscriber-to-trunk ratio correspondingly increases, we can intuitively expect some sizings to result in some call blockage. We can specify the number of calls we are willing to have blocked during the busy hour. This specification is known as the grade of service and represents the probability (P) of having a call blocked. If we specify a grade of service of 0.05 between the cities, we require a sufficient number of trunks so that only one call in 20, or five calls in every 100, will be blocked during the busy hour.

5.3.4 *Route Dimensioning Parameters*

To determine the number of trunks required to service a particular route, you can consider the use of several formulas. Each formula's utilization depends on the call arrival and holding time distribution, the number of traffic sources, and the handling of lost or blocked calls. Regardless of the formula employed, the resulting computation will provide the probability of call blockage or grade of service based on a given number of trunks and level of traffic intensity.

Concerning the number of traffic sources, you can consider the calling population as infinite or finite. If calls occur from a large subscriber population and subscribers tend to redial if blockage is encountered, the calling population can be considered infinite. The consideration of an infinite traffic source results in the probability of a call arrival becoming constant and does not make the call dependent on the state of traffic in the system. The two most commonly employed traffic dimensioning equations are both based on an infinite calling population.

Concerning the handling of lost calls, such calls can be considered cleared, delayed, or held. When such calls are considered held, it is assumed that the telephone subscriber, upon encountering a busy signal, immediately redials the desired party. The lost call-delayed concept assumes that each subscriber is placed in a waiting mechanism for service and forms the basis for queuing analysis. Because we can assume a service or non-service condition, we can disregard the lost call-delayed concept unless access to a network resource occurs through a data PBX or port selector that has queuing capability.

5.3.5 Traffic Dimensioning Formulas

The principal traffic dimensioning formula used in North America is based on the lost call–held concept and is commonly known as the Poisson formula. In Europe, traffic formulas are based on the assumption that a subscriber encountering a busy signal will hang up the telephone and wait a certain amount of time prior to redialing. The erlang B formula is based on this lost call-cleared concept.

5.4 The Erlang Traffic Formula

The most commonly used telephone traffic dimensioning equation is the erlang B formula. This formula is predominantly used outside the North American continent. In addition to assuming that data traffic originates from an infinite number of sources, this formula is based on the lost call-cleared concept. This assumption is equivalent to stating that traffic offered to but not carried by one or more trunks vanishes, and this is the key difference between this formula and the Poisson formula. The latter formula assumes that lost calls are held, and it is used for telephone dimensioning mainly in North America. Because data communications system users can be characterized by either the lost call-cleared or lost call-held concept, both traffic formulas and their application to data networks are discussed in this chapter.

If E is used to denote the traffic intensity in erlangs and T represents the number of trunks, channels, or ports designed to support the traffic, the probability $P(T,E)$ represents the probability that T trunks are busy when a traffic intensity of E erlangs is offered to those trunks. The probability is equivalent to specifying a grade of service and can be expressed by the erlang traffic formula as follows:

$$P(T,E) = \frac{\dfrac{E^T}{T!}}{1 + \dfrac{E^1}{1!} + \dfrac{E^2}{2!} + \dfrac{E^3}{3!} + \ldots + \dfrac{E^T}{T!}} = \frac{\dfrac{E^T}{T!}}{\displaystyle\sum_{I=0}^{T} \dfrac{E^1}{i!}}$$

where:

$$T! = T * (T - 1) \times (T - 2) \ldots 3 * 2 * 1$$

and

$$0! = 1$$

A list of factorials and their values is presented in Table 5.3 to assist readers in computing specific grades of service based on a given traffic intensity and trunk quantity.

Table 5.3   Factorial Values

N	Factorial N	N	Factorial N
1	1	51	1.551118753287382E+66
2	2	52	8.065817517094390E+67
3	6	53	4.274883284060024E+69
4	24	54	2.308436973392413E+71
5	120	55	1.269640335365826E+73
6	720	56	7.109985878048632E+74
7	5040	57	4.052691950487723E+76
8	40320	58	2.350561331282879E+78
9	362880	59	1.386831185456898E+80
10	3628800	60	8.320987112741390E+81
11	39916800	61	5.075802138772246E+83
12	479001600	62	3.146997326038794E+85
13	6227020800	63	1.982608315404440E+87
14	87178291200	64	1.268869321858841E+89
15	1307674368000	65	8.247650592082472E+90
16	20922789888000	66	5.443449390774432E+92
17	355687428096000	67	3.647111091818871E+94
18	6402373705728000	68	2.480035542436830E+96
19	1.216451004088320E+17	69	1.711224524281413E+98
20	2.432902008176640E+18	70	1.197857166966989E+100
21	5.109094217170944E+19	71	8.504785885678624E+101
22	1.124000727777608E+21	72	6.123445837688612E+103
23	2.585201673888498E+22	73	4.470115461512686E+105
24	6.204484017332394E+23	74	3.307885441519387E+107
25	1.551121004333098E+25	75	2.480914081139540E+109
26	4.032914611266057E+26	76	1.855494701666051E+111
27	1.088886945041835E+28	77	1.451830920282859E+113
28	3.048883446117138E+29	78	1.132428117820629E+115
29	8.841761993739701E+30	79	8.946182130782980E+116
30	2.652528598121911E+32	80	7.156945704626380E+118
31	8.222838654177924E+33	81	5.797126020747369E+120
32	2.631308369336936E+35	82	4.753643337012843E+122
33	8.683317618811889E+36	83	3.045523969720660E+124
34	2.952327990396041E+38	84	3.314240134565354E+126
35	1.033314796638614E+40	85	2.817104114380549E+128
36	3.719933267899013E+41	86	2.422709538367274E+130
37	1.376375309122635E+43	87	2.107757298379527E+132
38	5.230226174666010E+44	88	1.854826422573984E+134
39	2.036788208119745E+46	89	1.650795516090847E+136
40	8.159152832478980E+47	90	1.485715964481761E+138
41	3.345252661316380E+49	91	1.352001527678403E+140
42	1.405006117752880E+51	92	1.243841405464131E+142
43	6.041526306837884E+52	93	1.156772507081641E+144
44	2.658271574788450E+54	94	1.087366156656743E+146

Table 5.3   Factorial Values   (continued)

N	Factorial N	N	Factorial N
45	1.196222208654802E+56	95	1.032997848823906E+148
46	5.502622159812089E+57	96	9.916779348709491E+149
47	2.586232415111683E+59	97	9.619275968248216E+151
48	1.241391559253607E+61	98	9.426890448883248E+153
49	6.082818640342679E+62	99	9.332621544394415E+155
50	3.041409320171338E+64	100	9.332621544394418E+157

To illustrate the use of the erlang traffic formula, assume that a traffic intensity of 3 erlangs is offered to a three-position rotary. The grade of service is calculated as follows:

$$P(T,E) = \frac{\dfrac{E^T}{T!}}{\displaystyle\sum_{i=0}^{T}\dfrac{E^i}{T!}} = \frac{\dfrac{3^3}{3\times2\times1}}{\dfrac{3^0}{0!}+\dfrac{3^1}{1!}+\dfrac{3^2}{2!}+\dfrac{3^3}{3!}} = 0.346$$

This means that, on average during the busy hour, 34.6 out of every 100 calls will encounter a busy signal and for most organizations will represent an undesirable grade of service.

5.4.1 Computing Lost Traffic

Based on the computed grade of service, we can compute the traffic lost during the busy hour. Here, the traffic lost (e) is the traffic intensity multiplied by the grade of service. Thus, the traffic lost by position 3 is:

$$e_3 = E \times P(3,3) = 3\times0.345 = 1.038 \text{ erlangs}$$

Now let us assume the rotary is expanded to four positions. The grade of service then becomes:

$$P(4,3) = \frac{\dfrac{3^4}{4\times3\times2\times1}}{\dfrac{3^0}{0!}+\dfrac{3^1}{1!}+\dfrac{3^2}{2!}+\dfrac{3^3}{3!}+\dfrac{3^4}{4!}} = 0.2061$$

This expansion improves the grade of service so that approximately one in five calls now receives a busy signal during the busy hour. The traffic lost by position 4 now becomes:

$$e_4 = E * P(4,3) = 3 * 0.2061 = 0.6183 \text{ erlangs}$$

Note that the traffic carried by the fourth position is equal to the difference between the traffic lost by the three-position rotary and the traffic lost by the four-position rotary. That is:

traffic carried by position 4 = 1.038 - 0.6183 = 0.4197 erlangs

Based upon the preceding, we can calculate both the traffic carried and the traffic lost by each position of an n-position rotary. The results of the traffic computations are obtainable once we know the number of positions on the rotary and the traffic intensity offered to the rotary group. As previously noted, the traffic lost by position $n(e_n)$ can be expressed in terms of the grade of service and traffic intensity as follows:

$$e_n = E * P(T_n, E)$$

Substituting the preceding in the erlang formula gives:

$$= E \times \frac{n!}{\sum\limits_{i=0}^{n} \dfrac{E^i}{i!}}$$

where e_n is the traffic lost by the nth position on the rotary.

Because the traffic carried by any rotary position is the difference between the traffic offered to the position and the traffic lost by the position, we can easily compute the traffic carried by each rotary position. To do so, let us proceed as follows.

Let e_{n-1} equal the traffic lost by position n–1. Then, e_{n-1} becomes the traffic that is offered to position n on the rotary. Thus, the traffic carried by position n is equivalent to $e_{n-1} - e_n$. In the case of the first rotary position on a four-position rotary, the traffic lost becomes:

$$e_1 = E \times \frac{\dfrac{E^1}{1!}}{1 + \dfrac{E^1}{1!}} = \frac{E^2}{1 + E}$$

Then, the traffic carried by the first rotary position is the difference between the traffic intensity offered to the rotary group (E) and the traffic lost by the first position. That is, if T_{Cn} is the traffic carried by position n, then:

$$T_{C1} = E - e_1 = E - \frac{E^2}{1 + E} = \frac{E}{1 + E}$$

For the second rotary position, traffic lost by that position is:

$$e_1 = E \times \frac{\dfrac{E^2}{2!}}{1 + \dfrac{E^1}{1!} + \dfrac{E^2}{2!}} = \frac{E^3}{2 + 2E + E^2}$$

135

Table 5.4 Traffic Lost and Traffic Carried by Rotary Position

Rotary Position	Traffic Lost	Traffic Carried
1	$e_1 = \dfrac{E^2}{1+E}$	$E - e_1 = \dfrac{E}{1+E}$
2	$e_1 = \dfrac{E^3}{2^2 + E^2}$	$e_1 - e_2 = \dfrac{E^3}{1+E} - \dfrac{E^3}{2 + 2E = E^2}$
3	$e_3 = \dfrac{E^4}{6 + 6E + 3E^2 + E^3}$	$e_1 - e_3 = \dfrac{E^3}{2 + 2E + E^2} - \dfrac{E^4}{6 + 6E + 5E^2 + E^3}$
4	$e_1 = \dfrac{E^5}{24 + 24E + 12E^2 + 4E^3 + E^4}$	$e_3 - e_4 = \dfrac{E^4}{6 + 6E + 5E^2 + E^3} - \dfrac{E^5}{24 + 24E + 12E^2 + 4E^3 + E^4}$

Then, the traffic carried by the second position on the rotary is $e_1 - e_2$, or:

$$e_1 - e_2 = \frac{E^2}{1+E} = \frac{E^2}{2 + 2E + E^2}$$

We can continue this process to compute both the traffic carried as well as the traffic lost by each rotary position. Table 5.4 summarizes the formulas used to obtain the traffic lost and traffic carried for each position of a four-position rotary group.

5.4.2 Traffic Analysis Program

To assist readers in performing the computations required to determine the grade of service and traffic distribution over each port on a rotary group, a program was developed using the Microsoft QuickBasic compiler. Table 5.5 contains the listing of the traffic analysis program that can be used to analyze rotaries containing up to 60 positions. For rotaries beyond 60 positions, the program can be altered; however, execution time will considerably increase. This program is contained on the file TRAFFIC.BAS in the directory BASIC at the Web address previously referenced in this book.

For readers not familiar with the Microsoft Basic compiler, several entries in the program listing contained in Table 5.5 may warrant an explanation. Due to this, we examine the program listing to provide all readers with a firm understanding of statements that may be different from the basic interpreter or compiler they are using, as well as to obtain a better understanding of the logical construction of the program.

The $DYNAMIC statement in the second program line allocates memory to arrays as required. The FACTORIAL# statement allocates 61 elements (0 through 60) for the array that will contain the values of factorial

Table 5.5   Traffic Analyzer Program Listing

```
REM Traffic Analyzer Program
REM $DYNAMIC
DIM FACTORIAL#(60)
DIM TL#(60), TC#(60)
REM E is the offered load in Erlangs
REM PORT is the number of ports, dial in lines or trunks
REM GOS is the grade of service for port or channel PORT with traffic
E
REM TL# is an array that holds traffic lost by port number
REM TC# is an array that holds traffic carried by port number
CLS
PRINT TAB(25); "Traffic Analyzer"
PRINT
PRINT "This program computes the grade of service and the traffic
carried"
PRINT "and lost by each port or channel in an n position rotary type
group"
PRINT
INPUT "Enter traffic intensity in Erlangs"; E#
1 INPUT "Enter number of ports -maximum 60"; PORT
IF PORT > 60 OR PORT < 1 GOTO 1
GOSUB 100   'compute factorial 1 TO PORT
REM Compute the grade of service
                PORT# = PORT
                N# = (E# ^ PORT#)/FACTORIAL#(PORT)
                    D# = 0
                    FOR S = 0 TO PORT
                    S# = S
                    D# = D# + (E# ^ S#)/FACTORIAL#(S)
                    NEXT S
                GOS# = N#/D#
REM Compute the traffic lost by port
        FOR S = 1 TO PORT
                S# = S
                LN# = E# * (E# ^ S#/FACTORIAL#(S))
                LD# = 0
```

Table 5.5 Traffic Analyzer Program Listing (continued)

```
FOR S1 = 0 TO S
                    S1# = S1
                    LD# = LD# + E# ^ S1#/FACTORIAL#(S1)
                    NEXT S1
                    TL#(S) = LN#/LD#
              NEXT S
REM Compute the traffic carried by port
        FOR I = 1 TO PORT
              IF I = 1 THEN
                    TC#(I) = E# - TL#(1)
                    ELSE
                    TC#(I) = TL#(I - 1) - TL#(I)
                    END IF
        NEXT I
REM Output results
PRINT
PRINT "TOTAL TRAFFIC OFFERED"; E#; "ERLANGS TO"; PORT; "PORTS
PROVIDES A";
PRINT USING "##.####"; GOS#;
PRINT " GRADE OF SERVICE"
PRINT
PRINT TAB(25); "TRAFFIC DISTRIBUTION"
PRINT
PRINT "PORT#   TRAFFIC OFFERED   TRAFFIC CARRIED    TRAFFIC LOST"
PRINT
FOR I = 1 TO PORT
        PRINT USING "##"; I;
        PRINT USING "       ###.#####"; E#;
        PRINT USING "       ###.#####"; TC#(I);
        PRINT USING "       ###.#####"; TL#(I)
        E# = E# - TC#(I)
NEXT I
PRINT
PRINT "TRAFFIC LOST BY LAST PORT IS ";
PRINT USING "###.##### "; TL#(PORT);
PRINT "ERLANGS"
```

Table 5.5   Traffic Analyzer Program Listing   (continued)

```
PRINT

PRINT "GRADE OF SERVICE IS EQUIVALENT TO 1 IN ";

PRINT USING "#####  "; INT((1/GOS#) +.5);

PRINT "CALLS RECEIVING A BUSY SIGNAL"

END

REM subroutine to compute factorials

100 FOR I = 1 TO PORT

        p# = 1

                FOR J = I TO 1 STEP -1

                p# = p# * J

                NEXT J

        FACTORIAL#(I) = p#

        NEXT I

        FACTORIAL#(0) = 1

        RETURN
```

0 through factorial 60. Note that the variable suffix # (hash sign) is used in Microsoft Basic to denote a double precision variable. Similar to FACTORIAL#, TL#, and TC# are arrays that are used to hold the double precision values of traffic lost and traffic carried by each port.

After the traffic intensity in erlangs (assigned to the variable E#) and the number of ports (assigned to the variable PORT) are entered, the program branches to the subroutine beginning at statement number 100. This subroutine computes the values of factorial 0 through the number assigned to PORT and stores those factorial values in the array FACTORIAL#.

After computing the factorial values, the program computes the grade of service using the equations previously described in this chapter. Similarly, the traffic lost and carried by each port is computed by computerizing the previously described equations to Basic language statements.

To illustrate the equivalency of a grade of service (stored in the variable GOS#) to 1 in N calls obtaining a busy signal GOS# is first divided into 1. Next, 0.5 is added to the result to raise its value to the next highest number prior to taking the integer value of the computation. This is necessary because the INT function rounds down the result obtained by dividing GOS# into unity.

The result of the execution of the traffic analyzer program using a traffic intensity of 3 erlangs being presented to a four-position rotary is contained in

Table 5.6   Traffic Analyzer Program Execution

```
                           Traffic Analyzer
This program computes the grade of service and the traffic carried
and lost by each port or channel in an n position rotary type group
Enter traffic intensity in Erlangs? 3
Enter number of ports -maximum 60? 4
TOTAL TRAFFIC OFFERED 3 ERLANGS TO 4 PORTS PROVIDES A 0.2061 GRADE
OF SERVICE
                         TRAFFIC DISTRIBUTION
PORT#    TRAFFIC OFFERED    TRAFFIC CARRIED    TRAFFIC LOST
 1          3.00000           0.75000           2.25000
 2          2.25000           0.66176           1.58824
 3          1.58824           0.54977           1.03846
 4          1.03846           0.42014           0.61832
TRAFFIC LOST BY LAST PORT IS    0.61832 ERLANGS
GRADE OF SERVICE IS EQUIVALENT TO 1 IN 5 CALLS RECEIVING A BUSY SIGNAL
```

Table 5.6. Note that the grade of service is 0.2061, which is approximately equivalent to one in five calls receiving a busy signal.

Through the use of the traffic analyzer program, you can vary the traffic intensity and/or the number of ports on the rotary group to study the resulting traffic distribution and grade of service. To illustrate this, assume you want to analyze the effect of increasing the rotary group to five positions. Here, you could simply rerun the traffic analyzer program as illustrated in Table 5.7. Note that when the rotary group is expanded to five positions, the grade of service is approximately equivalent to one in nine calls receiving a busy signal. In addition, you can use multiple executions of the traffic analyzer program to determine the change in the traffic lost by the last port in a port grouping as you increase or decrease the number of ports to service a given traffic intensity. In comparing the executions of the program displayed in Table 5.6 and Table 5.7, note that an increase in the number of ports from three to five decreased the traffic lost by the last port from 0.61832 to 0.33016 erlangs. Thus, you can use this program as a "devil's advocate" to determine "what if" information without having to actually install or remove equipment and perform the line measurements normally associated with sizing such equipment.

5.4.3   Traffic Capacity Planning

There are three methods by which the erlang distribution equation can be used for capacity planning purposes. The first method, as previously

Table 5.7   Analyzing the Effect of Port Expansion

```
                        Traffic Analyzer
This program computes the grade of service and the traffic carried
and lost by each port or channel in an n-position rotary type group.
Enter traffic intensity in Erlangs? 3
Enter number of ports - maximum 60? 5
TOTAL TRAFFIC OFFERED 3 ERLANGS TO 5 PORTS PROVIDES A 0.1101 GRADE
OF SERVICE
                        TRAFFIC DISTRIBUTION
```

PORT#	TRAFFIC OFFERED	TRAFFIC CARRIED	TRAFFIC LOST
1	3.00000	0.75000	2.25000
2	2.25000	0.66176	1.58824
3	1.58824	0.54977	1.03846
4	1.03846	0.42014	0.61832
5	0.61832	0.28816	0.33016

```
TRAFFIC LOST BY LAST PORT IS 0.33016 ERLANGS
GRADE OF SERVICE IS EQUIVALENT TO 1 IN 9 CALLS RECEIVING A BUSY SIGNAL
```

illustrated, uses the erlang distribution equation to compute a grade of service based on a defined traffic intensity and number of ports or channels. Using the value of the computed grade of service, you can then accept it or alter the traffic intensity and/or number of ports to obtain a desired grade of service.

A second method by which the erlang formula can be used is to determine the amount of traffic that can be serviced by a given number of ports or channels to provide a predefined grade of service. Using the erlang formula in this manner involves a trial-and-error process because different traffic intensity values must be substituted into the formula to determine if it results in the desired grade of service. And because this process can be quite laborious, a computer program was developed to generate a table of traffic intensities that can be serviced by a varying number of ports or channels to provide predefined grades of service.

Table 5.8 contains a program listing of a Traffic Capacity Planner Program, which was also developed using the Microsoft QuickBasic Compiler. You will find this program in the file CAPACITY.BAS in the directory BASIC at the Web URL previously mentioned in this book. This program computes and displays the traffic intensity that can be offered to 1 to 40 ports to obtain 0.01, 0.02, 0.04, and 0.08 grades of service you can easily vary both the grades of service and/or number of ports.

Table 5.8   Traffic Capacity Planner Program

```
REM Traffic Capacity Planner Program

REM $DYNAMIC

DIM FACTORIAL#(60)

DIM E#(4, 40)

DIM GOS(10)

REM E is the offered load in Erlangs

REM E#(I,S) contains resulting traffic for GOS of I when S ports
used

REM PORT is the number of ports, dial in lines or trunks

REM GOS is the grade of service for port or channel PORT with
traffic E

MAXPORT = 40

CLS

FOR I = 1 TO 4

READ GOS(I)

NEXT I

DATA.01,.02,.04,.08

LPRINT TAB(25); "Capacity Planner"

LPRINT

LPRINT "This program computes and displays a table containing the
traffic"

LPRINT "carrying capacity for a group of ports that will result
in"

LPRINT "                  a predefined grade of service"

LPRINT

        LPRINT

        LPRINT " NUMBER OF PORTS          TRAFFIC SUPPORTED IN
ERLANGS PER PORT"

        LPRINT "                          FOR INDICATED GRADE
OF SERVICE"

        LPRINT TAB(30);

        LPRINT USING "#.###    #.###   "; GOS(1); GOS(2);

        LPRINT USING "#.###    #.### "; GOS(3); GOS(4)

        LPRINT

GOSUB 100   'compute factorial 1 TO factorial MAXPORT

REM vary grade of service from.01 to.08 or 1 in 100 to 1 in 12.5
calls busy
```

Table 5.8   Traffic Capacity Planner Program   (continued)

```
FOR I = 1 TO 4
        GOS# = GOS(I)
        REM Vary ports from 1 to MAXPORT
            FOR PORT = 1 TO MAXPORT
                    REM Find traffic in Erlangs that provides GOS
                        LOW# = 1
                        HIGH# = 100000
                          TRY# = (LOW# + HIGH#)/2
1  E# = TRY#/1000
PORT# = PORT
                        N# = (E# ^ PORT#)/FACTORIAL#(PORT)
                        D# = 0
                        FOR S = 0 TO PORT
                        S# = S
                        D# = D# + (E# ^ S#)/FACTORIAL#(S)
                        NEXT S
                        IF ABS(GOS# - N#/D#) <.0005 THEN GOTO 5
                        IF GOS# - N#/D# < 0 THEN
                                OLD# = TRY#
                            TRY# = TRY# - ((TRY# - LOW#)/2)
                                GOTO 1
                          ELSEIF GOS# - N#/D# > 0 THEN
                                TRY# = (TRY# + OLD#)/2
                                GOTO 1
                        END IF
5 E#(I, PORT) = TRY#/1000
NEXT PORT
                        NEXT I
REM output results
        FOR S = 1 TO MAXPORT
                LPRINT TAB(4); S;
                 LPRINT TAB(29);
            LPRINT USING "##.### ##.###  "; E#(1, S); E#(2, S);
              LPRINT USING "##.###  ##.###"; E#(3, S); E#(4, S)
                NEXT S
        END
```

143

Table 5.8   Traffic Capacity Planner Program   (continued)

```
REM subroutine to compute factorials
100 FOR I = 1 TO MAXPORT
        p# = 1
                FOR J = I TO 1 STEP -1
                p# = p# * J
                NEXT J
        FACTORIAL#(I) = p#
        NEXT I
        FACTORIAL#(0) = 1
        RETURN
```

To vary the grades of service, the DATA statement should be changed. To increase the number of ports, the variable MAXPORT's value of 40 should be changed. When the number of grades of service and/or number of ports are increased, the DIM E#(4,40) statement should be increased to reflect the revised number of grades of service and/or ports for which the traffic intensity is to be computed. If the number of ports increases beyond 60, you should increase the size of the FACTORIAL#(60) array as well as have patience as the computations become lengthy. A word of caution is in order for readers who may require an expansion of the size of arrays. If the total number of elements in your program will exceed 64K, you must use the /AH option when invoking Microsoft's QuickBasic compiler. The reader is referred to Microsoft's QuickBasic manual for information concerning the use of the /AH option.

The modifications required to change the program to compute the traffic supported by 1 to 44 ports or channels for grades of service ranging from 0.01 to 0.55 or 1 in 100 to 55 in 100 calls receiving a busy signal in increments of 0.005 are contained in Table 5.9. This illustration contains the revised Traffic Capacity Planner Program listing that readers can compare to the program listing contained in Table 5.8 to denote the use of two additional FOR-NEXT statements that permit the use of only one DATA statement.

To speed up the computations of the trial-and-error procedure, the program was written to increment or decrement trials by one half of the previously used value. When the grade of service and the computed grade of service differ by less than 0.0005, a match is considered to have occurred and the traffic intensity used to compute the grade of service is placed into the E# array.

Table 5.9   Revised Traffic Planner Capacity Program

```
REM Traffic Capacity Planner Program

REM $DYNAMIC

DIM FACTORIAL#(60)

DIM E#(4, 40)

DIM GOS(10)

REM E is the offered load in Erlangs

REM E#(I,S) contains resulting traffic for GOS of I when S ports
used

REM PORT is the number of ports, dial in lines or trunks

REM GOS is the grade of service for port or channel PORT with
traffic E

MAXPORT = 44

CLS

FOR I = 1 TO 4

READ GOS(I)

NEXT I

DATA -.01,-.005,.00,.005

FOR TT = 1 TO 25

FOR K= 1 TO 4

GOS(K) = GOS(K) + 2/100

NEXT K

LPRINT TAB(30); "Capacity Planner"

LPRINT

LPRINT "This program computes and displays a table containing the
traffic"

LPRINT "carrying capacity for a group of ports that will result
in"

LPRINT "                    a predefined grade of service"

LPRINT

        LPRINT

        LPRINT " NUMBER OF PORTS            TRAFFIC SUPPORTED IN
ERLANGS PER PORT"

        LPRINT "                              FOR INDICATED GRADE
OF SERVICE"

        LPRINT TAB(30);

        LPRINT USING "#.###    #.###    "; GOS(1); GOS(2);

        LPRINT USING "#.###    #.### "; GOS(3); GOS(4)

        LPRINT
```

Table 5.9   Revised Traffic Planner Capacity Program   (continued)

```
GOSUB 100   'compute factorial 1 TO factorial MAXPORT
REM vary grade of service from.01 to.08 or 1 in 100 to 1 in 12.5
calls busy
          FOR I = 1 TO 4
          GOS# = GOS(I)
          REM Vary ports from 1 to MAXPORT
               FOR PORT = 1 TO MAXPORT
                      REM Find traffic in Erlangs that provides GOS
                          LOW# = 1
                          HIGH# = 100000
                           TRY# = (LOW# + HIGH#)/2
1   E# = TRY#/1000
PORT# = PORT
                          N# = (E# ^ PORT#)/FACTORIAL#(PORT)
                          D# = 0
                          FOR S = 0 TO PORT
                          S# = S
                          D# = D# + (E# ^ S#)/FACTORIAL#(S)
                          NEXT S
                          IF ABS(GOS# - N#/D#) <.0005 THEN GOTO 5
                          IF GOS# - (N#/D#) < 0 THEN
                                    HIGH# = TRY#
                               TRY# = TRY# - ((TRY# - LOW#)/2)
                                    GOTO 1
                          ELSEIF GOS# - N#/D# > 0 THEN
                               TRY# = (TRY# + HIGH#)/2
                               GOTO 1
                          END IF
5 E#(I, PORT) = TRY#/1000
NEXT PORT
                               NEXT I
REM output results
          FOR S = 1 TO MAXPORT
                  LPRINT TAB(4); S;
                  LPRINT TAB(29);
               LPRINT USING "##.###  ##.###  "; E#(1, S); E#(2, S);
                LPRINT USING "##.###  ##.###"; E#(3, S); E#(4, S)
                  NEXT S
```

Table 5.9   Revised Traffic Planner Capacity Program   (continued)

```
REM Skip to next page
        FOR I = 1 TO 12
        LPRINT
        NEXT I
NEXT TT
END
REM subroutine to compute factorials
100 FOR I = 1 TO MAXPORT
        p# = 1
                FOR J = I TO 1 STEP -1
                p# = p# * J
                NEXT J
        FACTORIAL#(I) = p#
        NEXT I
        FACTORIAL#(0) = 1
        RETURN
```

Table 5.10 illustrates the output produced from the execution of the Capacity Planner Program listed in Table 5.8. In examining the traffic support by grade of service, you will note that a large group of ports is more efficient with respect to their traffic capacity support for a given grade of service than small groups of ports. Similarly, a small reduction in the number of ports from a large group of ports has a much more pronounced effect on traffic capacity support than a similar reduction in the number of ports from a smaller group of ports. To illustrate the preceding, consider the 0.01 grade of service. Four groups of ten ports support a total traffic intensity of 17.684 (4.471 * 4) erlangs. In comparison, one 40-port group supports a total of 28.877 erlangs. Based on this, it is more than efficient to have one large rotary group than several smaller rotary groups, and readers may wish to consider this important concept of equipment sizing prior to breaking rotary or port groups into subgroups designed to service individual groups of end users. This concept also explains why it would be better to have one rotary group connected to V.90 modems operating at 56 Kbps that can also service end-user 33.6-Kbps transmission requirements than separate rotary groups.

5.4.4   Traffic Tables

A third method by which the erlang formula can be used is through the generation of a series of tables that indicate grades of service based on

Table 5.10 Capacity Planner Program Execution

```
                        Capacity Planner
This program computes and displays a table containing the traffic
carrying capacity for a group of ports that will result in
a predefined grade of service
```

NUMBER OF PORTS	TRAFFIC SUPPORTED IN ERLANGS PER PORT			
	FOR INDICATED GRADE OF SERVICE			
	0.010	0.020	0.040	0.080
1	0.010	0.020	0.042	0.086
2	0.151	0.221	0.332	0.514
3	0.450	0.599	0.812	1.127
4	0.880	1.100	1.398	1.849
5	1.368	1.649	2.052	2.629
6	1.924	2.271	2.773	3.462
7	2.484	2.931	3.517	4.327
8	3.126	3.610	4.293	5.216
9	3.786	4.327	5.088	6.105
10	4.471	5.088	5.891	7.032
11	5.128	5.860	6.733	7.966
12	5.860	6.593	7.571	8.906
13	6.593	7.393	8.449	9.857
14	7.335	8.204	9.303	10.832
15	8.076	9.012	10.175	11.782
16	8.871	9.857	11.045	12.772
17	9.614	10.683	11.969	13.763
18	10.431	11.491	12.877	14.727
19	11.176	12.306	13.735	15.739
20	12.016	13.184	14.668	16.731
21	12.772	14.063	15.585	17.741
22	13.624	14.901	16.480	18.751
23	14.420	15.770	17.442	19.751
24	15.262	16.633	18.386	20.780
25	16.151	17.510	19.252	21.790
26	17.030	18.386	20.188	22.802
27	17.881	19.227	21.192	23.795
28	18.604	20.188	22.090	24.805
29	19.557	21.027	23.072	25.855
30	20.348	21.876	24.030	26.876

Table 5.10   Capacity Planner Program Execution   (continued)

31	21.192	22.892	24.903	27.906
32	21.973	23.748	25.855	28.936
33	22.892	24.610	26.821	29.987
34	23.841	25.544	27.797	30.986
35	24.610	26.368	28.712	32.048
36	25.544	27.363	29.685	33.070
37	26.368	28.263	30.642	34.069
38	27.247	29.106	31.664	35.157
39	28.126	30.045	32.557	36.187
40	28.877	31.047	33.526	37.208

specific traffic loads and a given number of ports or channels. Once again, a computer program was developed to facilitate the required computations.

Table 5.11 contains the Microsoft QuickBasic program listing of a program that was written to compute a table of grades of service based on a given traffic intensity and port or channel size using the erlang distribution. This program is stored on the file ERLANG.BAS under the BASIC directory at the Web URL previously indicated in this book.

The execution of the ERLANG.BAS program results in the generation of a data file named ERLANG.DAT that contains the grades of service for traffic intensities ranging from 0.5 to 40 erlangs for groups of up to 60 ports or channels. This program, like other programs developed to assist in traffic computations, can be easily modified to obtain grades of service for a different range of traffic intensities or larger number of ports or channels. A comprehensive table is contained on the file ERLANG.DAT at the indicated Web URL. This table lists grades of service based on traffic intensities up to 77.5 erlangs in increments of 0.5 erlangs. Because the data file is in ASCII format, you can use any data processor capable of reading ASCII files to manipulate the entries to meet their specific requirements or you can use the DOS redirect feature to print the file. Concerning the latter, you can enter the DOS command:

```
TYPE ERLANG.DAT > LPT1:
```

to direct the contents of the file ERLANG.DAT to your printer. These tables can be used to reduce many sizing problems to a simple lookup procedure to determine equipment and/or facility size once the concepts involved in the use of the tables are understood. Thus, we will next focus our attention on the use of traffic tables and their use in the equipment sizing process.

Table 5.11   Program to Generate Table of Grades of Service Using the Erlang Distribution

```
REM $DYNAMIC

DIM FACTORIAL#(60)

DIM E#(80), B#(80, 80)

REM E is the offered load in Erlangs

REM S is the number of ports, dial in lines or trunks

REM B(i,j) contains grade of service for port or channel i with
traffic j

OPEN "D:ERLANG.DAT" FOR OUTPUT AS #1

GOSUB 100    'compute factorial 1 TO 60

C = 0

FOR I = 5 TO 400 STEP 5

        C = C + 1

        E# = I/10

        E#(C) = E#

                FOR S = 1 TO 60

                        SX# = S

                        N# = (E# ^ SX#)/FACTORIAL#(S)

                        D# = 1

                        FOR D1 = 1 TO S

                        D1X# = D1

                        D# = D# + (E# ^ D1X#)/FACTORIAL#(D1)

                        NEXT D1

                B#(S, C) = N#/D#

                NEXT S

    NEXT I

    FOR I = 1 TO 80 STEP 5   'print 16 pages 5 entries per page

            PRINT #1, "                        ERLANG B DISTRIBUTION"

            PRINT #1, "         PROBABILITY ALL PORTS ARE BUSY WHEN
CALL ATTEMPTED"

            PRINT #1, "                      WHICH IS THE GRADE OF SERVICE"

            PRINT #1,

            PRINT #1, "PORT #                   TRAFFIC IN ERLANGS"

            PRINT #1,

        PRINT #1, USING "    ##.##      ##.##"; E#(I); E#(I + 1);

            PRINT #1, USING "     ##.## "; E#(I + 2);

        PRINT #1, USING "    ##.##      ##.##"; E#(I + 3); E#(I + 4)

            PRINT #1,
```

Table 5.11   Program to Generate Table of Grades of Service Using the Erlang Distribution   (continued)

```
FOR S = 1 TO 60

                    IF B#(S, I + 4) <.00001# GOTO 50
                    PRINT #1, USING "##      #.##### "; S; B#(S, I);
                    PRINT #1, USING "   #.##### "; B#(S, I + 1);
                    PRINT #1, USING "   #.##### "; B#(S, I + 2);
                    PRINT #1, USING "    #.##### "; B#(S, I + 3);
                    PRINT #1, USING "   #.##### "; B#(S, I + 4)
          NEXT S
50        REM space to top of page
          FOR LINECOUNT = 1 TO (66 - S)
          PRINT #1,
          NEXT LINECOUNT
NEXT I
CLOSE #1
END
REM subroutine to compute factorials
100 FOR I = 1 TO 60
        p# = 1
                    FOR j = I TO 1 STEP -1
                    p# = p# * j
                    NEXT j
        FACTORIAL#(I) = p#
        NEXT I
        RETURN
```

In examining the program listing contained in Table 5.11, note that although the program was written to store output on a file, the program can be easily modified to direct output to a printer. This can be accomplished by removing the statement OPEN "D:ERLANG.DAT" FOR OUTPUT AS #1 and changing all PRINT #1 entries to LPRINT.

Extracts from the execution of the ERLANG.BAS program are listed in Table 5.12. While the use of the erlang B formula is normally employed for telephone dimensioning, it can be easily adapted to sizing data communications equipment. As an example of the use of Table 5.12, consider the following situation. Suppose one desires to provide customers with a grade

Table 5.12　Erlang B Distribution Extracts

Port No.	Traffic in erlangs				
	5.50	6.00	6.50	7.00	7.50
1	0.84615	0.85714	0.86667	0.87500	0.88235
2	0.69942	0.72000	0.73799	0.75385	0.76792
3	0.56184	0.59016	0.61523	0.63755	0.65751
4	0.43583	0.46957	0.49994	0.52734	0.55214
5	0.32406	0.36040	0.39391	0.42472	0.45302
6	0.22902	0.26492	0.29910	0.33133	0.36154
7	0.15250	0.18505	0.21737	0.24887	0.27921
8	0.09490	0.12188	0.15010	0.17882	0.20746
9	0.05481	0.07514	0.09780	0.12210	0.14740
10	0.02927	0.04314	0.05977	0.07874	0.09954
11	0.01442	0.02299	0.03412	0.04772	0.06356
12	0.00657	0.01136	0.01814	0.02708	0.03821
13	0.00277	0.00522	0.00899	0.01437	0.02157
14	0.00109	0.00223	0.00416	0.00713	0.01142
15	0.00040	0.00089	0.00180	0.00332	0.00568

Probability that all ports are busy when call attempted, which is the grade of service.

of service of 0.1 when the specific traffic intensity is 7.5 erlangs. From Table 5.12, ten channels or trunks would be required because the use of the table requires one to interpolate and round to the highest port or channel. Thus, if it was desired to offer a 0.01 grade of service when the traffic intensity was 7 erlangs, you could read down the 7.0 erlang column and determine that between 13 and 14 channels are required. Because you cannot install a fraction of a trunk or channel, 14 channels would be required, as we round to the highest channel number.

5.4.4.1 Access Controller Sizing. In applying the erlang B formula to access controller sizing, an analogy can be made between telephone network trunks and controller ports. Let us assume that a survey of users in a geographic area has indicated that during the busy hour, normally six personal computer users would be active. This would represent a traffic intensity of 6 erlangs. Suppose we wish to size the access controller to ensure that, at most, only one out of every 100 calls to the device encounters a busy signal. Then our desired grade of service becomes 0.01. From Table 5.12, the 6-erlang column indicates that to obtain a 0.01136 grade of service would require 12 channels or ports, while a 0.00522 grade of service would result if the device had 13 channels. Based on the preceding data, the access controller would be configured for 13 channels, as illustrated in Figure 5.4.

From a practical consideration, the erlang B formula assumption that lost calls are cleared and traffic not carried vanishes can be interpreted as

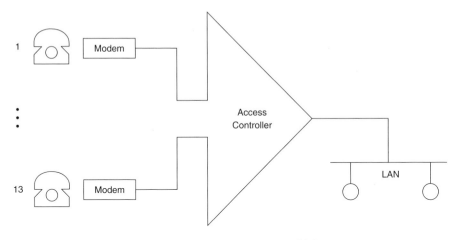

Figure 5.4   Access Controller Sizing

---

traffic overflowing one dial-in port is switched to the next port on the telephone company rotary as each dial-in port becomes busy. Thus, traffic overflowing dial-in port n is offered to port n + 1 and the traffic lost by the nth dial-in port, e_n, is the total traffic offered to the entire group of dial-in ports multiplied by the probability that all dial-in ports are busy. Thus,

$$e_n = E \times P(T_n, E)$$

where E is the traffic intensity in erlangs and n the number of ports or channels. For the first dial-in port, when n is 1, the proportion of traffic blocked becomes:

$$e_1 = \frac{E}{1 + E}$$

For the second dial-in port, the proportion of traffic lost by that port becomes:

$$e_2 = \frac{E^2/2!}{1 + (E^1/1!) + (E^2/2!)}$$

In general, the proportion of traffic lost by the nth port can be expressed as:

$$e_n = \frac{E^n/n!}{1 + (E^1/1!) + \dots (E^n/n!)}$$

From the preceding we note that we can analyze the traffic lost by each port on the access controller in the same manner as our previous discussion concerning the computation of lost traffic. In fact, the formulas contained in Table 5.12 for traffic lost and traffic carried by rotary position are applicable to each rotary position on the access controller. To verify this, let us reduce the complexity of calculations by analyzing the data traffic carried by a group of four dial-in ports connected to a four-channel access controller when a traffic intensity of 3 erlangs is offered to the group.

For the first dial-in port, the proportion of lost traffic becomes:

$$P_1 = \frac{3}{1+3} = 0.75$$

The proportion of lost traffic on the first port multiplied by the offered traffic provides the actual amount of lost traffic on port 1. Thus,

$$e_1 + P_1 * E = \frac{E}{1+E} * E = \frac{E2}{1+E} = 2.25 \text{ erlangs}$$

The total traffic carried on the first access controller port is the difference between the total traffic offered to that port and the traffic that overflows or is lost to the first port. Thus, the total traffic carried by port 1 is:

$$3 - 2.25 = 0.75 \text{ erlangs}$$

Because we consider the rotary a device that will pass traffic lost from port 1 to the remaining ports, we can compute the traffic lost by the second port in a similar manner. Substituting in the formula to determine the proportion of traffic lost, we obtain for the second port:

$$P_2 = \frac{E^2/2!}{1 + \left(E^1/1!\right) + \left(E^2/2!\right)} = 0.5294$$

The amount of traffic lost by the second port, e_2, becomes:

$$e_2 - p_2 * E = 0.5294 * 3 = 1.588 \text{ erlangs}$$

The traffic carried by the second port is the difference between the traffic lost by the first port and the traffic lost by the second port; thus:

$$e_1 - e_2 = 2.25 - 1.588 = 0.662 \text{ erlangs}$$

A summary of individual port traffic statistics is presented in Table 5.13 for the four-port access controller based on a traffic intensity of 3 erlangs offered to the device. Note that the computation results contained in Table 5.13 are within a small fraction of the results computed by the traffic analyzer program execution displayed in Table 5.6. The differences

154

Table 5.13 Individual Port Traffic Statistics

Port	Proportion of Lost Traffic	Amount of Lost Traffic	Traffic Carried
1	0.7500	2.2500	0.3462
2	0.5294	1.5880	0.6620
3	0.3462	1.0380	0.5500
4	0.2061	0.6813	0.4197

between the two can be attributed to the accuracy of the author's hand calculator versus the use of double precision in the program developed by the author. From Table 5.13, the traffic carried by all four ports totaled 2.3817 erlangs. Because 3 erlangs were offered to the access controller ports, then 0.6183 erlangs were lost. The proportion of traffic lost to the group of four ports is e_4/E or 0.6183/3, which is 0.2061. If you examine the ERLANG.DAT file, at the column for a traffic intensity of 3 erlangs and a row of four channels, you will note a similar 0.2061 grade of service. These calculations become extremely important from a financial standpoint if a table lookup results in a device dimensioning that requires an access controller expansion nest to be obtained to service one or only a few ports. Under such circumstances, you may wish to analyze a few of the individual high-order ports to see what the effect of the omission of one or more of those ports will have upon the system.

If data tables are available, the previous individual calculations are greatly simplified. From such tables the grade of service for channels 1 through 4 with a traffic intensity of 3 erlangs is the proportion of traffic lost to each port. Thus, if tables are available, you only have to multiply the grade of service by the traffic intensity to determine the traffic lost to each port.

5.5   The Poisson Formula

The number of arrivals per unit time at a service location can vary randomly according to one or many probability distributions. The Poisson distribution is a discrete probability distribution because it relates to the number of arrivals per unit time. The general model or formula for this probability distribution is given by the following equation:

$$P(r) = \frac{e^{-n}(r)^r}{r!}$$

where:
    r = number of arrivals
    p(r) = probability of arrivals
    n = mean of arrival rate
    e = base of natural logarithms (2.71828)
    r! = r factorial = r(r − 1)*(r − 2)*...*3 * 2 * 1

Table 5.14 Poisson Distribution Arrival (Rate of Two Per Unit Time)

Number of Arrivals per Period	Probability
0	0.1358
1	0.2707
2	0.2707
3	0.1805
4	0.0902
5	0.0361
6	0.0120
7	0.0034
8	0.0009
9	0.0002

The Poisson distribution corresponds to the assumption of random arrivals because each arrival is assumed to be independent of other arrivals and also independent of the state of the system. One interesting characteristic of the Poisson distribution is that its mean is equal to its variance. This means that by specifying the mean of the distribution, the entire distribution is specified.

5.5.1 Access Controller Sizing

As an example of the application of the Poisson distribution, let us consider an access controller where user calls arrive at a rate of two per unit period of time. From the Poisson formula, we obtain:

$$P(r) = \frac{2.71828 - 2 \times 2r}{r!}$$

Substituting the values 0, 1, 2, ..., 9 for r, we obtain the probability of arrivals listed in Table 5.14, rounding to four decimal places. The probability of arrivals in excess of nine per unit period of time can be computed but is a very small value and was thus eliminated from consideration.

The probability of the arrival rate being less than or equal to some specific number, n, is the sum of the probabilities of the arrival rate being 0, 1, 2, ..., n. This can be expressed mathematically as follows:

$$P(r <= n) = P(R = 0) + P(r = 1) + P(r = 2) + ... + P(r = n)$$

This can be expressed in sigma notation (the mathematical shorthand for expressing "sums" of numbers) as:

$$P(r <= n) = \sum_{r=0}^{n} \frac{e^{-n} \times n^{r}}{r!}$$

To determine the probability of four or fewer arrivals per unit period of time, we obtain:

$$P(r <= n) = \sum_{r=0}^{4} \left[\left(e^{-2} 2^{r} \right) / r! \right]$$

$$P(r <= 4) = P(r = 0) + P(r = 1) + P(r = 2) + P(r = 3) + P(r = 4)$$

$$= 0.1358 + 0.2707 + 0.2707 + 0.1804 + 0.0902$$

$$= 0.9478$$

From the preceding, almost 95 percent of the time four or fewer calls will arrive at the access controller at the same time, given an arrival rate or traffic intensity of 2. The probability that a number of calls in excess of four arrives during the period is equal to 1 minus the probability of four or fewer calls arriving, which is the grade of service. Thus, the grade of service when a traffic intensity of 2 erlangs is offered to four ports is:

$$P(r > 4) = 1 - P(r < 4) = 1 - 0.9478 = 0.0522$$

If four calls arrive and are being processed, any additional calls are lost and cannot be handled by the access controller. The probability of this occurring is 0.0522 for a four-channel access controller, given a traffic intensity of 2 erlangs. In general, when E erlangs of traffic are offered to a service area containing n channels, the probability that the service area will fail to handle the traffic is given by:

$$P(r >= n) = \sum_{r=n+1}^{n} \frac{e^{-e} \times E^{r}}{r!}$$

Although commonly known as the Poisson traffic formula, the preceding equation is also known as the Molina equation after the American who first applied it to traffic theory. Because the number of channels or ports is always finite, it is often easier to compute the probability that the number of channels cannot support the traffic intensity in terms of their support. This is because the probability of support plus the probability of not supporting a given traffic intensity must equal unity. Thus, we can rewrite the Molina or Poisson traffic formula as:

$$P(r > n) = \sum_{r=0}^{n} \frac{e^{-E} \times E^{r}}{r!}$$

To facilitate equipment and facility sizing using the Poisson traffic formula, another program was written in Microsoft QuickBasic. Table 5.15 contains the program listing of the file labeled POISSON.BAS, which is provided at the referenced Web address. This program generates a data file labeled POISSON.DAT, which contains a table of grades of service for traffic intensities ranging from 0.5 to 80 erlangs when lost calls are assumed to be held and thus follow the Poisson distribution. Both files are located in the directory BASIC at the Web address mentioned in this book.

To execute the POISSON.BAT program using Microsoft's QuickBasic, you must execute that compiler using its /AH option. That option allows dynamic arrays to exceed 64 K.

If you require the generation of a smaller set of tables or wish to alter the increments of traffic in erlangs, both modifications can be easily accomplished. Altering the number of tables requires changing the size of the E# and B# arrays, the statements FOR I = 5 to 800 STEP 5, E# = I/10, and I = 1 TO 160 STEP 5. The FOR I = 5 TO 800 STEP 5 statement controls the number of different traffic loads that will be computed. Because E# is set to I divided by 10, the program listing computes traffic from 0.5 to 80 erlangs in increments of 0.5 erlangs. Thus, you can change the FOR statement or the statement E# = I/10 or both to alter the number of traffic loads and their values. Finally, you must alter the statement I = 1 TO 160 STEP 5 if you change the previously referenced FOR statement. This is because the FOR I = 1 TO STEP 160 STEP 5 statement controls the printing of output. As included in the POISSON.BAS listing, the FOR I = 1 TO 160 STEP 5 statement results in the printing of 32 pages with five entries per page.

Similar to ERLANG.DAT, the file POISSON.DAT is available for downloading in the directory BASIC at the previously indicated Web URL. This file is in ASCII format and can be directed to your printer by the command TYPE POISSON.DAT>LPT1: or it can be imported into a word processor that is capable of reading ASCII files. The POISSON.DAT file contains grade of service computations based on a traffic intensity of 0.5 to 80 erlangs in increments of 0.5 erlangs.

5.5.2 Formula Comparison and Utilization

To contrast the difference between erlang B and Poisson formulas, let us return to the LAN access controller examples previously considered. When 6 erlangs of traffic are offered and it is desired that the grade of service should be 0.01, 13 channels are required when the erlang B formula is employed. If the Poisson formula is used, an excerpt of one of the tables produced by executing the POISSON.BAS program would appear as indicated in Table 5.16. Using this table, a grade of service of 0.01 for a traffic intensity of 6 erlangs results in a required channel capacity somewhere between 9 and 10. Rounding to the next highest number results in a requirement for

Table 5.15   POISSON.BAS Program Listing

```
'$DYNAMIC
OPEN "A:POISSON.DAT" FOR OUTPUT AS #1
DIM FACTORIAL#(60)
DIM E#(180), B#(160, 160)
REM E is the offered load in Erlangs
REM S is the number of ports, dial in lines or trunks
REM B(i,j) contains grade of service for port or channel i with
traffic j
GOSUB 100   'compute factorial 1 TO 60
C = 0
FOR I = 5 TO 800 STEP 5
        C = C + 1
        E# = I/10
        E#(C) = E#
                K = 0
                FOR S = 0 TO 59    'vary port number
                        K = K + 1
                        SX# = S
                        D# = 0
                        FOR X = 0 TO S
                        D1X# = X
                        D# = D# + (E# ^ D1X#)/(FACTORIAL#(X) *
2.71828 ^ E#)
                        NEXT X
                B#(K, C) = 1# - D#
                B#(X, C) = ABS(B#(K, C))
                NEXT S
  NEXT I
  FOR I = 1 TO 160 STEP 5  ' print 32 pages 5 entries per page
        PRINT #1, "                        POISSON   DISTRIBUTION"
        PRINT #1, "      PROBABILITY ALL PORTS ARE BUSY WHEN CALL
ATTEMPTED"
        PRINT #1, "                WHICH IS THE GRADE OF SERVICE"
        PRINT #1,
        PRINT #1, "PORT #                TRAFFIC IN ERLANGS"
        PRINT #1,
        PRINT #1, USING "    ##.##        ##.##"; E#(I); E#(I + 1);
```

Table 5.15   POISSON.BAS Program Listing   (continued)

```
PRINT #1, USING "          ##.##"; E#(I + 2);

    PRINT #1, USING "        ##.##        ##.##"; E#(I + 3); E#(I + 4)

    PRINT #1,

    FOR S = 1 TO 60

          IF B#(S, I + 4) <.00001# GOTO 50

          PRINT #1, USING "##  #.##### "; S; B#(S, I);

          PRINT #1, USING "     #.#####"; B#(S, I + 1);

          PRINT #1, USING "     #.#####"; B#(S, I + 2);

          PRINT #1, USING "     #.#####"; B#(S, I + 3);

          PRINT #1, USING "     #.#####"; B#(S, I + 4)

    NEXT S

50    REM space to top of page

    FOR LINECOUNT = 1 TO (66 - S)

    PRINT #1,

    NEXT LINECOUNT

NEXT I

CLOSE #1

END

REM subroutine to compute factorials

100 FOR I = 1 TO 60

    p# = 1

          FOR j = I TO 1 STEP -1

          p# = p# * j

          NEXT j

    FACTORIAL#(I) = p#

    NEXT I

    FACTORIAL#(0) = 1#

    RETURN
```

10 channels. Now let us compare what happens at a higher traffic intensity. For a traffic intensity of 10 erlangs and the same 0.01 grade of service, you will note that 19 channels will be required when the erlang B formula is used. If the Poisson formula is used, you will note that a 0.01 grade of service based on 10 erlangs of traffic requires between 18 and 19 channels. Rounding to the next highest channel results in the Poisson formula providing the same value as provided through the use of the erlang B formula.

In general, the Poisson formula produces a more conservative sizing at lower traffic intensities than the erlang B formula. At higher traffic

Table 5.16   Poisson B Distribution Extracts

Port No.	Traffic in erlangs				
	5.50	6.00	6.50	7.00	7.50
1	0.99591	0.99752	0.99850	0.99909	0.99945
2	0.97344	0.98265	0.98872	0.99270	0.99530
3	0.91162	0.93803	0.95696	0.97036	0.07974
4	0.79830	0.84880	0.88815	0.91823	0.94085
5	0.64248	0.71494	0.77633	0.82701	0.86794
6	0.47108	0.55432	0.63096	0.69929	0.75856
7	0.31396	0.39369	0.47347	0.55029	0.62184
8	0.19051	0.25602	0.32724	0.40128	0.47536
9	0.10564	0.15276	0.20842	0.27091	0.33803
10	0.05377	0.08392	0.12261	0.16950	0.22359
11	0.02525	0.04262	0.06683	0.09852	0.13776
12	0.01098	0.02009	0.03388	0.05335	0.07924
13	0.00445	0.00882	0.01602	0.02700	0.04266
14	0.00168	0.00362	0.00710	0.01281	0.02156
15	0.00060	0.00140	0.00295	0.00571	0.01026

Probability that all ports are busy when call attempted, which is the grade of service.

intensities, the results are reversed. The selection of the appropriate formula depends on how one visualizes the calling pattern of users of the communications network.

5.5.3   Economic Constraints

In the previous dimensioning exercises, the number of ports or channels selected was based on a defined level of grade of service. Although we want to size equipment to have a high efficiency and keep network users happy, we must also consider the economics of dimensioning. One method that can be used for economic analysis is the assignment of a dollar value to each erlang-hour of traffic.

For a company such as an Internet service provider, the assignment of a dollar value to each erlang-hour of traffic may be a simple matter. Here, the average revenue per one-hour session could be computed and used as the dollar value assigned to each erlang-hour of traffic. For other organizations, the average hourly usage of employees waiting service could be employed.

As an example of the economics involved in sizing, let us assume lost calls are held, resulting in traffic following a Poisson distribution, and that 7.5 erlangs of traffic can be expected during the busy hour. Let us suppose we desire initially to offer a 0.02 grade of service. From the extract of the execution of the Poisson distribution program presented in Table 5.14, between 14 and 15 channels would be required. Rounding to the highest number, 15 channels would be selected to provide the desired 0.02 grade of service, which is equivalent to one call in 50 obtaining a busy signal.

LAN access controllers normally consist of a base unit that contains a number of channels or ports and an expansion chassis into which dual-port adapter cards are normally inserted to expand the capacity of the controller. Many times, you may desire to compare the potential revenue loss in comparison to expanding the access controller beyond a certain capacity. As an example of this, consider the data in Table 5.16, which indicates that when the traffic intensity is 5.5 erlangs, a 12-channel access controller would provide an equivalent grade of service. This means that during the busy hour, 2 erlangs of traffic would be lost and the network designer could then compare the cost of three additional ports on the access controller and additional modems and dial-in lines — if access to the access controller is over the switched network — to the loss of revenue by not being able to service the busy-hour traffic.

5.6 Applying the Equipment Sizing Process

Many methods are available for end users to obtain data traffic statistics required for sizing communications equipment. Two of the most commonly used methods are based on user surveys and computer accounting information.

End-user surveys normally require each user to estimate the number of originated calls to a network access point for average and peak traffic situations as well as the call duration in minutes or fractions of an hour, on a daily basis. By accumulating the traffic data for a group of users in a particular geographic area, you then can obtain the traffic that the access controller will be required to support.

Suppose a new application is under consideration at a geographic area currently not served by a firm's data communications network. For this application, ten PCs with the anticipated data traffic denoted in Table 5.17 are to be installed at five small offices in the greater metropolitan area of a city. If each PC user will dial a centrally located LAN access controller, how many dial-in lines, auto-answer modems, and access controller ports are required to provide users with a 98 percent probability of accessing the network upon dialing the LAN access controller? What would happen if a 90 percent probability of access were acceptable?

For the ten PCs listed in Table 5.17, the average daily and peak daily traffic are easily computed. These figures can be obtained by multiplying the number of calls originated each day by the call duration and summing the values for the appropriate average and peak periods. Doing so, you obtain 480 minutes of average daily traffic and 1200 minutes of peak traffic.

Table 5.17   PC Traffic Survey

PC	Calls Originated per Day		Call Duration (minutes)	
	Average	Peak	Average	Peak
A	3	6	15	30
B	2	3	30	60
C	5	5	10	15
D	2	3	15	15
E	2	4	15	30
F	2	4	15	30
G	3	3	15	35
H	4	6	30	30
I	2	3	20	25
J	2	2	15	60

Dividing those numbers by 60 results in 8 erlangs average daily traffic and 20 erlangs peak daily traffic.

Prior to sizing, some additional knowledge and assumptions concerning PC traffic will be necessary. First, from the data contained in most survey forms, information regarding busy-hour traffic is nonexistent, although such information is critical for equipment sizing. Although survey forms can be tailored to obtain the number of calls and call duration by specific time intervals, for most users the completion of such precise estimates is a guess at best.

Busy-hour traffic can normally be estimated accurately from historical or computer billing and accounting type data, or from the use of a network management system that logs usage data. Suppose that the use of one of those sources shows a busy-hour traffic equal to twice the average daily traffic based upon an eight-hour normal operational shift. Then the traffic would be (8/8) * 2 or 2 erlangs, while the busy-hour peak traffic would be (20/8) * 2, or 5 erlangs.

The next process in the sizing procedure is to determine the appropriate sizing formula to apply to the problem. If we assume that users encountering a busy signal will tend to redial the telephone numbers associated with the access controller, the Poisson formula will be applicable. From Table 5.18, the 7.0-erlang traffic column shows a 0.01656 probability (1.65 percent) of all channels busy for a device containing six channels, 0.05265 for five channels, and 0.14288 for four channels. Thus, to obtain a 98 percent probability of access based on the daily average traffic would require six channels, while a 90 percent probability of access would require five channels.

Table 5.18 Poisson Distribution Program Extract

Port No.	Traffic in erlangs				
	5.50	6.00	6.50	7.00	7.50
1	0.39347	0.63212	0.77687	0.86466	0.91791
2	0.09020	0.26424	0.44217	0.59399	0.71270
3	0.01439	0.08030	0.19115	0.32332	0.45619
4	0.00175	0.01899	0.06564	0.14288	0.24242
5	0.00017	0.00366	0.01857	0.05265	0.10882
6	0.00001	0.00059	0.00446	0.01656	0.04202
7	0.00000	0.00008	0.00093	0.00453	0.01419
8	0.00000	0.00001	0.00017	0.00110	0.00425
9	0.00000	0.00000	0.00003	0.00024	0.00114
10	0.00000	0.00000	0.00000	0.00005	0.00028
11	0.00000	0.00000	0.00000	0.00001	0.00006
12	0.00000	0.00000	0.00000	0.00000	0.00001

Probability that all ports are busy when call attempted, which is the grade of service.

If we want to size the equipment based on the daily peak traffic load, how would sizing differ? We now would use a 5-erlang traffic column contained in the sizing tables. From the table, 11 channels would provide a 0.01369 probability (1.37 percent) of encountering a busy signal, while 10 channels would provide a 0.03182 probability. To obtain a 98 percent probability of access statistically would require 11 channels. Because there are only ten terminals, logic would override statistics and ten channels, or one channel per personal computer, would suffice. It should be noted that the statistical approach is based on a level of traffic that can be generated from an infinite number of computers. Thus, you must also use logic and recognize the limits of the statistical approach when sizing equipment. Because a 0.06809 probability of encountering a busy signal is associated with nine channels and a 0.13337 probability with eight channels, nine channels would be required to obtain a 90 percent probability of access.

In Table 5.19, the sizing required for average and peak daily traffic is listed for both 90 percent and 98 percent probability of obtaining access. Note that the difference between supporting the average and peak traffic loads is four channels for both the 90 percent and 98 percent probability of access scenarios, although peak traffic is 2.5 times average traffic.

Table 5.19 Channel Requirements Summary

Probability of Access (%)	Daily Average	Traffic Peak
90	5	9
98	6	10

The last process in the sizing procedure is to determine the number of channels and associated equipment to install. Whether to support the average or peak load will depend on the critical nature of the application, funds availability, how often peak daily traffic can be expected, and perhaps organizational politics. If peak traffic occurs once per month, we could normally size equipment for the average daily traffic expected. If peak traffic was expected to occur twice each day, we would normally size equipment based upon peak traffic. Traffic between these extremes may require that the final step in the sizing procedure be one of human judgment, incorporating knowledge of economics, and the application into the decision process.

Chapter 6
Using the Availability Level as a Decision Criterion

In Chapter 4 the application of queuing theory to determining transmission delays through remote bridges and routers was examined. As noted in that chapter, you can use queuing theory to compare the use of single versus multiple circuits used to connect remote bridges and routers. In doing so, you examined the use of single and multiple circuits from a performance perspective, leaving until this chapter a discussion of availability issues.

One of the more important decisions that network managers and LAN administrators face is determining whether to install single or multiple port devices such as remote bridges and routers. By understanding how availability is computed, you obtain the knowledge necessary to determine whether or not the cost of additional bridge or router ports, communications equipment, and transmission facilities is worthwhile with respect to the additional level of network availability obtained through the use of different communications configurations.

This chapter focuses attention on the use of the availability level of different network configurations as a decision criterion. That decision criteria can range from the direct selection of one configuration over another based upon their level of availability to the use of several selection parameters, to include such additional parameters as performance and cost.

6.1 Availability

In the same way that "one person's passion is another person's poison," there are different ways in which you can look at and define *availability*. Thus, to alleviate any possibility of confusion, let us first define the term as it relates to both components and systems. Once this is accomplished, we can examine its applicability to different local area network (LAN) communications configurations.

6.1.1 Component Availability

The availability of an individual component can be expressed in two ways that are directly related to one another. First, as a percentage, availability can be defined as the operational time of a device divided by the total time, with the result multiplied by 100. This is indicated by the following equation:

$$A\% = \frac{\text{operational time}}{\text{total time}} * 100$$

where A% is availability expressed as a percent.

For example, consider a leased line modem or DSU that normally operates continuously 24 hours per day. Over a one-year period of time, let us assume that the modem failed once and required eight hours to repair. During the year, the modem was available for use 365 days * 24 hours/day – 8 hours, or 8752 hours. Thus, the modem was operational 8752 hours during a period of 8760 hours. Using the availability formula, we obtain:

$$A\% = \frac{8752}{8760} * 100 = 99.91\%$$

6.1.2 MTBF and MTTR

Now let us define two commonly used terms and discuss their relationship to operational time and total time. The first term, Mean Time Before Failure (MTBF), is the average operational time of a device prior to its failure. Thus, MTBF is equivalent to the operational time of a device.

Once a device has failed, you must initiate actions to effect its repair. The interval from the time the device fails until the time the device is repaired is known as the time to repair and the average of each repair time is known as the Mean Time To Repair (MTTR). Because the total time is MTBF + MTTR, we can rewrite the availability formula as follows:

$$A\% = \frac{\text{MTBF}}{\text{MTBF} + \text{MTTR}} * 100$$

It is important to remember the M in MTBF and MTTR, as you must use the average or mean time before failure and average or mean time to repair. Otherwise, your calculations are subject to error. For example, if your device failure occurred halfway through the year, you might be tempted to assign 4380 hours to the MTBF. Then, you would compute availability as:

$$A\% = \frac{4380}{4380 + 8} * 100 = 99.91\%$$

The problem with the above computation is the fact that only one failure occurred, which results in the MTBF not actually representing a mean. Although the computed MTBF is correct for one particular device, as sure as the sun rises in the East, the MTBF would be different for a second device, different for a third device, etc. Thus, if you are attempting to obtain an availability level for a number of devices installed or to be installed, you, in effect, will compute an average level of availability through the use of an average MTBF. Thus, the next logical question is: How do you obtain average MTBF information for a communications device? Fortunately, many vendors provide MTBF information for the products they manufacture that you can use instead of waiting for a significant period of time to obtain appropriate information. Although many published MTBF statistics can be used as is, certain statistics may represent extrapolations that deserve a degree of elaboration. When vendors introduce a new product and quote an MTBF of 50,000, 100,000, or more hours, they obviously did not operate that device for that length of time. Instead, they either extrapolated MTBF statistics based on the improvements made to a previously manufactured product or based their statistics on the MTBF values of individual components.

If you note an asterisk next to an MTBF figure and the footnote indicates extrapolation, you should probably question the MTBF value. After all, if the MTBF of some device is indicated as 100,000 hours or almost 12 years, why is the warranty period typically one or two years? In such situations, you might wish to consider using the warranty period as the MTBF value instead of an extrapolated MTBF value. Concerning the MTTR, this number is also provided by the manufacturer but normally requires a degree of modification to be realistic.

Most manufacturers quote an MTTR figure based on the time required to repair a device once a repair person is on-site. Thus, you must consider the location where your equipment is to be installed and travel time from a vendor's location to your location. If your organization has a maintenance contract that guarantees a service call within a predefined period after notification of an equipment failure, you can use that time period and add it to the MTTR. For example, assume the specification sheet for a vendor's T1 channel service unit (CSU) listed an MTBF of 16,500 hours and an MTTR of two hours. If you anticipate installing the device in Macon, Georgia, and the nearest vendor service office is located in the northern suburbs of Atlanta, you would probably add four to six hours to the MTTR time. This addition would reflect the time required for a repair person in Atlanta to receive notification that he or she should service a failed device in Macon, complete his or her work in Atlanta, and travel to the site in Macon. While this may not be significant when an MTBF exceeds a year, suppose your equipment location was Boise, Idaho, and the CSU vendor used next-day delivery to ship a replacement device, in effect repairing by replacement.

In this situation, you may have to add 24 hours or more to the time required to swap CSUs to obtain a more realistic MTTR value.

6.1.3 System Availability

In communications, a system is considered to represent a collection of devices connected through the use of one or more transmission facilities that form a given topology. Thus, to determine the availability of a system, you must consider the availability of each device and transmission facility as well as the overall topology of the system. Concerning the latter, the structure of the system in which components are connected in serial or in parallel will affect the overall availability of that system. To illustrate the effect of topology on system availability, several basic LAN structures in which devices are connected in series and in parallel will be examined.

6.1.4 Devices Connected in Series

The top portion of Figure 6.1 illustrates the connection of n components in series. In this and subsequent illustrations, a component will be considered to represent either a physical network device or a transmission facility connecting two devices. Thus, the boxes labeled A_1, A_2, and A_3 could represent the availability of a data service unit (DSU; A_1), the availability of a leased line (A_2), and the availability of a second DSU (A_3).

The availability of n components connected in series is computed by multiplying the availability of each individual component. Mathematically, this is expressed as follows for n components:

$$A = \prod_{i=1}^{n} A_i$$

To illustrate the computation of a system in which components are arranged in series, consider the Token Ring network connected to an Ethernet LAN via the use of two remote bridges or routers and a pair of DSUs. This networking system is illustrated in the lower portion of Figure 6.1.

Let us assume that each remote bridge has an MTBF of one year, or 8760 hours, and any failure would be corrected by the manufacturer shipping a replacement unit to each location where a bridge or router is installed. Thus, we might assume a worst-case MTTR of 48 hours to allow for the time between reporting a failure and the arrival and installation of a replacement unit. Similarly, let us assume an MTBF of 8760 hours and an MTTR of 48 hours for each DSU. For the transmission line, most communications carriers specify a 99.5 percent availability level for digital circuits, so using a slightly lower level of 99.4 percent for the communications carrier serving our location would appear reasonable. Based on the preceding, the availability of the communications system, A_S, which

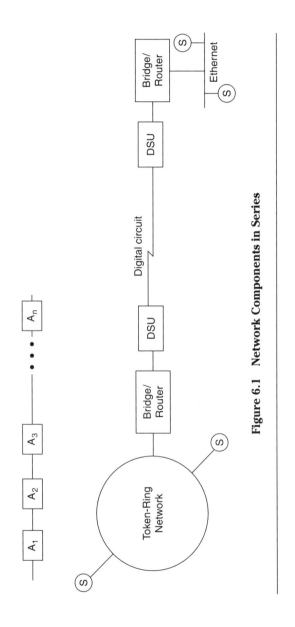

Figure 6.1 Network Components in Series

enables a user on a Token Ring network to access the Ethernet network and vice versa via a pair of single-port bridges or routers, then becomes:

$$A_S\% = [(Bridge_A)^2 * (DSU_A)^2 * Line_D] * 100$$

where:
> $Bridge_A$ = availability level of each bridge
> DSU_A = availability level of each DSU
> $Line_D$ = availability level of the digital circuit connecting the two locations

Because the availability of each component equals the MTBF divided by the sum of the MTBF and the MTTR, we obtain:

$$A_A\% = \left[\left(\frac{8760}{8808}\right)^2 * \left(\frac{8760}{8808}\right)^2 * 0.994 \right] * 100 = 97.25\%$$

This means that 2.75 percent of the time $(100 - 97.25)$ in which an attempt is made to use the communications system the failure of one or more components will render the system inoperative.

6.1.5 Devices Connected in Parallel

Figure 6.2a illustrates n devices connected in parallel. If only one device out of n is required to provide communications at any point in time, then the availability of the system as a percentage becomes:

$$A_S\% = \left(1 - \prod_{i=1}^{n} \left(1 - A_i\right) \right) * 100$$

For example, assume two devices, each having an availability level of 99 percent, are operated in parallel. Then, the availability level of the resulting parallel system becomes:

$$A_S\% = \left(1 - \prod_{i=1}^{2} \left(1 - A_i\right) \right) * 100$$

Substituting, we obtain:

$$A_S\% = [1 - (1 - 0.99) * (1 - 0.99)] * 100 = 99.99$$

Because communications within and between networks normally traverse multiple components, the use of parallel transmission paths normally involves multiple components on each path. Figures 6.2b and 6.2c illustrate two methods by which alternative paths could be provided to connect the Token Ring and Ethernet networks together.

(a) n components connected in parallel

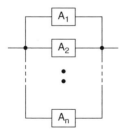

(b) Using dual single port bridges or routers

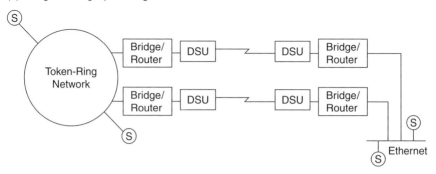

(c) Using single dual-port bridges or routers

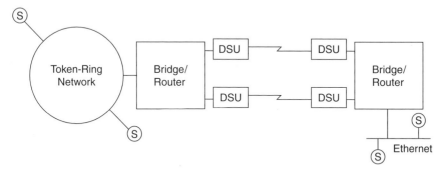

Figure 6.2   Connecting Devices in Parallel

Readers should note that transparent bridging supported by Ethernet networks precludes the use of closed loops that physically occur through the use of dual bridges or multi-port bridges illustrated in Figure 6.2b and 6.2c. However, if we assume that only one path operates at a single point in time, the use of two paths in which one only becomes active if the other becomes inactive is supported by transparent bridging. If routers are used instead of bridges, because they operate at the network layer, we do not have to concern ourselves with closed loops as they are only applicable to data-link layer 2 operations.

In the topology illustrated in Figure 6.2b, duplicate remote bridges or routers, DSUs, and transmission paths were assumed to be installed. In Figure 6.2c, it was assumed that your organization could obtain a very reliable remote bridge or router and preferred to expend funds on parallel communications circuits and DSUs because the failure rate of long-distance communications facilities normally exceeds the failure rate of the equipment.

For simplicity, let us assume that the availability level of each component illustrated in Figure 6.2b is 0.9. For each parallel path, you can consider the traversal of the path to encounter five components: two bridges or routers, two DSUs, and the communications line. Thus, the upper path containing five devices in series would have an availability level of $0.9 * 0.9 * 0.9 * 0.9 * 0.9$, or 0.59049. Similarly, the lower path would have a level of availability of 0.59049. Thus, you have now reduced the network structure to two parallel paths, each having an availability level of 0.59049. If A_1 is the availability level of path 1 and A_2 is the availability level of the second path, system availability, A_S, becomes:

$$A_S\% = \left(1 - \prod_{i=1}^{2}\left(1 - A_i\right)\right) * 100$$

Thus:

$$A_S\% = [1 - (1 - A_1)(1 - A_2)] * 100$$

Simplifying the above equation by multiplying the terms and substituting 0.59049 for A_1 and A_2, you obtain:

$$A_S\% = (A_1 + A_2 - A_1 * A_2) * 100 = 83.23$$

6.1.6 Mixed Topologies

Now let us focus attention on the network configuration illustrated in Figure 6.2c, in which a common bridge or router at each LAN location provides access to duplicate transmission facilities. To compute the availability of this communications system, you can treat each bridge or router as a serial element, while the two DSUs and the communications line between each DSU represent parallel routes of three serial devices.

Figure 6.3 illustrates how you can consider the communications system previously illustrated in Figure 6.2c as a sequence of serial and parallel elements. By combining groups of serial and parallel elements, you can easily compute the overall level of availability for the communications

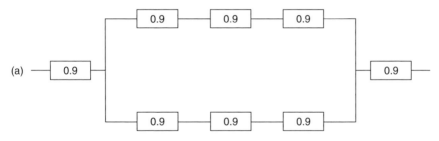

(a)

Availability of three serial devices = 0.9*0.9*0.9 = 0.729

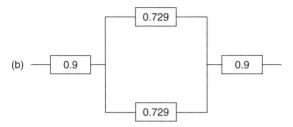

(b)

Availability of two parallel devices = (0.729 + 0.729) - 0.729*0.729 = 0.926

(c)

Availability of three serial devices = 0.9*0.926*0.9 = 0.75

(d)

Figure 6.3   Computing the Availability of a Mixed Serial and Parallel Transmission System

system as indicated in the four parts of Figure 6.3. In Figure 6.3a, the three serial elements of each parallel circuit are combined, including the two DSUs and communications line, to obtain a serial availability level of (0.9 $*$ 0.9 $*$ 0.9), or 0.729. Next, in Figure 6.3b, the two parallel paths are combined to obtain a joint availability of [(0.729 + 0.729) – (0.729 $*$ 0.729)], or 0.926. Finally, in Figure 6.3c, the joint availability of the parallel transmission paths is treated as a serial element with the two bridges or routers, obtaining a system availability of 0.75, which is shown in Figure 6.3d. Note that at a uniform 90 percent level of availability for each device, the use of single bridges or routers in place of dual bridges or routers lowers the system availability by approximately 8 percent. That is, the system availability obtained through the use of dual single-port bridges or routers illustrated in Figure 6.2b was computed to be 83.23 percent. In comparison,

Table 6.1   System Availability Comparison

Component Availability	System Availability	
	Single-Multiport Bridge or Router	Parallel Single-Port Bridges or Router
0.90	0.7505	0.8323
0.91	0.7778	0.8586
0.92	0.8049	0.8838
0.93	0.8318	0.9073
0.94	0.8582	0.9292
0.95	0.8841	0.9488
0.96	0.9094	0.9659
0.97	0.9337	0.9800
0.98	0.9571	0.9908
0.99	0.9792	0.9976
0.999	0.9980	0.9999

the system availability obtained from the use of single dual-port bridges or routers illustrated in Figure 6.2c was determined to be 75 percent.

6.1.7   Dual Hardware versus Dual Transmission Facilities

In the above calculations, assuming a uniform component availability of 0.90, the system availability of the dual network illustrated in Figure 6.2b was computed to be 83.23 percent, while the availability of the network illustrated in Figure 6.2c was computed to be 75 percent. Although the difference in availability of over 8 percent could probably justify the extra cost associated with dual bridges for organizations with critical applications, what happens to the difference in the availability of each network as the availability level of each component increases?

Table 6.1 compares the system availability for the use of single multi-port and parallel single-port bridge networks as component availability increases from 0.90 to 0.999. In examining the entries in Table 6.1, you will note that the difference between the availability level of each network decreases as component availability increases. In fact, the 8 percent difference in the availability of each system at a component availability level of 0.9 decreases to under 4 percent at a component availability level of 0.98 and to under 2 percent at a component availability level of 0.99. Most modern communications devices have a component availability level close to 0.999, which, by the way, usually exceeds the availability level of a transmission facility by 0.005. Thus, the use of dual bridges or dual routers instead of multi-port bridges or routers may be limited to increasing network availability by one tenth of 1 percent. This means you must balance the gain in availability against the cost of redundant bridges or routers.

176

Concerning cost, although bridges vary considerably with respect to features and price, at the end of 2002 their average price was approximately $1000. In comparison, the incremental cost of a dual-port bridge versus a single-port bridge was typically less than $500. Because you require two bridges to link geographically separated networks, the cost difference between the use of dual single-port bridges and single dual-port bridges is approximately (1000 − 500) ∗ 2, or $1000. Thus, in this example you would have to decide if an increase in network availability by approximately one tenth of 1 percent is worth $1000.

If you apply the preceding economic analysis to routers, the cost disparity between different network configurations becomes more pronounced. For example, a middle-range router might cost $5000, while the incremental cost of a dual-port router can be expected to add approximately $750 to the cost of the device. Then, the cost difference between dual single-port routers and single dual-port routers becomes (5000 − 750) ∗ 2, or $8500. Thus, when routers are used, your decision criterion could be one of deciding if an increase in network availability of approximately 0.1 percent is worth $8500.

If your organization operates a reservation system in which a minute of downtime could result in the loss of thousands to tens of thousands of dollars of revenue, the additional cost would probably be most acceptable. If your organization uses your network for interoffice electronic mail transmissions, you might prefer to save the $1000 and use dual-port bridges instead of dual single-port bridges or save $8500 if you were using routers for interconnecting your offices. This is because a gain of 0.1 percent of availability based on an eight-hour workday with 22 workdays per month would only produce 2.1 additional hours of availability per year. At a cost of approximately $500 when bridges are used or over $4250 when routers are used for the additional availability, it might be more economical to simply delay non-urgent mail and use the telephone for urgent communications.

6.1.8 *Evaluating Disk Mirroring*

Another area where the use of availability computations can be valuable with respect to LAN performance is in the area of evaluating the advantage associated with a disk mirroring system. To illustrate the use of availability in evaluating the practicality of a disk mirroring system, let us compare different file server equipment structures.

The top portion of Figure 6.4a illustrates the use of a conventional disk subsystem installed in a file server. In this example, data transmitted from a workstation flows across the network media into the file server and through its controller onto the disk. Thus, the conventional disk subsystem from the perspective of availability can be schematically represented as three components in series: the file server, controller, and disk.

Enhancing LAN Performance, Fourth Edition

(a) Conventional disk system

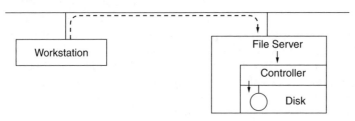

(b) Mirrored disk drives and dual controllers

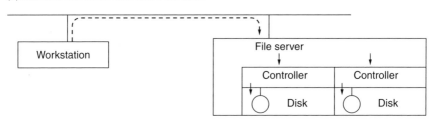

Figure 6.4   Comparing Data Flow Using Conventional and Mirrored Disk Systems on a File Server

The rationale for including the file server when computing the availability level of a disk system is the fact that the failure of the server terminates access to the disk. Although you might be tempted to compare availability levels of different disk systems without considering the availability level of the file server, by including the server you obtain a more realistic real-life comparison.

Figure 6.4b illustrates the dataflow when a file server has dual controllers and dual disks installed, a configuration commonly referred to as a fully mirrored disk subsystem.

A schematic representation, from the perspective of availability, for the mirrored disk drives and dual controllers is shown in Figure 6.5. Note that the file server can be considered to be placed in series with two pairs of parallel arranged devices: the controller and disk drive. Thus, if the file server fails, access to either drive is blocked, which represents reality.

Because we need availability levels of the file server, controller, and disk to compare single and mirrored disk systems, let us make some assumptions. Let us assume the file server is expected to fail once every three years and will require replacement via Express Mail, UPS, or another service within a 48-hour notification period. Thus, the availability of the file server becomes:

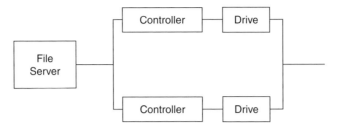

Figure 6.5   A Schematic Representation of a Fully Mirrored Disk Subsystem from the Perspective of Its Availability

---

$$A\% = \frac{8760 * 3}{8760 * 3 + 48} * 100 = 99.82$$

For the disk controller, let us assume it is very reliable and might fail once in a five-year period and its replacement will require 24 hours. Thus, the availability of the disk controller becomes:

$$A\% = \frac{8760 * 5}{8760 * 5 + 24} * 100 = 99.95$$

Although disk vendors commonly quote a MTBF of 100,000 hours or more, from practical experience my file server disks seem to need replacement on the average once every 2.5 years. When they fail, their replacement involves more than installing new hardware as the last backup must be moved onto the disk. Again, from this author's experience, the ordering of a replacement disk, its arrival and installation, accompanied by a full restore, can result in an average MTTR of 36 hours. Thus, I would compute the availability of disks I use as follows:

$$A\% = \frac{8760 * 2.5}{8760 * 2.5 + 36} * 100 = 99.84$$

Now that we have an availability level for each component, we can compare the availability level of the single and fully mirrored disk systems.

6.1.8.1   Single Disk System. The single disk system can be represented by three components in series. Hence, its availability becomes:

$$A_s\% = (0.9982) * (0.9995) * (0.9984) * 100 = 99.61$$

6.1.8.2   Mirrored Disk System. For the fully mirrored disk system, the availability of a controller and disk in series becomes:

$$A\% = (0.9995) * (0.9984) * 100 = 99.79$$

The fully mirrored system consists of two parallel paths of a controller and disk in series. Thus, the availability of each of those parallel paths becomes:

$$A\% = [(0.9979 + 0.9979) - (0.9979)(0.9979)] * 100 = 99.99956$$

When we consider the availability of the file server, the availability of the fully mirrored disk subsystem, to include the computer its components reside in, becomes:

$$A_s\% = (0.9982)(0.9999956) * 100 = 99.82$$

In comparing the availability level of a single disk subsystem versus fully redundant mirrored disks with dual controllers, note that availability has increased from 99.61 percent to 99.82 percent. By itself, this increase of 0.21 percent may not be meaningful, so let us attempt to consider it from an operational perspective. Over a three-year period, not considering a leap year in that period, there are 8760 * 3, or 26,280 hours. By increasing availability by 0.21 percent, we can expect to gain 26280×0.0021, or 55.2 hours of equipment life prior to a failure occurring that terminates access to data. Whether or not the additional operational time is worth the additional cost associated with installing a fully mirrored disk subsystem obviously depends on its additional cost as well as the actual MTBF and MTTR values you would use in your computations. However, the preceding information provides you with a methodology you can easily alter to analyze the equipment you may be considering.

6.2 Automating Availability Computations

As noted in the first section of this chapter, the computation of system availability can be reduced to a series of computations for devices in series and parallel. To facilitate the computations involved in determining serial and parallel component availability, the program AVAIL.BAS was developed. Table 6.2 lists the statements in that BASIC language program.

6.2.1 Program AVAIL.BAS

The program AVAIL.BAS can be used to compute the availability levels for components connected in series or in parallel. In fact, by selecting the program's BOTH option, the program will first compute the availability level of components connected in series and then compute the availability level of components connected in parallel.

To facilitate data entry, the program permits you to enter data in either of two ways. You can enter data concerning the availability level of individual components as a percent, or you can enter MTBF and MTTR values. For either data entry method, the program accepts a maximum of ten component availability level values, which should be more than sufficient for essentially all network configurations. In the event you require the computation of more than ten component availability level values, you can easily modify

Table 6.2 Program Listing of AVAIL.BAS

```
CLS :  REM PROGRAM AVAIL.BAS
PRINT "PROGRAM AVAIL.BAS TO COMPUTE AVAILABILITY LEVELS"
PRINT
PRINT "INDICATE COMPUTATIONS DESIRED "
PRINT "     S)ERIAL"
PRINT "     P)ARALLEL"
PRINT "     B)OTH SERIAL AND PARALLEL"
AGN: INPUT "ENTER THE TYPE OF COMPUTATIONS DESIRED      : ," COMP$
IF COMP$ <> "S" AND COMP$ <> "P" AND COMP$ <> "B" THEN GOTO AGN:
IF COMP$ = "B" THEN TRY$ = "A"
IF COMP$ = "B" THEN COMP$ = "S"
GOSUB DENTER
IF COMP$ = "S" THEN GOSUB SCOMPUTE
IF COMP$ = "P" THEN GOSUB PCOMPUTE
IF TRY$ = "A" THEN COMP$ = "P"
IF TRY$ = "A" THEN GOSUB DENTER
IF TRY$ = "A" THEN GOSUB PCOMPUTE
STOP
DENTER:
        IF COMP$ = "P" THEN GOTO PAR
        INPUT "ENTER NUMBER OF COMPONENTS IN SERIAL -MAX 10   : ," C
        IF COMP$ = "S" THEN GOTO SER
PAR:    INPUT "ENTER NUMBER OF COMPONENTS IN PARALLEL - MAX 10 : ," C
SER:    PRINT : PRINT "HOW DO YOU WANT TO ENTER DATA ?"
        PRINT "AS  P)ERCENT e.g., 12.5"
        PRINT "AS  M)TBF AND MTTR"
        INPUT "ENTER DATA ENTRY METHOD -P OR M              : ," D$
        IF D$ <> "P" AND D$ <> "M" THEN GOTO DENTER
        IF D$ = "M" GOTO MENTRY
FOR I = 1 TO C
        PRINT "FOR COMPONENT"; I;
        INPUT "ENTER PERCENT AVAILABILITY       : ," A(I)
        A(I) = A(I)/100
        NEXT I
        RETURN
```

181

Table 6.2   Program Listing of AVAIL.BAS   (continued)

```
MENTRY:
        FOR I = 1 TO C
        PRINT "FOR COMPONENT"; I;
        INPUT "ENTER MTBF AND MTTR VALUES        : ," MTBF(I), MTTR(I)
        A(I) = MTBF(I)/(MTBF(I) + MTTR(I))
        NEXT I
        RETURN
SCOMPUTE:
        IF COMP$ = "P" GOTO PCOMPUTE
        PROD = 1
        FOR I = 1 TO C
        PROD = PROD * A(I)
        NEXT I
        PRINT USING "AVAILABILITY OF ## "; C;
        PRINT USING " DEVICES IN SERIES = ##.#####"; PROD * 100
        RETURN
PCOMPUTE:
        PROD = 1
        FOR I = 1 TO C
        PROD(I) = (1 - A(I))
        PROD = PROD * PROD(I)
        NEXT I
        AVAIL = 1 - PROD
        PRINT USING "AVAILABILITY OF ##"; C;
        PRINT USING " DEVICES IN PARALLEL = ##.#####"; AVAIL * 100
        RETURN
END
```

AVAIL.BAS. To do so, you would simply add a DIM statement at the beginning of the program, which would contain a value for each array used in the program that reflects the highest number of components you intend to analyze. Because BASIC automatically dimensions all arrays to ten elements, no DIM statement was required in AVAIL.BAS.

6.2.2   Program Execution

Because the best way to illustrate the use of a computer program is to execute the program, let us do so. In doing so, let us assume our network

Table 6.3 Program AVAIL.BAS to Compute Availability Levels

```
INDICATE COMPUTATIONS DESIRED

    S)ERIAL

    P)ARALLEL

    B)OTH SERIAL AND PARALLEL

ENTER THE TYPE OF COMPUTATIONS DESIRED        : S

ENTER NUMBER OF COMPONENTS IN SERIAL -MAX 10  : 5

HOW DO YOU WANT TO ENTER DATA ?

AS  P)ERCENT e.g., 12.5

AS  M)TBF AND MTTR

ENTER DATA ENTRY METHOD -P OR M               : P

FOR COMPONENT 1 ENTER PERCENT AVAILABILITY    : 99.9

FOR COMPONENT 2 ENTER PERCENT AVAILABILITY    : 99.9

FOR COMPONENT 3 ENTER PERCENT AVAILABILITY    : 99.85

FOR COMPONENT 4 ENTER PERCENT AVAILABILITY    : 99.9

FOR COMPONENT 5 ENTER PERCENT AVAILABILITY    : 99.9

AVAILABILITY OF 5 DEVICES IN SERIES = 99.45120
```

configuration consists of two sets of five components connected in series, with each set routed parallel to the other set of components. Let us also assume that we have component availability expressed as a percent for one set of components and as MTBF and MTTR data for the second set of components.

Table 6.3 illustrates the execution of AVAIL.BAS to compute the availability of five serially connected components when availability for each component is available as a percent. In this example, it was assumed that four components each had an availability level of 99.9 percent, while one component had an availability level of 99.85 percent. As noted at the bottom of Table 6.3, the availability level of the five devices in series was computed as 99.45 percent.

Table 6.4 illustrates the execution of the program AVAIL.BAS to compute the availability of five serially connected components when you wish to use and have available MTBF and MTTR data. In this example, it was assumed that four network components each had an MTBF of 8000 hours and an MTTR of 24 hours. Concerning the latter, it was assumed that repair is accomplished by replacement and that your organization uses Express Mail, Federal Express, or a similar overnight service to deliver a new device that will be used to replace a failed device. Because your presumed experience is that the average time from failure notification to the replacement

Table 6.4 Program AVAIL.BAS to Compute Availability Levels

```
INDICATE COMPUTATIONS DESIRED

      S) ERIAL

      P) ARALLEL

      B) OTH SERIAL AND PARALLEL

ENTER THE TYPE OF COMPUTATIONS DESIRED           : S

ENTER NUMBER OF COMPONENTS IN SERIAL -MAX 10     : 5

HOW DO YOU WANT TO ENTER DATA ?

AS   P) ERCENT e.g., 12.5

AS   M) TBF AND MTTR

ENTER DATA ENTRY METHOD -P OR M                  : M

FOR COMPONENT 1 ENTER MTBF AND MTTR VALUES       : 8000,24

FOR COMPONENT 2 ENTER MTBF AND MTTR VALUES       : 8000,24

FOR COMPONENT 3 ENTER MTBF AND MTTR VALUES       : 720,2

FOR COMPONENT 4 ENTER MTBF AND MTTR VALUES       : 8000,48

FOR COMPONENT 5 ENTER MTBF AND MTTR VALUES       : 8000,48

AVAILABILITY OF 5 DEVICES IN SERIES = 97.94843
```

of the failed device is 24 hours, 24 hours was for each of four MTTR values. For one component an MTBF of 720 hours and an MTBR of two hours was used. This availability setting is representative of many digital transmission lines, because there are $24 * 30$, or 720 hours in a "typical" month, and one two-hour failure provides an approximate 99.7 percent level of line availability. As indicated at the bottom of Table 6.4, the availability level of this second set of five devices connected in series was computed to be 97.95 percent.

Now that you have determined the availability level of each set of serially connected devices, you can compute system availability by treating each resulting computed value as two devices in parallel. Thus, you can use AVAIL.BAS one more time to compute the system availability level of your two sets of five serially connected devices. To do so, you will execute AVAIL.BAS and select the parallel computation option.

Table 6.5 illustrates the execution of AVAIL.BAS in which the parallel option was selected. Because your previous executions of AVAIL.BAS resulted in two availability levels expressed as a percent, you will now select the percent data entry method for the parallel component computations. As indicated in Table 6.5, entering the results of the previous serial availability levels results in the availability level of 99.98874 percent. This represents the system availability level of the two sets of five serially

Table 6.5   Program AVAIL.BAS to Compute Availability Levels

```
INDICATE COMPUTATIONS DESIRED

     S)ERIAL

     P)ARALLEL

     B)OTH SERIAL AND PARALLEL

ENTER THE TYPE OF COMPUTATIONS DESIRED          : P

ENTER NUMBER OF COMPONENTS IN PARALLEL - MAX 10 : 2

HOW DO YOU WANT TO ENTER DATA ?

AS   P)ERCENT e.g., 12.5

AS   M)TBF AND MTTR

ENTER DATA ENTRY METHOD -P OR M                 : P

FOR COMPONENT 1 ENTER PERCENT AVAILABILITY      : 99.4512

FOR COMPONENT 2 ENTER PERCENT AVAILABILITY      : 97.94843

AVAILABILITY OF 2 DEVICES IN PARALLEL = 99.98874
```

connected components whose individual availability levels were previously specified. As indicated by this short example, you can use the program AVAIL.BAS to simplify the computations associated with different network structures because those structures can be considered to represent a mixture of devices connected in series or parallel.

6.2.3   The Availability Spreadsheet Template

To facilitate availability computations, a template named AVAIL was created using Microsoft's Excel spreadsheet. This template is illustrated in Figure 6.6 and can be obtained at the Web URL mentioned in this book as the file AVAIL in the directory EXCEL.

In examining the EXCEL AVAIL template shown in Figure 6.6, note that the template permits you to compute availability based on a percent or expressed in terms of MTBF and MTTR periods of time. Also note that the cell entries in the columns labeled Component Availability and MTBF and MTTR contain the values #na. In Microsoft's Excel, #na represents the condition "no value is available." In the spreadsheet template, #na was used to prevent division by zero conditions from occurring and would be replaced by actual availability data you would enter as you begin to use this template.

To illustrate the use of this Excel template, let us assume you want to determine the level of availability of two pairs of five components, with each sequence of components connected in series while the pairs provide a parallel routing topology. To facilitate providing a comparison to a previous computation presented in this chapter, let us assume that the level of availability of each component is 0.9. Then, you would first enter 0.9 in the

185

	A	B	C	D	E	F
1	**Availability Levels**					
2						
3	**Availability as a percent**					
4	**Number of Components**	**Component Availability**	**Serial Availability**	**Parallel Availability**		
5	1	#na	#na	N/A		
6	2	#na	#VALUE!	#VALUE!		
7	3	#na	#VALUE!	#VALUE!		
8	4	#na	#VALUE!	#VALUE!		
9	5	#na	#VALUE!	#VALUE!		
10	6	#na	#VALUE!	#VALUE!		
11	7	#na	#VALUE!	#VALUE!		
12	8	#na	#VALUE!	#VALUE!		
13	9	#na	#VALUE!	#VALUE!		
14	10	#na	#VALUE!	#VALUE!		
15						
16	**Availability in terms of MTBF & MTTR**					
17	**Number of Components**	**MTBF**	**MTTR**	**Individual Availability**	**Serial Availability**	**Parallel Availability**
18	1	#na	#na	#VALUE!	#VALUE!	#REF!
19	2	#na	#na	#VALUE!	#VALUE!	#REF!
20	3	#na	#na	#VALUE!	#VALUE!	#REF!
21	4	#na	#na	#VALUE!	#VALUE!	#REF!
22	5	#na	#na	#VALUE!	#VALUE!	#REF!
23	6	#na	#na	#VALUE!	#VALUE!	#REF!
24	7	#na	#na	#VALUE!	#VALUE!	#REF!
25	8	#na	#na	#VALUE!	#VALUE!	#REF!
26	9	#na	#na	#VALUE!	#VALUE!	#REF!
27	10	#na	#na	#VALUE!	#VALUE!	#VALUE!
28						
29						

Figure 6.6   Availability Levels: Base Template

component availability column for the first five components, obtaining a value of 0.59049 for the availability level of five components connected serially. This is illustrated in Figure 6.7, which indicates the entry of values for the five components and the resulting computations for serial availability and parallel availability. Note that for five components, the serial availability is indicated as 0.59049 in the column labeled Serial Availability at the top of the model being exercised. Because we previously specified that there are two pairs of five serially configured components in parallel, we would next reenter the previously computed serial availability values twice to compute the resulting level of availability for parallel components. This is illustrated in Figure 6.8.

In examining Figure 6.8, note that 0.59049 was entered as the component availability for components 1 and 2 as we want to compute parallel availability for two sequences of five components in series. Reading across the

	A	B	C	D	E	F
1	**Availability Levels**					
2						
3	Availability as a percent					
4	Number of Components	Component Availability	Serial Availability	Parallel Availability		
5	1	0.90000	0.90000	N/A		
6	2	0.90000	0.81000	0.99000		
7	3	0.90000	0.72900	0.99900		
8	4	0.90000	0.65610	0.99990		
9	5	0.90000	0.59049	0.99999		
10	6	#na	#VALUE!	#VALUE!		
11	7	#na	#VALUE!	#VALUE!		
12	8	#na	#VALUE!	#VALUE!		
13	9	#na	#VALUE!	#VALUE!		
14	10	#na	#VALUE!	#VALUE!		
15						
16	Availability in terms of MTBF & MTTR					
17	Number of Components	MTBF	MTTR	Individual Availability	Serial Availability	Parallel Availability
18	1	#na	#na	#VALUE!	#VALUE!	#REF!
19	2	#na	#na	#VALUE!	#VALUE!	#REF!
20	3	#na	#na	#VALUE!	#VALUE!	#REF!
21	4	#na	#na	#VALUE!	#VALUE!	#REF!
22	5	#na	#na	#VALUE!	#VALUE!	#REF!
23	6	#na	#na	#VALUE!	#VALUE!	#REF!
24	7	#na	#na	#VALUE!	#VALUE!	#REF!
25	8	#na	#na	#VALUE!	#VALUE!	#REF!
26	9	#na	#na	#VALUE!	#VALUE!	#REF!
27	10	#na	#na	#VALUE!	#VALUE!	#VALUE!
28						

Figure 6.7   Availability Levels: Entry of Values and Resulting Computations

Component 2 row to the column labeled Parallel Availability, you will note the value 0.83230. This indicates that two pairs of five components routed in series with individual component availability levels of 0.9 have a parallel level of availability of 83.23 percent. While this spreadsheet template may require the entry of a few sequences of data, it provides you with the ability to easily compute the availability levels of components connected in series and in parallel.

Enhancing LAN Performance, Fourth Edition

	A	B	C	D	E	F
1			**Availability Levels**			
2						
3	**Availability as a percent**					
4	**Number of Components**	**Component Availability**	**Serial Availability**	**Parallel Availability**		
5	1	0.59049	0.59049	N/A		
6	2	0.59049	0.34868	0.83230		
7	3	0.90000	0.31381	0.98323		
8	4	0.90000	0.28243	0.99832		
9	5	0.90000	0.25419	0.99983		
10	6	#na	#VALUE!	#VALUE!		
11	7	#na	#VALUE!	#VALUE!		
12	8	#na	#VALUE!	#VALUE!		
13	9	#na	#VALUE!	#VALUE!		
14	10	#na	#VALUE!	#VALUE!		
15						
16	**Availability in terms of MTBF & MTTR**					
17	**Number of Components**	**MTBF**	**MTTR**	**Individual Availability**	**Serial Availability**	**Parallel Availability**
18	1	#na	#na	#VALUE!	#VALUE!	#REF!
19	2	#na	#na	#VALUE!	#VALUE!	#REF!
20	3	#na	#na	#VALUE!	#VALUE!	#REF!
21	4	#na	#na	#VALUE!	#VALUE!	#REF!
22	5	#na	#na	#VALUE!	#VALUE!	#REF!
23	6	#na	#na	#VALUE!	#VALUE!	#REF!
24	7	#na	#na	#VALUE!	#VALUE!	#REF!
25	8	#na	#na	#VALUE!	#VALUE!	#REF!
26	9	#na	#na	#VALUE!	#VALUE!	#REF!
27	10	#na	#na	#VALUE!	#VALUE!	#VALUE!
28						

Figure 6.8 Availability Levels: Reentering Computed Serial Availability Values Twice

Chapter 7
Estimating Ethernet Network Performance

In Chapters 4 and 6, several models were developed and exercised to compute transmission delays, buffer memory requirements, and availability levels associated with the use of remote bridges and routers.

In Chapter 4, you did not have to consider the types of local area networks (LANs) to be connected other than noting that transmission delays and buffer memory requirement computations were based on several average frame sizes assumed to be flowing on a network. This enabled us to develop general models that can be tailored to a specific network environment by exercising a model with the appropriate frame size monitored or estimated to be carried by a network.

In Chapter 6, it was noted that the availability level of different network configurations are independent of the types of LANs to be connected. In this chapter we begin to focus attention on the performance requirements of specific types of LANs by examining the CSMA/CD access protocol. This will enable us to construct a model that reflects the transfer of frames on Ethernet, Fast Ethernet, and Gigabit Ethernet networks at different levels of network utilization. This, in turn, will provide us with a foundation for computing the maximum frame forwarding rate required to be supported by a bridge, router, or switch connected to an Ethernet network to ensure the device is fully capable of supporting the maximum level of Ethernet transmission. Similar to preceding chapters, both BASIC language programs and an Excel spreadsheet model will be developed and executed to facilitate exercising the mathematical models developed in this chapter.

7.1 CSMA/CD Network Performance

Ethernet is a Carrier Sense Multiple Access with Collision Detection (CSMA/CD) network. Each station on the network listens for a carrier and attempts to transmit data when it senses the absence of that signal. Unfortunately, two stations may attempt to simultaneously transmit data, resulting in the occurrence of a collision. Even when one station thinks there is no carrier, it is quite possible that a carrier signal is propagating down the transmission path. Thus, a station transmitting data when its sampling of the line indicates the absence of a carrier may also result in a collision.

Because of the random nature of collisions, Ethernet bus performance is not deterministic and performance characteristics and message transmission delays are not predictable. However, over a period of time, you can determine average and peak utilization, data elements that you can use to split one Ethernet LAN into two or more LANs via the use of bridges or other network devices to increase individual network performance.

7.1.1 Determining the Network Frame Rate

In this section we compute the frame rate on Ethernet, 100BASE-TX Fast Ethernet, and Gigabit Ethernet networks. Because the frame flow on 100BASE-TX is ten times that of the 10BASE-T Ethernet network operating at 10 Mbps, we will first focus our computations on the lower-speed network. Once we compute the frame rate on 10 Mbps Ethernet, we will simply multiply the result by 10 to determine the frame rate on Fast Ethernet.

Although we will perform a similar operation for Gigabit Ethernet by multiplying Ethernet results by 100, we will also note that this process is only applicable to certain types of frames. That is, Gigabit Ethernet requires carrier extension technology to insure the transmission of a minimum length frame, which was described earlier in this book and which will be reviewed in this chapter when we consider the Gigabit Ethernet frame rate.

Table 7.1   IEEE 802.3 (Ethernet) Frame Format

Preamble	Destination Address	Source Address	Length or Type	Data	Frame Check Sequence
8	6	6	2	$46 \le n \le 1500$	4

Frame Size (bytes)

Field	Minimum Size Frame	Maximum Size Frame
Preamble	8	8
Destination Address	6	6
Source Address	6	6
Length or Type	2	2
Data	46	1500
Frame Check Sequence	4	4
Total Size	72	1526

The top portion of Table 7.1 illustrates the IEEE 802.3 (Ethernet) frame format. In this illustration, the seven-byte preamble field and the one-byte start of frame delimiter field were combined into a common eight-byte preamble field for simplicity. In actuality, the preamble field used by Ethernet is an eight-byte sequence of alternating 1's and 0's, while the IEEE 802.3 frame format uses a seven-byte preamble field of alternating 1's and 0's. The start of frame delimiter one-byte field used in IEEE 802.3 frames follows a seven-byte preamble field and the sequence of alternating 1's and 0's, but ends with two set bits instead of the 1 and 0 used in the Ethernet preamble field. Because computations required to estimate Ethernet network and bridge and router performance are based on frame length and not frame composition, the use of a common eight-byte preamble field, while not technically correct from a frame composition basis, does not affect our computations. As indicated by the tabulation of frame field lengths in the lower portion of Table 7.1, the frame size can vary from a minimum of 72 to a maximum of 1526 bytes.

Under Ethernet and IEEE 802.3 standards, there is a dead time of 9.6 microseconds (μs) between frames. Using the frame size and dead time between frames, you can compute the maximum number of frames per second that can flow on an Ethernet network. For our example, let us assume we have a 10-Mbps LAN, such as a 10BASE-2, 10BASE-5, or 10BASE-T network. Here, the bit time then becomes $1/10^7$ or 100 nanoseconds (ns).

Now let us assume that all frames are at the maximum length of 1526 bytes. Then, the time per frame becomes:

$$9.6\,\mu sec + 1526\ bytes * \frac{8\ bits}{byte} * \frac{100\ nsec}{bit} = 1.23\ msec$$

Because one 1526-byte frame requires 1.23 ms, then in one second there can be 1/1.23 ms or approximately 812 maximum sized frames. Thus, the maximum transmission rate on an Ethernet network is 812 frames per second when information is transferred in 1500-byte units within a sequence of frames. One example of a situation in which data would be transferred in 1500-byte units is when a workstation downloads a file from a server or transfers a file to another workstation or to a server. When this type of data transfer occurs, the data field of a large number of sequential frames would be filled to their maximum size of 1500 bytes. If the last portion of the file being transferred is less than 1500 bytes, then the data field of the last frame used to transport the file would be less than 1500 bytes in length.

Now that the maximum number of frames that can traverse an Ethernet network when the data field is at its maximum size has been determined, let us compute the frame rate when the data field is at its minimum length.

Table 7.2 Ethernet Frame Processing Capability (Frames per Second)

Network Type	Average Frame Size (bytes)	Frames per Second	
		50% load	100% load
Ethernet	1526	406	812
	72	7440	14880
Fast Ethernet	1526	4060	8120
	72	74400	148800

When that situation occurs, the data field contains up to 46 characters of information, because PAD characters are required to fill the data field to a minimum length of 46 characters. This results in a minimum size Ethernet frame being 72 characters in length.

For a minimum frame length of 72 bytes, the time per frame is: 9.6 μs + 72 bytes * 8 bits/byte * 100 ms/bit, or $67.2 * 10^{-6}$ seconds. Thus, in one second there can be a maximum of $1/67.2 * 10^{-6}$, or 14,880 minimum-size 72-byte frames.

Table 7.2 summarizes the frame processing requirements for a 10-Mbps Ethernet network under 50 percent and 100 percent load conditions based upon minimum and maximum frame sizes. Note that those frame processing requirements define the frame examination (filtering) operating rate of a bridge, switch, or router port connected to an Ethernet network operating at 10 Mbps. That rate indicates the number of frames per second a device connected to a 10-Mbps Ethernet LAN must be capable of examining under heavy (50 percent load) and full (100 percent load) traffic conditions. Those frame processing requirements also define the maximum frame forwarding rate for a bridge, switch, or router connected to a single network, because if all frames were routed off the network, the forwarding rate would equal the filtering rate.

As an example of the potential utilization of information contained in Table 7.2, assume you were considering the acquisition of a two-port 10BASE-T bridge. That bridge must have a filtering capability at or above 29,780 72-byte frames per second to ensure it is capable of examining every frame that can flow on a 10BASE-T network connected to each port. Similarly, under a worst-case operational scenario, the bridge must be capable of forwarding 29,780 72-byte frames per second through the bridge to ensure that no frames requiring forwarding are lost.

7.1.1.1 Gigabit Ethernet Considerations. As discussed in Chapter 2, Gigabit Ethernet uses carrier extension technology to ensure that the minimum length frame is 512 bytes, not including its preamble and start of frame delimiter (SFD) fields. Figure 7.1 provides a review of the format of a Gigabit Ethernet frame, to include its carrier extension variable field.

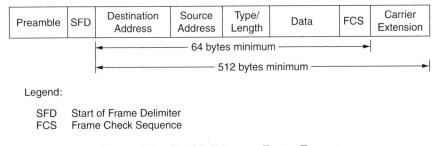

Legend:

SFD   Start of Frame Delimiter
FCS   Frame Check Sequence

Figure 7.1   Gigabit Ethernet Frame Format

Concerning the latter, the carrier extension field will vary in length from a maximum of 448 bytes when a minimum-length 64-byte frame is formed, to 0 bytes when a frame with an information field equal to or greater than 494 bytes in length is transmitted. Note that the actual frame length flowing on the media includes preamble and SFD fields, requiring a minimum length frame of 520 bytes for Gigabit Ethernet.

For a Gigabit Ethernet minimum length frame of 520 bytes, the time per frame computations use a dead time of 0.096 µs between frames and a bit duration of 1 ns. Thus, for a minimum frame length of 520 bytes, the time per frame becomes:

$$0.096 \text{ µs} + 520 \text{ bytes} * 8 \text{ bits/byte} * 1 \text{ ns/bit} = 4.256 \text{ µs}$$

Then, in one second, there can be a maximum of 1/4.256 µs or 234,962 minimum-size 520-byte frames. To compute the maximum number of maximum length frames that can flow on a Gigabit Ethernet network, we would use a frame length of 1526 bytes, to include the preamble and start of frame delimiter fields. Doing so, the time required to transmit a maximum-length Gigabit Ethernet frame becomes:

$$0.096 \text{ µs} + 1526 \text{ bytes} * 8 \text{ bits/byte} * 1 \text{ ns/bit} = 12.304 \text{ µs}$$

Thus, in one second, there can be a maximum of $1/12.304 \times 10^{-6}$ or 81,200 maximum-length frames per second. Table 7.3 summarizes the Gigabit Ethernet frame processing capability.

Table 7.3   Gigabit Ethernet Frame Processing Capability (Frames per Second)

Average Frame Size (bytes)	Frames per Second	
	50% load	100% load
520	117481	234962
1526	40600	81200

193

If you compare the entries in Table 7.2 and Table 7.3, you will note that Ethernet supports a data flow of 14,880 minimum-length frames per second, while Gigabit Ethernet's support for 520-byte minimum-length frames, which in effect could be 72 byte frames with a 448-byte carrier extension, is limited to 234,962 frames per second. This is 15.79 times the capability of a 10-Mbps Ethernet. If we compare Fast Ethernet's minimum-length frame per second rate of 14,800 to Gigabit Ethernet's rate of 234,962, the ratio decreases to 1.579:1. Thus, instead of obtaining a 100:1 and 10:1 ratio, we obtain 15.79:1 and 1.579:1 ratios, which indicates that for interactive query response applications the use of Gigabit Ethernet can be expected to provide less than a 60 percent improvement over Fast Ethernet instead of a ten-fold improvement!

7.1.1.2 Jumbo Frame Extension. Perhaps because of the previously developed Gigabit Ethernet computations, Alteon Networks introduced a Gigabit Ethernet extended frame transmission capability for its network adapters and Gigabit switch ports. This technology is being used under license or via original equipment manufacturer (OEM) agreements by other vendors and represents a technology that is gaining acceptance as "a mechanism to enhance the performance of Gigabit Ethernet." Whether or not jumbo frame technology provides a significant improvement in Gigabit performance can be determined by putting pen to paper to perform a series of computations.

Under Alteon Networks' jumbo frames technology, Ethernet frames are extended to permit an information field up to 9,000 bytes in length. This extension provides the ability to transport up to six times the maximum information transported by one standardized maximum-length frame while only requiring one set of overhead bytes for framing of the information field. To obtain an appreciation of the performance capability of jumbo frames, let us first compute the maximum number of maximum-length frames that can be transmitted on a Gigabit network.

The time required to transmit a jumbo Gigabit Ethernet frames is:

$$0.096 \text{ μs} + 9000 \text{ bytes} * 8 \text{ bits/byte} * 1 \text{ ns/bit} = 72.096 \text{ μs}$$

Then, in one second, $1/72.096 \times 10^{-6}$, or 13870 frames can be transmitted.

We can compare Gigabit Ethernet maximum-length frames to jumbo frames by examining their data transfer capability. Because 81,274 maximum-length Gigabit frames can be transmitted per second and each frame can transport 1500 bytes in its information field, we obtain a maximum data transfer capability of 81,274 frames/second * 1500 bytes/frame, or 121,911,000 bytes/second. At 8 bits per byte, we obtain a maximum data transfer of 121,911,000 bytes/second * 8 bits/byte, or 0.975288 Gbps. When jumbo frames are used, we can transmit 13,870 frames per second. Because the information field is now 9,000 bytes, this results in a maximum data transfer capability of 13,870 frames/second * 9000 bytes/frame * 8 bits/byte, or 0.99864 Gbps. Based upon the preceding, the use of jumbo frames can be expected to provide an increase in data transfer capability of approximately 23 Kbps (998.640 Mbps – 975.288 Mbps) for sustained file transfers and other applications that can fill jumbo frames. Whether or not the 23-Kbps increase in data transfer is worth a proprietary solution is left up to the reader to determine. However, it should be noted that the use of jumbo frames is only applicable to full-duplex Gigabit Ethernet where one end of the connection is a switch port that also supports jumbo frame technology. When we turn our attention to LAN switches later in this book, we will also discuss the use of jumbo frame support by switches. Now that we have an appreciation for Ethernet, Fast Ethernet, and Gigabit Ethernet frame processing requirements of bridges and routers, let us turn our attention to several BASIC programs to compute a series of bridge, switch, and router frame processing requirements.

7.1.2 Program EPERFORM.BAS

From the two sets of computations previously performed in this section, Ethernet bridge, switch, and router processing requirements and 50- and 100-percent network load conditions were determined. To facilitate performing additional computations, a general model of Ethernet network device processing requirements will be developed that will be incorporated into a BASIC language program. That program, which we will appropriately name EPERFORM.BAS, will be exercised by varying the Ethernet frame size from its minimum frame length of 72 bytes to its maximum frame length of 1526 bytes. Once again, it is important to note that the frame length will be varied from 72 bytes to 1526 bytes as we must include the preamble and start of frame delimiter fields, which collectively add 8 bytes to the MAC frame length. This addition is necessary because both fields are included with each frame that flows on the network and affects the maximum number of frames that can be transmitted per unit time. Similar to other BASIC language programs, EPERFORM.BAS can be located in the directory BASIC at the Web URL previously noted in this book.

To develop a general model that provides the maximum number of frames that can be transmitted on an Ethernet network, we can simply replace the specific frame length used in prior computations by the variable FLENGTH. Then, we obtain the maximum frame rate in frames per second (FPS) under a 100-percent network load by exercising the following equation:

$$\text{Ethernet 100\% load frame rate} = \frac{1}{9.6\ \mu\text{sec} + \text{FLENGTH} * 8\ \text{bits/byte} * 100\ \text{nsec/bit}}$$

Enhancing LAN Performance, Fourth Edition

Table 7.4   Program Listing of EPERFORM.BAS

```
REM PROGRAM EPERFORM.BAS

LPRINT "THIS PROGRAM COMPUTES ETHERNET BRIDGE FRAME PROCESSING
REQUIREMENTS"

LPRINT "        BASED UPON VARYING AVERAGE ETHERNET FRAME LENGTHS"

LPRINT

LPRINT "AVERAGE FRAME LENGTH        FRAME PROCESSING REQUIREMENT"

LPRINT "                           50% LOAD      100% LOAD"

LPRINT

FOR J = 1 TO 12 STEP 3

READ A, B, C

DATA 72,72,1,80,100,20,125,1500,25,1526,1526,1

FOR FLENGTH = A TO B STEP C

FPS = 1/(.0000096 + FLENGTH * 8 *.0000001)

LPRINT USING "    #####    "; FLENGTH;

LPRINT USING "                ######.##   ######.##"; FPS/2; FPS

NEXT FLENGTH

NEXT J

END
```

Table 7.4 lists the contents of the program EPERFORM.BAS developed to exercise the previously developed Ethernet frame rate model for frame lengths varying from 72 to 1526 bytes in length under 50- and 100-percent load conditions. In this program, the FOR J loop was used to define four sets of variables for use by the FOR FLENGTH loop, which performs the computations required to determine Ethernet frame processing requirements based on different frame lengths. The variable FPS computes the frame per second rate based on a bit duration of 100 ms (0.0000001), which represents the bit duration of a 10-Mbps Ethernet network. You can either lower the bit duration by a factor of 10 and change the interframe gap from 0.0000096 to 0.00000096 to compute a table of frame rates for Fast Ethernet, or multiply the results obtained from the execution of the unmodified program by 10. To facilitate determining the frame processing requirements of a Fast Ethernet network, the previously described modifications were made, with the modified program stored as the file FSTPRFM.BAS in the BASIC directory at the previously noted Web URL.

The first iteration of the J loop simply sets FLENGTH to compute the frame processing requirements for a frame length of 72 bytes. The second iteration of the J loop results in the FLENGTH loop computing the frame processing requirement for frame lengths from 80 to 100 bytes in increments of 20 bytes. The third iteration of the J loop results in the FLENGTH loop computing the frame processing requirements for frame lengths from 125 to 1500 bytes in increments of 25 bytes. Finally, the fourth iteration completes the computations for the maximum frame length of 1526 bytes.

Table 7.5 lists the results obtained from the execution of the program EPERFORM.BAS. Using monitoring equipment, such as a protocol analyzer, you can determine the average frame length transmitted on your network. Then you can use that data in conjunction with the frame processing requirements columns listed in Table 7.5 to determine the frame processing requirements for your specific network environment.

As indicated in the footnote in Table 7.5, by multiplying an entry in either frame processing column by 10 you can obtain the frame processing requirement for a 100BASE-TX Fast Ethernet network. As an alternative, you can execute the program FSTPRFM.EXE to generate a display similar to the one shown in Table 7.5 for the Fast Ethernet bridge frame processing requirements.

Due to improvements in bridge, switch, and router frame processing resulting from the incorporation of low-cost, high-performance microprocessors, such as the Intel Pentium series, today you should be able to obtain networking devices with a processing capability that exceeds the frame processing requirements for all Ethernet frame lengths. Thus, the data listed in Table 7.5 is primarily of value for deciding whether or not you should continue to use older bridges and routers as your network operation changes. If you are using or considering the installation of Fast Ethernet, the frame processing requirements listed in Table 7.5 increase by a factor of ten. Under such circumstances, the ability of some networking devices may not be capable of supporting a 100-percent load requirement. This is especially true if you anticipate adding a new adapter card and driver to support 100BASE-T operations in an existing PC-based bridge. Thus, you should carefully examine the frame processing capability of bridges, switches, and routers prior to using them for Fast Ethernet applications.

7.1.2.1 Program GBITPFRM.BAS. To provide you with the ability to determine the frame processing requirements of bridges, switches, and routers that have a Gigabit Ethernet interface, the program GBITPFRM.BAS was developed. Table 7.6 lists the statements in the program. Note that there are two key changes when comparing this program to the program EPERFORM.BAS listed in Table 7.4. First, for any frame length under 520 bytes, the frame length variable GLENGTH is set to 520 bytes for computing the FPS value. Second, the FPS computation uses a dead time of $9.6 * 10^{-8}$ sec and a bit duration of 100 ns associated with 10-Mbps Ethernet. Table 7.7 contains the results of the execution of the previously described program.

Table 7.5   Execution of Program EPERFORM.BAS

THIS PROGRAM COMPUTES ETHERNET BRIDGE FRAME PROCESSING REQUIREMENTS
        BASED UPON VARYING AVERAGE ETHERNET FRAME LENGTHS

AVERAGE FRAME LENGTH	FRAME PROCESSING REQUIREMENT	
	50% LOAD	100% LOAD
72	7440.48	14880.95
80	6793.48	13586.96
100	5580.36	11160.71
125	4562.04	9124.09
150	3858.02	7716.05
175	3342.25	6684.49
200	2948.11	5896.23
225	2637.13	5274.26
250	2385.50	4770.99
275	2177.70	4355.40
300	2003.21	4006.41
325	1854.60	3709.20
350	1726.52	3453.04
375	1614.99	3229.97
400	1516.99	3033.98
425	1430.21	2860.41
450	1352.81	2705.63
475	1283.37	2566.74
500	1220.70	2441.41
525	1163.87	2327.75
550	1112.10	2224.20
575	1064.74	2129.47
600	1021.24	2042.48
625	981.16	1962.32
650	944.11	1888.22
675	909.75	1819.51
700	877.81	1755.62
725	848.03	1696.07
750	820.21	1640.42
775	794.16	1588.31
800	769.70	1539.41
825	746.71	1493.43
850	725.06	1450.12

Table 7.5   Execution of Program EPERFORM.BAS   (continued)

AVERAGE FRAME LENGTH	FRAME PROCESSING REQUIREMENT	
	50% LOAD	100% LOAD
875	704.62	1409.24
900	685.31	1370.61
925	667.02	1334.04
950	649.69	1299.38
975	633.23	1266.46
1000	617.59	1235.18
1025	602.70	1205.40
1050	588.51	1177.02
1075	574.98	1149.95
1100	562.05	1124.10
1125	549.69	1099.38
1150	537.87	1075.73
1175	526.54	1053.07
1200	515.68	1031.35
1225	505.25	1010.51
1250	495.25	990.49
1275	485.63	971.25
1300	476.37	952.74
1325	467.46	934.93
1350	458.88	917.77
1375	450.61	901.23
1400	442.63	885.27
1425	434.93	869.87
1450	427.50	854.99
1475	420.31	840.62
1500	413.36	826.72
1526	406.37	812.74

Another area in which the data presented in Table 7.5 and Table 7.7 can be extremely valuable is in evaluating bridges, switches, and routers. Suppose you were evaluating two bridges manufactured by the well-known vendors "X" and "Y." Let us assume vendor X's sales literature lists an Ethernet frame processing capability of 15,000 frames per second without specifying the average frame length, while vendor Y's sales literature lists an Ethernet frame processing capability of 20,000 frames per second, also

Table 7.6   Program Listing of GBITPFRM.BAS

```
REM PROGRAM GBITPFRM.BAS

LPRINT "THIS PROGRAM COMPUTES GIGABIT ETHERNET BRIDGE FRAME
PROCESSING"

LPRINT "REQUIREMENTS BASED UPON VARYING AVERAGE ETHERNET FRAME
LENGTHS"

LPRINT

LPRINT "AVERAGE FRAME LENGTH        FRAME PROCESSING REQUIREMENT"

LPRINT "                              50% LOAD      100% LOAD"

LPRINT

FOR J = 1 TO 12 STEP 3

READ A, B, C

DATA 72,72,1,80,100,20,125,1500,25,1526,1526,1

FOR FLENGTH = A TO B STEP C

IF FLENGTH < 520 THEN GLENGTH = 520 ELSE GLENGTH = FLENGTH

FPS = 1/(9.599999999999999D-08 + GLENGTH * 8 *.000000001#)

LPRINT USING "   #####    "; FLENGTH;

LPRINT USING "              ######.##   ######.##"; FPS/2; FPS

NEXT FLENGTH

NEXT J

END
```

without specifying the average frame length. Which vendor product provides a higher level of capability?

Because each vendor's frame processing rate exceeds 14,880 frames per second, both have the ability to process a fully loaded Ethernet network. Thus, the higher processing capability of vendor Y is irrelevant and you should consider both products to be equivalent with respect to their frame processing capability.

Now let us assume that instead of working with legacy Ethernet, your organization is considering installing a Gigabit Ethernet backbone. Let us further assume that you are evaluating the capability of several switch vendors concerning their ability to support a Gigabit Ethernet uplink. Based on the evaluation of two switch vendor products, you noted that vendor X indicates a maximum frame processing capability of 200,000 frames per second while vendor Y, whose product costs 40 percent more, claims a frame processing capability of 500,000 frames per second. Without referring to Table 7.7, your first impression might be that you are obtaining a 150-percent performance increase from vendor Y for a 40-percent increase

Table 7.7   Execution Results of Program GBITPFRM.BAS

```
THIS PROGRAM COMPUTES GIGABIT ETHERNET BRIDGE FRAME PROCESSING
REQUIREMENTS BASED UPON VARYING AVERAGE ETHERNET FRAME LENGTHS
AVERAGE FRAME LENGTH          FRAME PROCESSING REQUIREMENT
                              50% LOAD      100% LOAD
```

AVERAGE FRAME LENGTH	50% LOAD	100% LOAD
72	117481.20	234962.41
80	117481.20	234962.41
100	117481.20	234962.41
125	117481.20	234962.41
150	117481.20	234962.41
175	117481.20	234962.41
200	117481.20	234962.41
225	117481.20	234962.41
250	117481.20	234962.41
275	117481.20	234962.41
300	117481.20	234962.41
325	117481.20	234962.41
350	117481.20	234962.41
375	117481.20	234962.41
400	117481.20	234962.41
425	117481.20	234962.41
450	117481.20	234962.41
475	117481.20	234962.41
500	117481.20	234962.41
525	116387.34	232774.67
550	111209.96	222419.92
575	106473.59	212947.19
600	102124.18	204248.36
625	98116.17	196232.34
650	94410.88	188821.75
675	90975.26	181950.52
700	87780.90	175561.80
725	84803.26	169606.52
750	82021.00	164042.00
775	79415.50	158831.00
800	76970.45	153940.89
825	74671.45	149342.89
850	72505.80	145011.59

Table 7.7   Execution Results of Program GBITPFRM.BAS   (continued)

AVERAGE FRAME LENGTH	FRAME PROCESSING REQUIREMENT	
	50% LOAD	100% LOAD
875	70462.23	140924.47
900	68530.70	137061.41
925	66702.24	133404.48
950	64968.82	129937.63
975	63323.20	126646.41
1000	61758.89	123517.79
1025	60270.01	120540.02
1050	58851.22	117702.45
1075	57497.70	114995.40
1100	56205.04	112410.07
1125	54969.22	109938.44
1150	53786.57	107573.15
1175	52653.75	105307.50
1200	51567.66	103135.31
1225	50525.46	101050.93
1250	49524.56	99049.13
1275	48562.55	97125.09
1300	47637.20	95274.39
1325	46746.45	93492.90
1350	45888.40	91776.80
1375	45061.29	90122.57
1400	44263.46	88526.91
1425	43493.39	86986.78
1450	42749.66	85499.31
1475	42030.93	84061.87
1500	41335.98	82671.96
1526	40637.19	81274.38

in cost. However, upon examining the frame rate obtainable on a Gigabit Ethernet network, you now realize it is limited to a maximum of 234,962 frames per second. Thus, the achievable performance difference between the two products is actually 17.48 percent, whereas the cost difference is 40 percent. This means that vendor Y's product is not the bargain it appears to be!

7.1.3   The Actual Ethernet Operating Rate

Now that the maximum number of frames that can be carried on 10-Mbps, 100-Mbps, and 1-Gbps Ethernet LANs has been determined, that information can be used to determine the utilization of the LAN. To do so we must recognize that the actual number of bits that can be carried on an Ethernet LAN will always be less than its operating rate due to the dead time between frames. For example, to compute the actual number of bits transmitted in one second using the maximum-length frame, you must subtract the number of bits that cannot be transmitted during the 812 slots of dead time (9.6 µs for a 10-Mbps Ethernet) from the LAN operating rate. Then, when 1526-byte frames are transmitted, the actual maximum Ethernet network data transfer operating rate becomes:

$$10 \text{ Mbps} - \frac{9.6 \text{ µsec}}{100 \text{ nsec}} * 812 = 9,922,048 \text{ bps}$$

Thus, for 100-percent utilization of a 10-Mbps Ethernet when a maximum frame size of 1526 bytes is used, 9.922 Mbps must be transmitted in one second. For a Fast Ethernet LAN, idle characters are transmitted between frames, which in effect results in a dead time between frames. That dead time is one tenth that of a 10-Mbps Ethernet, or 0.96 µs, while the bit duration is reduced to 10 ns. Thus, the actual maximum 100-Mbps Fast Ethernet data transfer operating rate when 1526-byte frames are transmitted becomes:

$$100 \text{ Mbps} - \frac{.96 \text{ µsec}}{10 \text{ ns}} * 8127 = 99,220,480 \text{ bps}$$

We can perform a similar computation for Gigabit Ethernet, adjusting the dead time between frames, its bit duration, and the number of frames transportable per second as follows for maximum length frames:

$$1000 \text{ Mbps} - \frac{0.096 \text{ µsec}}{1 \text{ ns}} * 81275 = 992,197,600 \text{ bps}$$

Because many inexpensive test devices are capable of counting frames, bits, or both frames and bits, using such equipment with knowledge of the maximum achievable data transfer rate on the network provides us with the ability to compute its utilization. In addition, you may be able to defer the purchase of a more expensive LAN performance analyzer, which, due to the prices of such equipment, may result in considerable savings.

7.1.4   Network Utilization

To illustrate the computations required to determine the level of Ethernet network utilization, let us assume that the monitoring of an Ethernet LAN indicates that during 10 minutes of monitoring, a total of 280,000 frames with an average data field length of 100 bytes were counted. The average frame length, including 100 data bytes, would be 126 bytes due to the 26 overhead bytes required to transport each frame. Then the average number of frames per second would be computed as follows:

$$\frac{280,000 \text{ frames}/10 \text{ minutes}}{\dfrac{60 \text{ sec}}{\text{minute}} * 10 \text{ minutes}} = 466.67 \text{ frames per second}$$

The number of bits flowing on the network is computed by multiplying the frame size by 8 bits/byte and then multiplying the result by the frame size. Thus, 126 bytes/frame * 8 bits/byte * 466.67 frames/second is 470,403 bits. Then, the utilization in percent would be 470,403/9,922,048 * 100, or 4.74.

Based on readily available performance statistics, a 100-node Ethernet can normally be expected to have an average utilization under 2 percent, with worst second, minute, and hour percentages of 40, 15 to 20, and 3 to 5, respectively. Similar utilization levels may not be applicable to 100-Mbps Fast Ethernet networks because such networks operate at ten times the rate of 10BASE-T LANs. This means that they can support a significant increase in traffic prior to reaching a higher level of utilization.

These preceding performance statistics represent the activity on a typical Ethernet network in that, at any particular time, many network users are performing local processing, such as composing a memorandum or an electronic message. Other network users may be reading a manual, talking on the telephone, or performing an activity completely unrelated to network usage. Thus, only a few people are actually transmitting or receiving information using the network. Concerning those people, one network user may be transmitting a short electronic mail message of a few hundred characters while another network user might be downloading a file from the server or accessing a server facility. Thus, a typical 2-percent level of network utilization on a 10-Mbps Ethernet network equates to a data transfer of 9,922,048 * 0.02, or approximately 198 Kbps. At this data transfer rate, many people can be sending electronic messages, interacting with the file server, and performing file transfer operations.

On a Fast Ethernet network, a 2-percent level of network utilization equates to a data transfer rate ten times that of a 10-Mbps Ethernet network, or approximately 1.98 Mbps. To put this number in perspective, let us assume that the typical length of an electronic mail message is 1000 characters, or 8000 bits. This means that at a 2-percent level of network utilization, a 100-Mbps Fast Ethernet network could support the transfer of almost 250 1000-character electronic mail messages per second!

When a number of network users initiate file transfers, you can expect a short peak level of utilization to approach or surpass 40 percent on a 10-Mbps

Ethernet network. Because a 640-Kbyte file transfer will require less than 0.07 seconds at 10 Mbps, many file transfers will rapidly be completed, which eliminates the potential for one file transfer overlapping another file transfer operation if two people initiate a file transfer just a second or two apart from one another. This explains why the worst minute utilization of a 10-Mbps Ethernet network is typically reduced to a range between 15 and 20 percent in comparison to a worst second utilization of 40 percent. Because our previous computation is much better than the typical worst minute utilization, it would appear that the monitored LAN is not overloaded. However, an extension of monitoring of several hours of activity during peak periods should be considered to ensure that utilization peaks were not inadvertently missed.

When we consider the level of utilization on a Gigabit Ethernet backbone network, it is important to remember that all frames with a length below 520 bytes are extended to a length of 520 bytes via carrier extension technology. This means that the performance level of Gigabit Ethernet can be taxed by a large amount of query-response traffic flowing onto a backbone Gigabit Ethernet LAN. You can see this by noting from Table 7.7 that the maximum number of frames a Gigabit Ethernet can transport is limited to 234,962 per second for all frames less than or equal to 520 bytes in length. In comparison, a Fast Ethernet LAN can support the transmission of 148,800 72-byte frames per second. This means that it becomes theoretically possible for two Fast Ethernet LANs joined via a Gigabit Ethernet backbone to saturate the backbone, although the Gigabit network theoretically should be capable of supporting ten Fast Ethernet LANs. When we examine the use of LAN switches later in this book, we will also turn our attention to the use of Gigabit Ethernet as a backbone network.

7.1.5 *Information Transfer Rate*

Although knowledge concerning the average frame length and frame rate is important, by themselves they do not provide definitive information concerning the rate at which information can be transferred on a network. This is because a portion of an Ethernet frame represents overhead and does not carry actual data. Thus, to obtain a more realistic indication of the ability of an Ethernet network to transfer information, you must compute the information transfer rate in bits per second (bps). This calculation is performed by first subtracting 26 bytes from the frame length for frames with a data field of 46 or more bytes, as there are 26 overhead bytes in each frame. Next, you would multiply the frame rate by the adjusted frame length and then multiply the result by 8 to obtain the information transfer rate in bits per second.

Table 7.8 lists the statements contained in a program named EITR.BAS. This program was developed to compute the information transfer rate in

Enhancing LAN Performance, Fourth Edition

Table 7.8   Program Listing of EITR.BAS

```
CLS
REM PROGRAM EITR.BAS
PRINT "INFORMATION TRANSFER RATE VERSUS AVERAGE FRAME LENGTH"
PRINT
PRINT "AVERAGE FRAME    100% LOAD    INFORMATION TRANSFER"
PRINT " LENGTH          FRAMES/SEC    RATE IN BPS          "
FOR J = 1 TO 12 STEP 3
READ A, B, C
DATA 72,72,1,80,100,20,125,1500,125,1526,1526,1
FOR FLENGTH = A TO B STEP C
FPS = 1/(.0000096 + FLENGTH * 8 *.0000001)
PRINT USING "#####          ######"; FLENGTH; FPS;
PRINT USING "          ########"; FPS * (FLENGTH - 26) * 8
NEXT FLENGTH
NEXT J
END
```

bps based on 16 average frame lengths and their corresponding frame transfer rates. Readers will note that the program EITR.BAS represents a simple modification to the previously developed program EPERFORM.BAS. Similar to the method noted for modifying the program EPERFORM.BAS for computing Fast Ethernet statistics, you can modify the program listing contained in Table 7.8. That is, you would change the computation for the variable FPS (frames per second) by modifying the interframe gap time and bit duration as indicated earlier in this chapter when the coding for the program EPERFORM.BAS was described. The previously described changes are included on the file FEITR.BAS, located in the BASIC directory at the noted Web URL, while the executable version of that file is named FEITR.EXE in that directory.

The results of the execution of EITR.BAS are listed in Table 7.9. To obtain the frames per second and information transfer rate for Fast Ethernet, you can multiply the entries in the second and third columns of Table 7.9 by 10 or execute the program FEITR.

In examining the data contained in Table 7.9, let us focus attention on the information transfer rate in the third column. Note that at an average frame length of 72 bytes, the information transfer rate is approximately 5.48 Mbps, or slightly more than half the Ethernet 10-Mbps operating rate. At an average frame length of 1526 bytes in which all frames are the maximum

206

Table 7.9   Information Transfer Rate versus Average Frame Length

Average Frame Length	100% Load Frames/Sec	Information Transfer Rate (bps)
72	14881	5476191
80	13587	5869565
100	11161	6607143
125	9124	7226278
250	4771	8549618
375	3230	9018088
500	2441	9257812
625	1962	9403454
750	1640	9501312
875	1409	9571590
1000	1235	9624506
1125	1099	9665787
1250	990	9698891
1375	901	9726027
1500	827	9748677
1526	813	9752926

length, the information transfer rate increases to approximately 9.75 Mbps. This explains why a large 10-Mbps Ethernet network can safely handle many simultaneous file transfer operations without degradation. A file transfer increases the average frame length, which increases the ability of an Ethernet network to transport information.

To illustrate how the information transfer rate depends on the average frame length, the results obtained from the execution of EITR.BAS were plotted as a line graph in Figure 7.2. In examining the entries on the y-axis of Figure 7.2, note that they range up to 10 Mbps, representing the information transfer rate on a 10-Mbps Ethernet network. Because Figure 7.2 is based on the plot of column 3 versus column 1 from Table 7.9, you can simply multiply the y-axis values by 10 to obtain a plot of the frame length versus the information transfer rate for 100-Mbps Fast Ethernet.

7.1.5.1 Gigabit Ethernet Considerations. One of the more interesting aspects of networking is its resemblance, on occasion, to a magician, with a comparison between products many times appearing as an illusion when you probe deeper. We can vividly note one illusion by comparing the information transfer rate of Gigabit Ethernet to Fast Ethernet and conventional or legacy 10-Mbps Ethernet.

As previously noted, Gigabit frames less than 512 bytes in length, not including the preamble and start of frame delimiter fields, are extended to a

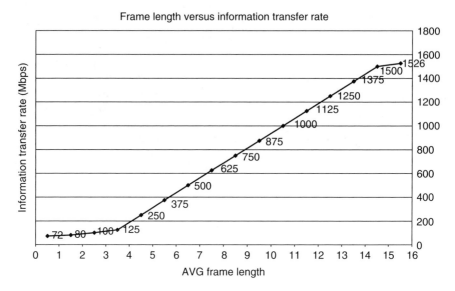

Figure 7.2   Frame Length versus Information Transfer Rate

length of 512 bytes through carrier extension technology. Thus, the actual information transfer capacity of a Gigabit frame depends on its length.

Table 7.10 contains the program listing of GITR.BAS, which was developed to compute the information transfer rate of Gigabit Ethernet based on a range of frame lengths. Note that when the frame length is less than 500, that value plus 8 is subtracted from 512 to determine the number of carrier extensions. Because we are working with frames that include the preamble and start of frame delimiter fields, an additional 8 bytes is subtracted to determine the number of carrier extensions. Next, the LPRINT statement subtracts the number of carrier extensions plus 26 overhead Ethernet bytes from the fixed Gigabit frame length of 520 bytes for all frames less than or equal to 520 and multiplies that amount by 8 to compute the number of information transporting bits in a frame. Multiplying that number by the variable FPS results in the information transfer rate for all frames up to 520 bytes in length. When frames exceed 520 bytes in length, the second series of LPRINT statements is invoked. This results in the frame length being decremented by the 26 overhead bytes in order to compute the information transfer rate. Table 7.11 illustrates the results obtained from the execution of the program GITR.BAS.

In examining the entries in Table 7.11, note that the information transfer rate of Gigabit Ethernet is only approximately 20 times that of 10-Mbps Ethernet for minimal-length frames. Because Fast Ethernet has ten times the information transfer rate of legacy Ethernet, this also means that Gigabit

Table 7.10   Program Listing of GITR.BAS

```
REM PROGRAM GITR.BAS

LPRINT "THIS PROGRAM COMPUTES GIGABIT ETHERNET INFORMATION TRANSFER
RATE"

LPRINT

LPRINT

LPRINT "AVERAGE FRAME        100% LOAD          INFORMATION TRANSFER"

LPRINT "  LENGTH             FRAMES/SEC          RATE IN BPS"

LPRINT

FOR J = 1 TO 12 STEP 3

READ A, B, C

DATA 72,72,1,80,100,20,125,1500,25,1526,1526,1

FOR FLENGTH = A TO B STEP C

IF FLENGTH < 520 THEN GLENGTH = 520 ELSE GLENGTH = FLENGTH

FPS = 1/(9.599999999999999D-08 + GLENGTH * 8 *.000000001#)

IF FLENGTH > 520 GOTO SKIP

CARRIEREXT = 512 - (FLENGTH + 8)

LPRINT USING "   #####           ########## "; FLENGTH; FPS;

LPRINT USING "               ########## "; FPS * (520 - (CARRIEREXT
+ 26)) * 8

GOTO SKIP1

SKIP: LPRINT USING "   #####           ########  "; FLENGTH; FPS;

LPRINT USING "               ########## "; FPS * (FLENGTH - 26) * 8

SKIP1:

NEXT FLENGTH

NEXT J

END
```

Ethernet only provides approximately twice the information transfer capability of Fast Ethernet when the average frame length is relatively small. Because many people might assume that Gigabit Ethernet always provides a ten-fold increase in information transfer in comparison to Fast Ethernet, this is a relatively good example of an illusion of networking!

In our examination of the overhead associated with the composition of Ethernet frames in Chapter 2, we noted that relatively short frames have a relatively large overhead, owing to the necessity to use pad characters to fill a data field to a minimum of 46 characters. At that time, we noted that by composing a client screen to accept several items of information rather than perform separate queries, we could enhance the efficiency of

Table 7.11   Execution Results of Program GITR.BAS

THIS PROGRAM COMPUTES GIGABIT ETHERNET INFORMATION TRANSFER RATE

AVERAGE FRAME LENGTH	100% LOAD FRAMES/SEC	INFORMATION TRANSFER RATE IN BPS
72	234962	116541352
80	234962	131578944
100	234962	169172928
125	234962	216165408
150	234962	263157888
175	234962	310150368
200	234962	357142848
225	234962	404135328
250	234962	451127808
275	234962	498120288
300	234962	545112768
325	234962	592105280
350	234962	639097728
375	234962	686090240
400	234962	733082688
425	234962	780075200
450	234962	827067648
475	234962	874060160
500	234962	921052608
525	232775	929236480
550	222420	932384320
575	212947	935264064
600	204248	937908480
625	196232	940345408
650	188822	942598144
675	181951	944687104
700	175562	946629184
725	169607	948439616
750	164042	950131264
775	158831	951715328
800	153941	953201984
825	149343	954599744
850	145012	955916416

Table 7.11   Execution Results of Program GITR.BAS   (continued)

AVERAGE FRAME LENGTH	100% LOAD FRAMES/SEC	INFORMATION TRANSFER RATE IN BPS
875	140924	957158976
900	137061	958333376
925	133404	959445056
950	129938	960499008
975	126646	961499520
1000	123518	962450624
1025	120540	963355776
1050	117702	964218432
1075	114995	965041408
1100	112410	965827328
1125	109938	966578752
1150	107573	967297728
1175	105308	967986560
1200	103135	968646848
1225	101051	969280512
1250	99049	969889024
1275	97125	970473920
1300	95274	971036608
1325	93493	971578176
1350	91777	972099840
1375	90123	972602752
1400	88527	973087808
1425	86987	973556032
1450	85499	974008192
1475	84062	974445184
1500	82672	974867776
1526	81274	975292608

Ethernet frames, as they would transport larger data fields. At that time we did not notice an optimum data field size other than the fact that a minimum data field of 1500 characters is the most efficient.

In examining Figure 7.2, note that for a frame length between 375 and 625 characters, including frame overhead characters, you can achieve an information transfer rate between 9 and 9.5 Mbps. A similar graph is applicable for Fast Ethernet, with the y-axis increased in value by a factor of 10. Thus, for both Ethernet and Fast Ethernet, you can achieve a very high level of information transfer when frames are between 375 and 625 characters in length. This indicates that by attempting to keep your client queries to that range, you can significantly increase the network information transfer rate to over 90 percent of that obtainable by a maximum-length frame. Thus, a frame length between 375 and 625 characters would be an appropriate range to make programmers developing client/server applications aware of as a design goal to increase the transmission efficiency of client/server applications.

Because Gigabit Ethernet primarily represents a backbone network technology, your hard efforts involved in developing client queries that flow in frames between 375 and 625 characters in length can cause a degree of harm if data is uplinked onto a Gigabit network. This is because you will note from Table 7.11 that the information transfer rate of Gigabit Ethernet begins to exceed 900 Mbps only when the frame length exceeds 500 bytes. Thus, the development of client/server applications may require you to investigate both the efficiency of frames on the network that clients use as well as a backbone network that may be used to connect clients to enterprise servers.

7.2 Using Bridges to Adjust the Network

One of the most valuable indicators of poor network response time, other than user complaints, is a high level of utilization. When Ethernet utilization climbs above 50 to 60 percent for long periods of time, either a large number of file transfers are hogging the network or network traffic has grown to the point where you may wish to modify the LAN to increase its performance. One of the most common methods used to improve LAN performance is to split the network into smaller segments through the use of one or more bridges.

Figure 7.3 illustrates the potential use of a local bridge to split an Ethernet into two smaller segments, thereby reducing the traffic on each of the resulting subnets. The maximum number of devices placed on each subnet depends on the traffic generated by each device, with a higher level of device traffic resulting in a lower limit on the number of devices per segment prior to network performance becoming unacceptable. By using a LAN protocol analyzer, you can obtain an accurate measurement of traffic per device, which can assist you in determining both when and where to subdivide the LAN. However, once a decision is made to employ the use of one or more local bridges, you should estimate their performance requirements to ensure the equipment you acquire does not become a bottleneck. To do so, you should ensure that the filtering and forwarding rate of a bridge under consideration at a minimum exceeds the frame processing rate associated with the average frame length monitored or estimated to be carried on your linked networks. As previously discussed in this

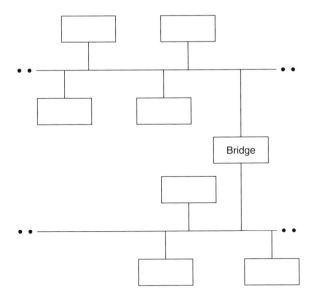

Figure 7.3   Using a Bridge to Improve Ethernet LAN Performance

chapter, most modern Ethernet bridges fabricated using high-performance Intel Pentium microprocessors or similar hardware will provide a level of frame processing that provides the ability to filter and forward frames under 100-percent loading without becoming a bottleneck. However, if you are using or considering the use of 100-Mbps Fast Ethernet or Gigabit Ethernet, you should carefully check the filtering and forwarding rates of bridges against the 100-percent frame load that a Fast Ethernet or Gigabit Ethernet network can provide. With a load rate ten times that of 10-Mbps Ethernet, many bridges are only capable of supporting a percentage of the maximum frame rate of a Fast Ethernet network. Similarly, some modern bridges and many of the latest network switches may not be capable of supporting the maximum Gigabit frame load. This situation also holds true for some servers that use the 32-bit Peripheral Component Interface (PCI) bus, which is severely taxed to achieve a frame transfer rate approaching the maximum Gigabit Ethernet frame transfer rate.

7.2.1   *Predicting Throughput*

Until now, it was assumed that the operating rate of each LAN linked by a bridge is the same. However, in many organizations, this may not be true due to the implementation of LANs at different times using different technology. Thus, the accounting department could be using a 10-Mbps Ethernet 10BASE-T LAN, while the personnel department might be using a Fast Ethernet CSMA/CD network operating at 100 Mbps.

Figure 7.4   Linking LANs with Different Operating Rates

7.2.2   Linked LANs

Suppose you wanted to interconnect the two LANs via the use of a local bridge. To predict throughput between LANs, let us use the network configuration illustrated in Figure 7.4. Here, the operating rate of LAN A is assumed to be R_1 bps, while the operating rate of LAN B is assumed to be R_2 bps.

In one second, R_1 bits can be transferred on LAN A and R_2 bits can be transferred on LAN B. Similarly, it takes $1/R_1$ seconds to transfer one bit on LAN A and $1/R_2$ seconds to transfer one bit on LAN B. Thus, the time, $1/R_T$, to transfer one bit across the bridge from LAN A to LAN B, ignoring the transfer time at the bridge, is given by:

$$\frac{1}{R_T} = \frac{1}{R_1} + \frac{1}{R_2}$$

or

$$R_T = \frac{1}{\dfrac{1}{R_1} + \dfrac{1}{R_2}}$$

Previously, we computed that a 10-Mbps Ethernet would support a maximum transfer of 812 maximum-sized frames per second. If we assume that the second LAN operating at 100 Mbps is a Fast Ethernet network, we would compute its transfer rate to be approximately 8130 maximum-sized frames per second. Thus, the throughput in frames per second would become:

$$R_T = \frac{1}{\dfrac{1}{812} + \dfrac{1}{8130}} = 738 \text{ frames per second}$$

It should be noted that the preceding computation represents a best-case scenario in which it is assumed that one station has full access to the bandwidth of each network as well as the resources of the bridge. Unfortunately, this is usually the exception rather than the rule, unless some inter-LAN activity is performed at 3 a.m.! Thus, you will want to adjust this frame transfer rate and the key question becomes how to do so. Fortunately, there are a number of low-cost LAN monitoring software products, such as Triticom Corporation's EtherVision and TokenVision software programs and WildPackets Etherpeek. Using such products, you can determine the average number of stations active on a network.

Suppose there were three users on LAN A transmitting data at any given time and two users on LAN B. Then you would adjust the previous computations to reflect the fact that several users share the bandwidth of each linked network. To do so, the maximum transfer rate on LAN A would become 812/3, or about 271 frames per second, while the maximum transfer rate on LAN B would become 8130/2, or approximately 4065 frames per second. Then, the expected throughput, which considers the fact that the bandwidth on each network is shared, becomes:

$$R_T = \frac{1}{\frac{1}{271} + \frac{1}{4165}} = 354 \text{ frames per second}$$

7.2.3   Estimating Data Transfer Time

Knowing the transfer rate between LANs can help us answer many common questions as well as provide us with a mechanism for determining whether or not the location of application programs on different servers should be altered. For example, suppose a program was located on a server on LAN B which suddenly became popular for use by workstations on LAN A. If the program required 768 Kbytes of storage, we could estimate the minimum transfer time required to load that program and, depending on the results of our calculation, we might want to move the program onto a server on LAN A. For this example, the data transfer rate would be 738 frames/second * 1500 bytes/frame, or 1,107,000 bytes per second. Dividing the data to be transferred by the data transfer rate, we obtain:

$$\frac{768 \text{ K bytes} * 1024 \text{ bytes/K}}{1,107,000 \frac{\text{bytes}}{\text{second}}} = 0.71 \text{ seconds}$$

Similar to our prior notation concerning the computation of the frame rate between linked LANs, the above transfer time computation represents a best-case scenario. That is, it would take 0.71 seconds to transfer the 768-Kbyte file if no other users required the bandwidth of each LAN during the file transfer activity. However, as previously noted, it was assumed that the use of a software monitoring program indicated that three users were actively performing network-related activities on LAN A and two users were performing network-related activities on LAN B. Thus, a more realistic transfer time computation would use a frame rate of 369 frames per second. In modifying our computations, the transfer rate would be

369 frames/second * 1500 bytes/frame, or 553,500 bytes per second. By dividing the data to be transferred by the data transfer rate, we obtain:

$$\frac{768 \text{ K bytes} * 1024 \text{ bytes/K}}{553,500 \text{ bytes/second}} = 1.42 \text{ seconds}$$

Here, 1.42 seconds represents the average transfer time between networks, while the 0.71-second transfer time represents the optimum transfer time.

7.2.4   Considering Remote Connections

We can extend our analysis of Ethernet frames and the process by which we can estimate data transfer time by considering the frame rate supported by different wide area network (WAN) line speeds. For example, let us consider a pair of remote bridges or routers connected by a 9.6-Kbps line. The time per frame for a 72-byte frame at 9.6 Kbps is:

$9.6 * 10^{-6} + 72 * 8 * 0.0001041$ seconds/bit = 0.0599712 seconds per frame.

Thus, in one second, the number of frames is 1/0.0599712, or 16.67 frames per second. Table 7.12 compares the frame-per-second rate supported by different link speeds for minimum- and maximum-size Ethernet frames. As expected, the frame transmission rate supported by a 10-Mbps link for minimum- and maximum-size frames is exactly the same as the frame processing requirements under 100 percent loading as previously indicated in Table 7.2.

In examining Table 7.12, readers should note that the entries in this table do not consider the effect of the overhead of a protocol used to transport frames between two networks. Thus, readers should decrease the frame-per-second rate by approximately 20 percent for all link speeds through 1.536 Mbps. The reason the 10-Mbps rate should not be adjusted is because it represents a local bridge connection that does not require the use of a WAN protocol to transport frames. Readers should also note that the link speed of 1.536 Mbps represents a T1 transmission facility that

Table 7.12   Link Speed versus Frame Rate

Link Speed	Frames Per Second	
	Minimum	Maximum
9.6 Kbps	16.67	.79
19.2 Kbps	33.38	1.58
56.0 Kbps	97.44	4.60
64.0 Kbps	111.17	5.25
1.536 Mbps	2815.31	136.34
10 Mbps	14880	812

operates at 1.544 Mbps. However, because the framing bits on a T1 circuit use 8 Kbps, the effective line speed available for the transmission of data is 1.536 Mbps.

Another note concerning the entries in Table 7.12 are their applicabiltiy to different types of Ethernet networks. Because Fast Ethernet frames vary in length from a minimum of 72 bytes to a maximum of 1526 bytes, the entries in the referenced table for link speeds up through 1.536 Mbps are also applicable to Fast Ethernet. Although Gigabit Ethernet requires a minimum frame length of 520 bytes to include the preamble and start of frame delimiter fields, when transferred via a WAN, carrier extension symbols are stripped from the frame. Thus, the frames-per-second rates for minimum- and maximum-length frames shown in Table 7.12 for WAN speeds up to 1.536 Mbps are also applicable for Gigabit Ethernet frames.

Once you determine the frame transfer rate supported by a remote connection, you can use a precise value based on knowledge of the average frame rate monitored or estimated to be carried by the network only if that rate falls between the frame rate range noted in Table 7.12. Otherwise, you would use the range of frame rates listed in Table 7.12 in your computations to obtain a range of transfer times. For example, assume you wish to link two LANs via the use of remote bridges, as illustrated in Figure 7.5a. If the DSUs operate at 56 Kbps, they are able to support a frame transmission rate between 4.6 and 97.44 frames per second prior to adjusting the rate downward by 20 percent to account for the WAN protocol overhead. If you monitored LAN A and determined that the average frame rate was 250, you could not use that value as the potential frame rate between LANs because it would exceed the transmission capacity of the circuit. Without prior knowledge obtained from monitoring the circuit, you would also use the range of frame rates listed in Table 7.12 and adjust them downward by 20 percent to account for the WAN protocol overhead. For either situation, you would then estimate the data transfer time between stations on one network from another by considering the operating rate of each network and the remote connection. Figure 7.5b illustrates the operating rate components for the network topology shown in Figure 7.5a.

To determine the frame transfer rate between remotely connected networks, you would then solve the following equation:

$$\frac{1}{R_T} = \frac{1}{R_1} + \frac{1}{R_2} + \frac{1}{R_3}$$

Solving for R_T, we obtain:

$$R_T = \frac{R_1 R_2 R_3}{R_2 R_3 + R_1 R_3 + R_2 R_3}$$

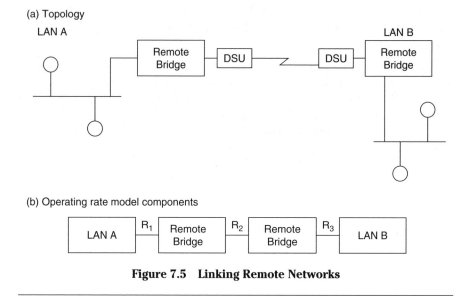

Figure 7.5   Linking Remote Networks

Using specific values for R_1, R_2, and R_3, you would determine R_T, which would provide the frame transfer rate between networks. Then, knowing the file size and average frame rate, you could compute the transfer time in the same manner as previously computed.

As indicated in this chapter, you can use your knowledge of the structure and operation of Ethernet LANs to compute a number of performance measurements. Some of those measurements provide a basis for selecting an appropriately performing bridge or router, while other calculations provide the ability to estimate the time required to load programs across a bridge connecting LANs operating at different data rates. These calculations also provide the tools necessary to adjust the configuration of LANs and recognize the need to move application programs to different servers to increase network performance.

7.2.4.1   The Excel Model LANTRUPT. To facilitate LAN throughput computations, an Excel model was developed that is stored on the file LANTRUPT located in the Excel directory at the Web URL indicated in this book and an example of the model is shown in Figure 7.6. In examining the LAN throughput predictor model shown in Figure 7.6, note that you can adjust LAN operating rates and the average number of network users on each network. Also note that you can enter specific frame rates for each LAN in the cells that currently contain the entry #na. Those two entries were used to prevent a division by zero computation and should be replaced by specific frame rates if you wish to determine an expected throughput based upon specific Ethernet frame rates determined from monitoring each network.

LAN THROUGHPUT PREDICTOR

	LAN A	LAN B
LAN operating rate in Mbps:	0	100
Average number of network users:	1	1

Ethernet LAN frame rates

	LAN A	LAN B
Minumum length frames:	14880	148800
Maximum length frames:	812	8120
Other	#na	#na

Throughput prediction: Expected Throughput (FPS)

Minimum length frames:	13527.27
Maximum length frames:	738.1818
Other	# VALUE!

Figure 7.6   LAN Throughput Predictor

Chapter 8
Estimating Token Ring Network Performance

Chapter 7 focused on Ethernet network performance and developed a mathematical model to determine the frame rate based on different frame lengths. The results of that model were then used to determine the information transfer capability of a 10-Mbps Ethernet network based on different frame sizes. As you might intuitively expect, the use of larger frames provided a higher information transfer capability because each Ethernet frame is separated from preceding and succeeding frames by a uniform time gap. Thus, longer frames were expected to be more efficient and this was determined to be true.

In this chapter, our attention will turn to Token Ring network performance in a similar manner to our method of examining Ethernet performance. That is, we will first develop a model that is representative of the flow of data on a Token Ring network. Then we will exercise the model both manually as well as through the use of a BASIC language program to determine the frame rate as a function of the number of stations on the network and the ring length as well as several other variables. In doing so, we will note that the performance models for CSMA/CD and Token Ring networks considerably differ due to the basic differences between each network access protocol.

In a CSMA/CD network, the transmission of a frame is read by all stations without one station's reading activity delaying another station's reading activity. In a Token Ring network, the opposite is true, because station n must process a token or frame prior to passing it onto station n+1 on the network. Thus, the Token Ring model developed in this chapter will considerably differ from the previously developed Ethernet model presented in Chapter 7. A second area of difference concerns the cabling structure of Ethernet and Token Ring networks. Most Ethernet bus-based networks use a fraction of the cabling used in the star-bus topology of a Token Ring network. Thus, propagation delay time plays a much more meaningful role in determining network performance and results in our inclusion of the speed at which tokens and frames traverse the cable in the Token Ring model we develop in this chapter.

8.1 Token Ring Traffic Modeling

In comparison to Ethernet, the modeling of a Token Ring network can be much more complex. This is because the frame rate depends on the number of nodes in a network, the token holding time per node, the type of wire used for cabling and ring length, and the type of adapter used as a ring interface unit.

The number of nodes and their cabling govern both token propagation time and holding time as a token flows around the ring. The type of adapter used governs the maximum frame rate supported. This rate can vary between vendors as well as within a vendor's product line. For example, Texas Instruments' original MAC code permitted a maximum transmission of 2200 64-Kbyte frames per second. New software from that vendor raised the frame rate to 3300, and a more recent release known as Turbo MAC 2.1 increased it to 4000 frames per second.

The type of cabling and ring length governs the propagation delay associated with the flow of tokens and frames around the ring. Although the data rate around a ring is consistent at either 4 Mbps or 16 Mbps, tokens and frames do not flow instantaneously around the ring and are delayed based upon the distance they must traverse and the type of cabling used. In addition, a slight delay is encountered at each node because the token must be examined to determine its status.

8.1.1 Model Development

In developing a model to determine Token Ring frame rates, let us assume there are N stations on the network. Then, on average, a token will travel N/2 stations until it is grabbed and converted into a frame. Similarly, a frame can be expected to travel N/2 stations until it reaches its destination and another N/2 stations until it returns to the origination station and is reconverted into a token.

As mentioned at the beginning of this chapter, the performance of a Token Ring network typically depends more on the total network cable length than an Ethernet network. Thus, in developing a model of Token Ring network performance, a mechanism is required to equate cable length to the propagation delay of electrons flowing on the cable. To do so, let us start with the well-known velocity of light.

8.1.2 Propagation Delay

In free space, the velocity of light is 186,000 miles per second. In twisted pair cable, the speed of electrons is approximately 62 percent of the velocity of light in free space. Thus, electrons will travel at approximately 186,000 * 0.62, or 115,320 miles per second. Because there are 5280 feet in a mile, this rate is equivalent to 608,889,600 feet per second, or approximately 609 feet per microsecond. Then, to traverse 1000 feet of cable would require $1000/609 * 10^6$, or approximately $1.64 * 10^{-6}$ seconds.

At a Token Ring operating rate of 4 Mbps, the bit duration is 1/4,000,000, or $2.5 * 10^{-7}$ seconds. At a network operating rate of 16 Mbps, the bit duration is 1/16,000,000, or $0.625 * 10^{-7}$ seconds. Because the time required for electrons to traverse 1000 feet of cable is $1.64 * 10^{-6}$ seconds, the cable propagation delay time per 100 feet of cable can be converted into a bit time delay to simplify computations. At a Token Ring operating rate of 4 Mbps, the bit time delay per 1000 feet of cable becomes $1.64 * 10^{-6}/2.5 * 10^{-7}$, or 6.56 bit times. When the Token Ring network operates at 16 Mbps, the bit time delay per 1000 feet of cable becomes $1.64 * 10^{-6}/.625 * 10^{-7}$, or 26.24 bit times.

8.1.3 4-Mbps Model

In developing a Token Ring performance model, let us commence the effort by assuming that the network operates at 4 Mbps. Once we develop this model and use it to perform a series of manual calculations, we will then construct a general model applicable to both 4- and 16-Mbps networks. That model will then be used as a basis for developing a BASIC language program that will be used to generate a comprehensive series of tables contained at the Web URL as well as two tables in this chapter whose entries we examine in detail. The tables contained at the Web URL can be used to facilitate determining the frame flow on a Token Ring network because they enable the frame flow computations to be supplemented by a table lookup process. The tables in this chapter can be considered to represent extracts from the comprehensive table and their use serves as a guide to the use of the comprehensive series of tables.

For the development of a 4-Mbps Token Ring performance model, let us start with the flow of a token as indicated by the following steps in the model development process.

1. Given a Token Ring network with N stations, a free token travels, on average, N/2 stations until it is grabbed and converted into a frame.
2. Each station adds a 2.5-bit time delay to examine the token. At a 4-Mbps ring operating rate, a bit time equals $2.5 * 10^{-7}$ seconds. Thus, each station induces a delay of $2.5 * 2.5 * 10^{-7}$, or $6.25 * 10^{-7}$ seconds.
3. The token consists of 3 bytes, or 24 bits. The time required for the token to be placed onto the ring is:

$$24 * 2.5 * 10^{-7} \text{ seconds/bit} = 60 * 10^{-7} \text{ seconds}$$

4. The time for the token to be placed onto the ring and flow around half the ring until it is grabbed is the sum of the times of step 2 and step 3. This time then becomes:

$$N/2 * 6.25 * 10^{-7} + 60 * 10^{-7}$$

5. Once a token is grabbed, it is converted into a frame. On average, the frame will travel $N/2$ stations to its destination. A frame containing 64 bytes of information consists of 85 bytes because 21 bytes of overhead, including starting and ending delimiters, source and destination addresses, and other control information must be included in the frame. Thus, the time required to place the frame on the ring becomes:

85 bytes $* 8$ bits/byte $* 2.5 * 10^{-7}$ seconds/bit $= 1.7 * 10^{-4}$ seconds

6. If the network contains N stations, the frame must traverse $N/2$ stations, on average, to reach its destination. Thus, the time required for the frame to be placed onto the ring and traverse half the ring becomes:

$$1.7 * 10^{-4} + N/2 * 6.25 * 10^{-7} \text{ seconds}$$

7. The total token and frame time from numbers 4 and 6 above is:

$$N/2 * 6.25 * 10^{-7} + 60 * 10^{-7} + N/2 * 6.25 * 10^{-7} + 1.7 * 10^{-4}$$

$$\text{or } N * 6.25 * 10^{-7} + 60 * 10^{-7} + 1.7 * 10^{-4} \text{ seconds}$$

8. Once the frame reaches its destination, it must traverse another $N/2$ stations, on average, to return to its originating station, which then removes it from the network. When this occurs, the origination station generates a new token onto the network and the previously described process is repeated. The time for the frame to again traverse half the network becomes:

$$N/2 * 6.25 * 10^{-7} \text{ seconds}$$

This time must be added to the time in step 7. Doing so, we obtain:

$$N * 9.375 * 10^{-7} + 60 * 10^{-7} + 1.7 * 10^{-4} \text{ seconds}$$

9. To consider the effect of propagation delay time as tokens and frames flow in the cable, we must consider the sum of the ring length and twice the sum of all lobe distances. Here, we must double the lobe distances because the token will flow to and from each workstation on the lobe. If we let C equal the number of thousands of feet of cable, we obtain the time in seconds to traverse the ring as:

$$N * 9.375 * 10^{-7} + 60 * 10^{-7} + 1.7 * 10^{-4} + 1.64 * 10^{-6} * C$$

which equals:

$$N * 9.375 * 10^{-7} + 1.76 * 10^{-4} + 1.64 * 10^{-6} * C$$

where:

N = number of stations

C = thousands of feet of cable

8.1.4 Exercising the Model

To illustrate the use of the previously developed Token Ring performance model, let us assume a Token Ring network of 50 stations has 8000 feet of cable. Then, the time for a token and frame to circulate the ring becomes:

$$50 * 9.375 * 10^{-7} + 1.76 * 10^{-4} + 1.64 * 10^{-6} * 8$$

$$= 468.75 * 10^{-7} + 1.76 * 10^{-4} + 13.12 * 10^{-6}$$

$$= 0.46875 * 10^{-4} + 1.76 * 10^{-4} + 0.1312 * 10^{-4}$$

$$= 2.36 * 10^{-4} \text{ seconds}$$

Then, in 1 second there will be, on average, $1/2.36 * 10^{-4}$, or 4237 64-byte information frames that can flow on a Token Ring network containing 50 stations and a total of 8000 feet of cable.

8.1.5 Network Modification

To illustrate the use of the previously developed model in determining the effect of cabling and network stations on the frame rate, let us now consider what happens when the network is reduced in size. Suppose the number of workstations is halved to 25 and the total cable distance reduced to 4000 feet. Then, with N = 25 and C = 4, the time for a token and frame to flow around the ring becomes:

$$25 * 9.375 * 10^{-7} + 1.76 * 10^{-4} + 1.64 * 10^{-6} * 4$$

$$= 0.234375 * 10^{-4} + 1.76 * 10^{-4} + 0.0656 * 10^{-4}$$

$$= 2.06 * 10^{-4} \text{ seconds}$$

Thus, in 1 second there will be, on average, $1/2.06 * 10^{-4}$, or 4854 64-byte information frames. As we would intuitively expect, as the number of stations and cable distance decrease, the transmission capacity of the ring increases.

8.1.6 Varying the Frame Size

Now let us examine the effect of transmitting larger information frames. Suppose we transmit 4000-byte information frames. Here, a total of 4021 bytes is required. Thus, the time required for the frame to be placed on the ring becomes:

$$4021 * 8 * 2.5 * 10^{-7}, \text{ or } 80.42 * 10^{-4} \text{ seconds}$$

Then, the total token and frame time becomes:

$$N * 9.375 * 10^{-7} + 60 * 10^{-7} + 80.42 * 10^{-4} + 1.64 * 10^{-6} * C$$

Again, let us assume the number of stations, N, is 50, while the cabling distance is 8000 feet. Thus, we obtain the token and frame revolution time as follows:

$$50 * 9.375 * 10^{-7} + 60 * 10^{-7} + 80.42 * 10^{-4} + 1.6 * 10^{-6} * 8$$

$$= 0.46875 * 10^{-4} + .06 * 10^{-4} + 80.42 * 10^{-4} + .1312 * 10^{-4}$$

$$= 81.08 * 10^{-4} \text{ seconds}$$

Then, in 1 second there will be $1/81.08 * 10^{-4}$ or 123.3 frames. Because each frame contains 4000 bytes of information, the effective operating rate becomes $123.3 * 4000 * 8$, or 3.946 Mbps for a 50-station Token Ring network with 8000 feet of cable using 4000 character information frames. In comparison, a similar Token Ring network using 64-byte information frames would have a frame rate of 4237 frames per second. However, this rate would be equivalent to an information transfer rate of $4237 * 64 * 8$, or 2.169 Mbps. Thus, larger frame sizes provide a more efficient data transportation capability.

The preceding computations, which represent the use of a simplified model of a 4-Mbps Token-Ring network, indicate an important concept. That is, the frame length, cabling distance, and number of network stations govern the maximum frame rate that can flow on a Token Ring network. This tells us that when a network becomes saturated due to heavy usage, you should consider breaking larger networks into two or more subnets interconnected by bridges to improve Token Ring network performance. The preceding is a simplified model due to the fact that the model does not include the effect of the flow of network management frames which, when they flow on the network, preclude the transfer of data. For example, every seven seconds, the active monitor transmits an Active Monitor Present frame for which all other stations respond with a Standby Monitor Present frame. Because the frame rate on a Token Ring network will range from over 100 frames per second when the frame length approaches the maximum size frame length on a 4-Mbps network to many thousands of frames per second when the minimum length frame is transmitted, the effect of the Active Monitor Present frames and responding Standby Monitor Present frame every seven seconds is negligible upon network performance. This is because those two frames are relatively short and would result in a maximum of 260 frames every seven seconds, during which approximately 15,000 or more similar length frames could be transported on the network. Thus, the use of a simplified model does not materially affect our model.

8.1.7 Adapter Card Considerations

One of the more interesting aspects of Token Ring frame rates is that the majority of adapter cards from different vendors that use the Texas Instruments chip set support a maximum frame rate of 4000 frames per second. This indicates that a further constraint on the number of nodes and cable length is the adapter cards used in a network. In 1991, Madge Systems introduced an adapter card capable of transmitting approximately 12 thousand 64-byte frames per second. Thus, using that firm's adapter card or other higher-performance adapter cards manufactured by other vendors can significantly improve the performance of a Token Ring network. However, the use of such "high-performance" adapter cards is irrelevant when a network grows in size in terms of the number of network stations and cable distance. In such situations, the capability of high-performance network adapter cards cannot be effectively used.

Now that we have developed and exercised a mathematical model to determine the frame rate on a 4-Mbps Token Ring network, we will use our prior effort to develop a general model for 4- and 16-Mbps networks. In doing so, let us use BASIC language variables so that we can exercise our model through its incorporation into a BASIC language program.

8.1.8 General Model Development

To denote the difference between 4- and 16-Mbps networks, let us use the array variable BITTIME(I). Then, we can assign the value 1/4,000,000 to BITTIME(1) to represent the bit time duration on a 4-Mbps Token Ring network and the value 1/16,000,000 to BITTIME(2) to represent the bit time duration on a 16-Mbps network.

Referring to our previous nine-step approach used in the development of a 4-Mbps Token Ring performance model, step 2 computed the station delay. Using the variable S.DELAY to represent the station delay, we obtain:

$$S.DELAY = 2.5 * BITTIME(I)$$

In step 3 we determined the time to place a token on the ring. Using the variable T.PLACEMENT to represent the token placement time, we obtain:

$$T.PLACEMENT = 24 * BITTIME(I)$$

Then, using the variable H.TRINGFLOW to represent the time for a token to be placed on the network and traverse half the ring (step 4 in our earlier model), we obtain:

$$H.TRINGFLOW = (N/2) * S.DELAY + T.PLACEMENT$$

Once a token is grabbed, it is converted into a frame. Because the time required to place the frame onto the ring depends on the length of the frame, let us use the array variable FRAMELENGTH(F) to denote different frame lengths. In actuality, let us assign different information field values to each FRAMELENGTH(F) value and add 21 bytes to represent the overhead per frame. Then, if we use the variable FRAMETIME to denote the time required to place a frame on the ring, we obtain:

$$FRAMETIME = (FRAMELENGTH(F) + 21) * 8 * BITTIME(I)$$

As noted in step 6 in our prior model, the frame must traverse N/2 stations, on average, to reach its destination. If we denote the variable H.FRAMEFLOW to represent the time required for the frame to be placed on the ring and flow N/2 stations down the ring, we obtain:

$$H.FRAMEFLOW = (N/2) * S.DELAY + FRAMETIME$$

If we use the variable C to denote the cable length (ring plus twice each lobe distance) in 1000-foot increments and the variable C.PROPTIME to denote the propagation delay time, we obtain:

$$C.PROPTIME = C * 1.64E{-06}$$

Then, to compute the frame rate using the variable FPS, we obtain:

$$FPS = 1/(TOTAL.TIME + C.PROPTIME)$$

8.1.9 Program TPERFORM.BAS

To facilitate the execution of our general Token Ring performance model, the program TPERFORM.BAS was developed. This program, whose statements are listed in Table 8.1, can be used to generate a series of tables that indicates the frame rate based upon the network operating rate, number of stations on the network, average frame length, and network cable length in 1000-foot increments. As previously noted, the frame length is specified in terms of the information field to which 21 bytes representing frame overhead are added.

In examining the program listing of TPERFORM.BAS, note that the FOR-NEXT loops that vary the number of stations, frame length, and cable length would result in 910 frame rate computations for each ring operating rate. Rather than place a large set of tables in this chapter, the results obtained from the execution of TPERFORM.BAS were placed in the BASIC directory at the previously noted Web URL. In addition, readers can modify the entries in the DATA statement to initialize a specific frame length more applicable to their network, or change the FOR-NEXT loop variable values for N and/or C to obtain information concerning the frame rate for a specific number of stations or cable length that is not in the table.

To provide readers with an example of the ease with which TPERFORM.BAS can be modified as well as data we can use to further discuss Token Ring performance, let us modify the program. By changing the FOR N loop

Table 8.1   Program Listing of TPERFORM.BAS

```
REM PROGRAM TPERFORM.BAS
        CLS
REM THIS PROGRAM GENERATES A SERIES OF TABLES INDICATING THE FRAME
REM RATE ON A TOKEN-RING NETWORK BASED UPON THE NETWORK OPERATING
REM RATE, NUMBER OF STATIONS, AVERAGE FRAME LENGTH AND TOTAL NETWORK
REM CABLE LENGTH
    FOR K = 1 TO 7                      ' initialize frame lenghts
    READ FRAMELENGTH(K)
    NEXT K
    DATA 64,128,256,512,1024,2048,4096
    BITTIME(1) = 1/4000000        ' initialize bit duration
    BITTIME(2) = 1/16000000
    RATE$(1) = "4MBPS"            ' initialize network rate
    RATE$(2) = "16MBPS"
START:

    LCOUNT = 0                    ' initialize line count
    FOR I = 1 TO 2                ' vary network operating rate
    IF I = 1 THEN GOTO NXT
    FOR LC = 1 TO 50 - LCOUNT: LPRINT : NEXT LC: LCOUNT = 0
NXT: GOSUB HOUTPT                 ' print page header
    FOR N = 10 TO 260 STEP 10     ' vary number of stations
    FOR F = 1 TO 7 STEP 1         ' vary frame length (bytes)
    FOR C = 2 TO 10 STEP 2 ' vary cable length (per 1000 feet)
    S.DELAY = 2.5 * BITTIME(I)
    T.PLACEMENT = 24 * BITTIME(I)
    H.TRINGFLOW = (N/2) * S.DELAY + T.PLACEMENT
    FRAMETIME = (FRAMELENGTH(F) + 21) * 8 * BITTIME(I)
    H.FRAMEFLOW = (N/2) * S.DELAY + FRAMETIME
    TOTAL.TIME = H.TRINGFLOW + H.FRAMEFLOW + (N/2) * S.DELAY
    C.PROPTIME = C *.00000164#
    FPS = 1/(TOTAL.TIME + C.PROPTIME)
    GOSUB DOUTPT
    NEXT C
    NEXT F
    NEXT N
    NEXT I
    END
```

Table 8.1   Program Listing of TPERFORM.BAS (continued)

```
HOUTPT:
     LPRINT "FRAME RATE OF A "; RATE$(I); " TOKEN-RING NETWORK"
     LPRINT "BASED UPON THE NETWORK OPERATING RATE, NUMBER OF"
     LPRINT "STATIONS, FRAME LENGTH AND TOTAL CABLE LENGTH "
     LPRINT
     LPRINT "NUMBER OF   AVG FRAME    CABLE LENGTH   FRAME RATE"
     LPRINT "STATIONS     LENGTH        X000 FEET      IN FPS"
     RETURN
DOUTPT:
     IF LCOUNT < 50 THEN GOTO SKIP
     FOR LC = 1 TO 10                    ' move to top of next page
     LPRINT
     NEXT LC
     LCOUNT = 0
     GOSUB HOUTPT
SKIP: LPRINT USING "   ####      ######"; N; FRAMELENGTH(F);
      LPRINT USING "              ###"; C;
      LPRINT USING "       ######## "; FPS
      LCOUNT = LCOUNT + 1
      RETURN
```

parameters to 40 TO 50 STEP 5 and the FOR 5 loop parameters to 1 TO 2 STEP 1, the printed outputs contained in Table 8.2 and Table 8.3 are obtained.

8.1.10   General Observations

In reviewing the results of the frame rate computations represented in Table 8.2, let us first examine the effect of a change in the average frame length versus a change in the cable length of a network. This will enable us to determine the relative effect of the average frame length versus cable distance for a network with a given number of stations.

For a 40-station network with an average frame length of 64 bytes, note that each increase in network cabling by 2000 feet results in a decrease in the frame rate ranging from 69 (4613 – 4544) to 63 (4413 – 4350) frames per second. Note that a 40-station network with an average frame length of 128 bytes has a decrease in the frame rate ranging from 27 (2900 – 2873) to 26 (2820 – 2794) frames per second as the cable length increases in 2000-foot increments from 2000 to 10,000 feet. When the average frame length is 64 bytes, a decrease in frame flow of 64 frames per second per 2000-foot

Table 8.2 Frame Rate of a 4-Mbps Token Ring Network

Number of Stations	Avg Frame Length	Cable Length × 1000 Feet	Frame Rate (fps)
40	64	2	4613
40	64	4	4544
40	64	6	4477
40	64	8	4413
40	64	10	4350
40	128	2	2900
40	128	4	2873
40	128	6	2846
40	128	8	2820
40	128	10	2794
45	64	2	4515
45	64	4	4449
45	64	6	4385
45	64	8	4323
45	64	10	4263
45	128	2	2861
45	128	4	2835
45	128	6	2809
45	128	8	2783
45	128	10	2758
50	64	2	4422
50	64	4	4359
50	64	6	4297
50	64	8	4237
50	64	10	4179
50	128	2	2824
50	128	4	2798
50	128	6	2772
50	128	8	2747
50	128	10	2723

Frame rate of a 4-Mbps Token Ring network based on the network operating rate, number of stations, frame length, and total cable length.

cable length increase is equivalent to $64 * 64 * 8$, or a decrease of 32,768 bits per second in the information flow capability of the network. When the average frame length is 128 bytes, a decrease in frame flow of 26 frames per second due to a cable length increase of 2000 feet results in a decrease of $128 * 26 * 8$, or 26,628 bits per second in the flow of information. Thus, as the average frame length increases, the effect of an increase in the amount of cabling used in the network slightly decreases.

Table 8.3 Frame Rate of a 16-Mbps Token Ring Network

Number of Stations	Avg Frame Length	Cable Length ×1000 Feet	Frame Rate (fps)
40	64	2	17651
40	64	4	16685
40	64	6	15819
40	64	8	15039
40	64	10	14332
40	128	2	11280
40	128	4	10877
40	128	6	10503
40	128	8	10153
40	128	10	9826
45	64	2	17293
45	64	4	16365
45	64	6	15531
45	64	8	14778
45	64	10	14095
45	128	2	11133
45	128	4	10740
45	128	6	10375
45	128	8	10033
45	128	10	9714
50	64	2	16950
50	64	4	16057
50	64	6	15253
50	64	8	14527
50	64	10	13866
50	128	2	10989
50	128	4	10607
50	128	6	10250
50	128	8	9917
50	128	10	9604

Frame rate of a 16-Mbps Token Ring network based on the network operating rate, number of stations, frame length, and total cable length.

Now let us examine the frame rate as the average frame length increases and the number of stations remains fixed. Note that for a 40-station network, an increase in the average frame rate from 64 to 128 bytes for a cable length of 2000 feet results in a decrease in the frame rate of 1713 (4613 – 2900) frames per second. For a cable length of 10,000 feet, an increase in the average frame length from 64 to 128 bytes for a 40-station network results in a decrease in the frame rate of 1556 (4350 – 2794) frames per second. Thus, the effect of the frame length on the frame rate exceeds the effect of the cable length.

Now let us turn our attention to observing the effect of an increase in the number of network stations with a fixed average frame length and cable length. For a 40-station network that has an average frame length of 64 bytes and a cable length of 2000 feet, the frame rate is 4613 frames per second. When the number of stations is increased to 45, the frame rate drops to 4515, a decrease of almost 100 frames per second. On a per-station-increase basis, this results in a decrease of approximately 20 frames per second when the average frame length is 64 bytes. Note that this decrease in the frame rate is slightly less than the decrease in the frame rate as the network cable distance increases from 2000 to 10,000 feet. This means that each increase in the number of stations has a lesser effect on network performance than an increase of 8000 feet in the cabling used in a network. Although these figures slightly differ as the number of stations on a network increases, you can use the preceding as a general guide for configuring and expanding Token Ring networks. That is, by limiting your network cabling distance, you may be able to alleviate the effect of an increase in the number of network stations on network performance.

8.1.11 Station Effect on Network Performance

To obtain a more detailed understanding of the effect of an increase in the number of network stations on network performance, the comprehensive series of tables contained in the BASIC directory at the noted Web URL was used to extract data. In doing so, the frame rate for 4- and 16-Mbps Token Ring networks was extracted for 64-byte frame lengths and 10,000 feet of cable as the number of network stations varied from 10 to 260 in increments of ten stations. Table 8.4 contains the frame rate information extracted from the comprehensive table.

In examining the frame rates for 4- and 16-Mbps networks listed in Table 8.4, note that the number of stations has a considerable effect on the information flow on a Token Ring network. For example, a ten-station 4-Mbps network supports a frame rate of 4956 frames per second, which is equivalent to an information transfer rate of 4956 frames/second * 64 bytes/frame * 8 bits/byte, or 2.537 Mbps. For a 260-station network, the frame rate is reduced to 2293 frames per second, which is equivalent to an information transfer rate of 2293 frames/second * 64 bytes/frame * 8 bits/byte, or 1.174 Mbps. Turning our attention to the frame rates listed in Table 8.4 for a 16-Mbps Token Ring network, note that a ten-station network supports an information flow of 15,938 frames/second * 64 bytes/frame * 8 bits/byte, or 8.16 Mbps. When the number of stations is increased to 260, the information rate decreases to 8241 frames/second * 64 bytes/frame * 8 bits/byte, or 4.219 Mbps. Although the primary reason a Token Ring network

Table 8.4   Frame Rate versus Number of Network Stations

Number of Stations	Frame Rate (fps)	
	4 Mbps	16 Mbps
10	4956	15938
20	4736	15364
30	4535	14830
40	4350	14332
50	4179	13866
60	4022	13430
70	3876	13020
80	3740	12634
90	3613	12271
100	3495	11928
110	3384	11603
120	3280	11296
130	3182	11005
140	3090	10728
150	3003	10465
160	2921	10215
170	2843	9976
180	2769	9748
190	2699	9530
200	2632	9322
210	2569	9123
220	2508	8932
230	2451	8748
240	2396	8573
250	2343	8404
260	2293	8241

Based on a 64-byte average frame length and 10,000 feet of network cabling.

supports a maximum of 260 network stations is based on jitter of the bits flowing on the network, the approximate halving of the information transfer capability is another important consideration for limiting the number of stations on a network.

8.2   Bridge and Router Performance Requirements

The first section in this chapter focused attention on the development of mathematical models to estimate the flow of data on 4- and 16-Mbps Token Ring networks. This section uses the previously obtained knowledge about Token Ring performance to examine the flow of data between networks

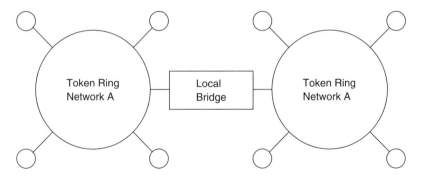

Figure 8.1   Using a Local Token Ring Bridge

when bridges are used. In doing so, we obtain answers to such questions as: What is the forwarding and filtering rate required to be supported by a Token Ring bridge or router prior to that device becoming a potential network bottleneck? What effect does the use of different types of WAN transmission facilities have on the data transfer capability of Token Ring remote bridges and routers? Because the use of WAN transmission facilities is only applicable to remote bridges and routers, let us first examine the required level of performance of a local bridge and then focus on the use of remote bridges and routers.

8.2.1   Local Bridges

Figure 8.1 illustrates the use of a local bridge to connect two Token Ring networks. Here, each Token Ring network can operate at either 4 or 16 Mbps, resulting in three distinct mixtures of network operating speeds the bridge must support: 4 and 4 Mbps, 4 and 16 Mbps, and 16 and 16 Mbps. Thus, the level of performance required by a local bridge linking Token Ring networks will depend on the average frame length, total cable length, number of stations, and the operating rate of each network. Obtaining this information will provide the frame rate in frames per second that you can expect each network to carry. Then, the frame processing capability of the local bridge should equal the sum of the frame rate expected to be carried by each Token Ring network or the bridge will become a network bottleneck.

8.2.2   Considering a Performance Range

Because the average frame length carried on a network varies by time and the number of stations on a network expands and contracts in tandem with personnel changes and corporate policy, instead of determining one number, you may prefer to work with a range of values. As an alternative, you may wish to select a network situation in which a bridge meeting the frame rate requirements of a certain networking scenario can be expected to satisfy a large variance in future changes to each Token Ring network to be interconnected. For example, assume you have a 4-Mbps and a 16-Mbps Token Ring network you wish to locally connect and, through monitoring, determined that the average frame length on each network was 128 bytes. Assuming the 4-Mbps network has 50 stations and the 16-Mbps network has 80 stations and each network uses 6000 feet of cable, you would use the Token Ring table at the Web URL to determine that the expected frame rate on the 4-Mbps network is 2772 fps (frames per second) while the expected frame rate on the 16-Mbps network is 9561 fps. Then, the local bridge should have a frame filtering capability equal to the sum of each network expected frame rate, or 12,333 fps. However, what happens if either network changes?

8.2.3 Considering the Effect of Network Changes

If the number of stations and length of network cabling increases, the frame rate on the network decreases. Thus, an increase in either or both of those variables has no effect on a bridge acquired to support the frame rate of smaller networks. Similarly, an increase in the average frame length results in a decrease in the frame rate on each network. Because the most variable factor is the average frame length, you may wish to consider selecting a lower average frame length, which in effect increases the network frame rate. In doing so, you are adding a margin of safety to the processing requirements of a local Token Ring bridge. For example, lowering the average frame length to 64 bytes while keeping the number of stations and cable length of the network constant results in the 4-Mbps network being projected to have a frame rate of 4297 fps, while the 16-Mbps network has its frame rate projection increased to 13,776 fps. Then, the local bridge you would use to connect the two networks should have the capability to process 18,073 64-byte frames per second. Concerning the bridge forwarding rate, under a worst-case scenario, assume that each frame on each network for a short period of time is routed to the other network. Then, the forwarding rate of the local bridge should equal its filtering rate to ensure the bridge will not become a network bottleneck and cannot congest the flow of data between networks.

8.2.4 Remote Bridges and Routers

As previously noted, the performance requirement for a local bridge is simply the sum of the frame rate on each connected network. That aggregate number of frames per second provides you with the overall frame processing rate a local bridge must exceed prior to it becoming a potential network bottleneck. In turning our attention to remote bridges and routers used to connect two geographically dispersed Token Ring networks, we must consider the operating rate of the WAN transmission facility used to connect networks. Unless that transmission facility operates at the network operating rate, a condition that essentially only occurs when a local bridge is used, the transmission facility functions as a filter, which reduces the maximum potential forwarding rate of frames routed from one network to the other network.

8.2.5 Wide Area Network Operating Rate

There are three key variables that govern the frame rate that can be achieved on a wide area transmission facility used to interconnect remotely located Token Ring networks. Those variables include the frame lengths, WAN operating rate, and the overhead of the transmission protocol used to transport frames between networks. Because the protocol overhead can vary, based on the type of protocol used by a bridge or router manufacturer as well as by their use of data compression, we will first examine the maximum frame rate based on different frame lengths without considering the effect of the protocol or presence or absence of data compression.

8.2.6 Program TRWAN.BAS

To facilitate the computation of frame rates based on different average frame lengths, the BASIC language program TRWAN.BAS was developed. Table 8.5 lists the statements in that program, which computes the frame rate for average frame lengths of 64, 128, 256, 512, 1024, 2048, and 4096 bytes. In actuality, the program adds 21 bytes to each frame length to correspond to the overhead bytes that are wrapped around the information field. Thus, the average frame length actually represents the length of the information field. The WAN operating rates, which vary from 4800 bps to 1.536 Mbps, represent commonly available analog leased line operating rates (through 19,200 bps) and commonly available digital leased line operating rates. Table 8.6 illustrates the table generated from the execution of that program.

In examining the entries in Table 8.6, note that the T1 operating rate of 1.536 Mbps represents the T1 speed of 1.544 Mbps less the 8000 bps used for T1 framing. Also note that at the 1.536-Mbps rate and an average frame length of 64 bytes, the maximum frame rate of 2259 fps is less than the frame rate of 2293 fps for a 260-station, 4-Mbps Token Ring network constructed using 10,000 feet of cable. Thus, the WAN operating rate of a high-speed T1 circuit can be expected to function as a bottleneck for the transfer of data between Token Ring networks without considering the effect of the overhead of the transmission protocol or the use of data compression to enhance transmission efficiency.

8.2.6.1 Protocol Overhead. To illustrate the effect of a protocol's overhead on the maximum frame rate supported by different WAN operating rates, let us revise the program TRWAN.BAS. If we assume the WAN protocol

Table 8.5   TRWAN.BAS Program Listing

```
REM PROGRAM TRWAN.BAS

REM THIS PROGRAM COMPUTES THE MAXIMUM FRAME RATE THAT A WIDE AREA

REM NETWORK TRANSMISSION FACILITY CAN CARRY BETWEEN TWO REMOTE
BRIDGES

CLS

DIM MFPS(9, 7)                                    'max frames per sec

FOR I = 1 TO 9

READ RATE(I)

NEXT I

DATA 4800,9600,19200,56000,64000,128000,256000,512000,1536000

FOR I = 1 TO 7

READ FLENGTH(I)

NEXT I

DATA 64,128,256,512,1024,2048,4096

FOR I = 1 TO 9

FOR J = 1 TO 7

MFPS(I, J) = (RATE(I)/8)/(FLENGTH(J) + 21)

NEXT J

NEXT I

PRINT "WAN RATE    - - - - MAXIMUM FRAME RATE PER SECOND - - - - - -"

PRINT "  BPS              BASED UPON AVERAGE FRAME LENGTH IN BYTES"

PRINT "              64        128       256       512       1024
2048    4096 "

PRINT

J = 1

FOR I = 1 TO 9

PRINT USING " ######## "; RATE(I);

PRINT USING " #####.## #####.## #####.##"; MFPS(I, 1); MFPS(I, 2);
MFPS(I, 3);

PRINT USING " #####.## #####.##"; MFPS(I, 4); MFPS(I, 5);

PRINT USING " #####.## #####.##"; MFPS(I, 6); MFPS(I, 7)

NEXT I

END
```

Table 8.6   Results Obtained from Executing TRWAN.BAS

WAN RATE BPS	— — — — MAXIMUM FRAME RATE PER SECOND — — — — — — BASED UPON AVERAGE FRAME LENGTH IN BYTES						
	64	128	256	512	1024	2048	4096
4800	7.06	4.03	2.17	1.13	0.57	0.29	0.15
9600	14.12	8.05	4.33	2.25	1.15	0.58	0.29
19200	28.24	16.11	8.66	4.50	2.30	1.16	0.58
56000	82.35	46.98	25.27	13.13	6.70	3.38	1.70
64000	94.12	53.69	28.88	15.01	7.66	3.87	1.94
128000	188.24	107.38	57.76	30.02	15.31	7.73	3.89
256000	376.47	214.77	115.52	60.04	30.62	15.47	7.77
512000	752.94	429.53	231.05	120.08	61.24	30.93	15.55
1536000	2258.82	1288.59	693.14	360.23	183.73	92.80	46.64

overhead is 20 percent, change the computation of the two-dimensional array MFPS to:

$$MFPS(I,J) = (RATE(I)/8)/((FLENGTH(J) + 21) * 1.2)$$

If you want to examine the effect of a different overhead percentage, change the multiplier 1.2 to 1.15 for computing a 15-percent protocol overhead, to 1.10 for a 10-percent protocol overhead, and so on. Table 8.7 lists the results obtained by executing the program TRWAN.BAS in which a protocol overhead of 20 percent was used for frame rate computations.

8.2.6.2   Data Compression. Due to the ability of data compression to reduce redundancies contained within the information field of a Token Ring frame, the use of this technology increases the efficiency of the WAN transmission facility. Since 1990, several vendors have introduced compression performing remote bridges as well as added this capability to routers. Although the effect of compression depends on the level of data redundancy, which changes from frame to frame, most vendors advertise an average compression ratio of 2:1 for their products. What this means is that the logical data carried by the information field on the average is doubled within the physical information field. Thus, to consider the effect of data compression on the frame rate transfer capability of the WAN transmission facility, you would modify the computation of MFPS (I,J) in the program TRWAN.BAS as follows:

$$MFPS(I,J) = (RATE(I)/8)/(FLENGTH(J) * K + 21)$$

where K represents the reciprocal of the average data compression ratio. To consider both the effect of data compression and protocol overhead on

Table 8.7   Results Obtained from Executing Program TRWAN.BAS with a 20-percent Protocol Overhead

ADJUSTED FRAME RATE BASED UPON 20 PERCENT WAN PROTOCOL OVERHEAD

WAN RATE — — — — MAXIMUM FRAME RATE PER SECOND — — — — — —

BPS   BASED UPON AVERAGE FRAME LENGTH IN BYTES

	64	128	256	512	1024	2048	4096
4800	5.88	3.36	1.81	0.94	0.48	0.24	0.12
9600	11.76	6.71	3.61	1.88	0.96	0.48	0.24
19200	23.53	13.42	7.22	3.75	1.91	0.97	0.49
56000	68.63	39.15	21.06	10.94	5.58	2.82	1.42
64000	78.43	44.74	24.07	12.51	6.38	3.22	1.62
128000	156.86	89.49	48.13	25.02	12.76	6.44	3.24
256000	313.73	178.97	96.27	50.03	25.52	12.89	6.48
512000	627.45	357.94	192.54	100.06	51.04	25.78	12.95
1536000	1882.35	1073.83	577.62	300.19	153.11	77.33	38.86

the frame transfer rate of the WAN transmission facility, you would modify the computation of MFPS(I,J) as follows:

$$MFPS(I,J) = (RATE(I)/8)/((FLENGTH(J) * K + 21) * P)$$

where K represents the reciprocal of the average data compression ratio and P represents the average protocol overhead.

To illustrate the use of the revised computation of MFPS(I,J), let us assume that the average data compression ratio is 2 and the expected protocol overhead is 15 percent. Then, K has a value of 1/2 or 0.5, while P has a value of 1.15. Table 8.8 illustrates the tabulation of frame rates obtained by modifying the computation of MFPS(I,J) as previously discussed and then re-executing the program TRWAN.BAS. In comparing the tabulations contained in Tables 8.4, 8.5, and 8.6, you will note that the key to reducing the potential of the WAN transmission facility from functioning as a network bottleneck is obtained by the application of data compression. In fact, at certain operational states, the WAN transmission facility may no longer be a bottleneck. For example, from Table 8.8 you will note that a T1 circuit is capable of transporting 3150 64-byte frames per second based on a data compression ratio of 2 and a protocol overhead of 15 percent. In comparison, we previously noted that the frame rate on a 260-station, 4-Mbps Token Ring network constructed using 10,000 feet of cable is 2293 frames per second. Thus, this WAN link connected to compression performing remote bridges would have the capability to transfer a greater number of frames per second than the 4-Mbps Token Ring network could generate. Readers can modify the program TRWAN.BAS and use it in conjunction

Table 8.8 Results Obtained from Executing TRWAN.BAS Using a Data Compression Ratio of 2 and a Protocol Overhead of 15 Percent

WAN RATE	— — — — MAXIMUM FRAME RATE PER SECOND — — — — — —						
BPS	BASED UPON AVERAGE FRAME LENGTH IN BYTES						
	64	128	256	512	1024	2048	4096
4800	9.84	6.14	3.50	1.88	0.98	0.50	0.25
9600	19.69	12.28	7.00	3.77	1.96	1.00	0.50
19200	39.38	24.55	14.01	7.53	3.92	2.00	1.01
56000	114.85	71.61	40.85	21.97	11.42	5.82	2.94
64000	131.26	81.84	46.69	25.11	13.05	6.66	3.36
128000	262.51	163.68	93.38	50.23	26.10	13.31	6.72
256000	525.02	327.37	186.75	100.46	52.21	26.63	13.45
512000	1050.04	654.73	373.50	200.91	104.41	53.26	26.90
1536000	3150.12	1964.19	1120.51	602.73	313.24	159.77	80.69

with the entries in Table 8.8 to determine the most appropriate WAN operating rate based on the topology, size, and operating rates of networks to be connected as well as the transmission protocol overhead and the expected gain in transmission efficiency due to the use of compression performing bridges or routers, assuming this feature is included in the remote bridges or routers you are using or anticipate acquiring.

8.2.7 Traffic Flow between Interconnected Networks

Now that mathematical models have been developed to estimate the frame flow on individual Token Ring networks and through the use of remote bridges and routers connected via the use of different types of WAN transmission facilities, let us focus attention on the traffic flow between remotely located interconnected networks. In doing so, we will use the model presented in Chapter 7, in which the total traffic flow, R_T, between networks has the following relationship to the frame rates on networks 1 (R_1) and 2 (R_2) and the WAN transmission facility frame transfer rate, which we will denote as R_3:

$$\frac{1}{R_T} = \frac{1}{R_1} + \frac{1}{R_2} + \frac{1}{R_3}$$

or

$$R_T = \frac{R_1 R_2 R_3}{R_2 R_3 + R_1 R_3 + R_1 R_2}$$

To illustrate the use of the preceding equation, let us assume you wish to download a 640-Kbyte file from a server located on a 16-Mbps Token Ring network that has 200 stations and 10,000 feet of cable to a 4-Mbps Token Ring network that has 50 stations and 4000 feet of cable, while the remote bridges or routers connecting each network use a 64-Kbps transmission facility. Because a file transfer uses the largest size frame available for most of the transfer, the transfer would take place using 4500-byte frames, which is the largest information field length supported by both 4- and 16-Mbps Token Ring networks. From the Token Ring table, the closest entries we can locate govern the frame rate for a frame length of 4096 bytes. From the table, the maximum frame rate supported by a 4-Mbps network with 50 stations and 4000 feet of cable is 121 fps, while the maximum frame rate on a 16-Mbps network with 200 stations and 10.000 feet of cable is 471 fps. From Table 8.7 we note that the maximum frame rate supported by a 56-Kbps digital circuit with a 20-percent protocol overhead is 1.42 fps when the average frame length is 4500 bytes. Using our formula to find the transfer rate, we obtain:

$$R_T = \frac{121 * 471 * 1.42}{471 * 1.42 + 121 * 1.42 + 121 * 471} = 1.399 \text{ fps}$$

Similar to our notation in Chapter 7, the previously computed value of R_T represents a best-case scenario in that it assumes the transfer of data from one network to another occurs without other stations on each network using the network or requesting inter-network transmission. Suppose the use of a monitoring program on each network indicated that at any time an average of three workstations were using the transmission facilities of each network and two workstations were using inter-network transmission. Then, you would adjust the values of R_1 and R_2 by dividing each by 3 and adjust the value of R_3 by dividing its value by 2. Doing so, we obtain:

$$R_T = \frac{\left(121/3\right)\left(471/3\right)\left(1.42/2\right)}{\left(471/3\right) * \left(1.42/2\right) + \left(121/3\right) * \left(1.42/2\right) + \left(121/3\right) * \left(471/3\right)} = .69 \text{ fps}$$

Based on the preceding, you can expect a best-case frame flow between networks of 1.399 frames per second and an average frame flow between networks of 0.69 frames per second.

Based on an information field of 4096 bytes, the maximum flow of information between networks is 4096 bytes/frame * 1.399 frames/second, or 5730 bytes per second. Then, the optimum transfer time of a 640-Kbyte file would become:

$$\frac{640 \text{ K} * 1024 \text{ bytes/K}}{4096 \text{ bytes/frame} * 1.399 \text{ frames/second}} = 114 \text{ seconds}$$

To compute the average file transfer time, we would use the average transfer rate of 0.69 frames per second. Using an information field of 4096 bytes and a frame rate of 0.69 frames per second, the average information transfer capability between networks becomes 4096 bytes/frame * 0.69 frames/second. Then, the average transfer time to move a 640-Kbyte file between networks becomes:

$$\frac{640\text{ K} * 1024\text{ bytes/K}}{2826\text{ bytes/second}} = 232\text{ seconds}$$

This indicates that the transmission time to move a 640-Kbyte file between two Token Ring networks connected by a pair of remote bridges or routers using a 56-Kbps WAN transmission facility can be expected, on average, to require 232 seconds, or slightly under four minutes. In a best-case scenario, the transfer time will require 114 seconds, or slightly under two minutes. Both timings are based on the network characteristics previously discussed and will obviously change if either network or the WAN transmission rate changes.

You can extend the previous computations to determine a peak transmission time by monitoring each network to determine the peak number of users performing network activity at a given period of time. Once you obtain this information, you would then adjust the values for R_1, R_2, and R_3 similar to the manner in which those values were adjusted to determine the average frame transfer rate between networks. By considering the peak traffic on each network, your computation for R_T would result in a worst-case frame transfer rate that, when used to compute the file transfer time, would provide the maximum transfer time.

Whether or not the optimum, average, and peak transfer times are acceptable depends on your organization and "its need for speed." While an increase in the WAN operating rate will have a significant effect on the ability to transfer frames between networks, it is not without cost. Thus, you may wish to perform a cost analysis to determine if a reduction in file transfer time or an increase in the transfer capability of the WAN is worth the expense associated with obtaining a higher WAN transmission capability. In addition, you should consider the relationship of file transfer activity in the form of programs and data files to the transfer of relatively short electronic messages in the form of files. For example, if the primary use of the Internet is to transport short e-mail files, would an additional expense of $1000 or more per month to reduce the transfer time of a message from three seconds to one second be worthwhile? Considering the fact that it may take a second or two for a person to move his or her hand to the keyboard and press a key to open the mail, I would probably defer the expense. However, the answer to such questions are for you to decide. In doing so, you can use the models provided in this book to determine transfer rates and transfer times, and then use that information in conjunction with the cost of communications equipment and transmission facilities as your decision criteria.

Chapter 9
ATM Performance

This chapter examines ATM with respect to its performance. In doing so we build upon our base of knowledge concerning ATM previously presented in Chapter 2, our examination of the application of waiting line analysis presented in Chapter 4, and knowledge of Ethernet performance obtained in Chapter 7.

In Chapter 2 we discussed four ATM Adaption Layer (AAL) services as well as obtained a general overview of the basic 53-byte ATM cell. In this chapter we probe deeper into each AAL, examining the segmentation process that results in the format of the AAL cell and its effect on AAL cell data transport capability. Once this is accomplished, we turn our attention to LAN Emulation and develop a general model and exercise that model to examine the effect of LAN Emulation on ATM performance. In doing so we apply waiting line analysis to ATM to obtain an appreciation for and understanding of the effect of queuing on the LAN Emulation process.

9.1   AAL Cell Variations

In Chapter 2 we noted that there are four AALs: AAL-1, AAL-2, AAL-3/4, and AAL-5. Each AAL uses a predefined cell format when it segments data from high layers into ATM cells. In this section we examine the segmentation process and the resulting cell formats obtained from the use of different AALs as well as their potential effect on ATM performance.

9.1.1   AAL-1

AAL-1 is used to support a constant bit rate connection that has a timing relationship between source and destination. During the segmentation process, the convergence layer segments each protocol data unit (PDU) into 48-byte entities that contain a one-byte header with three fields. That header is placed within the payload area of each cell, reducing the payload to 47 bytes of user data.

Figure 9.1 illustrates the AAL-1 cell format. Note that the one-bit convergence sublayer indicator (CSI) is followed by a three-bit sequence number (SN) field and a four-bit sequence number protection (SNP) field. The SN is used to detect cell insertion and cell loss, while the SNP is used to correct errors that occur in the sequence number.

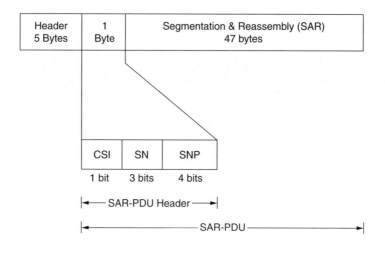

Legend:

CSI   Convergence Sublayer Indicator
SN   Sequence Number
SNP   Sequence Number Protection

Figure 9.1   AAL-1 Cell Format

9.1.2   AAL-2

AAL-2 is used to transfer time-dependent variable bit rate data. To do so, AAL-2 transmits timing information with the data, enabling the timing dependency to be recovered at the cell destination. As data is segmented at the AAL-2 layer, a header and trailer are added to each cell's payload, resulting in 46 bytes being available in the payload to actually transport data. Figure 9.2 illustrates the AAL-2 cell format. The AAL-2 header contains two fields: a sequence number (SN) used to detect inserted or lost cells and an information type (IT) field. The latter has one of three values: Beginning of Message (BOM), Continuation of Message (COM), or End of Message (EOM). The trailer also contains two fields: a length indicator (LI) field that contains the number of data bytes in a partially filled cell and a cyclic redundancy check (CRC) field that is used by the SAR sublayer to correct errors.

9.1.3   AAL-3/4

AAL-3 was developed to support time-independent variable rate data while AAL-4 was developed to transport time-independent variable bit rate data in a connectionless mode. Due to similarities between the two, they were combined into a common AAL referred to as AAL-3/4.

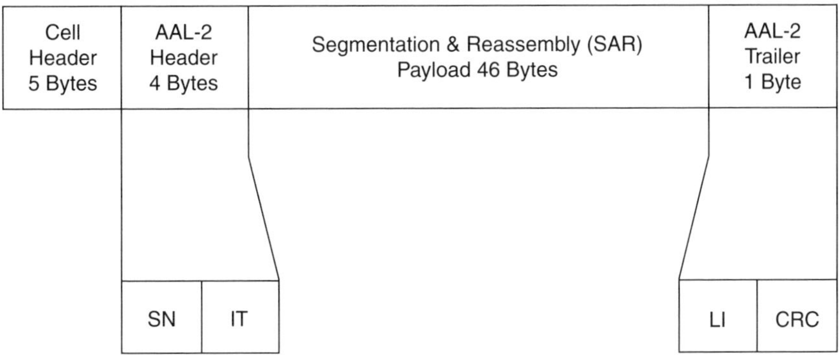

Cell Header 5 Bytes	AAL-2 Header 4 Bytes	Segmentation & Reassembly (SAR) Payload 46 Bytes	AAL-2 Trailer 1 Byte

	SN	IT			LI	CRC

Legend:

SN	Sequence Number
IT	Information Type
LI	Length Indicator
CRC	Cyclic Redundancy Check

Figure 9.2   AAL-2 Cell Format

Figure 9.3 illustrates the steps in the flow of data associated with AAL-3/4. First, data from the upper user layer is passed in the form of a service data unit (SDU) to the convergence sublayer of the AAL. At this point, AAL-3/4 subdivides the convergence sublayer into a service specific convergence sublayer (SSCS) and a common part convergence sublayer (CPCS). The upper layer SDU is passed through the SSCS unchanged. In comparison, the CPCS adds a four-byte header, a four-byte trailer, and up to three bytes of padding to ensure that the entire PDU is divisible by 4. The CPCS-PDU is then passed on to the segmentation and reassembly (SAR) sublayer of the AAL, where the entire PDU, to include the added header, trailer, and any pads, are segmented into 44-byte pieces. The SAR adds a two-byte header and a two-byte trailer to each segment, resulting in a 48-byte payload that contains 44 bytes of data.

The CPCS header contains three fields. The first field is the common part indicator (CPI) field, which indicates that the payload is part of the common part. The second field is the begin tag (Btag) field, which marks the start of the protocol data unit, while the third field, the buffer allocation size (BAsize), informs the receiver of the amount of buffer space required to accommodate the message.

Similar to the header, the trailer also contains three fields. The first field is an alignment (AL) field. This field is a byte filler that is employed to make the header and trailer the same length at four bytes each. The second field in the trailer is an end tag (Etag), which is used to mark the end of the PDU.

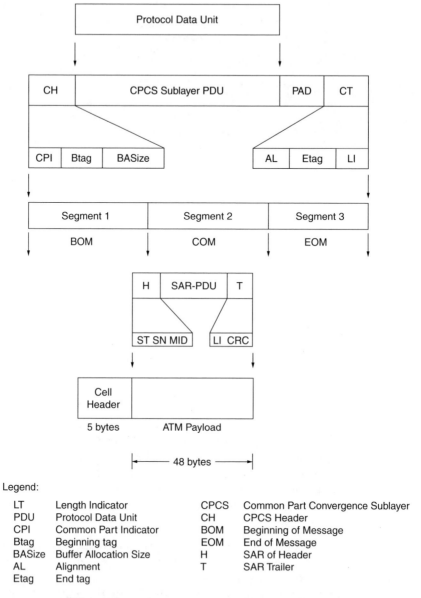

Figure 9.3   AAL-3/4 Data Flow and Cell Formation

The third field is the length indicator (LI), which indicates the length of the PDU payload.

At the SAR sublayer, a header and trailer are added to each segment. The header contains information concerning the segment order, while the trailer includes a CRC field. The lower portion of Figure 9.3 illustrates the AAL-3/4 SAR-PDU format prior to an ATM cell being formed. Note that the header contains three fields: a two-bit segment type (ST) field that indicates one of four segment types, a four-bit sequence number (SN) field, and a ten-bit multiplexing identification (MID) field. The latter is used to multiplex two or more CPCS connections onto a single ATM layer connection. The SAR trailer contains two fields: a six bit length indicator (LI) field that indicates the number of bytes contained in the payload portion of the segment and a ten-bit CRC. Based on the preceding, not only is AAL-3/4 relatively complex, but, in addition, its 44-byte payload capacity adversely affects data transfer.

9.1.4 AAL-5

The complexity of AAL-3/4 as well as its relatively high overhead of four bytes for every 48 bytes of ATM user information resulted in the requirement for a simplified AAL. That requirement was met by AAL-5, which places headers and trailers onto the convergence sublayer PDU instead of the SAR-PDU. Other "tricks" employed by AAL-5 to reduce overhead include assuming data is sequenced by the user and the use of the payload type indication (PTI) bit in the cell header to indicate the last cell in a transmission sequence. These "tricks" eliminate the necessity to include the SN and LI fields in each cell; however, they are included in some cells as they are used in fields in the common part convergence sublayer (CPCS), which is passed to the SAR-PDU prior to segmentation into a series of cells.

Figure 9.4 illustrates the formation of an AAL-5 cell. Note that the CPCS-PDU trailer winds up placed in the cell transporting the end of message (EOM), which means that its eight-byte trailer only reduces the payload in the last cell in a sequence. Assuming an average of three cells per sequence, this results in 8/3, or an average payload reduction of 2.55 bytes. The actual payload reduction depends on the length of the cell sequence. Because the LI field is two bytes in length, this means the number of cells can be up to 65,535. Thus, when the cell sequence is 1, the payload reduction is 8 bytes/1, which results in a payload capacity of 40 bytes for a worst-case scenario. If the cell sequence is 65,535, then the payload reduction is 8 bytes/65,535, or 0.000122 bytes, resulting in a best-case payload capacity of 47.9998 bytes.

9.1.5 Payload Capacity

To illustrate the effect of different AALs on ATM payload capacity, let us begin with the common ATM line operating rate of 155.520 Mbps. Every 27th ATM cell is used to convey operational, administrative, and maintenance (OAM) information and is not available to transport data. This means that 155.520/27 or 5.76 Mbps is used for OAM, resulting in a line operating rate of 149.76 Mbps available for ATM cells transporting data.

249

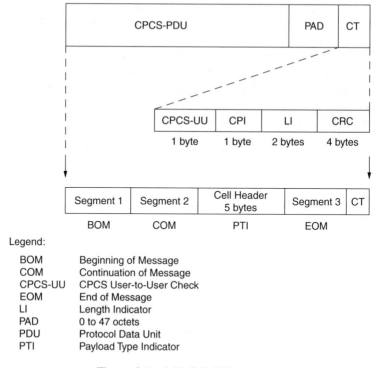

Figure 9.4   AAL-5 Cell Formation

Each ATM cell has a five-byte header, reducing the payload area to 48 bytes. This means that for a best-case scenario, 149.76 Mbps * 48/53 or 135.63169 Mbps is available for the cell payload.

AAL-1 transports data using a one-byte header within the payload area. Thus, the payload capacity is reduced to 135.63169 * 47/48 or 132.80602 Mbps.

AAL-2 transports data using two bytes of overhead within the 48-byte payload, reducing the payload to 46 bytes. Thus, the payload capacity is reduced to 135.63169 Mbps * 46/48, or 129.98036 Mbps.

AAL-3/4 uses four bytes of overhead within the 48-byte ATM cell payload area, reducing the effective payload to 44 bytes. Thus, the effective payload capacity becomes:

135.63169 Mbps * 4/48 or 124.32904 Mbps

AAL-5 places its overhead into the CPCS-PDU, which results in the eight-byte trailer being contained in the cell transporting the EOM. As previously discussed, the eight bytes of overhead are contained in the last cell in the cell sequence. Because the cell sequence can vary from 1 to 65,535 cells,

Table 9.1   AAL Payload Capacity

AAL	Payload Capacity (Mbps)
AAL-1	132.80602
AAL-2	129.98036
AAL-3/4	124.32904
AAL-5	
Worst case	113.0264
Best case	135.63169
Possible average	128.32904

the reduction in the payload can range from a best case of 0.000122 bytes to a worst case of 8 bytes. Thus, the actual payload per cell can range from 40 bytes to 47.998 bytes.

Using a payload of 40 bytes, the payload capacity for AAL-5 becomes 135.63169 Mbps * 40/48, or 113.0264 Mbps. Using a payload of 47.9998 bytes, the payload capacity becomes 135.63169 Mbps * 47.9998/48, or 135.63112 Mbps. If we assume an average overhead of 2.66 bytes per 48 bytes of payload, this reduces the effective payload to 45.33 bytes. Then, the actual payload capacity for an AAL-5 payload becomes 135.63169 Mbps * 45.33/48, or 128.09565 Mbps. Table 9.1 summarizes payload capacity by AAL and indicates that not every AAL is created equal with respect to its payload capacity.

9.2   LAN Emulation

When ATM was initially deployed as a mechanism to provide a high-speed backbone for Ethernet or Token Ring networks, the incompatibilities between those networks with respect to addressing, connection operation, and broadcasting made it extremely difficult to use the newer technology. ATM is a connection-oriented technology that uses virtual paths (VPs) and virtual channels (VCs) to establish a route from source to destination. As a connection-oriented technology, there was no provision for learning addresses as performed by layer 2 bridges, resulting in the absence of a broadcasting mechanism in ATM. In comparison, Ethernet and Token Ring networks are connectionless networks that use layer 2 Media Access Control (MAC) addressing and include a broadcast mechanism built into each protocol. Figure 9.5 summarizes the key differences between ATM and different types of Ethernet and Token Ring networks connected via LAN switches to an ATM backbone.

9.2.1   Need for LANE

Prior to the development of LAN Emulation (LANE), network managers who wanted to use ATM as a high-speed backbone to interconnect layer 2-based

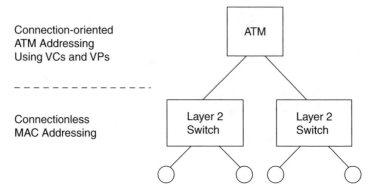

Figure 9.5   ATM versus Legacy LANs

LANs had to map ATM permanent virtual circuits (PVCs) using VP and VC identifiers to link layer 2 switches through the ATM backbone. Typically, each layer 2 switch would include one or more ATM cards, with both a layer 2 MAC address and an ATM address. The mapping of PVCs from each edge switch through the ATM backbone would provide layer 2 LAN users with the ability to both access ATM resources as well as pass data via an ATM backbone to other layer 2 LAN users, as illustrated in Figure 9.6. Although the mapping of PVCs worked, there were several problems associated with this technique. First, each time the network topology changed, the network would have to have the previously static connections reconfigured, substantially increasing the workload of network

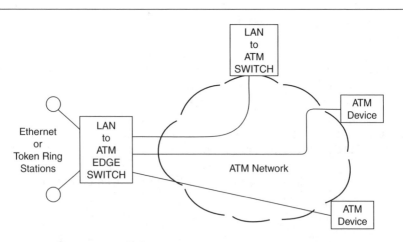

Figure 9.6   Manually Configuring PVCs to Enable LAN-to-ATM Interoperatility

managers. Second, to err is human and maintaining correct mappings is a time-consuming process that can be error-prone.

9.2.2   The LAN Emulation Process

Recognizing the deficiencies associated with the manual configuration of PVCs, the ATM Forum introduced an automated technique for mapping layer 2 MAC addresses to ATM addresses. This technique is referred to as LAN Emulation, with LANE Version 1.0 approved during 1995. LANE supports Ethernet to Ethernet via ATM, Ethernet to ATM, Token Ring to Token Ring via ATM, and Token Ring to ATM connectivity. Although FDDI is not directly supported by LANE, you can use a router or switch to bridge FDDI traffic onto a LANE emulation service by first converting its frames to either Ethernet or Token Ring.

9.2.2.1   Components. There are four key components associated with LAN Emulation. Those components include a LAN Emulation client (LEC), a LAN Emulation configuration server (LES), and a broadcast and unknown Server (BUS). Let us first review the general operation of each component prior to examining the emulation process.

9.2.2.2   LAN Emulation Client. The LAN Emulation client (LEC) resides on ATM attached devices, such as a layer 2 switch that has an uplink to an ATM switch. The LEC has two addresses —an IEEE 48-bit MAC address and a 20-byte ATM address — and serves as a portal to enable layer 2 LAN connectionless service to be transported via ATM's connection-oriented service. Functions performed by the LEC include address resolution, data forwarding, and the registration of MAC addresses with the LAN Emulation server.

9.2.2.3   LAN Emulation Server. The LAN Emulation server (LES) represents a database repository that contains MAC addresses and corresponding ATM addresses required to reach the MAC address. LECs register their ATM to MAC address translations with the LES. This enables other LECs to send address-resolution requests to the LES to obtain appropriate ATM addresses. Because there can be multiple LECs on an ATM network, a mechanism is required to point the LEC to the correct LES. That mechanism is in the form of a LAN Emulation configuration server (LECS).

9.2.2.4   LAN Emulation Configuration Server. As briefly mentioned earlier, an ATM network can have multiple LESs, each maintaining an independent network within the ATM network. Such networks are referred to as emulated LANs (ELANs) and form domains within the network. To point each LEC to the correct ELAN as well as the LES associated with the ELAN requires the use of a LAN Emulation configuration server (LECS).

The LECS maintains a database of ELANs and the ATM addresses of the LESs that control the ELANs. Thus, a LEC will first query a LECS to determine the address of the appropriate LES to use.

9.2.2.5   Broadcast and Unknown Server. When an LEC attempts to obtain an ATM address, it first checks its cache memory area. If the required address is not in cache, it sends an address-resolution request to the LES, which checks its database. If the desired address at this point in time is unknown, the address-resolution process requires a request containing the MAC address and requesting the ATM address to be broadcast to each LEC on the network. Because ATM is a connection-oriented protocol, it needs a mechanism to issue broadcasts not directly supported by the protocol. That mechanism is provided by the broadcast and unknown server (BUS), which is responsible for distributing broadcasts and multicasts.

Now that we have an appreciation for the components associated with LAN Emulation, we can probe deeper into the manner by which the process occurs. In doing so, we also develop a general model that we can exercise to examine the effect of the LAN Emulation process upon network performance. First we will omit the effect of queuing through LAN switches to develop a basic model concerning LAN Emulation. Once this is accomplished, we then consider the effect of queuing on the LAN Emulation process.

9.2.2.6   Operation and Model Development. To illustrate the LAN Emulation process, let us assume that several Ethernet switches are connected via the use of an ATM backbone, as illustrated in Figure 9.7. When each Ethernet switch is initialized, the LEC on each switch uses either a locally configured ATM address or a fixed address defined by the ATM Forum to locate the LECS. Either method results in the use of a pair of VPIs and VCIs, collectively referred to as a virtual channel connection (VCC). The LEC request shown as number 1 in Figure 9.7 results in the LECS checking its database to determine if the LEC can join the ELAN. Assuming it is permitted to do so, the LECS uses the same VCC to return the ATM address and the name of the LES for the ELAN to the LEC. This is indicated as number 2 in Figure 9.7.

At an ATM operating rate of 155.520 Mbps, one cell of 53 bytes requires:

$$\frac{53 \text{ bytes} * 8 \text{ bits/bytes}}{155.520 \text{ Mbps}} \text{ or } 2.7263 \times 10^{-6} \text{ seconds}$$

Therefore, without considering processing delay as the LECS checks its database, the minimum round-trip delay for the LEC to access the LECS and determine the LES to use is 5.45126×10^{-6} seconds, or 2 cell times ($2C_T$). Because the LEC should only require accessing the LECS once to locate its LES, this delay is not cumulative. Once the LECS response is received, the LEC tears down the previously established VCC to the LECS and initiates a new VCC to the LES to exchange information. This VCC represents

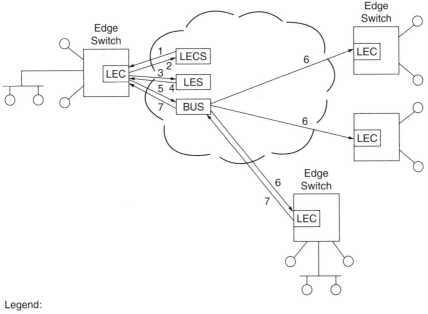

Legend:

LEC	LAN Emulation Client
LECS	LAN Emulation Configuration Server
LES	LAN Emulation Server
BUS	Broadcast and Unknown Server

Figure 9.7   The LANE Process

a bi-directional control VCC that will remain operational as long as the LEC continues to use the LES. Using this VCC, the LEC will also query the LES to determine the ATM address for the BUS. To do so, the LEC transmits an address-resolution request for the broadcast address hex FFFFFF and uses the received ATM address to establish a VCC to the BUS.

Returning to Figure 9.7, numbers 3 and 4 indicate the initial LEC querying of the LES and its response in which it returns the ATM address of the BUS, while number 5 indicates the establishment of a VCC from the LEC to the BUS. Assuming each action is near instantaneous and ignoring processing delays, a minimum of three cell durations must occur until the LEC learns the address of the BUS and establishes a VCC to it. Thus, the additional one-time delay becomes:

$$2.7263 \times 10^{-6} * 3 = 8.1789 \times 10^{-6} \text{ seconds}$$

This is equivalent to three cells times or $3C_T$. Now that the LEC knows the LES and BUS to use, let us assume a frame arrives at the switch that needs an ATM address to correctly flow over the ATM network to its destination.

255

The LEC reads the packet's destination MAC address and examines its forwarding tables in cache memory to determine if it has a corresponding ATM address. If an address is in cache memory, the LEC uses that address and begins segmenting the frame into cells for delivery via the ATM network. The LEC will only find a corresponding ATM address to the destination MAC address if it is currently communicating with the destination ATM device on behalf of another user. Otherwise, the LEC queries the LES to determine if the latter previously learned the ATM address that needs to be resolved. At nearly the same time, the LEC begins transmitting an address-resolution request to the BUS. This overlap cuts down on the time required to resolve the address if the LES cannot provide the address resolution. If the LES has the required address and begins to return it to the LEC, the latter stops transmission to the BUS and uses the address provided by the LES to connect directly to the destination address. When transmitting to the BUS, the LEC uses a LAN Emulation ARP (LE-ARP), in effect broadcasting the known MAC address to each LEC and having the LEC with the correct MAC address respond with its ATM address. Because the BUS performs broadcasting, the LEC sends a request to the BUS. The BUS has a two-way VCC to each LEC that is established during the initialization of each LEC as well as a one-way VCC to each LEC it uses for broadcasts. The BUS uses the one-way VCC to each LEC to broadcast its LE-ARP request and the response from the appropriate LEC then flows through the BUS to the originating LEC.

In continuing our model development, let us assume that P_1 is the probability that the LEC is communicating with the destination ATM device when it receives a LAN frame for forwarding over the network. Then, the probability is $1 - P_1$ that the LEC must access the LES.

Accessing the LES via a one-cell request requires $(1 - P_1) * 2.7263 \times 10^{-6}$ seconds or $(1 - P) * C_T$. Assuming the probability that the LES has learned the desired ATM address is P_2, then a one-cell response, again assuming no processing time, becomes:

$$P_2 * 2.7263 \times 10^{-6} \text{ seconds}$$

If P_2 is the probability that the LES can resolve the request, then $1 - P_2$ represents the probability that the LES cannot resolve the request. When this occurs, the LEC sends an LE-ARP to the BUS (number 5 in Figure 9.7), which issues a broadcast to each LEC (number 6 in Figure 9.7), with the LEC having the desired address returning the ATM address (number 7 in Figure 9.7) required to access the destination MAC address. Again assuming instantaneous processing, which while obviously not true, facilitates simplicity, the time required to resolve the ARP becomes:

$$(1 - P_2) * 2.7263 \times 10^{-6} * 2 \text{ seconds}$$

Table 9.2 LANE Delay Components

Activity	Delay
LEC-to-LECS access	$2C_T$
LEC-to-LES access and VCC setup to BUS	$3C_T$
LEC access to LES	$(1 - P_1)C_T$
LEC ARP request	$(1 - P_2)C_T * 2$

Note: C_T = cell time of 2.7263×10^{-6} seconds

P_1 = probability LEC is communicating with the destination MAC address

P_2 = probability LES learned the desired ATM address

or $(1 - P_2) * C_T * 2$, as we will assume a cell must flow in each direction, from the BUS to each LEC and back through the BUS to the LEC. Based on the preceding, the LANE delay components are listed in Table 9.2.

Based on the LANE delay components listed in Table 9.2, the cumulative delay due to the emulation process becomes:

$$2C_T + 3C_T + (1 - P_1)C_T * N + (1 - P_2)C_T * 2 * N \text{ seconds}$$

where N represents the number of addresses that need to be resolved and C_T represents the cell transmission time.

When a power failure occurs or switches are first initialized, we have a worst-case condition where P_1 and P_2 are initially 0. In comparison, when ATM switches and the LECs in edge devices have been operational for a period of time, both P_1 and P_2 approach and can reach a value of 1. Thus, let us exercise the preceding equation.

Figure 9.8 illustrates the execution of an EXCEL spreadsheet model for 100, 1000, and 10,000 addresses that require resolution during a backbone initialization procedure or after a power failure. Although the complexity of the emulation process makes it appear that the transmission time associated with the learning of appropriate addresses would be a time-consuming process, the relatively high operating rate of the backbone minimizes the effect of the learning process. In fact, for 10,000 address resolution, the transmission time is eight hundredths of a second for the worst-case condition where each address must be resolved!

Note that the preceding model did not include consideration of the effect of hundreds, thousands, or tens of thousands of MAC layer 2 devices attempting to transmit through an ATM backbone upon recovering from a power failure. In effect, we did not consider the effect of queuing delays that occur when a large number of stations must have MAC addresses resolved via a single uplink. Thus, let us continue our LANE model development by

	A	B	C	D	E
1	**Initialization Effect of LAN Emulation**				
2		Cell Time:	2.7263E-06		
3	P1	P2	N		Initialization Time
4	0.00	0.00	100		0.00083152
5	0.10	0.10	100		0.00074973
6	0.20	0.20	100		0.00066794
7	0.30	0.30	100		0.00058615
8	0.40	0.40	100		0.00050437
9	0.50	0.50	100		0.00042258
10	0.60	0.60	100		0.00034079
11	0.70	0.70	100		0.00025900
12	0.80	0.80	100		0.00017721
13	0.90	0.90	100		0.00009542
14	1.00	1.00	100		0.00001363
16	0.00	0.00	1000		0.00819253
17	0.10	0.10	1000		0.00737464
18	0.20	0.20	1000		0.00655675
19	0.30	0.30	1000		0.00573886
20	0.40	0.40	1000		0.00492097
21	0.50	0.50	1000		0.00410308
22	0.60	0.60	1000		0.00328519
23	0.70	0.70	1000		0.00246730
24	0.80	0.80	1000		0.00164941
25	0.90	0.90	1000		0.00083152
26	1.00	1.00	1000		0.00001363
28	0.00	0.00	10000		0.08180263
29	0.10	0.10	10000		0.07362373
30	0.20	0.20	10000		0.06544483
31	0.30	0.30	10000		0.05726593
32	0.40	0.40	10000		0.04908703
33	0.50	0.50	10000		0.04090813
34	0.60	0.60	10000		0.03272923
35	0.70	0.70	10000		0.02455033
36	0.80	0.80	10000		0.01637143
37	0.90	0.90	10000		0.00819253
38	1.00	1.00	10000		0.00001363

Figure 9.8   The Excel LAN Emulation Initialization Model

considering the effect of queuing through layer 2 switches as MAC stations contend for access to the ATM backbone.

9.2.3 Queuing Considerations

As previously mentioned, in the preceding LANE model there was one significant omission we will not attempt to address. That omission is the fact that we did not consider the effect of MAC stations becoming active

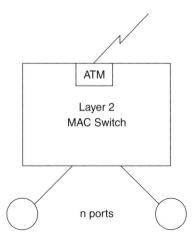

Figure 9.9   When n layer 2 MAC stations become active and require an address resolution, queues develop in the switch which introduce delays.

and contending for access to the LE-ARP process via a common port on the layer 2 MAC switch.

Figure 9.9 illustrates the contention of n ports on a layer 2 switch to the 155.52-Mbps ATM uplink port. The number of ports and the operating rate of each port will determine the waiting time in the system which will affect the overall delay in resolving MAC to ATM addresses.

At 155.52 Mbps, the cell slot time is $155.52 \times 10^{-6}/53 * 8$, or 355792 cells per second. However, one in every 27 cell slots is used for operations, administration, and maintenance (OAM). Thus, the cell slot rate available for actual traffic becomes $(26/27) * 366792$, or 353208 cells per second. This results in a service time of 1/353208, or 2.831 µs.

Due to possible wide variations concerning the number of LAN ports and their operating rates, let us define some common parameters to use to illustrate the effect of queuing on the LANE process. Let us assume that the switch contains 64 ports, resulting in 63 LAN ports and one ATM uplink. Further assume that each LAN port operates at 10 Mbps and an initial LAN frame containing a destination address that requires resolution results in an ATM cell that begins the emulation process. Then the following question: What is the delay through the switch associated with each address that needs to be resolved?

9.2.3.1   ATM Queuing Parameters.   Because ATM provides a constant service time, the formulas used to develop a queuing model are different from the model used earlier in this book. Table 9.3 lists the applicable

Table 9.3   Single-Channel, Single-Phase Formulas for Poisson Arrivals And Constant Service Times

Utilization	$P = \dfrac{\lambda}{\mu}$
Probability no activity in system	$P_0 = 1 - \dfrac{\lambda}{\mu}$
Length of queue	$Lq = \dfrac{(\lambda/\mu)^2}{2(1-\lambda/\mu)}$
Length of system	$L = Lq = \lambda/\mu$
Average waiting time in queue	$Wq = Lq/\lambda$
Average waiting time in system	$W = Wq + 1/\mu$

formulas for a single-phase, single-channel queuing system with Poisson arrivals and constant service rates.

If we assume layer 2 LAN stations are 10-Mbps Ethernet devices, then from Chapter 7 the frame rate in frames per second becomes:

$$1 / \left[9.6 \times 10^{-6} + \left(B * 8 \, \frac{\text{bits}}{\text{bytes}} * \frac{100\text{ns}}{\text{bit}} \right) \right]$$

where B is the frame length in bytes. The frame rate represents the maximum arrival rate of frames from one station that upon switch power-up.

If S represents the number of stations, and P_1 and P_2 represent the probability a station is active and has sustained activity, then the frame arrival rate can be expressed as follows:

$$\lambda = S * P_1 * P_2 * 1/((9.6 \times 10^{-6}) + (B * 8 * 100 \times 10^{-9}))$$

where B is the frame length in bits.

To facilitate our computations, another LANE spreadsheet model was developed. This model, which computes switch delay time, is shown in Figure 9.10 and is stored at the Web URL previously noted in this book on the file LANE2 in the directory EXCEL. In examining the entries in Figure 9.10, note that the top portion of the model computes a "probabilistic frame arrival rate" based upon a variable frame length and fixed probabilities that the station is active and has a sustained transfer rate. The latter probability recognizes the fact that only a portion of stations are transmitting at anywhere near a sustained level of activity.

The lower series of computations shown in Figure 9.10 first computes Lq, L, Wq, and W based upon the formulas presented in Table 9.3. Note that W represents the average frame waiting time in the system without considering that a frame must be buffered for the information to be used to form

	A	B	C	D	E	F	G	H
1	LAN EMULATION SWITCH DELAY TIME							
2								
3	Cell rate:	353208						
4								
5	Frame length (bytes)	Frame Rate (fps)	Number of LAN Layer 2 Stations	Maximum Frame Arrival Rate	Probability Station Active (P1)	Probability Sustained Activity (P2)	Probabilistic Frame Arrival Rate	
6	72	14881	63	937500	0.75	0.50	351563	
7	100	11161	63	703125	0.75	0.50	263672	
8	124	9191	63	579044	0.75	0.50	217142	
9	256	4664	63	293843	0.75	0.50	110191	
10	512	2385	63	150286	0.75	0.50	56357	
11	1024	1207	63	76014	0.75	0.50	28505	
12	1526	813	63	51203	0.75	0.50	19201	
13								
14	Frame length (bytes)	Lq	L	Wq	W	Frame to Cell Transfer Delay Time	Total Frame Delay Time	Total Delay per 10000 addresses
15	72	106.327762	107.323104	0.00030244	0.00030527	0.00006	0.00036287	3.62874606
16	100	1.099180	1.845686	0.00000417	0.00000700	0.00008	0.00008700	0.86999935
17	124	0.490540	1.105309	0.00000226	0.00000509	0.00010	0.00010429	1.04290271
18	256	0.070729	0.382702	0.00000064	0.00000347	0.00020	0.00020827	2.08273068
19	512	0.015146	0.174705	0.00000027	0.00000310	0.00041	0.00041270	4.12699945
20	1024	0.003542	0.084246	0.00000012	0.00000296	0.00082	0.00082216	8.22155466
21	1526	0.001563	0.055924	0.00000008	0.00000291	0.00122	0.00122371	12.2371257
22								

Figure 9.10   The Excel Model LANE2, which Computes the LANE Switch Delay Time

an appropriate cell. Thus, an additional delay time is involved because we must consider frame buffering. This time is computed by multiplying the frame length by 8 to obtain the number of bits in the frame and the result by 100 nanoseconds, which is the bit duration at a data rate of 10 Mbps. Thus, the results of the preceding computations are contained in the column labeled "Frame to Cell Transfer Delay Time." Next, the waiting time in the system is added to the frame to cell delay time to obtain the total frame delay time. The last column in the lower portion of the spreadsheet, which is labeled "Total Delay per 10000 Addresses," shows the frame delay time multiplied by 10,000. This column indicates LAN Emulation delay time attributable to the layer 2 switch. As indicated in Figure 9.10, a maximum delay of approximately 12 seconds could occur under worst-case conditions based upon the prior set of assumptions. Because no two LANE configurations are the same, you will more than likely want to consider varying the frame length, number of stations, and P_1 and P_2 to better reflect your organization's potential or existing use of LANE. When you do so, remember that your assumptions should always result in a probabilistic frame arrival rate less than the cell rate or infinite queues and meaningless results will occur.

While an approximate 12-second delay is not earth shattering, it illustrates the fact that self-healing cannot occur instantaneously under ATM and represents a potential sacrifice to enjoy the fruits of the technology.

In concluding our discussion of LANE, two items deserve mention. First, it should be noted that the LAN Emulation process uses AAL-5, which is the most efficient adaption layer in terms of the use of a 48-byte payload. A second item worth mentioning concerns some limitations of the LANE 1.0 process in addition to the time it takes. Those limitations include the fact that LANE 1.0 only supports a single LES, BUS, and LECS on a single ELAN, which limits its reliability because the failure of one or more servers can result in the entire network becoming inoperative with respect to its address resolution capability. A second major limitation of LANE 1.0 is the fact that it does not distinguish between different types of traffic. Thus, voice could get stuck behind file transfers. Recognizing the preceding problems resulted in the development of LANE 2.0. Under LANE 2.0, multiple LES, BUS, and LECS servers can operate on a single ELAN, increasing reliability and providing redundancy. In addition, LANE 2.0 supports quality of service, to include eight global classes of traffic. This feature enables LANE 2.0 to support constant bit rate (CBR), variable bit rate (VBR), and available bit rate (ABR) traffic in addition to the unspecified bit rate (UBR) traffic supported by LANE 1.0.

Chapter 10
Working with Images

Advances in the graphics capability of personal computers, coupled with low-cost digital cameras, has resulted in a significant increase in the use of image-based applications. From photographs of employees being digitized and incorporated into personnel databases to photographs of automobile accidents with a digital camera being uploaded by insurance agents to the home office, we are witnessing a literal explosion in the use of image-based applications. Because local area networks (LANs) primarily support personal computer-based applications, it should come as no surprise that the transmission of images via LAN media is also increasing. In addition, the explosion in the growth of the World Wide Web has had a considerable effect on the transmission of images on both an inter- and intra-LAN basis.

For LANs connected to the Internet, the "surfing" of Web sites can considerably increase the flow of images on the corporate LAN. Even without connecting the corporate LAN to the Internet, the establishment of corporate Web server-based help desks can result in an increase in the transport of images. Although the use of images a few years ago was basically a curiosity, today they are essentially a necessity.

This chapter focuses attention on techniques to enhance the storage and transmission of images. To obtain an appreciation for the problems associated with the use of images, we will briefly review their storage requirements, as their transmission time is proportional to their storage requirements. Once this is accomplished, we will compare and contrast the effect of transmitting images upon LAN bandwidth to the use of text-based applications. Doing so will provide information that not only explains the bandwidth problems associated with transmitting images on a LAN but, in addition, provides a foundation for discussing techniques you can consider to minimize the effect of images on LAN bandwidth and server storage capacity. The preceding information will form a foundation for examining a variety of techniques that you can consider to enhance the use of images on a LAN while minimizing their effect on other network users.

In concluding this chapter, we focus attention on a very practical problem most organizations will eventually face if they have not already done so. That problem is the selection of an optimal Web server connection rate to the Internet. Because Web pages are graphic intensive and many Internet service providers (ISPs) now bill based upon the level of utilization of circuits used to connect subscribers to the Internet, we also examine the effect of image compression on both the line operating rate and potential cost of the Internet connection.

10.1 Image Basics

Images can be categorized by the manner by in which they are stored, displayed, and manipulated. Images fall into two general categories: raster and vector.

10.1.1 Raster Images

A raster image or perhaps more correctly termed an image stored in a raster format is represented by a series of picture elements or pixels of equal size. The raster format breaks an image into a grid of pixels and records color information for each pixel.

The number of colors that can be represented by each pixel depends on the number of bits used to record each pixel, a term commonly referred to as the "pixel color depth." Because each pixel in a file will have the same color depth, the term is also commonly used as a reference to a file's color representation.

10.1.1.2 Color Depth. A raster image with a color depth of one bit per pixel is restricted to providing a black or white color representation as only two choices are available per bit position. Most raster image formats support more than one bit per pixel, permitting more than one level of color per image. Table 10.1 lists some common bits-per-pixel values supported by popular raster image formats and the corresponding maximum number of colors.

In examining the entries in Table 10.1, several items are worth discussing that may influence the manner by which you use images. First, the capability of many personal computers, to include most PCs manufactured prior to 1994, are limited to displaying a maximum of 256 colors. Second, a

Table 10.1   Maximum Color Support versus Bits-per-Pixel

Bits-per-Pixel	Maximum Number of Colors
1	2
2	4
4	16
8	256
16	32,768
24	16,777,216

color depth of 24 bits is commonly referred to as "true color" as human eyesight cannot normally distinguish colors beyond those supported by a 24-bit color depth. Although a few scanners now support a color depth of 32 bits per pixel, scanning at that color depth could result in a conversion to a lower color depth as some of the more commonly used raster file formats support a lesser number of bits per pixel.

10.1.2 Vector Images

A second category by which images are stored and displayed is based on the use of direct line segments in place of pixels. Those line segments are recorded as mathematical formulas, with the resulting shape referred to as a vector image. Although a vector image is scalable without distortion and normally results in significantly smaller files than raster-based files, vector data cannot reproduce photographic realistic images.

Photographs taken with a digital camera, scanned images, and creative art drawn using a pixel-based "paint" program are examples of raster images. In comparison, a series of algorithms that represent the positioning and placement of lines and arcs created using a computer-aided design (CAD) program would be stored as a vector image. Because employee pictures in personnel files, real estate applications that include photographs of interiors and exteriors of homes, and most World Wide Web pages are based on the use of raster images, the focus of this chapter is also upon this category of graphics representation. In addition, because the data storage requirements of raster-based images can exceed by several orders of magnitude the data storage requirements of vector-based images, it is the former type of image that can be expected to significantly consume LAN bandwidth. Thus, our focus on raster-based images will provide an understanding of where the majority of bandwidth-associated imaging problems arise, as well as enable a description of methods you can consider to alleviate those problems.

10.1.3 Why Images Are a Problem

To understand the data storage problem associated with the use of raster images, let us assume that you have just returned from the store with the results of your latest camera operation and noted a photograph that could be useful for incorporation into a server-based application. Off you go to your friend down the hall who has a scanner connected to his PC.

10.1.3.1 Storage Considerations. Let us assume your friend sets the resolution of his scanner to 300 dots per inch for both horizontal and vertical resolution. If your color photograph measures 3.5 by 5 inches, the scanned image will require 300×300 bits/inch times 17.5 square inches divided by 8 bits/byte for a total of 196,875 bytes of storage, without considering a color depth beyond one bit per pixel. If you selected a 256-color

Table 10.2   Text versus Image Storage

Type of File*	Data Storage (Bytes)
Image with color depth of 1	196,875
Image with color depth of 8	1,575,000
Image with color depth of 24	4,725,000
Screen of text with color depth of 8	4,000

* Image is a 3.5 × 5 inch photograph scanned at 300 × 300 bits/inch.

resolution scan, 8 bits per pixel would be required, while for true color, 24 bits per pixel would be required. Getting out your calculator, your computations would note that the data storage requirements to store the image with a 256-color resolution would be 1,575,000 bytes, while its true color storage would require 4,725,000 bytes. To place the previously described image storage requirements in perspective, consider a full screen of text where each character could be displayed in one of 256 colors. That screen would consist of 80 × 25 characters, for a total of 2000 bytes. Adding one color attribute byte to represent the color depth of each displayed character would result in a requirement to store 4000 bytes. Note that this is almost 1/400 of the data storage required for the previously described 256-color resolution image. Table 10.2 provides a comparison of the data storage requirements of the previously described image at three different color depths to a screen of text.

10.1.3.2 Transmission Delays. Although 10BASE-T Ethernet and Token Ring LANs operate at 10 and 16 Mbps, respectively, in actuality their bandwidth is shared among network users. This means that a network consisting of 200 users having an average of ten percent of its workstations attempting to use the LAN at any particular point in time results in a reduction of the average bandwidth to 10 Mbps/20 or 500 kbps per user on an Ethernet and 16 Mbps/20 or 800 kbps per user on a Token Ring network. Of course, this quick calculation does not consider the effect of collisions on an Ethernet, nor the flow of station management frames on a Token Ring network, which would further reduce the average bandwidth obtainable by each user. This also means that downloading the previously described 256-color image on the Ethernet LAN could require 1.575 Mbytes/500 kbps, or over three seconds. For the true color version of the image, the time would triple as the data storage required for a true color raster image is triple that of a 256-color image.

Although you might be tempted to say "so what" concerning a three- or nine-second delay, as other LAN users begin to work with applications that use images the delays become cumulative. For example, as five users near simultaneously query a visual database to retrieve the previously described 256-color image, the last person to press the Enter key or click on a Windows button could expect to encounter a delay exceeding 15 seconds. Just think what this does for time-sensitive frames, such as SNA data bound for a mainframe where delays of a few seconds can result in session timeouts. Fortunately, there are several methods you can consider to reduce the effect of images upon LAN performance. Some methods, such as LAN segmentation, adding switching hubs and boosting servers to Fast Ethernet, ATM or another high-speed technology, can result in a considerable expenditure of funds and may be ultimately necessary to implement. However, on occasion, there are other possible solutions to the problems resulting from the transportation of images on LANs that can be performed through software and in many instances may not require any additional expenditure of funds. Those possible solutions are based on the fact that scanning software as well as image viewing programs normally support multiple file formats. Some formats are limited to recording the image as is on a pixel-by-pixel basis, while other formats support the use of one or more compression algorithms to reduce the quantity of data prior to its actual storage. Because a good LAN manager or network administrator, like a shopper, likes a bargain, we first examine some of the more popular file formats used to store images, to include their support of different types of compression. Once this is accomplished, we describe and discuss several methods that can be used to adjust images, which reduces their effect on network bandwidth. Note that these methods may not be applicable to some applications, such as medical imaging where every pixel counts. However, for other applications, the loss of a small amount of resolution may be an acceptable trade-off for significantly reducing the storage required for an image as well as decreasing the time required to transport the image on a network. After examining the effect of image formats on storage, we turn our attention to other solutions that can be applicable to reducing the effect of transmitting images on other network users. Those solutions will involve the use of hardware and, as you might surmise, represent more expensive methods for supporting images than software-based solutions.

10.2 Examining Image Formats

Because images were first digitized and stored as files, over 50 formats were developed to standardize their recording and viewing. Table 10.3 provides a summary of the file format extension, file format source, and the support of different color depths for 30 commonly encountered raster images.

10.2.1 Common Formats

Of those images listed in Table 10.3, a core set of five probably represents a large majority of the methods by which images are stored and viewed. Table 10.4 includes a list of five file formats, as well as a more descriptive explanation of each file format than contained in Table 10.3.

Table 10.3 Common Raster Image File Extensions, Sources, and Color Depth Support

File Extension	Source	1	4	8 Gray	8 Color	24
BMP	Microsoft Windows RGB encoded	×	×	×	×	×
BMP	Microsoft Windows RLE encoded	×	×		×	×
BMP	OS/2 RGB encoded	×	×		×	×
CLP	Windows Clipboard	×	×		×	×
CUT	Dr. Italo				×	
DCX	Multiple PCX images		×	×	×	×
GIF	CompuServe	×	×	×	×	
IMG	Gem Paint	×	×		×	
JPG	Joint Picture Experts Group			×		×
MAC	MacPaint	×				
PCD	Kodak Photo CD					×
PCX	ZSoft PaintBrush	×				
PCX	ZSoft PaintBrush Version 2	×	×			
PCX	ZSoft PaintBrush Version 3	×	×			
PCX	ZSoft PaintBrush Version 5	×	×		×	×
PGM	UNIX			×		
PIC	PC Paint	×	×		×	
PCT	QuickDraw Picture			×	×	
RLE	Microsoft Windows		×		×	
TGA	True Vision (Targa)			×	×	×
TIF	Aldus Corp Huffman Compressed	×				
TIF	Aldus Corp No Compression	×	×	×	×	×
TIF	Aldus Corp Packed bits	×	×		×	×
TIF	Aldus Corp LZW compression	×	×	×	×	×
TIF	Aldus Corp G3 compression	×				
TIF	Aldus Corp G4 compression	×				
WMF	Windows Metafile	×	×	×	×	×
WPG	WordPerfect Version 5.0	×	×		×	
WPG	WordPerfect Version 5.1	×	×		×	
WPG	WordPerfect Version 6.x	×	×		×	×

10.2.1.1 BMP. The Microsoft Windows bitmap format (BMP) can store black & white and color images. Because one version of this format does not use any compression, resulting files can be extremely large; however, they provide a mechanism for comparing the storage efficiency of other image formats. An option supported by the BMP image format includes the use of a Run Length Encoding (RLE) compression scheme. Under RLE, repeated runs of pixels are compressed, which can result in a smaller BMP file. Although the use of RLE compression makes you expect that the

Table 10.4   Common Image File Formats

Extension	Description
BMP	The Microsoft Clipboard and file format, which stores images in a bitmap format and optionally supports RLE compression.
GIF	CompuServe's Graphical Interchange Format stores images using a 12-bit Lempel-Ziv Welch (LZW) lossless compression technique.
JPG	The Joint Picture Experts Group (JPEG) standardized the storage of images based on the ability of the user to specify the removal of details via a lossy compression method.
PCX	The ZSoft PaintBrush image format uses a run length limited (RLL) lossless compression method.
TIF	The Tag Image File Format (TIFF) represents a specification for the storage of images that was jointly written by Aldus Corporation and Microsoft. Although the copyright is held by Aldus, the specification is in the public domain. TIFF supports five compression methods — one lossy and four lossless.

resulting compressed image will be smaller than a noncompressed BMP image, this is not always the case. A "noisy" image, which has many translations of color depth, object changes, and other irregularities, may well result in an expansion of storage when compressed using BMP's RLE compression option. This expansion results from characters required to denote the occurrence of compression adding to the size of the file when runs of the same pixel color depth are relatively short.

Because RLE compression is fully reversible, there is no loss of image quality when the compressed data is decompressed by a BMP viewer. The RLE compression method is referred to as lossless compression because all pixels in the original image are restored upon decompression.

10.2.1.2   GIF. The CompuServe Graphical Interchange Format (GIF) represents one of the earliest developed image storage and viewing formats, with the first GIF standard developed in 1987, while a downward compatible standard was developed during 1989. GIF was widely used by electronic bulletin board systems as it was among the first to incorporate data compression, using a 12-bit Lempel Ziv Welch (LZW) technique. The LZW compression technique typically provides a 2:1 to 3:1 reduction in the amount of data storage required to store an image in comparison to storing it in its original bitmapped format.

LZW is one of several string-based compression methods that is fully reversible. That is, the decompression algorithm when applied to a previously compressed file results in the recreation of the original file on a bit-for-bit basis without any loss of data. Due to this, this type of compression is also known as *lossless compression*.

10.2.1.3 JPG. The Joint Picture Experts Group (JPEG) standardized a method of image storage and viewing based upon a series of compression methods. Although the technique is referred to as JPEG, the file extension resulting from an image stored using the JPEG technique is JPG, a carryover from the DOS and non-Windows 95 limitation of a three-character file extension.

JPEG image compression is based on the transformation of 8×8-pixel blocks of a true color image into luminance and chrominance levels. Each block is processed by a two-dimensional discrete cosine transformation to obtain 64 coefficients representing the block. Those coefficients are quantized by predefined tables for luminance and chrominance components, after which information about the block is packed into lower-frequency coefficients. This results in many coefficients being represented by 0's and 1's, which facilitates the compression of data representing the image.

Many imaging programs that support JPEG enable a user storing an image to adjust the quantization tables by defining a quality value. At the default of 75 used by most programs, relatively little picture degradation occurs; however, a significant amount of compression may be obtainable. At lower quality values, slightly better compression results are obtainable but a marked loss of image quality occurs when decompression occurs and the previously compressed image is viewed. Other imaging programs do not permit a user to directly alter the quantization tables by defining a quality value. Instead, they may internally define several quality values and associate those values with the terms "least," "moderate," and "highest" or similar meaning descriptors. Then, selecting a compression level descriptor results in the program using a predefined quality value.

The adjustment of JPEG quantization tables by specifying a quality value using a program compression descriptor, or using a program's default, results in a permanent loss of image details. Thus, the method of compression used by JPEG is referred to as lossy because decompression does not result in the exact reconstruction of the original image. However, while lossless compression is extremely important when working with data files that can include financial information, word processing files, and similar information, a small loss of image quality may not be perceptible to the human eye. Unlike the storage of data files, which must be compressed using a lossless compression method, a degree of lossy compression is typically tolerable when working with most images. The trick when using a lossy compression method is similar to having self-control at an "all-you-can-eat" buffet. That is, do not overindulge, for an excessive amount of lossy compression will result in a bad visual feeling from a distorted image. If you are using an imaging program that directly supports the entry of a quality value, care should be taken when selecting values under 50. At or under a quality value of 50, depending upon the image, you may begin to notice the

8-bit × 8-bit blocks as they begin to become more pronounced due to excessive pixel loss. As we shortly note, you can obtain a significant data reduction through the use of the default quality value of 75, resulting in an image essentially indistinguishable from the original.

10.2.1.4 PCX. The PCX image format was developed for the ZSoft PC PaintBrush image editing program and represents one of the first graphics formats used with the IBM PC and compatible computers. The PCX format is supported by many DOS and Windows based programs and supports color depths ranging from black and white to 24-bit true color.

PCX uses a run length compression method that results in a repetitive sequence of bits being replaced by a repeat count byte and a data byte. Run length compression is a lossless compression method that results in the recreation of an exact duplicate of the original image. The simplicity of the run length compression method results in coding and decoding operations occurring relatively fast; however, this compression method is, in general, inferior to the LZW compression method used in the GIF and supported as one of several compression methods by the TIFF image format described next.

10.2.1.5 TIF. The first Tag Image File Format (TIFF) specification was jointly developed by Aldus, Microsoft, and several scanner manufacturers during 1986 as a mechanism to standardize a file format for images used in desktop publishing. Since then, a number of specification revisions occurred that expanded TIFF support to digital video images and increased the number of compression methods that can be used to reduce image storage requirements.

TIFF supports five compression methods — four lossless and one lossy. Lossless compression methods supported include two types of ITU-T (formerly CCITT) Group 3 and one method of Group 4 compression primarily associated with the use of fax, and LZW compression. A lossy JPEG compression method was added in TIFF specification revision 6.0. A TIFF-compatible file generator program must support at least one compression method, while a reader should be capable of supporting all compression methods. Similar to JPEG, TIFF files are commonly stored using a three-character extension, which explains why the second F is not used.

Although the TIFF specification is supported by a large number of popular programs, there are a large number of options associated with the use of many programs that require some thought prior to clicking on a button or entering a command. Some programs use a default of no compression when TIFF is selected, which as previously discussed, will result in a maximum amount of storage used for the image. Other programs provide support for a large number of patterns that can be used for storing different types of images. Forgetting to set an appropriate compression

Figure 10.1   An 8 × 10-Inch Photograph of the Author's Daughter Stored as a Noncompressed TIF File

method or the selection of an unnecessary pattern can result in a file storage size that warms the heart of a disk drive manufacturer. When placed on a LAN, the noncompressed image can result in a minimum of some degraded performance being experienced by other network users. Adding to unintended effects, in some situations where large images or a large number of images are transmitted, the delays due to their transport can result in session timeouts as well as significantly degraded performance.

To obtain an appreciation of the effect of LAN-based images as well as techniques that can be used to minimize the effect of their storage and transmission requires an image with which to work. Due to the problems of copyright, this author decided not to use a picture of the Brooklyn Bridge, a famous museum, or another object that might be difficult to obtain permission to use. Instead, he used a photograph of his daughter as a basis for reviewing key concepts that will facilitate the use of images on a network.

Figure 10.1 illustrates the scanned image of an approximate 8 × 10-inch photograph of this author's daughter, Jessica Held Vanny. When stored using TIFF without being compressed, the file required 2,494,045 bytes of storage.

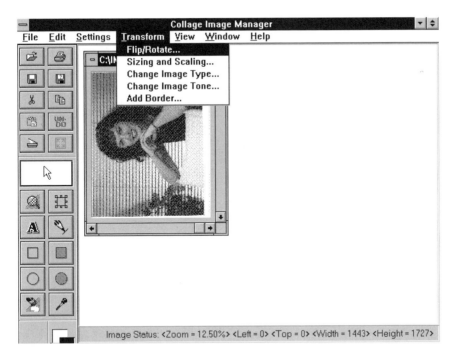

Image Status: <Zoom = 12.50%> <Left = 0> <Top = 0> <Width = 1443> <Height = 1727>

Figure 10.2   Using the Collage Image Manager to Rotate the Retrieved TIF Image 90°

10.2.2   *Comparing Storage Requirements*

To illustrate the differences in data storage resulting from the use of other image formats, the author used the Image Manager program, which is part of the Collage Complete image suite of programs from Inner Media, Inc., of Hollis, New Hampshire. Image Manager supports ten distinct file formats, permitting the original scan to be easily altered from its TIF format without having to rescan the photograph.

Figure 10.2 illustrates the Image Manager main screen after the previously scanned photograph was retrieved through the use of the program's File Open menu option. Because the photograph was scanned along its vertical axis, Figure 10.2 illustrates the initial selection of the program's Flip/Rotate option to reposition the image lengthwise to provide a more conventional view of the image. Figure 10.3 illustrates the result obtained by selecting a 90° clockwise rotation of the image. In the remainder of this chapter, we work with the image illustrated in Figure 10.3, transforming the TIF image format into other popular image formats so we can examine the effect of different formats on data storage requirements and transmission time on a network.

Figure 10.3 The Resulting Rotated Image that Will Form the Basis for Performing Several Image Conversations and Image Manipulation Operations

Figure 10.4 illustrates the Collage Image Manager program's "Save Image As" window with its image format box selected to illustrate the file formats supported by the program. Although the program supports ten distinct image file formats, it actually supports over 20 formats if you consider the fact that several formats include different sub-formats based upon the program's support of one or more compression methods for several formats. Although this author used the Collage Image Manager program to perform his conversions, it should be noted that there are numerous programs that provide this capability. Some programs, such as Paint Shop Pro, can be obtained from many Internet shareware Web sites, requiring the payment of a nominal fee after a typical 30-day trial period. Other programs, such as the Collage Complete suite or the popular Hijack suite, are well-known commercial programs advertised for sale in many trade publications or available for download directly from the vendor's Web site.

10.2.2.1 File Format Comparisons. Table 10.5 summarizes the storage requirements of different image file formats based on their conversion from the original scanned picture that was stored as a noncompressed TIF file. In examining the entries in Table 10.5, it should be noted that each image format was stored as a 256-level, true gray, 8-bit-per-pixel color type.

274

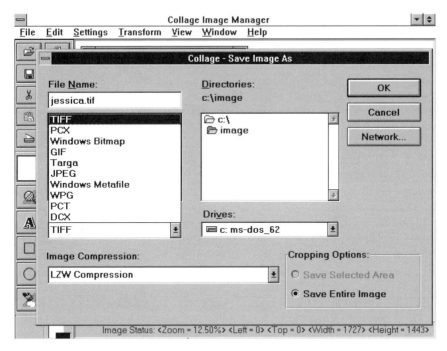

Figure 10.4   Through the Collage Image Manager's "Save Image As" Option You Can Store a File in a Different Format

Table 10.5   Comparing Image Format Storage Requirements

File Format	Description	Data Storage (Bytes)
TIF	TIFF noncompressed	2,494,095
TIF	TIFF LZW-compressed	1,950,970
BMP	Windows Bitmap non-compressed	2,781,122
BMP	Windows Bitmap RLE compression	2,494,582
DCX	Multiple PCX color images — no compression	2,634,995
GIF	CompuServe Graphics Interchange LZW compression	1,803,744
JPG	JPEG Least Compression	1,365,036
JPG	JPEG Moderate Compression	163,888
JPG	JPEG Highest Compression	84,973
PCT	Quick Draw Picture — no compression	2,571,200
PCX	PC PaintBrush — no compression	2,634,591
TGA	Targa — no compression	2,492,079
WMF	Windows Metafile	2,494,670

275

Also note that in comparing the data storage requirements of each image, the presence or absence of compression as well as the type of compression used can have a considerable effect. For example, the noncompressed TIF image required 2,494,095 bytes of storage, while the same image stored using TIF's lossless LZW compression technique required 1,950,970 bytes of storage. Thus, simply changing the TIF file format to support its lossless compression method, which has absolutely no effect on the clarity of the image when it is decoded, results in a (2,494,095 − 1,950,970)/2,494,095 or approximate 22 percent data storage reduction. Because transmission time is usually proportional to the size of a file under normal network operating conditions, you can reduce the transmission time of the image by 22 percent by storing it in a compressed form. As network utilization increases on an Ethernet LAN, the additional effect of collisions will be reduced by transmitting images in their compressed format. In certain situations, a reduction in the file size of an image by 20 percent might well result in a 100 percent or more reduction in the transmission time of an image on a heavily utilized local area network.

10.2.2.2 Examining Visual Image Differences. To illustrate the visual differences between the original image and several converted images, Figures 10.5 through 10.8 represent the printout of four converted image formats.

Figure 10.5 illustrates the display of the GIF image format of the author's daughter. Through the use of the lossless LZW compression technique, the data storage requirement of the file was reduced to approximately 1.8 Mbytes. While less than the noncompressed TIF file, this reduction is significantly more than the storage required when the original TIF image was converted to several types of JPG images which are discussed later in this section. From Table 10.5 you will note that other than the use of JPG file formats, GIF provides the best overall compression performance. Because the use of JPG can result in a considerable data reduction beyond that obtainable from lossless compression techniques, let us focus our attention on the results obtained from converting the original TIF image to JPG using different quality values.

10.2.2.3 Considering JPG. Figures 10.6 through 10.8 illustrate the printout of the image after it was converted to JPG by specifying least, moderate, and highest compression. These three compression descriptors correspond to quality values of 97, 90, and 70, respectively. If you compare Figures 10.6 through 10.8 to the original TIF image in Figure 10.1, focusing on the facial features of each image, you may notice a very slight difference between the JPG and TIF images. The difference becomes slightly more pronounced when comparing Figure 10.8 and Figure 10.1.

In comparing Figures 10.6 through 10.8 to Figure 10.1, it is important to note the application being used. For example, if your network user image

Figure 10.5   Display of the GIF Image Format of the Author's Daughter

operations are oriented to storing pictures of persons or places for a visual database application, a slight degree of image distortion may be an acceptable price to pay for the significant reduction in data storage that becomes obtainable. For our example, the data storage required for Figure 10.8 is 84,973 bytes, which as you will note from Table 10.5 is approximately 1/30th of the data storage required by the noncompressed TIF file shown in Figure 10.1. In comparison, if the images will be used in a desktop publishing application where clarity is of extreme importance, you would more than likely restrict compression to the lossless method. Similarly, when working with medical images, such as a chest x-ray where the loss of even one pixel could result in a misdiagnosis, you should never consider the use of a lossy compression method.

10.2.3 Additional Image Management Operations

Through the use of scanner software or an image management program, you obtain the ability to perform a variety of functions that affect the storage and transmission time of images. In addition to selecting an appropriate file format to include the use of compression, you can consider such

Figure 10.6   A Printout of the Image AFTER Its Conversion to JPG Using the Collage Image Manager's Least Compression Specification

operations as image cropping and color reduction, as well as changing the resolution of a scanned image.

10.2.3.1   Image Cropping. Image cropping provides you with the ability to eliminate unnecessary portions of an image that obviously reduces its storage requirements. To illustrate the effect of cropping, the compressed TIF and moderate compression JPG images were cropped. Figure 10.9 illustrates the cropped TIF image while Figure 10.10 illustrates the cropped JPG image. In comparing the cropped images to the original size images, you will note that the background eliminated is more than likely unnecessary if the image is to be stored on a photo-ID database used to provide guards with pictures of employees or for similar applications. The author's cropping effort reduced the TIF file to 1,156,975 bytes while the moderately compressed JPG file was reduced to 98,153 bytes of storage.

10.2.3.2   Color Reduction. Concerning color reduction, there are several questions persons working with images should be asked. First, do they

Figure 10.7   Printout of the File Stored Using Moderate JPG Compression

really require a true-color 24- or 32-bits-per-pixel image for applications that never see a printed page? For example, does it make sense to scan photographs of employees using a 24-bit-per-pixel color depth? Perhaps 256-color (8 bits per pixel) or even a 16-level true gray using 4 bits per pixel might be sufficient. In fact, once an image is placed on a server, you might wish to review its color depth with respect to its application through the use of an image management program. For example, returning to the Collage Image Manager program, Figure 10.11 illustrates the selection of the program's Change Image Type option window that was displayed by selecting the option from the program's Transform menu. In Figure 10.11 the NewType list was selected to provide readers with a visual indication of the color depth types supported by the program for TIF formatted files. Many times, you can significantly reduce the storage requirements of an image by changing its color depth.

Now that we have an appreciation for software-based techniques we can consider for altering the storage requirements and network transmission time of images, let us turn our attention to hardware-based techniques.

Figure 10.8   Printout of the File Stored Using the Highest JPG Compression Supported by the Collage Image Manager Program

10.3   Hardware Considerations

There are several hardware-based techniques you can consider to minimize the effect of images on LAN performance. Those techniques include LAN segmentation, upgrading LAN adapter cards to obtain a higher throughput for servers storing images, upgrading your LAN infrastructure to a new and higher bandwidth capable network, and using LAN switches. Because the use of LAN switches is the focus of Chapter 11, we focus our attention on the first three hardware-based techniques in the remainder of this chapter.

10.3.1   LAN Segmentation

A simple subdivision of a LAN into two or more segments connected by bridges may create more problems than it solves when working with images. To understand why this situation can occur, consider Figure 10.12, which shows two LAN segments interconnected through the use of a bridge, with one segment connected to a gateway that provides access to a mainframe for users connected to both network segments.

Figure 10.9   Cropped TIF File Using LZW Compression (Requires 1,156,975 Bytes of Storage)

If a user on either segment accesses an image application on server B, the transmission of the image can adversely affect users on both segments. In addition, depending on the size of the image and other user activity occurring on segment B, the additional bandwidth used by the image could delay an in-progress mainframe session to the point where it times out. If you can segregate images to server A and have a minimal number of users on segment B requiring access to server A, you can reduce and possibly eliminate the possibility of session timeouts. If you can place all users requiring access to image-based applications on one segment and inter-LAN traffic is primarily time-insensitive electronic mail, you could minimize the effect of image applications on segment B users. However, because many if

Figure 10.10   Cropped Moderately Compressed JPG File (Data Storage Reduced to 98,153 Bytes)

not most LAN users typically require access to a mixture of applications, it may not be possible to perform the previously mentioned segmentation. Instead, you may have to consider an alternative hardware approach, such as upgrading LAN adapter cards, upgrading your LAN infrastructure, or acquiring LAN switches.

10.3.2 Upgrading Adapter Cards

One of the key bottlenecks hindering network performance is the adapter card used in workstations and servers. For example, the data transfer capability of 10BASE-T Ethernet network interface cards (NICs) can easily

Figure 10.11   Collage Image Manager Change Image Type Window

vary from 300,000 bytes/sec to over 600,000 bytes/sec. If you do not know the transfer rate of your adapter, you can consider running a predefined test. To do so you should create a large file on your network server and download it to a workstation when you are the only user on the network. By clocking the transfer time and using that time as a divisor to the file size transferred, you can obtain a viable estimate of the NIC's maximum transfer rate. Then, if that rate appears low in comparison to the capability of other NICs, you should consider replacing server and workstation NICs for users who work with images. Because the replacement of NICs is significantly less costly than other hardware alternatives, you might consider placing this option at the top of your hardware list. Readers are referred to Section 6 in Chapter 13 for additional information concerning the performance of network adapter cards.

10.3.3   *Upgrading the LAN Infrastructure*

Although the title of this section can be considered applicable to the previous sections in this chapter, the author is using it here in the context of

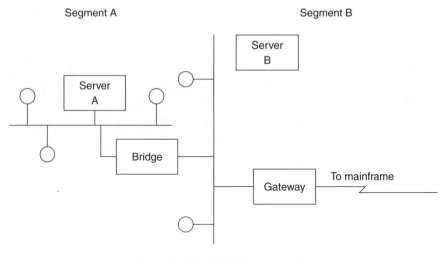

Figure 10.12   LAN Segmentation

upgrading an existing LAN infrastructure to a new and higher bandwidth capable network. This hardware solution might involve replacing a 10BASE-T network by a 100BASE-T, or a Token Ring network by an ATM network and obviously represents the most costly method for handling images. In fact, due to the cost associated with upgrading an entire existing LAN, it should normally be considered as a last resort, with the use of intelligent switching hubs normally providing a more economical method to support the effect of images being transported on LANs. Thus, readers are referred to Chapter 11 for detailed information concerning the operation and utilization of intelligent switches.

10.4   Web Server Considerations

During the past few years, the number of Web servers connected to the Internet has increased at an almost hyper-exponential growth rate. From a few thousand servers in 1995, the number of servers connected to the Internet is estimated to exceed several million as we enter the new millennium. Along with this increase in the employment of Web servers to provide corporations, academic, and government agencies with a presence on the Web is a pair of interrelated problems that result from the use of images. One problem is determining an appropriate WAN connection rate to the Internet from the LAN on which the server resides. A second problem involves examining and, when practical, altering Web page images to reduce the quantity of transmission to improve performance. As a side benefit, this action will decrease the cost of communications if your ISP bill is based on the level of utilization of the transmission facility connecting

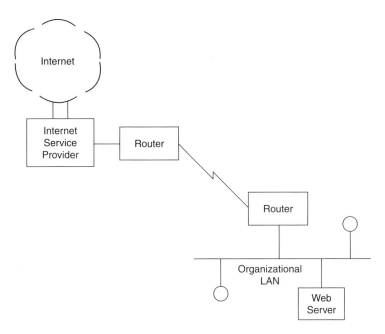

Figure 10.13   A Typical Web Server–Internet Connection

your organization's Web server to the Internet. In this section we examine both problems as well as methods to resolve those problems.

10.4.1 Determining a WAN Connection Rate

The selection of an appropriate WAN operating rate to connect your organization's Web server to the Internet can be considered to represent a double-edged sword, requiring a high degree of caution. To illustrate the problems associated with the selection of an appropriate WAN operating rate, consider Figure 10.13, which illustrates the manner by which most servers are connected to the Internet. In this example, a router attached to the organizational LAN on which the Web server resides is connected via leased line to a router at the ISP. If the WAN operating rate is too slow, your organization may lose visitors who, after attempting to access your site, simply give up and go elsewhere, or worse yet, forego a purchase if your site provides online sales. At the other extreme, let us assume you selected a WAN operating rate that greatly exceeds actual traffic requirements. In this situation, your organization will more than likely wind up paying for unused and perhaps unnecessary transmission capacity month after month. Thus, a methodology is required that can eliminate a degree of guessing that takes place when many organization attempt to select a Web server WAN connection rate.

**Table 10.6   Variables to Consider When
Selecting a Web Server WAN Connection Rate**

- Web server page structure
  - Use of text and graphics
  - Storage requirements per page
- Web page relationships
  - Estimated frequency of access per visit
- Information content and audience
- Expected hits during busy hour
- Other LAN connectivity requirements
  - Workstations
  - Servers

10.4.1.1   Variables to Consider. There are a number of variables you should consider when selecting a Web server WAN connection rate. Some variables can be easily quantified; however, as we will shortly note, other variables may require a degree of estimation.

Table 10.6 lists the major variables you should consider as input to a decision process concerning determining an appropriate Web server connection rate to the Internet. By discussing each of the entries in Table 10.6, we can obtain an appreciation for the use of these variables in the WAN operating rate selection process. Thus, let us examine each of the variables listed in Table 10.6 and how we might apply information about those variables to the WAN operating rate selection process.

10.4.1.1.1   Web Page Structure. The Web page structure variable is concerned with the relationship between the use of text and graphics on each page on your server. In examining the use of text and graphics, you should attempt to determine the storage requirements per Web page. In doing so, it is important to note that each object referenced on a stored page, such as a GIF or JPG image, is stored as a separate file. Thus, if a Web page contains nine icons, you must locate the size of nine images and add their cumulative storage to the storage of the Web page holding the text of the page.

10.4.1.1.2   Web Page Relationships. A second variable that warrants consideration is the relationship of Web pages to one another and an estimate of the frequency or probability of access per Web page per site visit. This means you should review how a Web surfer or customer might access your organization's home page and then jump to other pages on your server. In doing so, you would estimate how many times a user accessing the home page would access other pages. For example, if you believe a page would be accessed once by every three persons visiting your site, the page would have a probability of access of 0.33.

10.4.1.1.3   Information Content and Audience. You should examine the information content of your organization's Web server and its audience as this will probably provide you with an indication of its anticipated popularity. In doing so, you may wish to check with your marketing and public relations department to ascertain if there are any promotions or advertising planned that could affect Web server access and, if so, how access might be affected.

10.4.1.1.4 Determining Expected Hits. To correctly size the WAN transmission facility, you must consider the number of hits to your server during its peak or busy-hour period. If your organization does not already operate a server from which you can extrapolate such information, you may be able to use the information content, audience, and advertising and promotion information to query your ISP on page hits to other servers they support that appear to be similar in scope to your organization's planned server.

10.4.1.1.5 Other LAN Connectivity Requirements. If the Web server is not the only device on the LAN, you should consider the effect of other devices on the WAN operating rate. For example, if there are workstations or other servers on the LAN, their WAN transmission requirements must be considered. Now that we have an appreciation for the scope of the variables we should consider, let us turn our attention to the estimation process.

10.4.1.2 Estimating the WAN Operating Rate. There are six specific steps you should consider when attempting to estimate an appropriate operating rate to connect your organization's server to the Internet. Those steps are summarized in Table 10.7, where the sixth step, while not necessary for determining the WAN operating rate, is important to perform as it will indicate if the operating rate can be used to its full extent. To illustrate the use of the steps presented in Table 10.7, let us assume your organizational server will have a home page and three "order" pages, with each order page under the home page. Let us further assume that the home page contains 100 Kbytes of images and text, while each order page contains 25 K-bytes of text and images. Thus, these assumptions would result in completing the first step listed in Table 10.7.

Table 10.7   Steps in the WAN Operating Rate Estimation Process

1. Determine Web page storage, to include graphics and text.
2. Estimate probability of access per Web page.
3. Estimate average Web page storage based on items 1 and 2.
4. Estimate number of hits during the busy hour.
5. Multiply expected hits during busy hour by average storage for typical page. Add 15 percent for communications overhead and divide by 3600 seconds per hour to compute operating rate in bps.
6. Examine the LAN to determine if the server can use the LAN to keep up with the rate determined in step 5.

The second step in the WAN operating rate estimation process involves assigning a probability of access per Web page. Let us assume that for every hit on the home page, an order page will receive 0.3 hits. While 0.3 times the 3 order pages only equals 0.9, in this situation we are assuming that 10 percent of traffic to the home page will result in a browser operating decision that they either arrived by mistake, decided the product is not what they want after reading the home page, or decide upon another reason not to proceed further.

Under step 3 we want to estimate the average Web page storage based upon their retrieval. Thus, using the preceding assumptions, we obtain:

$$\frac{100 \text{ KB} \times 1 + 25 \text{ KB} \times .3 + 25 \text{ KB} \times .3 + 25 \text{ KB} \times .3}{1.9} = 64.47 \text{ KB}$$

Next, we need to estimate the number of hits expected during the busy hour. As previously mentioned, we can contact our ISP to obtain an estimate based upon the type of site content we plan to place on the server, contact our organization's marketing and PR departments, or extrapolate figures from usage on a different server. Let us assume that we determined that during the busy-hour we can expect 3000 hits on the server.

Moving on to step 5, we would first multiply 64.47 KB by 3000 hits per busy-hour and then add 15 percent for protocol overhead. Next, we would multiply the result by 8 bits/byte and divide the number by 3600 seconds in an hour to determine the data rate in bits per second (bps). Thus, we would compute the following:

$$\frac{64.47 \text{ KB/hour} * 1024 \text{ bytes/k} * 3000 \text{ hits} * 1.15 * 8 \text{ bits/byte}}{3600 \text{ sec/hour}} = 506,133 \text{ bps}$$

Based on the preceding computation, we would be inclined to order a 512-Kbps fractional T1 line to connect our server to the Internet. However, prior to doing so we should perform step 6, which involves examining the LAN to determine if it can support a data transfer of 506,133 bps from the server to the router for transmission to the Internet. To accomplish step 6, you would place a protocol analyzer on the existing LAN to determine the average frame length and frame rate on the network prior to providing Internet access. Suppose the existing frame rate is 620 frames per second and the average frame length is 120 bytes. Then, 620 frames/second * 120 bytes/frame * 8 bits/byte results in a data rate of 595,200 bps on the LAN. Obviously, an additional 506,133-bps transmission flowing from the server to the router via the LAN will not bring the LAN to saturation and the network can support the added transmission to the router.

10.4.2 *Images and Network Charges*

In concluding this chapter we turn our attention to the effect of images on the cost of an Internet connection. Let us assume that your Internet service provider bills for a corporate Internet connection based upon the operating rate of the leased line and its level of utilization, a billing technique many ISPs are beginning to employ. Let us further assume that the monthly charge of your ISP for a T1 line is $750 per month plus $0.01 per Mbyte of data transmitted onto the Internet.

To illustrate the potential effect of Web page images on network charges, let us assume that your organization's home page contains a picture in JPEG format of your firm's building, your CEO, or another object that results in 100,000 bytes being downloaded each time a person accesses your home page. If you import the picture into an image manipulation program and change its quality value slightly lower, you more than likely can reduce the size of the file by at least 20 percent, or 20,000 bytes, without adversely affecting its visual appeal. If your organization's Web site home page is accessed 15,000 times per week, this one simple action would reduce the quantity of data transmitted to the Internet by 20,000 bytes * 15,000, or 300 Mbytes per week. Over a four-week period, this results in the elimination of 1.2 Gbytes of traffic. At a cost of $0.10 per Mbyte, you just saved your organization $12 per month, or $144 on an annual basis for a few minutes of effort. If you continue your examination of other pages on your Web server and perform similar operations, it becomes possible to save several thousand dollars or more for a lightly utilized server, and possibly tens of thousands of dollars per year for a heavily utilized server by adjusting the quality scale of JPEG images, converting images into better formats with respect to their data storage requirements, or simply cropping images. Thus, images matter, especially when you have to pay for their transmission.

Chapter 11
Using Intelligent Switches

The expansion of local area networks (LANs), both in terms of the number of network users supported as well as in the number and type of applications they use, typically results in a considerable increase in the use of network bandwidth. This, in turn, can result in the occurrence of a variety of problems. Those problems can range from sluggish network performance being experienced by workstation users that marginally affects their productivity to the occurrence of session timeouts that terminate network-related work in progress, forcing users to redo previously performed operations or precluding users from performing certain types of network related activity.

Until the early 1990s the primary method employed to overcome the effect of network congestion was segmentation, subdividing a network into two or more entities interconnected by a bridge or router. Today, the network manager and LAN administrator have several options, to include the use of a higher operating rate network such as Fast Ethernet, Gigabit Ethernet, or ATM, or the use of intelligent switches. This chapter focuses attention on the latter, which are also referred to as switching hubs.

To obtain an appreciation for the role of intelligent switches, we first review the operation of conventional hubs, to include the bandwidth constraints associated with their use. Once this is accomplished, we focus our attention on the different operational methods supported by intelligent layer 2 switching hubs, to include the basic switching methods supported by different products that fall into this class of networking device. Using this information as a foundation we then explore the use of both Ethernet and Token Ring intelligent switching hubs, to include obtaining an understanding of the key features built into many products as well as why the presence of some features and the absence of other features can result in degraded performance instead of an expected improvement in performance. Due to this, we examine how the use of certain intelligent layer 2 switch features can result in network problems and how those problems can be alleviated through the use of other device features. Because we will obtain a detailed understanding of the operational effect of a comprehensive set of intelligent switching hub features, the information presented in this chapter can also be used as a guide for the evaluation of switching hubs.

With technological developments extending intelligent switching operations to higher layers in the OSI Reference Model, it is important to note the capabilities of these "upper layer" switches. Although their use does not directly affect performance on individual LANs, their use can significantly affect the flow of traffic between LANs. Due to this, we conclude this chapter by focusing our attention on layer 3 and layer 4 switches.

11.1 Conventional Hub Bottlenecks

This section examines why conventional hubs, which were developed to facilitate the cabling of network devices, also function as a bottleneck with respect to the use of network bandwidth. In doing so, we will discuss the operation of both Ethernet and Token Ring hubs, with the latter primarily referred to as a multistation access unit (MAU).

11.1.1 Ethernet Hub Operation

In an Ethernet environment, a single LAN is usually referred to as a segment, with large networks typically composed of multiple segments connected by a bridge or router. The early implementations of Ethernet in the form of 10BASE-5 and 10BASE-2 coaxial cable-based networks resulted in the use of a common medium to which workstations are attached. This is illustrated in Figure 11.1, which shows the cabling structure of a coaxial-based Ethernet network.

Based on the fact that the bandwidth of the media is shared with only one user able to transmit at any given time, the Ethernet LAN segment shown in Figure 11.1 is commonly referred to as a shared-media, shared-bandwidth network.

A change in the network topology and cabling structure of Ethernet resulted in the development of hub-centric 10BASE-T networks, in which

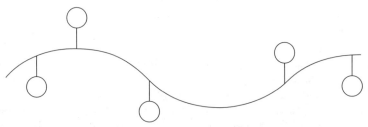

10BASE-5 and 10BASE-2 Ethernet networks consist of a coaxial run to which network devices are attached.

Figure 11.1   A Shared Media, Shared Bandwidth Ethernet LAN Segment

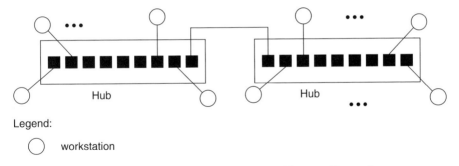

Figure 11.2   A Two-Hub 10BASE-T Ethernet Network

cabling from individual network devices to dedicated ports on the hub resulted in a star-wiring configuration. When two or more hubs are interconnected to a common network, the wiring topology resembles a star-bus structure as illustrated in Figure 11.2. Although the wiring topology changed, the use of hubs did not alter the fact that the network remained a shared-media, shared-bandwidth network.

To illustrate the problem associated with the use of a shared-media, shared-bandwidth network, let us examine the operation of a conventional Ethernet hub. This type of hub simply duplicates nodes attached to the hub. Figure 11.3 illustrates the data flow when one workstation (node 1) transmits a frame to another workstation, file server, gateway, or another network device that is either connected to the same hub or to another hub that is connected to the hub to which the data originator is connected. Because the hub functions as a data regenerator, the frame is repeated onto each connection to the hub to include interconnections to other hubs. This restricts dataflow to one workstation at a time, because

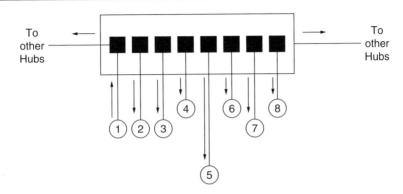

Figure 11.3   Conventional Hub Dataflow

293

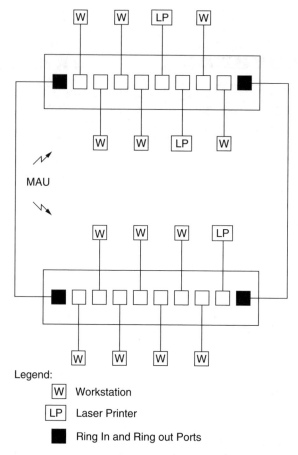

Legend:

[W] Workstation

[LP] Laser Printer

■ Ring In and Ring out Ports

Figure 11.4   The Connection of Token Ring MAUs Forms a Star-Ring Topology

collisions occur when two or more attempts to gain access to the media happen at the same time.

11.1.2 Token Ring Hub Operation

Although dataflow on a Token Ring network is circular, this type of network is also a shared-media, shared-bandwidth network. In a Token Ring network environment, hubs, referred to as multistation access units (MAUs), are connected via their Ring In and Ring Out ports to form a star-ring topology similar to that shown in Figure 11.4. The actual dataflow of a frame is from one device to the next, to include flowing down the cable, called a lobe, connecting the device to the MAU port, to an attached device and back to the port prior to flowing to the next port. Because only one frame can flow on the network at any point in time, access to the bandwidth is also shared. Thus, a Token Ring network also represents a shared-media, shared-bandwidth network.

11.1.3 Bottleneck Creation

Conventional Ethernet hubs create network bottlenecks because all traffic flows through a shared backplane in the hub. Thus, each device connected to an Ethernet hub competes for a slice of the bandwidth of the backplane. In a Token Ring environment, devices compete to acquire a token, resulting in the sharing of network bandwidth in a similar manner. The end result of this bandwidth sharing is an average transmission rate per device that is many times below the operating rate of the network. For example, consider a departmental 10BASE-T network operating at 10 Mbps and consisting of 12 interconnected eight-port hubs that supports a total of 96 devices. Then, the average slice of bandwidth available for each device is 10 Mbps/96, or approximately 104 Kbps. Note that although each device transmits and receives data at the LAN operating rate of 10 Mbps, their average data transfer capability is approximately 104 Kbps because each device must compete with 95 other devices to obtain access to the network. Similarly, a 96-node Token Ring network would result in each device attached to that network having an average data transfer capability of 4 Mbps/96 or 16 Mbps/96, depending on the operating rate of the network. This means that over a period of time, the addition of network users, the introduction of one or more graphic-based applications, or growth in the use of current applications can result in a severely taxed network. When this type of situation occurs, you can consider a variety of techniques to enhance network performance. Those techniques can include network segmentation through the use of a bridge or router, migrating your existing infrastructure to a different and higher operating rate technology, or employing intelligent switching hubs, which is the focus of this chapter.

11.2 Switching Operations

The development of intelligent switching hubs has its foundation, similar to many other areas of modern communications, in telephone technology. Shortly after the telephone was invented, the switchboard was developed to enable multiple simultaneous conversations to occur without requiring telephone wires to be installed in a complex matrix between subscribers. Later, telephone office switches were developed to route calls based upon the telephone number dialed, followed in a similar manner by the development of bridges in a LAN environment. Bridges can be considered to represent an elementary type of switch due to their limited number of ports and simplistic switching operation. That switching operation is based upon whether or not the destination address in a frame "read" on one port is known to reside on that port.

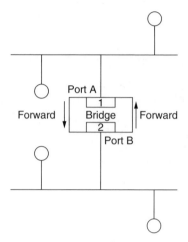

Port A operation:

1. Read source address of frames on LAN A to construct a table of source addresses associated with port 1.
2. Read destination address in frames and compare to addresses in source address table.
3. If address in table, output frame onto port associated with address.
4. If address not in table, flood frame.

Port B operation:

1. Read source address of frames on LAN B to construct a table of source addresses associated with port 2.
2. Read destination address in frames and compare to addresses in source and address table.
3. If address in table, output frame onto port associated with address.
4. If address not in table, flood frame.

Figure 11.5   Bridge Switching Operation

11.2.1 Bridge Switching

Figure 11.5 illustrates the basic operation of a bridge. If you compare the operations performed by a bridge with respect to each port, you will note they are nearly identical. The only difference concerns the port they forward frames to when the destination address of a frame is compared to a table of source addresses and no match occurs. When this situation occurs, the frame's destination is unknown. Thus, the bridge transmits copies of the frame onto all ports other than the port it was received on, a process referred to as flooding. If n networks are connected in serial via the use of n – 1 bridges, and a frame is transmitted on the network at one end of the interconnected group of networks to the network on the opposite end of the interconnected group of LANs, each bridge would perform a similar forwarding operation until the frame traversed n bridges and was placed onto the last network in the interconnected series. The simplicity associated with the operation of bridges makes them a popular networking device. However, most bridges are limited to forwarding or "switching" frames on a serial basis, from one port to another. This restricts the forwarding rate to the lowest network operating rate. For example, the connection of a 10-Mbps Ethernet network to a 16-Mbps Token Ring network via the use of a local bridge would reduce inter-network communications to a maximum operating rate of 10 Mbps, creating another network bottleneck.

11.2.2 The Layer 2 LAN Switch

Recognizing the limitations associated with the operation of bridges, vendors incorporated parallel switching technology into a device known as an intelligent switching hub. This device was based on matrix switches, which for decades have been successfully employed in telecommunications operations. By adding buffer memory to stored address tables, frames flowing on LANs connected to different ports could be simultaneously read and forwarded via the switch fabric to ports connected to other networks. Because the first series of devices operate based on layer 2 MAC addresses, they are commonly referred to as layer 2 switches.

11.2.2.1 Basic Components. Figure 11.6 illustrates the basic components of a four-port intelligent switch. Similar to a bridge that reads frames flowing on a network to construct a table of source addresses, the tables in an intelligent switch are normally learned by examining traffic flow. This allows the destination address to be compared to a table of destination addresses and associated port numbers. When a match occurs between

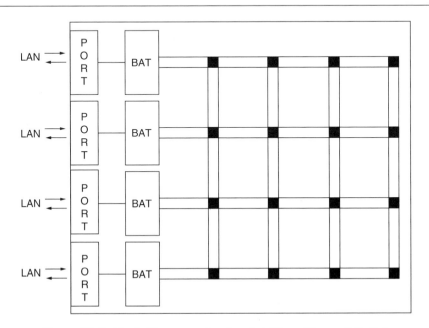

Figure 11.6   Basic Components of an Intelligent Layer 2 Switch

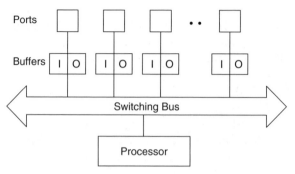

Ports

Buffers

Switching Bus

Processor

A shared-bus based switch passes all frames over a common bus, enabling all frames to be observed and enabling
statistics to be developed.

Figure 11.7   Shared Bus Switch

the destination address of a frame flowing on a network connected to a
port and the address in the port's address table, the frame is copied into
the switch. Then, the frame is routed through the switch fabric to the
destination port, where it is placed onto the network connected to that
port. If the destination port is in use due to a previously established
cross-connection between ports, the frame is maintained in the buffer until
it can be switched to its destination.

11.2.2.2 Switch Architecture. There are three common designs used to
develop different types of LAN switches, to include layer 2 devices. Those
designs that represent the architecture or switching method of the switch
include shared bus, shared memory, and crossbar.

11.2.2.2.1 Shared Bus. The shared bus switch architecture represents a
simple and cost-effective LAN switch design method. In this design,
illustrated in Figure 11.7, frames from each port are buffered while the
destination address is read. Frames are then output onto the bus with a
special header indicating the destination port. Each frame then flows into
an output buffer associated with the destination port and then out through
the port. The processor can represent a Reduced Instruction Set (RISC)
CPU or may be implemented via hardware. Some switches use the processor
to collect and maintain switch statistics as well as process frames. Other
switches simply use the processor to examine and forward frames.

While a shared bus architecture is relatively simple to implement, it is
not easily scalable. That is, at some operating rate, the hub reaches its
limit. Most shared bus switches are limited in the number of ports they can
support or port modules that can be added to the switch. While this switch
architecture is suitable for switching a limited number of 10- and 100-Mbps

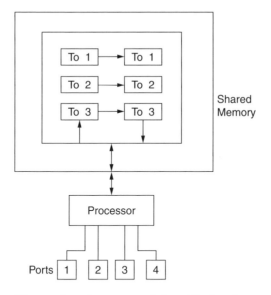

When a shared memory switch architecture is used, frames are placed into predefined locations in memory based upon their destination and extracted from those locations for delivery to the appropriate port.

Figure 11.8   Shared Memory Switch Architecture

---

ports, it is normally not used for Gigabit Ethernet and is commonly relegated to low-bandwidth applications. This is due to the fact that an input can be blocked from sending data if any other transaction is occurring on the bus.

11.2.2.2.2   Shared Memory. A second common switch design uses predefined areas of memory as buffer pools to place incoming frames and extract frames for output to specific ports. This type of switch design is referred to as a shared memory switch.

Figure 11.8 illustrates an example of a shared memory switch architecture. As frames flow into the switch, the destination address is read to determine the appropriate output port. After that information is obtained, the frame is placed into a buffer in a common memory area with the exact location corresponding to the destination port. A flag is set that informs an extraction process to extract the frame and send it to its destination.

Similar to a shared bus architecture, a shared memory design has limited scalability. That is, for the switch to run at full utilization, memory I/O capacity must occur at at least twice the sum of all individual port capacities.

Because memory has significantly declined in price, many switch vendors implemented a shared buffer memory design.

A variation of a shared memory design architecture is a multi-port shared memory design. Under this architecture, simultaneous memory access becomes possible for each or for several outputs, resulting in multiple paths between the processor and shared memory shown in Figure 11.8. However, because all data must pass through shared RAM, the maximum bandwidth becomes a function of the shared RAM data bus width and access time, making it both expensive and difficult to implement for switching beyond 20 Gbps.

11.2.2.2.3 Crossbar. A third switch design provides a route from each input port to each output port via the use of a matrix of switching elements. This type of switch design is referred to as a crossbar switch and resembles the matrix shown in Figure 11.6. As the destination address is read, the switch process sets up a cross-connection between input and output ports through the crossbar. Although a crossbar switch is more complex to design, its capacity can be scaled upward through the use of additional switching elements if the basic design permits expandability. Another benefit of a crossbar switch is the fact that it can support an extremely high rate of data transfer, making the design suitable for supporting Gigabit Ethernet beyond a limited number of ports.

11.2.2.3 Delay Times. Switching occurs on a frame-by-frame basis, with the cross-connection torn down after being established for routing one frame. Thus, frames can be interleaved from two or more ports to a common destination port with a minimum of delay. For example, consider a maximum-length Ethernet frame of 1526 bytes, to include a 1500-byte data field and 26 overhead bytes. At a 10-Mbps operating rate, each bit time is $1/10^7$ seconds, or 100 ns. For a 1526-byte frame, the minimum delay time if one frame precedes it in attempting to be routed to a common destination becomes:

$$1526 \text{ bytes} \times \frac{8 \text{ bits}}{\text{byte}} \times \frac{100 \text{ ns}}{\text{bit}} = 1.22 \text{ ms}$$

This computed delay time represents blocking resulting from frames on two service ports having a common destination and should not be confused with another delay time referred to as latency. Latency represents the delay associated with the physical transfer of a frame from one port via the switch to another port and is fixed based upon the architecture of the switch. In comparison, blocking delay depends on the number of frames from different ports attempting to access a common destination port and the method by which the switch is designed to respond to blocking. Some switches simply have large buffers for each port and service ports in a round-robin fashion when frames on two or more ports attempt to access a common destination port. This method of service is not similar to politics as it does not show favoritism; however, it also does not consider the fact that some attached networks may have operating rates different from other attached networks. Other switch designs recognize that port buffers are filled based upon both the number of frames having a destination address of a different network and the operating rate of the network. Such switch designs use a priority service scheme based on the occupancy of the port buffers in the switch.

11.2.2.4 Key Advantages of Use. A key advantage associated with the use of intelligent switching hubs results from their ability to support parallel switching, permitting multiple cross-connections between source and destination to occur simultaneously. Although shared bus and shared memory architectures only permit one frame at a time to be switched, the high operating rate of the switch in comparison to 10BASE-T or 100BASE-T operating rates of connected LAN devices can make it appear that simultaneous cross-connections are occurring although such cross connections occur one at a time. For example, a 100 MHz bus operates ten times faster than the sustained frame rate on a 10BASE-T network. Thus, a shared bus or shared memory switch can first read frames into buffers from two or more ports at 10 Mbps and operate on those frames internally at a much higher rate. Because a crossbar switch can support multiple simultaneous cross-connections between source and destination ports, it can support true parallel switching.

For example, if four 10BASE-T networks are connected to the four-port switch shown in Figure 11.6, two simultaneous cross-connections (each at 10 Mbps) could occur, resulting in an increase in bandwidth to 20 Mbps. Here, each cross-connection represents a dedicated 10-Mbps bandwidth for the duration of a frame. Thus, from a theoretical perspective, an N-port switching hub supporting a 10-Mbps operating rate on each port provides a throughput up to $N/2 * 10$ Mbps. For example, a 128-port switching hub would support a throughput up to $(128/2) * 10$ Mbps, or 640 Mbps. In comparison, a network constructed using a series of conventional hubs connected to one another would be limited to an operating rate of 10 Mbps, with each workstation on that network having an average bandwidth of 10 Mbps/128, or 78 Kbps.

11.2.2.5 Considering Connected Devices. One area many network managers and LAN administrators fail to consider when evaluating the bandwidth capacity of switches is the devices they will interconnect. For example, consider a 24-port switch in which each port operates at 100 Mbps. Let us assume that the switch will connect 20 workstations, three servers, and a router, with the latter connected to the Internet. What is the minimum backplane capacity of the switch required to prevent blocking?

Normally, if each port could communicate with another port other than itself, you can expect a maximum of 12 simultaneous cross-connections, each occurring at 100 Mbps. Thus, you might be tempted to require a backplane speed of 1.2 Gbps. However, in a client/server operational environment, your switch has 20 workstations communicating with three servers and a router, resulting in a maximum of four simultaneous cross-connections. Thus, by considering the devices to be connected to the switch, the minimum backplane speed required to prevent blocking is 400 Mbps, and not 1.2 Gbps!

Through the use of intelligent switches you can overcome the operating rate limitation of a LAN. In an Ethernet environment, the cross-connection through a switch represents a dedicated connection so there will never be a collision. This fact has enabled many switch vendors to use the collision wire-pair from conventional Ethernet to support simultaneous transmission in both directions between a connected node and switch port, resulting in a full-duplex transmission capability that will be discussed in more detail later in this chapter. In fact, a similar development permits a Token Ring switch to provide full-duplex transmission because, if there is only one station on a port, there is no need to pass tokens and repeat frames, thus raising the maximum bi-directional throughput between a Token Ring device and a switch port to 32 Mbps. Thus, the ability to support parallel switching as well as initiate dedicated cross-connections on a frame-by-frame basis can be considered the key advantages associated with the use of switches. Both parallel switching and dedicated cross-connections permit higher-bandwidth operations.

Now that we have an appreciation for the general operation of LAN switches, let us focus our attention on the different switching techniques that can be incorporated into this category of communications equipment.

11.2.3 Switching Techniques

Three switching techniques used by layer 2 LAN switches include (1) crosspoint, also referred to as cut-through or "on-the-fly;" (2) store-and-forward; and (3) a hybrid method that alternates between the first two methods based upon the frame error rate. As we will soon note, each technique has one or more advantages and disadvantages associated with its operation.

11.2.3.1 **Cross-Point Switching.** The operation of a cross-point switch is based on an examination of the destination of frames as they enter a port on the device. The switch uses the destination address as a decision criterion to obtain a port destination from a lookup table. Once a port destination is obtained, a cross-connection through the switch is initiated, resulting in the frame being routed to a destination port where it is placed onto a network for which its frame destination address resides. In actuality, there are usually two lookup tables in a switch. The first table, which is usually constructed dynamically, consists of source addresses of frames flowing on the network connected to the port. This enables the switch to construct a table of known devices. Then, the first comparison using the destination address in a frame is with the table of known source addresses. If the destination address matches an address in the table of known source addresses, this indicates that the frame's destination is on the current network and no switching operation is required. If the frame's destination address does not match an address in the table of known source addresses, this indicates that the frame is to be routed through the switch onto a different network. Then the switch will search a destination lookup table to obtain a port destination and initiate a cross-connection through the switch, routing the frame to a destination port where it is placed onto a network where a node with the indicated destination address resides.

Some switches use a single lookup table, with the destination address of each frame compared to the addresses in that table to determine whether or not switching is required: other switches use two tables as previously described. Another variation between switch designs concerns the number and location of lookup tables. Some switch designs result in each port having its own lookup table or set of tables, with a fixed amount of memory subdivided into a buffer area and lookup table similar to the buffer and address tables illustrated in Figure 11.6. Another switch design uses a common memory area that is logically subdivided for use by each port. Although this design makes more economical use of memory, the use of shared memory introduces delays that are avoided when memory is used with individual ports. However, from an upgrade perspective, it is easier to upgrade one memory area than a series of memory areas. Thus, you may wish to consider differences in upgradability versus very slight differences in latency.

The remainder of this section focuses attention on the operation of layer 2 LAN switches by assuming only one lookup table is used as it provides an easier mechanism to describe the basic operation of different switching methods. In addition, we will not differentiate performance based on the type and location of lookup tables because the overall switch design, to include the operation of custom designed integrated circuits, has a more pronounced effect on switch performance than the type and location of lookup tables.

Figure 11.9 illustrates the basic operation of cross-point or cut-through switching. In this technique, the destination address in a frame is read prior to the frame being stored (1). That address is forwarded to a lookup table (2) to determine the port destination address that is used by the switching fabric to initiate a cross-connection to the destination port (3). Because this switching method only requires the storage of a small portion of a frame until it is able to read the destination address and perform its

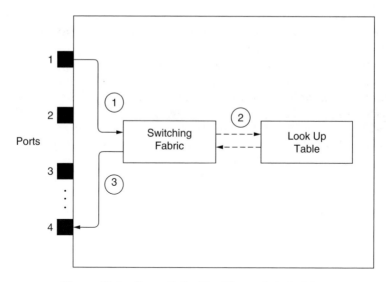

Figure 11.9   Cross-Point/Cut-Through Switching

table lookup operation to initiate switching to an appropriate output port, latency through the switch is minimized.

Latency functions as a brake on two-way frame exchanges. For example, in a client/server environment, the transmission of a frame by a work-station results in a server response. Thus, the minimum wait time is 2× latency for each client/server exchange, lowering the effective throughput of the switch. Because a cross-point switching technique results in a mini-mal amount of latency, the effect on throughput of the delay attributable to a switching hub using this switching technique is minimal.

We can compute the minimum amount of latency associated with a cross-point switch as follows. As a minimum, the switch must read 14 bytes (8 bytes for the preamble and 6 bytes for the destination address) prior to being able to initiate a search of its port-destination address table. At 10 Mbps, we obtain:

$$9.6\ \mu s + 14\ bytes * 8\ bits/byte * 100\ ns/bit$$

$$9.6 \times 10^{-6} + 112 * 100 * 10^{-9}$$

$$20.8 \times 10^{-6}\ seconds$$

Here, 9.6 μs represents the Ethernet interframe gap at an operating rate of 10 Mbps, while 100 ns/bit represents the bit duration of a 10-Mbps Ethernet LAN. Thus, the minimum one-way latency not counting switch overhead of a cut-through switch is 20.8×10^{-6} seconds, while the round-trip minimum latency would be twice that duration.

11.2.3.2 Store-and-Forward Switching. In comparison to a cut-through operating LAN switch, a store-and-forward switch first stores an entire frame in memory prior to operating on the data fields within the frame. Once the frame is stored, the switch checks the frame's integrity by performing a cyclic redundancy check (CRC) on the contents of the frame, comparing its computed CRC against the CRC contained in the frame's frame check sequence (FCS) field. If the two match, the frame is considered to be error-free and additional processing and switching will occur. Otherwise, the frame is considered to have one or more bits in error and will be discarded.

In addition to CRC checking, the storage of a frame permits filtering against various frame fields to occur. Although a few manufacturers of store-and-forward LAN switches support different types of filtering, the primary advantage advertised by such manufacturers is data integrity. Whether or not this is actually an advantage depends on how you view the additional latency introduced by the storage of a full frame in memory as well as the necessity for error checking. Concerning the latter, switches should operate error-free, so a store-and-forward switch only removes network errors that should be negligible to start with.

When a switch removes an errored frame, the originator will retransmit the frame after a period of time. Because an errored frame arriving at its destination network address is also discarded, many people question the necessity of error checking by a store-and-forward LAN switch. However, filtering capability, if offered, may be far more useful as you could use this capability, for example, to route protocols carried in frames to destination ports far easier than by frame destination address. This is especially true if you have hundreds or thousands of devices connected to a large LAN switch. You might set up two or three filters instead of entering a large number of destination addresses into the switch.

Figure 11.10 illustrates the operation of a store-and-forward layer 2 LAN switch. Note that a common switch design is to use shared buffer memory to store entire frames, which increases the latency associated with this type of switch. Because the minimum length of an Ethernet frame is 72 bytes, then the minimum one-way delay or latency, not counting the switch overhead associated with the lookup table and switching fabric operation, becomes:

$$96 \text{ } \mu s + 72 \text{ bytes} * 8 \text{ bits/byte} * 100 \text{ ns/bit}$$

$$9.6 * 10^{-6} + 576 * 100 * 10^{-9}$$

$$67.2 * 10^{-6} \text{ seconds}$$

Again, 9.6 μs represents the Ethernet interframe gap, while 100 ns/bit is the bit duration of a 10-Mbps Ethernet LAN. Thus, the minimum one-way latency of a store-and-forward Ethernet switch is 0.0000672 seconds, while

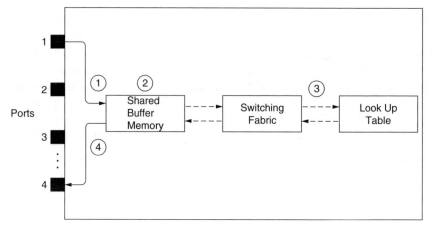

Figure 11.10   Store-and-Forward Switching

a round-trip minimum latency is twice that duration. For a maximum-length Ethernet frame with a data field of 1500 bytes, the frame length becomes 1526 bytes. Thus, the one-way maximum latency becomes:

$$96 \ \mu s + 1526 \ bytes * 8 \ bits/byte * 100 \ ns/bit$$

$$\text{or } 9.6 * 10^{-6} + 12208 * 100 * 10^{-9}$$

$$\text{or } 0.012304 \ seconds$$

When considering the use of a Token Ring store-and-forward switch, latency computations are more difficult as the time gap between frames, as noted in Chapter 9, depends on the number of stations on a ring connected to a switch on the port, the cable length of the ring to include twice its sum of lobe cable runs, and the LAN operating rate. If only one station is connected to a port, determining latency is simplified, as a ring is formed with the station and the port. Because the port acts as a participant on the ring, it can respond by passing the frame back to the originator with the delay essentially reduced to twice the latency through the switch. For example, a 2000-byte information field in a Token Ring frame requires a total of 2021 bytes, to include frame overhead. When received from a 16-Mbps Token Ring network, the frame would have a one-way latency of:

$$2021 \ bytes * \frac{8 \ bits}{byte} * \frac{1 \ second}{16 \times 10^{6} \ bit}$$

$$\text{or } 16168 \ bits \times 62.5 \ \frac{ns}{bit}$$

$$\text{or } 0.0010105 \ seconds$$

11.2.3.3 Hybrid Switching. A hybrid switch supports both cut-through and store-and-forward switching, selecting the switching method based upon monitoring the error rate encountered by reading the CRC at the end of each frame and comparing its value to a computed CRC performed "on-the-fly" on the fields protected by the CRC. Initially, the switch might set each port to a cut-through mode of operation. If too many bad frames are noted as occurring on the port, the switch will automatically set the frame processing mode to store-and-forward, permitting the CRC comparison to be performed prior to the frame being forwarded. This permits frames in error to be discarded without having them pass through the switch. Because the "switch," no pun intended, between cut-through and store-and-forward modes of operation occurs adaptively, another term used to reference the operation of this type of switch is "adaptive."

The major advantages of a hybrid switch are that it provides minimal latency when error rates are low and discards frames by adapting to a store-and-forward switching method so it can discard errored frames when the frame error rate rises. From an economic perspective, the hybrid switch can logically be expected to cost more than a cut-through or store-and-forward switch because its software development effort is more comprehensive. However, due to the competitive market for communications products, upon occasion its price may be reduced below competitive switch technologies.

In addition to being categorized by their switching technique, layer 2 LAN switches can be classified by their support of single or multiple addresses per port. The former method is referred to as port-based switching, while the latter switching method is referred to as segment-based switching.

11.2.3.4 Port-Based Switching. A layer 2 LAN switch that performs port-based switching only supports a single address per port. This restricts switching to one device per port; however, it results in a minimum amount of memory in the switch as well as provides for a relatively fast table lookup when the switch uses a destination address in a frame to obtain the port for initiating a cross-connect.

Figure 11.11 illustrates an example of the use of a port-based switching hub. In this example, M user workstations use the switch to contend for the resources of N servers. If $M > N$, then a switch connected to Ethernet 10-Mbps LANs can support a maximum throughput of $N/2 * 10$ Mbps, because up to $N/2$ simultaneous client/server frame flows can occur through the switch.

It is important to compare the maximum potential throughput through a switch to its rated backplane speed. If the maximum potential throughput is less than the rated backplane speed, the switch will not cause delays based upon the traffic being routed through the device. For example, consider a 64-port switch that has a backplane speed of 400 Mbps. If the

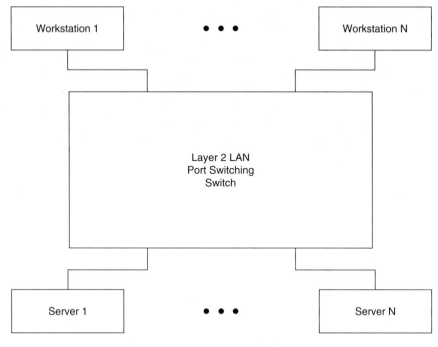

Figure 11.11   Port-Based Switching

maximum port rate is 10 Mbps, then the maximum throughput, assuming 32 active cross-connections were simultaneously established, becomes 320 Mbps. In this example, the switch has a backplane transfer capability sufficient to handle the worst-case data transfer scenario. Now let us assume that the maximum backplane data transfer capability is 200 Mbps. This would reduce the maximum number of simultaneous cross-connections capable of being serviced to 20 instead of 32 and adversely affect switch performance under certain operational conditions. However, as previously noted, it is also important to consider the types of devices to be connected to a switch. Simply dividing the number of ports by 2 and multiplying by the port data rate correctly provides the needed backplane speed without considering reality. That is, if your organization operates network devices in a client/server environment and you are connecting 20 workstations and four servers on a 24-port switch, then you can expect a maximum of four cross-connects, not 12. This makes a considerable difference when selecting a backplane speed to prevent blockage.

Because a port-based switching hub only has to store one address per port, search times are minimized. When combined with a pass-through or cut-through switching technique, this type of switch results in a minimal

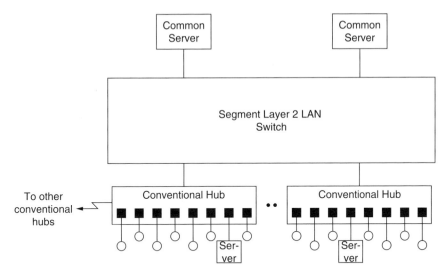

Figure 11.12   Segment-Based Switching

latency, to include the overhead of the switch in determining the destination port of a frame.

11.2.3.5   Segment-Based Switching. A segment-based switching technique requires a layer 2 LAN switch to support multiple addresses per port. Through the use of this type of switch, you achieve additional networking flexibility because you can connect other hubs to a single segment-based switch port.

Figure 11.12 illustrates an example of the use of a segment-based switching hub in an Ethernet environment. Two segments in the form of conventional hubs with multiple devices connected to each hub are shown in the lower portion of Figure 11.12. However, note that a segment can consist of a single device, resulting in the connection of one device to a port on a segment switch being similar to a connection on a port-based switch. However, unlike a port-based switch that is limited to supporting one address per port, the segment-based switch can, if necessary, support multiple devices connected to a port. Thus, the two servers connected to the switch at the top of Figure 11.12 could, if desired, be placed on a conventional hub or a high-speed hub, such as a 100BASE-T hub, which in turn would be connected to a single port on a segment-based switch.

In Figure 11.12, each conventional hub acts as a repeater, and forwards every frame transmitted on that hub to the switch, regardless of whether or not the frame requires the resources of the switch. The segment switch examines the destination address of each frame against addresses in its lookup table, only forwarding those frames that warrant being forwarded. Otherwise, frames are discarded as they are local to the conventional hub. Through the use of a segment-based switch, you can maintain the use of local servers with respect to existing LAN segments as well as install servers whose access is common to all network segments. The latter is illustrated in Figure 11.12 by the connection of two common servers shown at the top of the switch. If you obtain a store-and-forward segment switch that supports filtering, you could control access to common servers from individual workstations or by workstations on a particular segment. In addition, you can also use the filtering capability of a store-and-forward segment-based switch to control access from workstations located on one segment to workstations or servers located on another segment.

Now that we have an appreciation for the general operation and utilization of layer 2 LAN switches, let us examine how they are used in a networking environment.

11.2.4 Switch Operations

Although features incorporated into an Ethernet switch considerably differ between vendors as well as within vendor product lines, upon occasion we can categorize this communications device by the operating rate of the ports it supports. Doing so results in five basic types of Ethernet switches, which are listed in Table 11.1. Switches that are restricted to operating at a relatively low data rate are commonly used for departmental operations, while switches that support a mixed data rate are commonly used in a tiered network structure at a higher layer in the tier than switches that operate at a low uniform data rate. Concerning the latter, when used in a tiered network structure, the lower uniform operating rate switch is commonly used at the lower level in the tier.

11.2.4.1 Stand-Alone Usage. The basic use of a stand-alone switch is to support a workgroup that requires additional bandwidth beyond that available on a shared bandwidth LAN. Figure 11.13 illustrates the use of a switch to support a workgroup or small organizational department. As a workgroup expands or several workgroups are grouped together to form a department, most organizations will want to consider the use of a two-tiered switching network. The first or lower-level tier would represent

Table 11.1   Types of Ethernet Switches Based on Port Operating Rates

- All ports operate at 10 Mbps
- Mixed 10/100 Mbps port operation
- All ports operate at 100 Mbps
- Mixed 10/100/1000-Mbps port operation
- All ports operate at 1000 Mbps

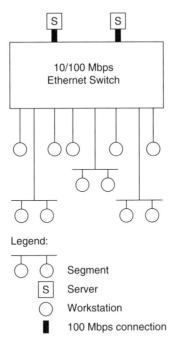

Figure 11.13   Support a Small Department or Workgroup

---

switches dedicated to supporting a specific workgroup, to include local servers. The upper tier would include one or more switches used to interconnect workgroup switches as well as provide workgroup users with access to departmental servers whose access crosses workgroup boundaries. Because the upper-tier switch or switches are used to interconnect workgroup switches, the upper-tier switches are commonly referred to as backbone switches.

11.2.4.2   Multi-Tier Network Construction. Figure 11.14 illustrates the generic use of a two-tiered Ethernet switch-based network. The switch at the higher tier functions as a backbone connectivity mechanism, which enables access to shared servers, commonly known as global servers, by users across departmental boundaries. Switches in the lower tier facilitate access to servers shared within a specific department. This hierarchical networking structure is commonly used with a higher-speed Ethernet switch such as a Fast Ethernet or Gigabit Ethernet switch, or with other types of backbone switches, such as FDDI and ATM, as well as with other types of lower-tier switches.

One common variation associated with the use of a tiered switch-based network is the placement of both departmental and global servers on an

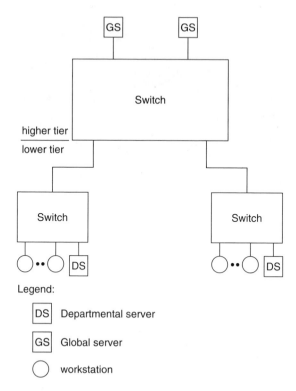

Figure 11.14 Generic Construction of a Two-Tiered Ethernet Switch-Based Network

upper-tier switch. This placement allows all servers to be co-located in a common area for ease of access and control, and is commonly referred to as a server farm. However, if an upper-tier switch should fail, access to all servers could be affected, representing a significant disadvantage of this design. A second major disadvantage is the fact that all traffic has to be routed through at least two switches when a server farm is constructed. In comparison, when servers primarily used by departmental employees are connected to a switch serving departmental users, most traffic remains local to the local switch at the bottom of the tier.

With the introduction of Gigabit Ethernet switches, it becomes possible to use this type of switch in either a multi-tier architecture as previously shown in Figure 11.14 or as a star-based backbone. Concerning the latter, Figure 11.15 illustrates the potential use of a Gigabit Ethernet switch that supports a mixture of 100-Mbps and 1-Gbps ports. In this example, the Gigabit Ethernet switch is shown being used to support two fat pipes or trunk groups, with one trunk group consisting of four 100-Mbps ports, while the second group consists of two 100-Mbps ports. Here, the term "fat pipe"

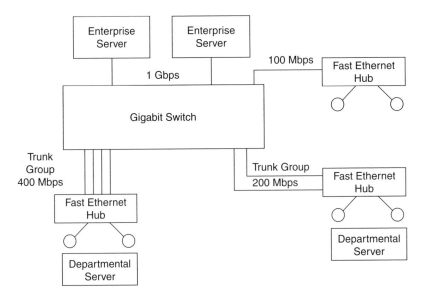

Figure 11.15   Using a Gigabit Ethernet Switch as a Star-Based Backbone Switch

represents a group of ports that operate as an entity to provide a higher level of throughput. When we review layer 2 LAN switch features later in this chapter, we also discuss fat pipes in more detail.

In examining Figure 11.15, note that enterprise servers are connected to the Gigabit switch, while department servers are connected to 100-Mbps Fast Ethernet hubs. By connecting 10BASE-T switching hubs to Fast Ethernet hubs, you could extend the star into a star-tiered network structure.

11.2.5 Switch Components

Regardless of the operating rate of each port on an Ethernet switch, most devices are designed in a similar manner. That is, most switches consist of a chassis into which a variety of cards are inserted, similar in many respects to the installation of cards into the system expansion slots of personal computers. Modular Ethernet switches that are scalable commonly support CPU, Logic, matrix, and port cards.

11.2.5.1   CPU Card. The CPU card commonly manages the switch, identifies the types of LANs attached to switch ports, and performs self tests and directed switch tests.

11.2.5.2   Logic Module. The logic module is commonly responsible for comparing the destination address of frames read on a port against a table of addresses it is responsible for maintaining. It is also responsible for

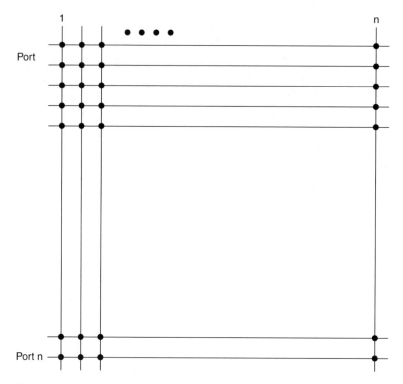

The matrix module of a switch with n ports can be considered to represent an n × n star wired backplane.

Figure 11.16   The Key to the Operation of a Switch Is a Matrix Module that Enables Each Port to be Cross-Connected to Other Ports

instructing the matrix module to initiate a crossbar switch once a comparison of addresses results in the selection of a destination port address.

11.2.5.3   Matrix Module. The matrix module of a switch can be considered to represent a crossbar of wires from each port to each port as illustrated in Figure 11.16. Upon receipt of an instruction from a logic module, the matrix module initiates a cross-connection between the source and destination port for the duration of the frame.

11.2.5.4   Port Module. The port module can be considered to represent a cluster of physical interfaces to which either individual stations or network segments are connected based upon whether the switch supports single or multiple MAC addresses per port. Some port modules permit a mixture of port cards to be inserted, resulting in, as an example, 10 and 100 Mbps as well as full-duplex connections to be supported. In comparison, other

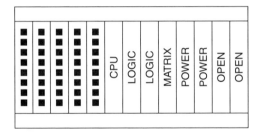

Figure 11.17 A Typical Ethernet Modular Switch Chassis Containing a Mixture of Port, CPU, Logic, Matrix, and Power Cards

---

port modules are only capable of supporting one type of LAN connection. In addition, there are significant differences between vendor port modules concerning the number of ports supported. Some modules are limited to supporting two or four ports, while other modules may support six, eight, or ten ports. It should be noted that many switches support other types of LAN port modules, such as Token Ring, FDDI, and even ATM.

11.2.5.5 Redundancy. In addition to the previously mentioned modules, most switches also support single and redundant power supply modules and may also support redundant matrix and logic modules. Figure 11.17 illustrates a typical Ethernet modular switch chassis showing the installation of 11 modules to include five 8-port modules to form a 40-port switch.

Now that we have an appreciation of the general operation and utilization of layer 2 LAN switches, let us examine those features that define their ability to provide different levels of operational capability. Once this has been accomplished, we turn our attention to Ethernet and Token Ring networking techniques using different types of switches.

11.3 Layer 2 LAN Switch

11.3.1 Layer 2 LAN Switch Features

There is literally an ever-expanding number of features being incorporated into Ethernet switches. These features range from providing such basic functions as port and segment switching to methods developed by some vendors to prevent erroneous frames from being transferred through the switch in a cut-through mode of operation. In this section we review 19 distinct switch features, as summarized in alphabetical order in Table 11.2.

The table of features presented was constructed not only to list features you should note, but, in addition, as a mechanism to facilitate the evaluation of switches. That is, you can indicate your requirement for a particular feature and then note whether or not that requirement can be satisfied by

Table 11.2   Ethernet Switch Features

Feature	Requirement	Vendor A	Vendor B
Address table size support:			
Addresses/port			
Addresses/switch			
Aging settings			
Architecture:			
ASIC based			
CISC based			
RISC based			
Auto-negotiation ports			
Backplane transfer capacity			
Error prevention			
Fat pipe and trunk group			
Filtering/forwarding rate support:			
Filtering rate			
Forwarding rate			
Flow control:			
Backpressure			
Software drivers			
802.3x flow control			
No control			
Full-duplex port operation			
Jabber control			
Latency			
Management			
Mirrored port			
Module insertion			
Port buffer size			
Port module support			
Spanning tree support			
Switch type:			
Port-based switch			
Segment-based switch			
Switching mode:			
Cut-through			
Store and forward			
Hybrid			
Virtual LAN support:			
Port based			
MAC based			
Layer 3 based			
Rule based			

different vendor products by replacing "Vendor A" and "Vendor B" by the names of switches you are evaluating. By duplicating this table, you can extend the two right-most columns to evaluate more than two products. As we examine each feature listed in Table 11.2, our degree of exploration will be based on whether or not the feature was previously described. If the feature was previously described in this chapter, we will limit our discussion to a brief review of the feature. Otherwise, we will discuss its operation in considerable detail.

11.3.1.1　Address Table Size Support. The ability of a switch to correctly forward packets to their intended recipient depends on the use of address tables. Similarly, the capability of a switch to support a defined number of workstations depends on the number of entries that can be placed in its address table. Thus, the address table size can be viewed as a constraint that affects the ability of a switch to support network devices.

There are two address table sizes you may have to consider: the number of addresses supported per port and the number of addresses supported per switch. The first address table constraint is only applicable for ports that support the connection of network segments. In comparison, the total number of addresses recognized per switch represents a constraint that affects the entire switch. Many Ethernet switches support up to 1024 addresses per port for segment-based support. Such switches may only support a total of 8192 addresses per switch. This means that a 16-port switch with eight fully populated segments could not support the use of the eight remaining ports as the switch would run out of address table entries. Thus, it is important to consider the number of addresses supported per port and per switch as well as match such data against the anticipated requirements.

11.3.1.2　Aging Settings. MAC addresses and their associated port are stored with a timestamp value. This provides the bridge with the ability to purge old entries to make room for new entries in the port-address table. Because a switch is a multi-port bridge, it also uses a timer to purge old entries from its port-address table. Some switches provide users with the ability to set the aging time within a wide range of values or to disable aging. Other switches have a series of predefined aging values from which a user can select.

11.3.1.3　Architecture. As previously noted, there are three basic methods used to construct LAN switches. Those methods include a bus-based design, shared memory, and a crossbar matrix design. The first two methods are typically simpler and less expensive to implement than a crossbar design. However, the crossbar design is more scalable as well as provides a true parallel switching capability.

11.3.1.4 Auto-Negotiation Ports. To provide a mechanism to migrate from 10 Mbps to 100 Mbps, National Semiconductor developed a chip set known as Nway; it provides an automatic data rate sensing capability as part of an auto-negotiation function. This capability enables a switch port to support either a 10- or 100-Mbps Ethernet attachment to the port; however, this feature only works when cabled to a 10/100-Mbps network adapter card. You may otherwise have to use the switch console to configure the operating rate of the port or the port may be fixed to a predefined operating rate.

11.3.1.5 Backplane Transfer Capacity. The backplane transfer capacity of a switch provides you with the ability to determine how well the device can support a large number of simultaneous cross-connections, as well as its ability to perform flooding. For example, consider a 64-port 10BASE-T switch with a backplane transfer capacity of 400 Mbps. Because the switch can support a maximum of 64/2 or 32 cross-connects, the switch's backplane must provide at least a 32 * 10 Mbps or 320 Mbps transfer capacity. However, when it encounters an unknown destination address on one port, the switch will output or flood the packet onto all ports other than the port on which the frame was received. Thus, to operate in a non-blocked mode to effect flooding, the switch must have a buffer transfer capacity of 64 * 10 Mbps, or 640 Mbps.

11.3.1.6 Error Prevention. Some switch designers recognize that the majority of runt frames (frames improperly terminated) result from a collision occurring during the time it takes to read the first 64 bytes of the frame. On a 10-Mbps Ethernet LAN, this is equivalent to a time of 51.2 μs. In a cut-through switch environment when latency is minimized, it becomes possible to pass runt frames to the destination. To preclude this from happening, some switch designers permit the user to introduce a 51.2-μs delay that provides sufficient time for the switch to verify that the frame is of sufficient length to have a high degree of probability that it is not a runt frame. Other switches that operate in the cut-through mode may simply impose a 51.2-μs delay at 10 Mbps to enable this error prevention feature. Regardless of the method used, the delay is only applicable to cut-through switches that support LAN segments, as single user ports do not generate collisions.

11.3.1.7 Fat Pipe and Trunk Group. A fat pipe is a term used to reference a high-speed port. When 10BASE-T switches were first introduced, the term actually referenced a group of two or more ports operating as an entity. Today, a fat pipe can reference a 100-Mbps port on a switch primarily consisting of 10-Mbps operating ports or a 155-Mbps ATM port on a 10/100 or 100-Mbps switch. In addition, some vendors retain the term "fat pipe" as a reference to a group of ports operating as an entity while other vendors use the term "trunk group" to represent a group of ports that function as an entity. However, to support a grouping of ports operating as a common entity requires the interconnected switches to be obtained from the same company as the method used to group ports is proprietary.

11.3.1.8 Filtering and Forwarding Rate Support. The ability of a switch to interpret a number of frame destination addresses during a defined time interval is referred to as its filtering rate. In comparison, the number of frames that must be routed through a switch during a predefined period of time is referred to as the forwarding rate. Both the filtering and forwarding rates govern the performance level of a switch with respect to its ability to interpret and route frames. When considering these two metrics, it is important to understand the maximum frame rate on an Ethernet LAN; this was discussed earlier in this book.

11.3.1.9 Flow Control. Flow control represents the orderly regulation of transmission. In a switched network environment there are a number of situations for which flow control can be used to prevent the loss of data and subsequent retransmissions which can create a cycle of lost data followed by retransmissions. The most common cause of lost data results from a data rate mismatch between source and destination ports. For example, consider a server connected to a switch via a Fast Ethernet 100-Mbps connection that responds to a client query when the client is connected to a switch port at 10 Mbps. Without the use of a buffer within the switch, this speed mismatch would always result in the loss of data. Through the use of a buffer, data can be transferred into the switch at 100 Mbps and transferred out at 10 Mbps. However, because the input rate is ten times the output rate, the buffer will rapidly fill. In addition, if the server is transferring a large quantity of data, the buffer could overflow, resulting in subsequent data sent to the switch being lost. Thus, unless the length of the buffer is infinite, an impossible situation, there would always be some probability that data could be lost.

Another common cause of lost data is when multiple source port inputs are contending for access to the same destination port. If each source and destination port operates at the same data rate, then only two source ports contending for access to the same destination port can result in the loss of data. Thus, a mechanism is required to regulate the flow of data through a switch. That mechanism is flow control.

All Ethernet switches this author is familiar with have either buffers in each port or centralized memory that functions as a buffer. The key difference between switch buffers is in the amount of memory used. Some switches have 128K, 256 Kbytes, or even 1 or 2 Mbytes per port, whereas other switches may support the temporary storage of 10 or 20 full-length Ethernet frames. To prevent buffer overflow, four techniques are used:

backpressure, proprietary software, IEEE 802.3x flow control, and no control. Thus, lets examine each technique.

11.3.1.10 Backpressure. Backpressure represents a technique by which a switch generates a false collision signal. In actuality, the switch port operates as if it detected a collision and initiates the transmission of a jam pattern. The jam pattern consists of 32 to 48 bits that can have any value other than the CRC value that corresponds to any partial frame transmitted before the jam.

The transmission of the jam pattern ensures that the collision lasts long enough to be detected by all stations on the network. In addition, the jam signal serves as a mechanism to cause non-transmitting stations to wait until the jam signal ends prior to attempting to transmit, thus alleviating additional potential collisions from occurring. Although the jam signal temporarily stops transmission, enabling the contents of buffers to be output, the signal also adversely affects all stations connected to the port. Thus, a network segment consisting of a number of stations connected to a switch port would result in all stations having their transmission capability suspended even when just one station was directing traffic to the switch.

Backpressure is commonly implemented based upon the level of buffer memory used. When buffer memory is filled to a predefined level, that level serves as a threshold for the switch to generate jam signals. Then, once the buffer is emptied beyond another lower level, that level serves as a threshold to disable backpressure operations.

11.3.1.11 Proprietary Software Drivers. Software drivers enable a switch to directly communicate with an attached device. This enables the switch to enable and disable the station's transmission capability. Currently, software drivers are available as a NetWare Loadable Module (NLM) for NetWare servers, and may be available for Windows 2000 by the time you read this book.

11.3.1.12 IEEE 802.3x Flow Control. During 1997, the IEEE standardized a method that provides flow control on full-duplex Ethernet connections. To provide this capability, a special "Pause" frame was defined that is transmitted by devices that want to stop the flow of data from the device at the opposite end of the link.

Figure 11.18 illustrates the format of the Pause frame. Because a full-duplex connection has a device on each end of the link, the use of a predefined destination address and operation code (OpCode) defines the frame as a Pause frame. The value following the OpCode defines the time in terms of slot times that the transmitting device wants its partner to pause. This initial pause time can be extended by additional Pause frames containing new slot time values or canceled by another Pause frame

Destination Address 01–C2–80–00–00–01 (6 bytes)	Source Address (6 bytes)	Type 8808 (2 bytes)	OpCod 0001 (2 bytes)	Pause time (slot times) (2 bytes)	Pad (42 bytes)

Figure 11.18   The IEEE 802.3x Pause Frame

containing a zero slot time value. The Pad field shown at the end of the Pause frame must have each of its 42 bytes set to zero.

Under the 802.3x standard, the use of Pause frames is auto-negotiated on copper media and can be manually configured for use on fiber links. The actual standard does not require a device capable of sending a Pause frame to actually do so. Instead, it provides a standard for recognizing a Pause frame as well as a mechanism for interpreting the contents of the frame so a receiver can correctly respond to it.

The IEEE 802.3x flow control standard is applicable to all versions of Ethernet from 10 Mbps to 1 Gbps; however, the primary purpose of this standard is to enable switches to be manufactured with a minimal amount of memory. By supporting the IEEE 802.3x standard, a switch with a limited amount of memory can generate Pause frames to regulate inbound traffic instead of having to drop frames when its buffer is full.

11.3.1.13   No Control. Many switch vendors rely on the fact that the previously described traffic patterns that can result in buffers overflowing and the loss of data have a relatively low probability of occurrence for any significant length of time. In addition, upper layers of the OSI Reference Model will retransmit lost packets. Thus, many switch vendors rely on the use of memory buffers and do not incorporate flow control into their products. Whether or not this is an appropriate solution will depend on the traffic you anticipate flowing through the switch.

11.3.1.14   Full-Duplex Port Operation. If a switch port only supports the connection of one station, a collision can never occur. Recognizing this fact, most Ethernet switch vendors now support full-duplex or bi-directional traffic flow by using two of the four wire connections for 10BASE-T for transmission in the opposite direction. Full-duplex support is available for 10BASE-T, Fast Ethernet, and Gigabit Ethernet connections. Because collisions can occur on a segment, switch ports used for segment-based switching cannot support full-duplex transmission.

In addition to providing a simultaneous bi-directional data flow capability, the use of full duplex permits an extension of cabling distances. For example, at 100 Mbps, the use of a fiber cable for full-duplex operations can support a distance of 2000 meters while only 412 meters is supported using half-duplex transmission via fiber.

Due to the higher cost of full-duplex ports (FDX) and adapter cards, you should carefully evaluate the potential use of FDX prior to using this capability. For example, most client workstations will obtain a minimal gain through the use of a full-duplex capability because humans operating computers rarely perform simultaneous two-way operations. Thus, other than speeding acknowledgments associated with the transfer of data, the use of an FDX connection for workstations represents an excessive capacity that should only be considered when vendors are competing for sales and, as such, they provide this capability as a standard. In comparison, the use of an FDX transmission capability to connect servers to switch ports enables a server to respond to one request while receiving a subsequent request. Thus, the ability to utilize the capability of FDX transmission is enhanced by using this capability on server-to-switch port connections.

Although vendors would like you to believe that FDX doubles your transmission capability, in actuality you will only obtain a fraction of this advertised throughput. This is because most network devices, to include servers that are provided with FDX transmission capability, only use that capability a fraction of the time.

11.3.1.15   Jabber Control. A jabber is an Ethernet frame whose length exceeds 1518 bytes. Jabbers are commonly caused by defective hardware or collisions, and can adversely affect a receiving device by its misinterpretation of data in the frame. A switch operating in the cut-through mode with jabber control will truncate the frame to an appropriate length. In comparison, a store-and-forward switch will normally automatically drop a jabbered frame.

11.3.1.16   Latency. When examining vendor specifications, the best word of advice is to be suspicious of latency notations, especially those concerning store-and-forward switches. Many vendors do not denote the length of the frame used for latency measurements, while some vendors use what might be referred to as creative accounting when computing latency. Thus, let us review the formal definition of latency.

Latency can be defined as the difference in time (t) from the first bit arriving at a source port to the first bit output on the destination port. Modern cut-through switches have a latency of approximately 40 µs, while store-and-forward switches have a latency between 80 and 90 µs for a 72-byte frame, and 1250 to 1300 ms for a maximum-length 1500-byte frame.

For a store-and-forward Ethernet switch, an entire frame is first stored. Because the maximum length of an Ethernet frame is 1526 bytes, this

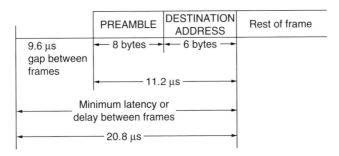

Figure 11.19 Switch Latency Includes a Built-In Delay Resulting from the Structure of the Ethernet Frame

means that the maximum latency for a store-and-forward 10-Mbps Ethernet switch is:

$$\frac{1526 \text{ bytes} * 8 \text{ bits/byte}}{10 \text{ Mbps}} \text{ or } 1.2208 \text{ μs}$$

plus the time required to perform a table lookup and cross-connection between source and destination ports. Because a 10-Mbps-Ethernet LAN has a 9.6-μs gap between frames, this means that the minimum delay time between frames flowing through a cut-through switch is 20.8 μs. Figure 11.19 illustrates the composition of this delay at a 10-Mbps operating rate. For a store-and-forward switch, considering the 9.6-μs gap between frames results in a maximum latency of 1230.4 μs plus the time required to perform a table lookup and initiate a cross-connection between source and destination ports.

11.3.1.17 Management. The most common method used to provide switch management involves the integration of RMON support for each switch port. This enables an SNMP console to obtain statistics from the RMON group or groups supported by each switch. Because the retrieval of statistics on a port-by-port basis can be time consuming, most switches that support RMON also create a database of statistics to facilitate their retrieval.

11.3.1.18 Mirrored Port. A mirrored port is a port that duplicates traffic on another port. For traffic analysis and intrusive testing, the ability to mirror data exiting the switch on one port to a port to which test equipment is connected can be a very valuable feature.

11.3.1.19 Module Insertion. Modular switches support two different methods of module insertion: switch power-down and hot insertion. As their names imply, a switch power-down method requires you to first deactivate the switch and literally bring it down. In comparison, the ability to perform hot insertions enables you to add modules to an operating switch without adversely affecting users.

11.3.1.20   Port Buffer Size. Switch designers incorporate buffer memory into port cards as a mechanism to compensate for the difference between the internal speed of the switch and the operating rate of an end station or segment connected to the port. Some switch designers increase the amount of buffer memory incorporated into port cards to use in conjunction with a flow control mechanism, while other switch designers can use port buffer memory as a substitute for flow control. If used only as a mechanism for speed compensation, the size of port buffers may be limited to a few thousand bytes of storage. When used in conjunction with a flow control mechanism or as a flow control mechanism, the amount of buffer memory per port may be up to 64, 128, or 256 Kbytes, perhaps even up to 1 or 2 Mbytes. Although you might expect more buffer memory to provide better results, this may not necessarily be true. For example, assume a workstation on a segment is connected to a port that has a large buffer with just enough free memory to accept one frame. When the workstation transmits a sequence of frames, only the first is able to be placed into the buffer. If the switch then initiates flow control as the contents of its port buffer is emptied, subsequent frames are barred from moving through the switch. When the switch disables flow control, it is possible that another station with data to transmit is able to gain access to the port prior to the station that sent frame one in a sequence of frames. Due to the delay in emptying the contents of a large buffer, it becomes possible that subsequent frames are sufficiently delayed as they move through a switch to a mainframe via a gateway that a time-dependent session could time-out. Thus, you should consider your network structure in conjunction with the operating rate of switch ports and the amount of buffer storage per port to determine if an extremely large amount of buffer storage could potentially result in session timeouts. Fortunately, most switch manufacturers limit port buffer memory to 128 Kbytes, which at 10 Mbps results in a maximum delay of:

$$\frac{128 * 1024 * 8 \text{ bits/byte}}{10 \text{ Mbps}}$$

or 0.10 seconds. At 100 Mbps, the maximum delay is reduced to 0.01 seconds, while at 1 Gbps the delay becomes 0.001 seconds.

11.3.1.21   Port Module Support. Although many Ethernet switches are limited to supporting only Ethernet networks, the type of networks supported can considerably differ between vendor products as well as within a specific vendor product line. Thus, you may wish to examine the support

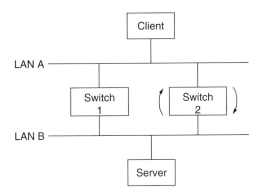

Figure 11.20   The Need for Loop Control

of port modules for connecting 10BASE-2, 10BASE-5, 10BASE-T, 100BASE-T LANs, and Gigabit Ethernet devices. In addition, if your organization supports different types of LANs or is considering the use of switches to form a tier structured network using a different type of high-speed backbone, you should examine port support for FDDI, full-duplex Token Ring, and ATM connectivity. Many modular Ethernet switches include the ability to add translating bridge modules, enabling support for several different types of networks through a common chassis.

11.3.1.22   Spanning Tree Support. Ethernet networks use the spanning tree algorithm to prevent loops that, if enabled, could result in the continuous replication of frames. In a bridged network, spanning tree support is accomplished by the use of bridge protocol data units (BPDUs) that enable bridges to select a root bridge and agree upon a network topology that precludes loops from occurring. Because a switch, in effect, represents a sophisticated bridge, we would want to preclude the use of multiple switches from forming a loop. For example, consider Figure 11.20, which illustrates the use of two switches to interconnect two LANs. If both switches were active, a frame from the client connected on LAN A destined to the server on LAN B would be placed back onto LAN A by Switch 1, causing a packet loop and the replication of the packet, a situation we want to avoid. By incorporating spanning tree support into each switch, they can communicate with one another to construct a topology that does not contain loops. For example, one switch in Figure 11.20 would place a port in a blocking mode while the other switch would have both ports in a forwarding mode of operation.

To obtain the ability to control the spanning tree, most switches permit a number of parameters to be altered from their management console. Those parameters include the forwarding delay, which governs the time the switch will wait prior to forwarding a packet, the aging time the switch waits for the receipt of a hello packet before initiating a topology change, the "Hello" time interval between the transmission of BPDU frames, and the path cost assigned to each port.

11.3.1.23 Switch Type. As previously discussed, a switch will either support one or multiple addresses per port. If it supports one address per port, it is a port-based switch. In comparison, if it supports multiple addresses per port, it is considered a segment-based switch even if only one end station is connected to some or all ports on the switch.

11.3.1.24 Switching Mode. Ethernet switches can be obtained to operate in a cut-through, store-and-forward, or hybrid operating mode. As previously discussed in this chapter, the hybrid mode of operation represents toggling between cut-through and store-and-forward based upon a frame error rate threshold. That is, a hybrid switch might initially be set to operate in a cut-through mode and compute the CRC for each frame on-the-fly, comparing its computed values to the CRCs appended to each frame. When a predefined frame error threshold is reached, the switch would change its operating mode to store-and-forward, enabling erroneous frames to be discarded. Some switch vendors reference a hybrid switch mode as an error-free cut-through operating mode.

11.3.1.25 Virtual LAN Support. A virtual LAN (vLAN) can be considered to represent a broadcast domain created through the association of switch ports, MAC addresses, or a network layer parameter. Thus, there are three basic types of vLAN creation methods you can evaluate when examining the functionality of an Ethernet switch. In addition, some vendors now offer a rules-based vLAN creation capability that enables users to have an almost infinite number of vLAN creation methods with the ability to go down to the bit level within a frame as a mechanism for vLAN associations.

11.3.2 Switched-Based Virtual LANs

As briefly mentioned in our review of switch features, a virtual LAN (vLAN) can be considered to represent a broadcast domain. This means that transmission generated by one station assigned to a vLAN is only received by those stations predefined by some criteria to be in the domain. Thus, to understand how vLANs operate requires us to examine how they are constructed.

11.3.2.1 Construction Basics. A vLAN is constructed by the logical grouping of two or more network nodes on a physical topology. To accomplish this logical grouping, you must use a vLAN-"aware" switching device. Those devices can include intelligent switches, which essentially perform bridging and operate at the Media Access Control (MAC) layer, or routers, which operate at the network layer, or layer 3, of the Open Systems Inter-connection (ISO) Reference Model. Although a switching device is required to develop a vLAN, in actuality it is the software used by the device that provides you with a vLAN capability. That is, a vLAN represents a sub-network or broadcast domain defined by software and not by the physical topology of a network. Instead, the physical topology of a network serves as a constraint for the software-based grouping of nodes into a logically defined network.

11.3.2.2 Implicit versus Explicit Tagging. The actual criteria used to define the logical grouping of nodes into a vLAN can be based on implicit or explicit tagging. Implicit tagging, which in effect eliminates the use of a special tagging field inserted into frames or packets, can be based on MAC address, port number of a switch used by a node, protocol, or another parameter that nodes can be logically grouped into. Because many vendors offering vLAN products use different construction techniques, interoperability between vendors may be difficult, if not impossible. In comparison, explicit tagging requires the addition of a field into a frame or packet header. This action can result in incompatibilities with certain types of vendor equipment as the extension of the length of a frame or packet beyond its maximum can result in the inability of such equipment to handle such frames or packets. Based on the preceding, the differences between implicit and explicit tagging can be considered akin to the prover-bial statement "between a rock and a hard place." Although standards can be expected to resolve many interoperability problems, network managers and administrators may not have the luxury of time to wait until such stan-dards are developed. Instead, you may wish to use existing equipment to develop vLANs to satisfy current and evolving organizational requirements.

11.3.3 Port-Grouping vLANs

As its name implies, a port-grouping vLAN represents a virtual LAN created by defining a group of ports on a switch or router to form a broadcast domain. Thus, another common name for this type of vLAN is a port-based virtual LAN.

11.3.3.1 Operation. Figure 11.21 illustrates the use of an intelligent LAN switch to create two vLANs based upon port groupings. In this example, the switch was configured to create one virtual LAN consisting of ports 0, 1, 5, and 6, while a second virtual LAN was created based upon the group-ing of ports 2, 3, 4, and 7 to form a second broadcast domain.

Advantages associated with the use of LAN switches for creating vLANs include the ability to use the switching capability of the switch, the ability to support multiple stations per port, and an internetworking capability. A key disadvantage associated with the use of port-based vLANs is the fact

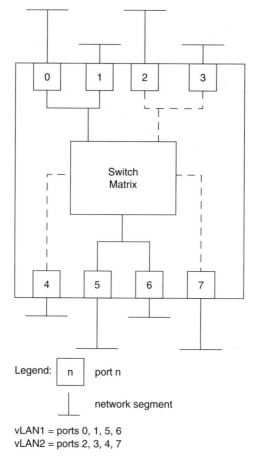

Legend:

| n | port n |

network segment

vLAN1 = ports 0, 1, 5, 6
vLAN2 = ports 2, 3, 4, 7

Figure 11.21   Creating Port-Grouping vLANs Using a LAN Switch

---

they are limited to supporting one vLAN per port. This means that moves from one vLAN to another will affect all stations connected to a particular switch port.

11.3.3.2 Supporting Inter-vLAN Communications. The use of multiple network interface cards (NICs) provides an easy-to-implement solution to obtaining an inter-vLAN communications capability when only a few vLANs must be linked. This method of inter-vLAN communications is applicable to all methods of vLAN creation; however, when a built-in routing capability is included in a LAN switch, you would probably prefer to use the routing capability rather than obtain and install additional hardware.

Figure 11.22 illustrates the use of a server with multiple NICs to provide support to two port-based vLANs. Not only does this method of multiple

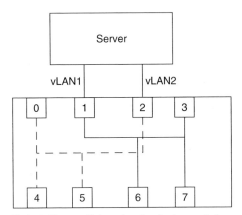

By installing multiple network adapter cards in a
server or workstation, a LAN device can
become a member of multiple vLANs.

Figure 11.22   Overcoming the Port-Based Constraint Where Stations Can Join Only a Single vLAN

vLAN support require additional hardware and the use of multiple ports on a switch or wiring hub, but, in addition, the number of NICs that can be installed in a station is typically limited to two or three. Thus, the use of a large switch with hundreds of ports configured for supporting three or more vLANs may not be capable of supporting inter-vLAN communications unless a router is connected to a switch port for each vLAN on the switch.

11.3.4 MAC-Based VLANs

Figure 11.23 illustrates the use of an 18-port switch to create two vLANs. In this example, 18 devices are shown connected to the switch via six ports, with four ports serving individual network segments. Thus, the LAN switch in this example is more accurately referenced as a segment switch with a MAC or layer 2 vLAN capability. This type of switch can range in capacity from small 8- or 16-port devices capable of supporting segments with up to 512 or 1024 total addresses, to large switches with hundreds of ports capable of supporting thousands of MAC addresses. For simplicity of illustration, we will use the six-port segment switch to denote the operation of layer 2 vLANs as well as their advantages and disadvantages.

In turning our attention to the vLANs shown in Figure 11.23, note that we will use the numeric or node addresses shown contained in circles as MAC addresses for simplicity of illustration. Thus, addresses 1 through 8 and 17 would be grouped into a broadcast domain representing vLAN1, while addresses 9 through 16 and 18 would be grouped into a second broadcast domain to represent vLAN2. At this point in time, you would be tempted to

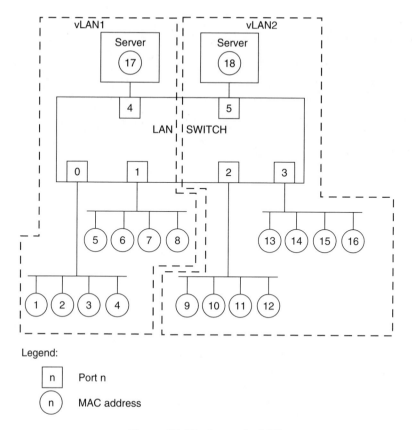

Legend:

n (box)	Port n
n (circle)	MAC address

Figure 11.23   Layer 2 vLAN

---

say "so what," as the use of MAC addresses in creating layer 2 vLANs resembles precisely the same effect as if you used a port-grouping method of vLAN creation. For example, using an intelligent hub with vLAN creation based upon port grouping would result in the same vLANs as those shown in Figure 11.23 when ports 0, 1, and 4 are assigned to one virtual LAN and ports 2, 3, and 5 to the second.

11.3.4.1 Flexibility. To indicate the greater flexibility associated with the use of equipment that supports layer 2 vLAN creation, let us assume users with network node addresses 7 and 8 were just transferred from the project associated with vLAN1 to the project associated with vLAN2. If you were using a port-grouping method of vLAN creation, you would have to physically re-cable nodes 7 and 8 to either the segment connected to port 2 or the segment connected to port 3. In comparison, when using a segment switch with a layer 2 vLAN creation capability, you would use the management port to delete addresses 7 and 8 from vLAN1 and add them to

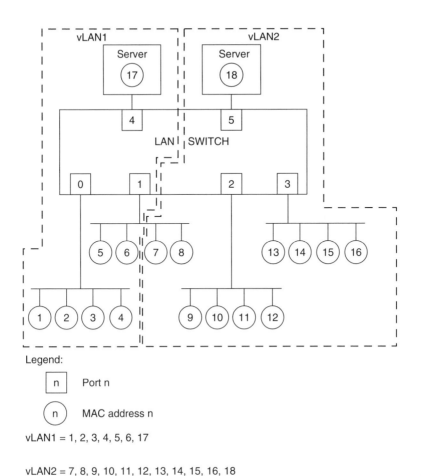

Figure 11.24   Moving Stations When Using a Layer 2 vLAN

vLAN2. The actual effort required to do so might be as simple as dragging MAC addresses from one vLAN to the other when using a GUI (graphical user interface) or entering one or more commands when using a command-line management system. The top of Figure 11.24 illustrates the result of the previously mentioned node transfer. The lower portion of Figure 11.24 shows the two vLAN layer 2 tables, indicating the movement of MAC addresses 7 and 8 to vLAN2.

Although the reassignment of stations 7 and 8 to vLAN2 is easily accomplished at the MAC layer, it should be noted that the "partitioning" of a segment into two vLANs can result in upper layer problems. This is because upper layer protocols, such as IP, require all stations on a segment to have the same network address. Some switches overcome this problem by dynamically altering the network address to correspond to the vLAN on which the station resides. Other switches without this capability restrict the creation of MAC-based vLANs to one device per port, in effect limiting the creation of vLANs to port-based switches.

11.3.4.2 Interswitch Communications. Similar to the port-grouping method of vLAN creation, a MAC-based vLAN is normally restricted to a single switch. However, some vendors include a management platform that enables multiple switches to support MAC addresses between closely located switches. Unfortunately, neither individual or closely located switches permit an expansion of vLANs outside the immediate area, resulting in the isolation of the virtual LANs from the remainder of the network. This deficiency can be alleviated in two ways. First, for inter-vLAN communications, you could install a second adapter card in a server and associate one MAC address with one vLAN while the second address is associated with the second virtual LAN. While this method is appropriate for a switch with two vLANs, you would require a different method to obtain interoperability when communications are required between a large number of virtual LANs. Similar to correcting the interoperability problem with the port-grouping method of vLAN creation, you would have to use routers to provide connectivity between MAC-based vLANs and the remainder of your network.

11.3.4.3 Router Restrictions. When using a router to provide connectivity between vLANs, there are several restrictions you must consider. Those restrictions typically include a requirement to use a separate switch port connection to the router for each virtual LAN and the inability to assign portions of segments to different vLANs. Concerning the former, unless the LAN switch either internally supports layer 3 routing or provides a "trunking" or "aggregation" capability that enables transmission from multiple vLANs to occur on a common port to the router, one port linking the switch to the router will be required for each vLAN. Because router and switch ports are relatively costly, internetworking of a large number of virtual LANs can become expensive. Concerning the latter, this requirement results from the fact that in a TCP/IP environment, routing occurs between segments. An example of inter-vLAN communications using a router is illustrated in Figure 11.25.

When inter-vLAN communications are required, the layer-2 switch transmits packets to the router via a port associated with the virtual LAN workstation requiring such communications. The router is responsible for determining the routed path to provide inter-vLAN communications, forwarding the packet back to the switch via an appropriate router-to-switch interface. Upon receipt of the packet, the switch uses bridging to forward the packet to its destination port.

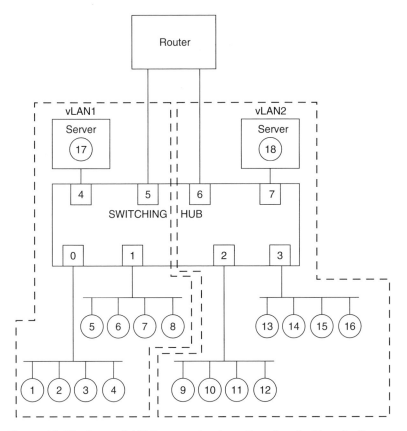

Figure 11.25 Inter-vLAN Communications Require the Use of a Router.
F

Returning to Figure 11.25, a workstation located in vLAN1 requiring communications with a workstation in vLAN2 would have its data transmitted by the switch on port 5 to the router. After processing the packet, the router would return the packet to the switch, with the packet entering the switch on port 6. Thereafter, the switch would use bridging to broadcast the packet to ports 2, 3, and 7, where it would be recognized by a destination node in vLAN2 and copied into an appropriate network interface card.

11.3.5 Layer 3-Based vLANs

A layer 3 based vLAN is constructed using information contained in the network layer header of packets. As such, this precludes the use of LAN switches that operate at the data-link layer from being capable of forming layer 3 vLANs. Thus, layer 3 vLAN creation is restricted to routers and LAN switches that provide a layer 3 routing capability.

Through the use of layer 3 operating switches and routers, there are a variety of methods that can be used to create layer 3 vLANs. Some of the more common methods supported resemble the criteria by which routers operate, such as IPX network numbers and IP subnets, AppleTalk domains, and layer 3 protocols.

The actual creation options associated with a layer 3 vLAN can vary considerably based upon the capability of the LAN switch or router used to form the virtual LAN. For example, some hardware products permit a subnet to be formed across a number of ports and may even provide the capability to allow more than one subnet to be associated with a network segment connected to the port of a LAN switch. In comparison, other LAN switches may be limited to creating vLANs based upon different layer 3 protocols.

11.3.5.1 Subnet-Based vLANs. Figure 11.26 illustrates the use of a layer 3 LAN switch to create two virtual LANs based upon IP network addresses. In examining the vLANs created through the use of the LAN switch, note that the first virtual LAN is associated with the subnet 198.78.55, which represents a Class C IP address, while the second vLAN is associated with the subnet 198.78.42, which represents a second Class C IP address. Also note that because it is assumed that the LAN switch supports the assignment of

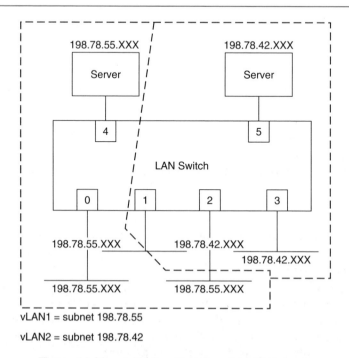

vLAN1 = subnet 198.78.55

vLAN2 = subnet 198.78.42

Figure 11.26   vLAN Creation Based on IP Subnets

more than one subnet per port, port 1 on the switch consists of stations assigned to either subnet. While some LAN switches support this subnetting capability, it is also important to note that other switches do not. Thus, a LAN switch that does not support multiple subnets per port would require stations to be re-cabled to other ports if it was desired to associate them to a different virtual LAN.

11.3.5.2 Protocol-Based vLANs. In addition to forming virtual LANs based on a network address, the use of the layer 3 transmission protocol as a method for vLAN creation provides a mechanism that enables vLAN formation to be based on the layer 3 protocol. Using this method of vLAN creation, it becomes relatively easy for stations to belong to multiple vLANs. To illustrate this concept, consider Figure 11.27, which illustrates the creation of two vLANs based on their layer 3 transmission protocol. In examining the stations shown in Figure 11.27, note that the circles with the uppercase I represent those stations configured for membership in the vLAN based upon the use of the IP protocol, while those stations represented by circles containing the uppercase X represent stations configured for membership in the vLAN that uses the IPX protocol as its membership criteria. Similarly, stations represented by circles containing the characters I/X represent stations operating dual protocol stacks that enable such stations to become members of both vLANs.

Two servers are shown at the top of the LAN switch illustrated in Figure 11.27. One server is shown operating dual IPX/IP stacks, which results in the server belonging to both vLANs. In comparison, the server on the upper right of the switch is configured to support IPX and could represent a NetWare file server restricted to membership in the vLAN associated with the IPX protocol.

11.3.5.3   Rule-Based vLANs. A recent addition to vLAN creation methods is based on the ability of LAN switches to look inside packets and use predefined fields, portions of fields, and even individual bit settings as a mechanism for the creation of a virtual LAN.

11.3.5.4   Capabilities. The ability to create virtual LANs via a rule-based methodology provides, no pun intended, a virtually unlimited virtual LAN creation capability. To illustrate a small number of the almost unlimited methods of vLAN creation, consider Table 11.3, which lists eight examples of rule-based vLAN creation methods. In examining the entries in Table 11.3, note that in addition to creating vLANs via the inclusion of specific field values within a packet, such as all IPX users with a specific network address, it is also possible to create vLANs using the exclusion of certain packet field values. The latter capability is illustrated by the next to last example in Table 11.3, which forms a vLAN consisting of all IPX traffic with a specific network address but excludes a specific node address.

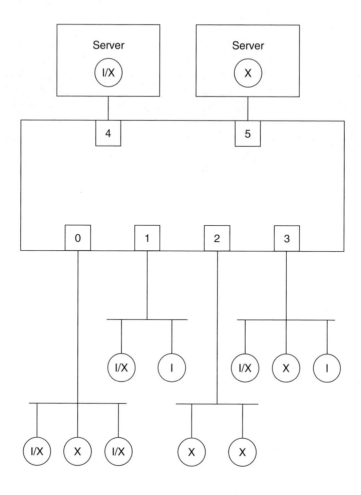

I = vLAN1 membership X = vLAN2 membership
I/X = membership in both LANs

Legend:

n	port n
I	IP Protocol used by station
X	IPX Protocol used by station
I/X	IPX and IP Protocols used by station

Figure 11.27   vLAN Creation Based on Protocol

Table 11.3   Rule-Based vLAN Creation Examples

- All IP users with a specific IP subnet address
- All IPX users with a specific network address
- All network users whose adapter cards were manufactured by the XYZ Corporation
- All traffic with a specific Ethernet Type field value
- All traffic with a specific SNAP field value
- All traffic with a specific SAP field value
- All IPX traffic with a specific network address but not a specific node address
- A specific IP address

11.3.5.5   Multicast Support. One rule-based vLAN creation example that deserves a degree of explanation to understand its capability is the last entry in Table 11.3. Although you might be tempted to think that the assignment of a single IP address to a vLAN represents a typographical mistake, in actuality it represents the ability to enable network stations to dynamically join an IP multicast group without adversely affecting the bandwidth available to other network users assigned to the same subnet, but located on different segments attached to a LAN switch. To understand why this occurs, let us digress and discuss the concept associated with IP multicast operations.

IP multicast references a set of specifications that allows an IP host to transmit one packet to multiple destinations. This one-to-many transmission method is accomplished using Class D IP addresses (224.0.0.0 to 239.255.255.255), which are mapped directly to data-link layer 2 multicast addresses. Through the use of IP multicasting, a term used to reference the use of Class D addresses, the need for an IP host to transmit multiple packets to multiple destinations is eliminated. This, in turn, permits more efficient use of backbone network bandwidth; however, the arrival of IP Class D addressed packets at a network destination, such as a router connected to an internal corporate network, can result in a bandwidth problem. This is because multicast transmission is commonly used for audio and/or video distribution of educational information, videoconferencing, news feeds, and financial reports, such as delivering stock prices. Due to the amount of traffic associated with multicast transmission, it could adversely affect multiple subnets linked together by a LAN switch that uses subnets for vLAN creation. By providing a "registration" capability that allows an individual LAN user to become a single-user vLAN associated with a Class D address, Class D packets can be routed to a specific segment even when several segments have the same subnet. Thus, this limits the effect of multicast transmission to a single segment.

11.3.6 Upper Layer Switching

In concluding this chapter, we briefly turn our attention to upper layer switches, a term used by this author to collectively denote switching performed at ISO Open System Interconnection (OSI) Reference Model layers above the data-link layer. Beginning in the latter portion of 1996, vendors introduced switching products that operate at layer 3, the network layer, and even layer 4, the transport layer. By 2002, vendors had extended switching capability to the application layer, layer 7 in the ISO Reference Model.

Switches operating above layer 2 are based on the need to provide network users with a higher degree of functionality. Although we can truthfully state that switches operating above layer 2 look deeper into the frame to examine higher layer packet data encapsulated in LAN frames, that is a simplistic view of such switches. To obtain a better appreciation for the operation and utilization of upper layer switches, let us first examine the rationale for the development of such switches.

11.3.6.1 Rationale. A layer 2 switch operates using MAC addresses. In doing so, it views all interconnected networks as flat, requiring flooding to occur when the destination address in a frame is unknown. Using a flat network view, the higher capacity of layer 2 LAN switches over traditional shared media hubs begins to be negated due to redundant traffic being carried over switch-based networks as well as broadcast storms occurring on such networks. As previously discussed in this chapter during our examination of virtual LANs, the introduction of vLAN capability to layer 2 LAN switches enabled users to partition a switch into broadcast domains, which alleviates some of the effect of broadcasts interfering with data transfer. However, unless you create a large number of vLANs, which introduces inter-vLAN communications problems, you will continue to have broadcast problems.

Another limitation of layer 2 switches is the fact that they are based on layer 2 addresses. This means that they are not capable of recognizing the structure of a hierarchical network nor taking advantage of that network structure.

Because layer 2 LAN switches operate considerably faster than routers that operate at the network layer, such switches achieve a high degree of penetration in isolated islands of corporate LANs. However, routers are still required to move packets between geographically separated networks or to collapse the layer 2 switch infrastructure using the router as a backbone device. An example of the latter is shown in Figure 11.28, where a router is used to link two switches together as well as provide a WAN connection to a distant network location.

One of the problems associated with using routers to collapse switch-based networks, provide inter-vLAN communications, and perform other functions is the fact that they are relatively slow in comparison to the operation of layer 2 switches. Conventional routers are software-based devices that use microprocessors to perform such traditional functions as

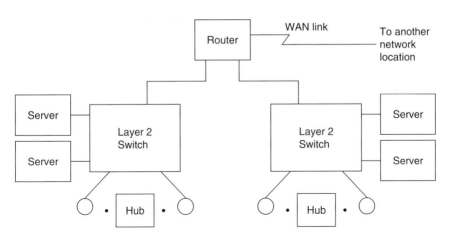

Figure 11.28   Using a Router to Interconnect Switches

looking up next-hop route information, modifying packet headers, and forwarding packets out an appropriate router port. As it operates at layer 3, a conventional router must update the time-to-live (TTL) field in IP packets, recalculate the frame check sequence (FCS), and perform other network-related functions that limit the number of packets per second that can be processed. Layer 2 switches commonly perform most tasks in hardware, using application specific integrated circuits (ASICs) to achieve frame processing rates in the millions of frames per second. In comparison, conventional routers may be hard-pressed to operate above 5000 packets per second as they perform the previously described operations via software.

The performance problems associated with routers used to interconnect layer 2 switches as well as the need to developing faster processing capabilities for internetworking applications, such as the use of routers to transmit packets on the Internet, resulted in the incorporation of several techniques to enhance the packet processing capability of routers. Those techniques include the use of ASICs and special headers appended to packets to identify traffic flows and facilitate their routing. The latter technique is more commonly referred to as tag switching and standardized as Multiprotocol Label Switching (MPLS). Now that we have an overview of the rationale for the development of higher layer switching, let us turn our attention to the methods used to obtain this capability.

11.3.6.2   Layer 3 Switching. When we discuss layer 3 switching, we are really talking about a wide range of products that operate at the network layer. Some products are LAN switches with a built-in simplistic routing capability that enables the switch to look into each frame to the network layer and make switching decisions based upon the type of protocol network address (as previously discussed during our examination of virtual LANs). Other layer 3 switching products are actually designed to forward packets at extremely high data rates beyond the capabilities of conventional routers. As such, they are manufactured for providing transmission over a wide area network in comparison to layer 3 LAN switches that provide a vLAN creation capability on a local area network. To obtain the high-speed packet processing capability, the second type of router either is designed to use ASICs for processing each packet or creates flows to facilitate the movement of packets. Thus, we can further categorize layer 3 switching by the manner by which packets are processed: packet by packet or flow based.

11.3.6.3 Packet-by-Packet Routing. When layer 3 switching uses a packet-by-packet routing method, the router, or perhaps a better term to use is the switch/router, examines each packet via hardware and forwards it to its destination using standardized routing protocols. Through the use of ASICs to perform a majority of traditional router functions as well as the replacement of a bus-based architecture by either a shared-memory or crossbar architecture, switch/router packet processing performance is significantly enhanced.

A key advantage of the switch/router that operates on a packet-by-packet basis is its compatibility with other routers in the network. Such switch/routers do not need to recognize special packet headers that are employed by the second type of layer 3 switch, one that uses flow-based routing.

11.3.6.4 Flow-Based Routing. Layer 3 flow-based switching was developed by Ipsilon Networks in 1996 and was shortly followed by other vendors that introduced their own methods for using network addresses for high-speed switch/router products. Here, the term "flow" represents a conversation between two end stations through a network. Flow-based switching requires tags to be appended to packets to expedite their delivery and was standardized as MPLS.

In flow-based routing, an initial packet or group of packets is identified to determine if they are flowing to a common destination and if the packet is part of a larger sequence of packets, with the latter occurring by examining packet sequence numbers and the window size negotiated during a TCP/IP session. During this initial flow learning process, the first or first few packets are routed. Once a flow is identified, a mechanism is used to inform all intermediate devices between flow points of the flow so they can use switching instead of routing.

One of the most popular methods used to identify a flow is to prefix a tag to the packet. This technique, which is referred to as tag switching, was initially used by Cisco Systems prior to the standardization of MPLS.

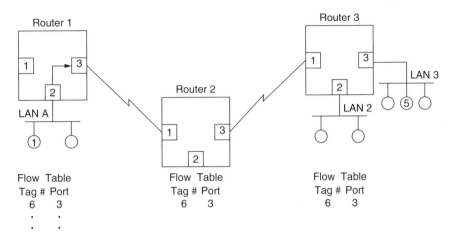

Figure 11.29 Flow-Based Routing Using Packet Tagging Assuming Flow from Station 1 on LAN A to Station 5 on LAN 3 Is Identified by Tag Number 6

Figure 11.29 illustrates an example of the partial construction of router flow tables assuming the use of packet tagging. In this example, assume a flow from station 1 on LAN A to station 5 on LAN 3 was identified and assigned a tag value of 6. Router 1 would prefix each packet inbound from port 2 that meets the flow criteria with tag number 6 and by examining its flow table switch packets with tag 6 out port 3. At router 2, packets inbound with a tag value of 6 would be switched out of port 3. In tag switching, each router between flow points only has to examine the tag to determine how to switch the incoming packet, significantly enhancing the packet per second processing rate of the switch/router. However, each router between flow points must be capable of supporting tag switching or another type of layer 3 forwarding based upon the type of forwarding used by the network.

Although flow-based routing can considerably enhance the packet processing rate of switch/routers, this method of routing originally represented proprietary solutions that did not provide interoperability between different vendor products. This situation changed with the standardization of MPLS.

A current limitation of flow-based routing is the fact that you cannot use such network applications as traceroute to determine the route to a destination because the use of tags or labels results in a proprietary route development mechanism through the network. However, if you need an extremely high packet processing capability, a flow-based layer 3 switching technique may provide the solution to your organization's processing requirements.

11.3.6.5 Layer 4 Switching. A layer 4 switch looks further into each packet, examining layer 4 information such as the contents of the TCP or the UDP header. Once this information is obtained, the layer 4 switch becomes capable of making decisions concerning the routing of traffic based upon the type of application being carried by the packet. Because a sequence of packets carrying a particular application results in a session of activity, another term for a layer 4 switch is a "session switch."

By examining the start of a transmission session via noting a SYN packet or a TCP start, the switch can be used to provide a number of functions that can be difficult, if not impossible, for layer 2 and layer 3 switches to perform. For example, by examining the TCP or UDP port numbers, a layer 4 switch can bind sessions to specific IP addresses based on the use of predefined criteria, such as the flow of traffic to two or more servers. To illustrate this, consider the use of the layer 4 LAN switch that is shown in Figure 11.30. In this example, the layer 4 switch can function as a load balancer or application distributor.

In the example illustrated in Figure 11.30, the layer 4 switch could function as a virtual IP (VIP) front end to the servers connected to the switch. Here, a VIP address would be configured for each server or group of servers that supports a single or a common application. Once the switch

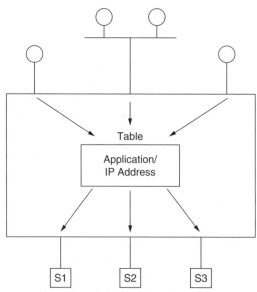

A layer 4 switch can switch packets based upon the application being transported.

Figure 11.30   Using a Layer 4 Switch

determines the appropriate server to satisfy a session, it binds the session to a specific IP address and substitutes the server's real IP address for the virtual IP address. Once the preceding is accomplished, the layer 4 switch forwards the connection request and subsequent packets, remapping the addresses of the packets until a session termination or FIN packets are encountered.

In general, layer 4 switches are slower than layer 2 switches because they must look further into the packet, requiring additional processing time. In addition, layer 4 switches are primarily designed for intranet applications. Thus, while layer 4 switches can provide a relatively high-speed packet processing capability, their layer 3 operations may be limited, with many routing protocols not supported by the switch.

Although the use of layer 4 switching is primarily to note application sessions and route those sessions to an appropriate port, it should be noted that when functioning as a traffic balancer, the switch represents a much more capable product than a hardware-based load balancer. Concerning the latter, a load balancer is typically a two to four LAN, one WAN port device that simply routes incoming Web traffic requests to mirrored servers. In comparison, a layer 4 switch can route all types of traffic and can range in size from a few ports to hundreds of ports.

11.3.6.6 Application Layer Switching. An application layer switch would appear to operate at layer 7 of the ISO Reference Model. While this assumption is correct for some protocol stacks, because an application in the TCP/IP protocol suite is identified by port number, application layer switching can occur at layer 4. Thus, in a TCP/IP environment, application layer switching occurs through the use of a layer 4 switch.

Chapter 12
LAN Monitoring Tools

In previous chapters in this book, we discussed, described, and developed mathematical models that you could exercise to determine the performance of a local area network (LAN) or the wide area network (WAN) transmission facility used to connect two geographically separated LANs. The use of many of the models developed in this book depends on one or more frame or packet characteristics, such as the average frame length, the number of frames flowing to a particular station per unit time, or a similar metric. In prior chapters we assumed the information could be obtained. In this chapter we discuss and describe two network monitoring tools you can use to obtain detailed information that can be used as input to one or more models previously developed in this book.

12.1 EtherPeek

EtherPeek, a product of WildPackets (formerly known as the AG Group) of Walnut Creek, California, is a comprehensive protocol analyzer that operates at and above the data-link layer of the OSI Reference Model. This program includes a large number of features that enable statistics to be gathered concerning the flow of Ethernet frames as well as higher layer packets contained in the frames. Readers can download a trial copy of EtherPeek from the WildPackets Web site (www.wildpackets.com).

12.1.1 Operational Overview

Figure 12.1 illustrates the initial screen display of EtherPeek in its capture mode. Note that at the upper-left corner of the display, the number of bytes available is shown as 2,097,152, which in effect represents 2048 Kbytes. This represents the default buffer area used by EtherPeek for capturing data. While this may appear to represent a large amount of recording capability, as we will soon note this amount of memory can be rapidly filled by frames on a heavily utilized LAN. Fortunately, EtherPeek includes several mechanisms that enable you to focus your packet capturing effort on specific types of packets.

You can tailor EtherPeek in several ways to satisfy your data capture and analysis effort. One way to overcome the inability to capture more than a short period of activity on a heavily utilized LAN is to increase the size of the capture buffer. This can be accomplished by selecting the Capture

Figure 12.1 The EtherPeek Capture Screen Display

Figure 12.2   Use the Capture Buffer Options Dialog Box to Adjust the Size of Packets Captured and the Amount of Memory Used for Packet Capturing

Buffer option from the Capture menu. Figure 12.2 illustrates the display of the resulting Capture Buffer Options dialog box.

12.1.1.1   Capture Buffer. In examining Figure 12.2, note that you can truncate the information captured for each packet by clicking on the box labeled "Limit each packet to." You can also adjust the buffer size from its default of 2048 Kbytes as well as select a continuous capture mode if you want to observe activity over a prolonged period of time on a heavily utilized LAN.

12.1.1.2   Filtering. Another technique you can use to control the capture of packets is to employ filtering, predefining specific types of packets you want captured.* An example is your LAN runs IP and NetWare, but because the latter is not routed to the Internet, you might want to limit statistics gathering to IP. By limiting the capture of packets to IP and defining a router IP address, you could significantly narrow the scope of packet capturing to determining the arrival rate of frames destined to the Internet. This would represent one of many general filtering methods you can employ through the use of the program's filtering capability. Now that we have a general appreciation for the use of filtering, let us examine some specific capabilities associated with the use of the program.

---

*For example, if your LAN runs IP and NetWare, you might want to limit statistics gathering to IP because NetWare is not routed to the Internet.

Figure 12.3 illustrates the EtherPeek Filters screen display resulting from the selection of the Filters option from the Capture menu. As indicated in the upper portion of the display, you can select packet filtering as one of three options. You can set the filter mode to ignore all filters, resulting in all packets being captured. As an alternative, you can set the filter mode so that only packets matching checked filters are captured (which is selected in Figure 12.3), or you can set the filter mode so that packets not matching checked filters are captured. The latter is equivalent to a boolean NOT operator.

Once you select the type of filters you want to employ for a specific protocol, you can further quantify filtering by either double-clicking on a selected protocol or clicking on the Add button. Either action results in the display of the dialog box labeled Filter Settings, which is shown in Figure 12.4.

As indicated in Figure 12.4, through the use of the Filter Settings dialog box you can select a variety of filtering options to control the types of packets that will be captured. Concerning basic filtering options, you can select address, protocol, offset, and error filtering. Address filtering allows you to filter based on the type of address, such as Ethernet, AppleTalk, IP, and DecNet. You can effect filtering based on a specific address, pair of addresses, or any source or destination address. Although all Ethernet addresses are shown for the IP filter illustrated in Figure 12.4, you could select a specific Ethernet or IP destination address to examine the flow of packets to a router if you need such information to examine the potential effect of different WAN operating rates on the queuing system formed by a router and its WAN transmission facility.

The protocol filter provides the ability to select certain types of protocols to filter. Although IP was previously selected, you could use the protocol filter option to select a certain type of IP protocol such as the Address Resolution Protocol (ARP). The offset filter option provides the ability to move to a specific location within a packet and specify the value of data for the filter matching criteria. The fourth type of filter is the error filter. As indicated in Figure 12.4, for Ethernet filtering, the program's error filter options include CRC and frame alignment errors and run and oversize packets.

12.1.1.3 Packet Capture. After selecting your filters and possibly modifying the default buffer settings, you are ready to initiate a packet capturing session. An example of a packet capturing session in which only IP packets are captured based on the previously shown general filter that was created is illustrated in Figure 12.5.

The packets captured that meet your predefined filtering criteria are listed in the order in which they are observed on the network. As indicated in Figure 12.5, packets are numbered sequentially and their source and

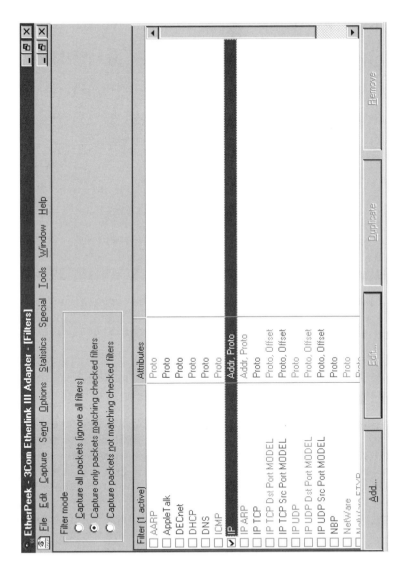

Figure 12.3 Use the EtherPeek Filters Screen to Control the Type Captured

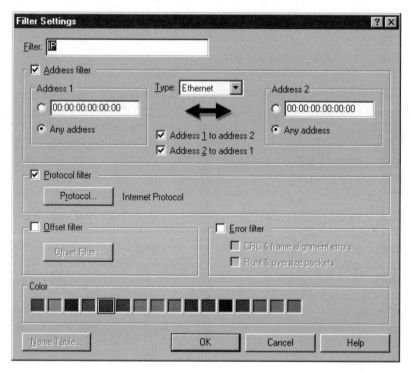

Figure 12.4   Use the Filter Settings Dialog Box to Set Values for up to Four Types of Filters

destination address, packet size, time of occurrence, and protocol are listed. As we will shortly note, there are several methods you can use to alter information displayed about each captured packet.

12.1.1.4 Display Options. In examining Figure 12.5, note the column labeled "Flag" that appears blank. In actuality, that field can display up to five characters that indicate the occurrence of certain types of predefined situations. Those situations can be observed through the Packet Flags tab in the program's Display Options dialog box, which is illustrated in Figure 12.6. In the Packet Flags tab shown in Figure 12.6, an asterisk (*) is shown and is used to indicate IEEE 802.3 Logical Link Control (LLC) packets, while the alphabetic characters C, F, R, and T are used to indicate CRC checksum errors, frame alignment errors, runt/oversize packet errors, and trigger packets, respectively. When any of these conditions occur, the appropriate character is displayed in the Flag field previously illustrated in Figure 12.6.

Returning briefly to Figure 12.5, note that during the monitoring period, a total of 6888 packets were received. This means that 688 packets flowing on the network were read. However, because a filter was employed, only

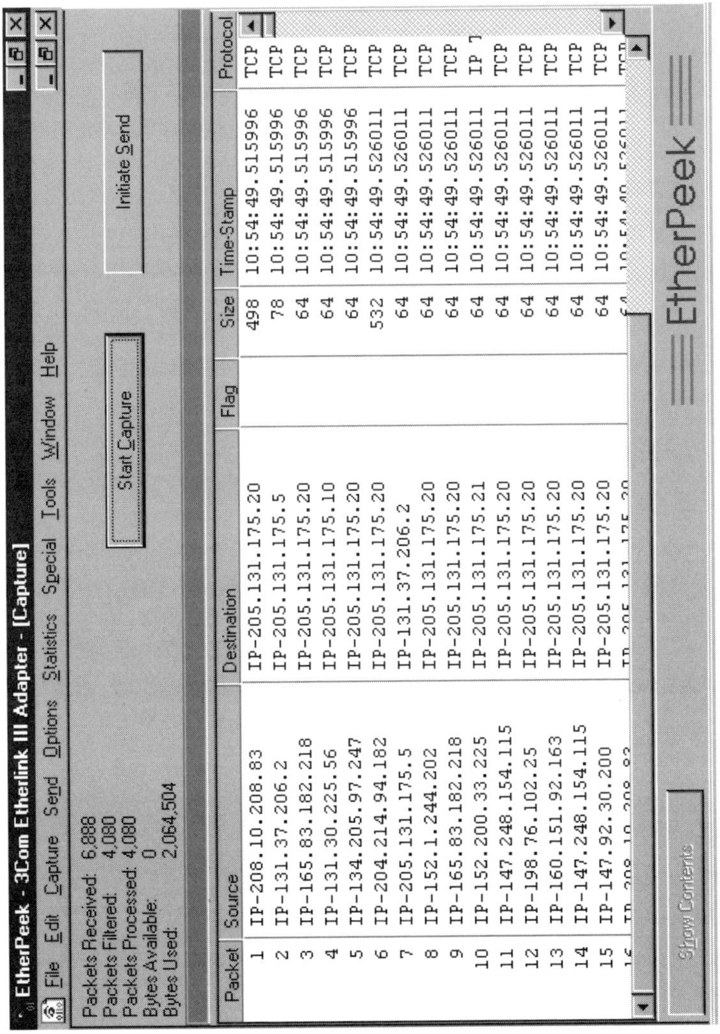

Figure 12.5   Captured Packets Meeting Your Filtering Criteria Are Listed by Time of Occurrence

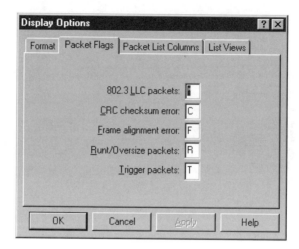

Figure 12.6   Use the Packet Flags Tab in the Display Options Dialog Box to Control the Display Indicator Used to Denote Five Predefined Conditions

4080 packets met the filtering criteria and were processed. Because continuous monitoring was not employed, the approximately 2 Mbytes of buffer space were used until the number of available bytes reached zero and packet capturing terminated.

Another display option you can use to control the display of packet information is the Packet List Columns tab located in the Display Options dialog box. Figure 12.7 provides a view of the default settings of the previously mentioned tab. Note that you can display a variety of other packet fields, such as source and destination port values, which can be extremely important when attempting to ascertain information about the application being transported.

12.1.2 Statistics

Although a major rationale for the use of EtherPeek or a similar packet analysis program is to decode the content of packets for the purpose of this book, our interest is oriented toward obtaining statistical information. This is because the models developed in this book are oriented toward metrics concerned with the flow of data instead of the contents of the data. Thus, we will conclude our examination of EtherPeek with a peek, no pun intended, at its statistics capability. However, prior to doing so, it should be mentioned that a key function of EtherPeek is its packet analysis capability. By double-clicking on a packet entry in the Packet Capture window, you can have the program decode the contents of the packet.

Returning to the topic of this section, through the Statistics menu you can view a variety of program-generated statistics. Figure 12.8 illustrates

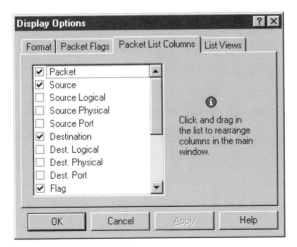

Figure 12.7   Use the Packet List Columns Tab to Control the Display of Packet Information on the Packet Capture Screen

the Source Node summary screen display that indicates by IP address the percentage of packets transmitted and the total number of packets transmitted during the previous packet capture session. You can also generate a similar set of statistics by destination node, as well as a summary by both source and destination nodes. Through the use of one or more of the previously mentioned displays, you can identify the percentage and number of packets transmitted by specific devices or to specific devices during the packet capture period, thus providing you with the ability to obtain information that can be valuable in developing queuing models.

In concluding this brief examination of EtherPeek, Figure 12.9 illustrates the program's Summary Statistics screen display. Note for each packet capture session the summary statistics display provides a summary of the distribution of packets by packet length as well as other information, such as the duration of the packet capture session, the total number of packets read, packets collected and multicast and broadcast packets. Also note that because the LAN monitored is a heavily utilized network, it only required six seconds to fill a 2-Mbyte packet buffer. Thus, to obtain a longer period of observation, you should more than likely consider employing a more narrowly focused filter as well as using a larger buffer size.

12.2   EtherVision

A second program readers can consider to obtain statistical information concerning the flow of data on their LANs is EtherVision, a product from Triticom of Eden Prairie, Minnesota. The Triticom Web site is located at www.triticom.com.

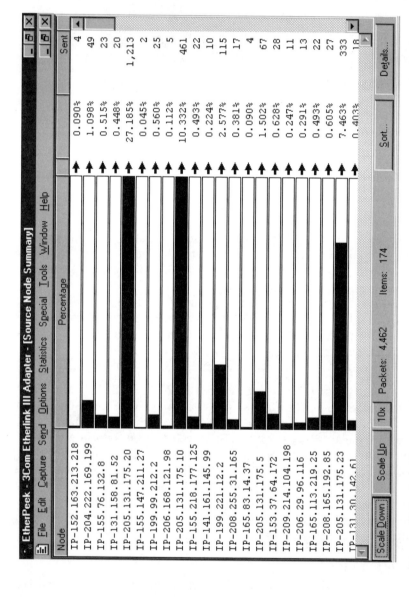

Figure 12.8 Use EtherPeek's Statistics Menu to Display Summary Statistics Based on the IP Address of Packets Transmitted, Packet Destinations, or Both

Stat	Current	Snapshot 1	Snapshot 2	Snapshot 3	Snapshot 4	Snapshot 5
Start Date	10/29/98	10/29/98	10/29/98	10/29/98	10/29/98	10/
Start Time	12:48:09 PM	11:09:13 AM	11:09:13 AM	11:09:13 AM	11:09:13 AM	11:09:
Duration	06s	09s	09s	09s	09s	
Total (p)	7,368	7,376	7,376	7,376	7,375	
Collected (p)	4,640	4,804	4,804	4,804	4,804	
Multicast Packets (p)	5	4	4	4	4	
Broadcast Packets (p)	5	4	4	4	4	
64 Byte Packets (p)	2,815	2,800	2,800	2,800	2,800	
64-127 Byte Packets (p)	66	68	68	68	63	
128-255 Byte Packets (p)	72	85	85	85	85	
256-511 Byte Packets (p)	317	319	319	319	319	
512-1023 Byte Packets (p)	432	716	716	716	715	
1024-1517 Byte Packets (p)	92	75	75	75	75	
1518 Byte Packets (p)	846	741	741	741	741	
Web URLs (p)	4,225	4,313	4,313	4,313	4,313	
TCP Checksum Error (p)	.	.	.	.	.	
ICMP Packets (p)	.	.	.	.	.	
ICMP Source Quench (p)	.	.	.	.	.	
ICMP Dest Unreach (p)	.	.	.	.	.	
ICMP Port Unreach (p)	.	.	.	.	.	
FTP Xfers Initiated (p)	.	1	1	1	1	

Figure 12.9 EtherPeek Summary Statistics Display Provides a Summary of Packets by Packet Length Interval

Figure 12.10   Use the EtherVision Available Options Menu to Monitor the Traffic Based on Source or Destination Address

12.2.1 Operation

Figure 12.10 illustrates the EtherVision Available Options menu when the program is initialized. Note that the first option, Monitor Traffic, results in two options. You can either monitor traffic based on the source address in each frame or the destination address in each frame. Similar to EtherPeek, EtherVision requires the use of a promiscuous LAN adapter card for its production version because the program needs to read each frame on the network. Unlike EtherPeek, which provides a packet decoding capability and operates at and above the data-link layer, EtherVision is restricted to operating at the data-link layer. While it can neither decode packets nor provide higher layer information, the program can provide summary statistics by station, which may be all you require for gathering information required by the models presented in this book.

12.2.2 Statistics

Figure 12.11 illustrates the EtherVision monitoring screen after an elapsed period of 73 seconds. Note that at this time the program discovered nine distinct source addresses and accumulated statistics concerning the number of frames transmitted by each station. Using a table of vendor hardware addresses, the program can identify the manufacturer of most LAN adapter cards by comparing the first three bytes in each address against entries in its table that represent registered vendor IDs. In addition, the program provides the ability to associate names to hardware addresses to facilitate the recognition of different stations. In the example shown in

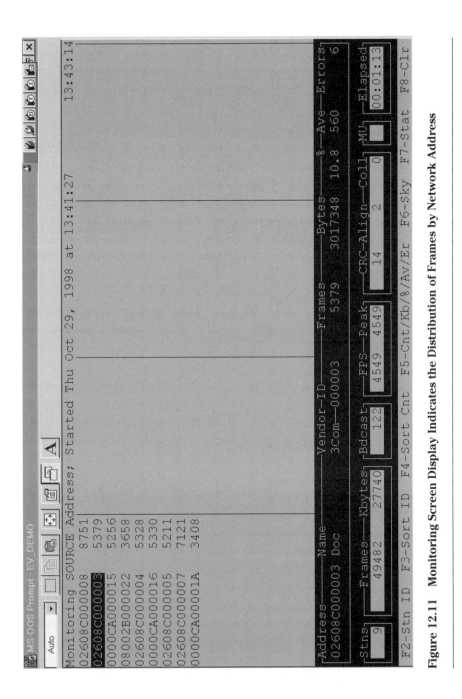

Figure 12.11   Monitoring Screen Display Indicates the Distribution of Frames by Network Address

Figure 12.11, the dark area near the bottom of the screen indicates that the highlighted address at the top of the screen has the name Doc, used a LAN adapter manufactured by 3 Com Corporation, and transmitted 10.8 percent of all the frames flowing on the LAN since monitoring commenced.

In concluding this brief review of EtherVision, we will examine its Statistics display, which is obtained by pressing the F7 key from the monitoring display. Figure 12.12 illustrates an example of this display. Note that this screen provides specific information about Ethernet frames, to include the total frames flowing on the network and their average size or length. This display also indicates the distribution of frame by length, network utilization, and other statistical information that can be used with one or more of the models previously developed in this book.

Regardless of the network monitoring tool utilized, it is important to note that the use of an appropriate tool can provide a literal window of observation concerning the activity on a network. By accumulating statistics, you can spot trends, gather metrics to exercise performance models, and obtain the ability to denote potential problems before they become problems. Thus, while this author will not recommend the use of a specific tool, he emphatically recommends the use of a network monitoring tool!

For readers who wish to contact the developers of the two programs discussed in this chapter, Table 12.1 lists their voice, fax, and postal addresses. In addition, the Web addresses of both vendors are listed as a point of reference concerning the latest versions of their products.

Table 12.1   Vendor Contacts

EtherPeek

WildPackets (formerly known as the AG Group, Inc.)

WildPackets Inc.
1340 Treat Blvd.
Suite 500
Walnut Creek, California 94597
Phone: (925) 937-3200, (800) 466-2447 (domestic)
Fax: (925) 937-3211
info@wildpackets.com
Web: http://www.wildpackets.com

EtherVision

Triticom

P.O. Box 46427
Eden Prairie, Minnesota 55344
Phone: (952) 829-8019
Fax: (952) 937-1998
info@triticom.com
Web: http://www.triticom.com

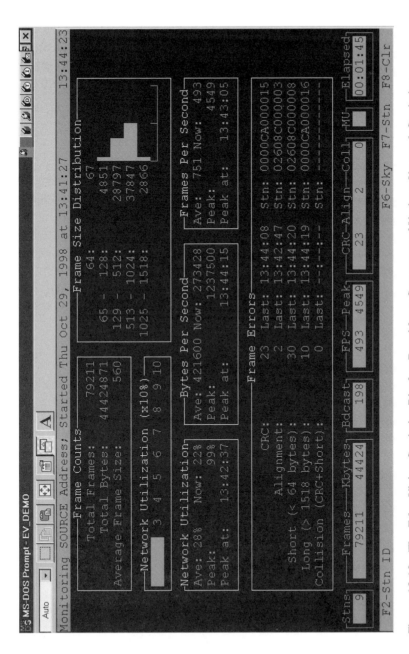

Figure 12.12 **The EtherVision Statistics Display Provides a Summary of Various Network Statistics**

Chapter 13
Transmission Optimization Techniques

Until now, the primary focus of this book was on the creation and use of mathematical models to predict the performance of different types of local area networks (LANs) and internetworking devices. In this chapter we turn our attention to the use of several optimization techniques that, when incorporated into bridges and routers, will enhance the efficiency of inter- and intra-network transmission. In addition, we will examine the use of different types of network interface cards or adapters which, when used in a workstation, enhance its ability to transfer information onto and receive information from the network.

The techniques examined in this chapter include the use of filtering, precedence and express queuing, data compression, frame truncation, and the switched telephone network to supplement the use of leased lines during peak transmission periods. Readers should note that most remote bridge and router manufacturers provide one or more of the techniques described in this chapter. However, readers should also note that the efficiency of the implementation of each technique varies between vendors. In addition, most vendors only provide a small subset of the techniques covered in this chapter. Because the value of each technique is based on your specific networking requirements, you will have to compare the operational results of each technique against your specific communications environment to determine which techniques provide a higher level of networking capability and then use this chapter as a guide in your equipment selection process.

In examining network interface cards (NICs), our focus is on the different hardware design features and the effect of those features on the data transfer capability of the adapter. You can also use this information as a guide to facilitate your equipment selection process.

13.1 Filtering

Filtering is the most common transmission optimization technique incorporated into remote bridges and routers. Although most devices support a predefined filtering capability in which source and/or destination frame addresses are entered into a filtering table during the equipment installation process, other devices permit an authorized administrator to dynamically change the filtering tables because few networks are static.

13.1.1 Local versus Remote Filtering

Through the use of filtering you can control the number and types of packets that are forwarded across a transmission circuit linking two remote bridges or routers. Although you can also use filtering to control the flow of data between two LANs connected by a local bridge, we focus our attention on the application of filtering by devices interconnected via wide area network (WAN) transmission facilities. This is because the application of filtering by devices connected via WAN transmission facilities directly affects the required transmission rate linking the filtering devices. Because the monthly cost of a wide area transmission facility is proportional to its operating rate, the ability to lower the required operating rate through the use of filtering can be expected to reduce your organization's transmission cost. In comparison, the use of filtering by a local bridge has a less significant effect. First, it usually has no effect on cost because local cabling links each network at the common local bridge, as illustrated at the top of Figure 13.1. Second, the use of filtering has a lesser effect on performance when performed by a local bridge than when performed by a remote bridge. This is because the WAN link connecting two remote bridges or routers operates at a fraction of the operating rate of each network. Thus, the removal of frames via filtering, as illustrated in the lower portion of Figure 13.1, has a more pronounced effect on a lower operating rate circuit than local cable connecting two higher operating rate LANs.

13.1.2 Filtering Methods

There are several types of filtering supported by bridges and routers. Two of the most common methods of filtering frames are based on the use of the address and service fields in a frame. If you are working with packets at layer 3, then the port field in an IP environment would replace the service field.

13.1.2.1 Address Field Filtering. The most basic type of filtering is performed by bridges that operate at the MAC sublayer of the OSI Reference Model's data-link layer. Operating at this layer, bridges are transparent to high-level protocols that function at the network layer of the OSI Reference Model. Thus, the primary mechanism used for filtering is based on the use of the

Local bridging

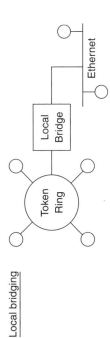

Filtering has no effect upon the cabling used to connect local networks. Since both networks operate at MBPS rates the removal of frames based on filtering usually has a negligible effect upon network performance.

Remote bridging

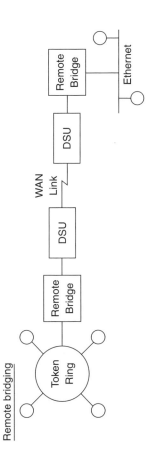

Filtering can have a significant effect upon the operating rate of a circuit connecting geographically dispersed networks since the WAN link normally operates at a fraction of each LAN operating rate.

Figure 13.1   Effect of Local versus Remote Bridge Filtering

destination and source address fields within Token Ring and Ethernet/IEEE 802.3 frames. For example, consider the IEEE Token Ring functional addresses listed in Table 2.5 in Chapter 2. Assume that you want to preclude the transmission of Token Ring functional address frames from being forwarded onto the Ethernet network illustrated in Figure 13.1, because those frames are normally irrelevant to stations on the Ethernet network. To do so, you would set your bridge to filter all frames with destination addresses equivalent to the block of destination addresses assigned by the IEEE to the Token Ring functional addresses listed in Table 2.5 (Chapter 2).

To illustrate the effect of functional address filtering, consider the active monitor address listed in Table 2.5 (Chapter 2). The active monitor on a Token Ring network transmits an active monitor frame every seven seconds, or 12,343 times each day. This frame is used to notify the standby monitors that the active monitor is operational and the frame is irrelevant to an Ethernet network. Thus, the filtering of just this one frame reduces the flow of data from a Token Ring network onto an Ethernet network by approximately 13,000 frames per day. Even when two Token Ring networks are interconnected active monitor frames should be filtered because each network has its own active monitor. Thus, this filtering example is applicable to both Token Ring-to Ethernet as well as Token Ring-to-Token Ring bridging.

13.1.2.2 Service Access Point Filtering. Filtering based on destination and source address fields is supported by essentially all bridges. A more sophisticated level of filtering supported by some bridges is based on the DSAP (destination services access point) and SSAP (source services access point) addresses carried within the information field of Token Ring and Ethernet/IEEE 802.3 frames.

Figure 13.2 illustrates the general format of the conversion of a Token Ring frame into an Ethernet frame. The DSAP and SSAP can be considered post office boxes that identify locations where information is left and received to and from higher level layers of the OSI Reference Model. For example, the transportation of an electronic mail message used by a higher network process would have a defined DSAP. Thus, a bridge that includes the capability to perform filtering based on DSAP and SSAP addresses would provide the ability to perform filtering at the application level, as well as add a degree of security to your network if you want to restrict the movement of frames carrying certain types of information between networks.

13.2 Precedence and Express Queuing

Chapter 4 examined the use of waiting line analysis or queuing to determine an optimum line operating rate to link remote bridges and routers, the effect of single and dual port equipment on network performance, and buffer memory requirements of network devices. In doing so, we assumed that the servicing of queues was based on a first-in, first-out basis. That is,

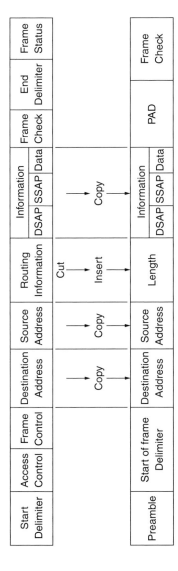

Figure 13.2 Token Ring to IEEE 802.3 Frame Conversion

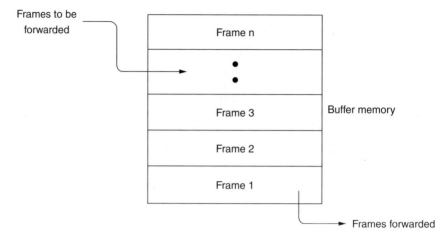

Figure 13.3 First-In, First-Out Queuing

---

the arrival of frame n followed by frame n+1 into a queue would result in a remote bridge or router transmitting frame n prior to transmitting frame n+1. Although most remote bridges and routers operate on a first-in, first-out service basis, other devices may support precedence and/or express queuing. In doing so, they provide a level of performance that may considerably exceed the performance of other devices that do not support such queuing options during periods of peak network activity. To illustrate the advantages of precedence and express queuing, let us first focus attention on the operation of first-in, first-out queuing and some of the problems associated with this queuing method.

13.2.1 First-In, First-Out Queuing

When first-in, first-out queuing is used, messages are queued in the order in which they are received. This is the simplest method of queuing, as a single physical and logical buffer area is used to store data and all messages are assumed to have the same priority of service. The software used by the bridge or router simply extracts each frame based on their position in the queue. Figure 13.3 illustrates first-in, first-out queuing.

13.2.2 Queuing Problems

The major problems associated with first-in, first-out queuing involve the effect of this queuing method on a mixture of interactive and batch transmission during peak network utilization periods. To illustrate the problems associated with first-in, first-out queuing, consider the network illustrated in Figure 13.4 in which a Token Ring network is connected to an Ethernet network through the use of a pair of remote bridges.

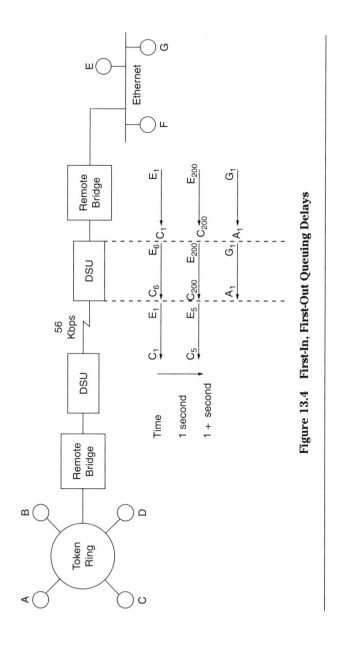

Figure 13.4   First-In, First-Out Queuing Delays

13.2.2.1   Mixing File Transfer and Interactive Sessions. Now assume that station E on the Ethernet initiates a file transfer to station C on the Token Ring. Also assume that the Ethernet network is a 10BASE-T network operating at 10 Mbps and the wide area network transmission facility operates at 56 Kbps.

If the stations on the Ethernet are IBM PC or compatible computers with industry standard architecture (ISA) Ethernet adapter boards, the maximum transfer rate is normally less than 300,000 bytes per second. Using that figure and assuming station E transmitted for one second in which each frame was the maximum length of 1500 information field bytes, not including frame overhead, a total of 300,000 bytes/1500 bytes per frame, or 200 frames, would be presented to the remote bridge. At 56 Kbps, the bridge would forward 56,000/(8 × 1500), or approximately 5 frames, not considering the WAN protocol and frame overhead. Thus, at the end of one second, there could be 195 frames in the bridge's buffer, as illustrated in the lower-right portion of Figure 13.4.

Now assume that at slightly after one second of time, station G on the Ethernet transmits a query to an application operating on station A on the Token Ring. The 195 frames in the buffer of the remote bridge would require approximately 40 seconds (195 frames × 1500 bytes/frame × 8 bits/byte/56,000 bps) to be emptied from the buffer and placed onto the line prior to the frame from station G being placed onto the line. Thus, first-in, first-out queuing can seriously degrade transmission from an Ethernet to another Ethernet or to a Token Ring network when file transfer and interactive transmission occurs between networks. The reverse situation, in which transmission is from a Token Ring to an Ethernet or between two Token Ring networks, does not result in as significant problems because a priority mechanism is built into the Token Ring frame, which results in a more equitable shared use of the network bandwidth than achievable on an Ethernet network.

13.2.2.2   Workstation Retransmissions. In the preceding example we noted the potential for the delay of 40 seconds until data from station G was transmitted. In actuality, this will almost never happen because most remote bridges and routers have installation guidelines that typically suggest that you configure buffer memory to store only a few seconds' worth of data. However, doing so results in a workstation attempting to transfer a file retransmitting frames that were not accepted by the bridge or router, adding to network traffic as well as the level of network utilization. This will have a detrimental effect on a series of stations attempting concurrent file transfer operations, as well as stations performing interactive client/server activities when file transfer operations are in effect. In certain situations, buffer queuing delays, added to frame retransmission time, can result in file transfer timeouts that result in the termination of the

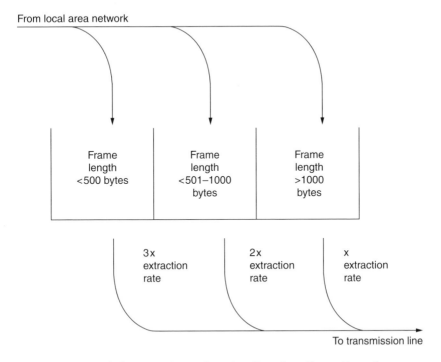

From local area network

Frame length <500 bytes

Frame length <501–1000 bytes

Frame length >1000 bytes

3x extraction rate

2x extraction rate

x extraction rate

To transmission line

Figure 13.5   Precedence Queuing Based on Frame Length

file transfer session. In other situations, random delays in interactive sessions will frustrate network users. Due to such problems, some remote bridge and router manufacturers have incorporated precedence queuing and express queuing into their products.

13.2.3 Precedence Queuing

Precedence queuing was probably the first method used by remote bridge and router manufacturers to enhance the transmission of inter- and intra-network traffic through device buffer memory. In precedence queuing, data entering a communications device, such as a remote bridge or router, is sorted by priority into separate queues as illustrated in Figure 13.5. Because a bridge operates at the MAC sublayer of the OSI Reference Model's data-link layer, a logical question many readers probably have concerns the method by which a bridge can recognize different frame priorities.

13.2.4 Methods Used

In actuality, until a few years ago a remote bridge performing precedence queuing did not look for a priority byte as there was none to look for. Instead, the bridge used one of two methods: examining the DSAP address in a frame or the frame length. The examination of DSAP addresses permits the bridge to recognize certain predefined applications and prioritize the routing of frames onto the WAN transmission facility based on those priorities. The second method, which is based on the frame length, presumes that interactive traffic is carried by shorter-length frames than file transfer and program load traffic. A few years ago, the IEEE 802.1p standard was promulgated, which, in conjunction with the 802.1q standard, added priority bits to a vLAN tag. Now, bridges and routers compatible with the new standard can examine the setting of frame priority bits to make precedence queuing decisions at layer 2.

13.2.5 Operation

Figure 13.5 illustrates the operation of precedence queuing based on frame length within the buffer area of a remote bridge. In this example, the physical buffer area is subdivided into logical partitions, with each partition used to queue frames whose length falls within a predefined range of values.

Frames from the attached LAN are placed into logical partitions based on the length of the frame. For an Ethernet network this could entail subdivision of the maximum length of 1500 bytes of the information field of that frame. Once logical queues are formed, the servicing of the queues can occur on a round-robin or priority basis. The lower portion of Figure 13.5 illustrates a priority extraction process. In this example, for every frame whose length exceeds 1000 bytes which is serviced and placed on the transmission line, two frames with a length of 501 to 1000 bytes and three frames whose length is less than or equal to 500 bytes are serviced from their queues and placed on the transmission line.

13.2.6 Express Queuing

Express queuing is a term used by one bridge and router manufacturer to represent the allocation of transmission bandwidth based on the destination address of frames in the queue as well as the number of frames with the same destination address in the queue. That is, under express queuing, transmission bandwidth is allocated so that in any given interval of time each destination address will be assigned to either a fixed portion of the WAN bandwidth or a smaller portion if there are fewer frames queued with that destination address. This technique recognizes the fact that interactive transmission is represented by a low rate of frame flow. Therefore, this type of transmission only requires a portion of the total transmission bandwidth to obtain an acceptable flow over the WAN transmission facility. The actual method by which bandwidth is allocated is based on an algorithm designed not only to provide interactive transmission priority service, but to also ensure that multiple concurrent file transfers share the majority of the remaining bandwidth in an equitable manner, which prevents timeouts from occurring.

13.3   Data Compression

Unless data is purely random, it contains a degree of redundancy. Data compression can be considered a process that uses one or more algorithms to reduce or eliminate data redundancies.

13.3.1   Compression Ratio

The efficiency of compression is referred to as the compression ratio, which represents the ratio of the number of original bytes in a frame to the number of compressed bytes. A high compression ratio represents either efficient compression, data with a high level of redundancy, or both.

Because data carried by information frames varies over time with respect to content and the amount of data redundancy, the compression ratio will vary with time. Normally, you can expect a compression performing remote bridge or router to have an average compression ratio between 2.0 and 2.5. Allowing for the fact that the WAN transmission protocol has a 10 to 20 percent overhead, the effect of compression typically results in the doubling of the information carrying capacity of a circuit. That is, as a general rule, you can expect a 56-Kbps digital circuit to transfer an average of 112 Kbps of LAN frame data when compression performing remote bridges or routers are used.

13.3.2   Compression Methods

There are three main categories into which compression methods fall: byte oriented, statistical, and table lookup or dictionary based.

13.3.2.1   Byte-Oriented Compression.   Byte-oriented compression techniques examine the bit composition of each byte, comparing the composition of the current byte to one or more succeeding bytes. If redundancies are noted, the algorithm replaces a series of bytes with a new sequence that eliminates those redundancies. A few of the more popular byte-oriented compression techniques include run length encoding, half-byte encoding, and null suppression.

Null suppression simply results in the substitution of a compression indicating character and null count character for a sequence of nulls. In comparison, run length encoding permits any character sequence to be reduced by the use of a three-character sequence to replace a repeated run of any character. The three-character sequence includes a compression-indicating character, the character in the run, and a count character.

Half-byte encoding is a compression technique that results in the replacement of a sequence of characters that has the same half-byte bit composition, such as a string of numerics, by encoding two numerics into a byte. Then, the reduced byte sequence is prefixed by a compression-indicating character and a count byte.

13.3.2.2 Statistical Compression. Statistical compression algorithms replace frequently occurring bytes by short codes and less frequently occurring bytes by longer codes. The net result of this replacement process is to reduce the average number of bits required to represent a character from 8 to a lesser number, typically between 4 and 5, resulting in a compression ratio of 2:1 or less. In replacing each fixed-length byte of 8 bits, the replacement process results in the use of a variable-length code. This variable-length code is constructed based on a statistical compression algorithm, with the Huffman coding technique being the most popular method employed. This technique results in the encoded compressed data bits having a prefix property that makes it instantaneously decodable. Thus, decompression performed according to the Huffman algorithm minimizes delays in comparison to the use of other compression methods. While this was an important consideration during the era of Intel 8088 microprocessors, the widespread availability of Intel Pentium and other modern high-performance microprocessors has reduced the decompression times associated with other compression techniques to the point where they do not adversely affect the throughput of data.

13.3.2.3 Dictionary-Based Compression. Because the replacement of frequently occurring bytes by short codes and less frequently occurring bytes by longer codes results in a reduction in the average number of bits required to represent a character, it is logical to assume that greater efficiencies can be obtained by substituting codes for strings of characters. This logic resulted in the development of dictionary-based compression algorithms in which transmitted data is placed into a dictionary and the location of characters and strings of characters (pointers) is transmitted instead of the actual data.

The most popular dictionary-based compression algorithm dates to the work of Jacob Ziv and Abraham Lempel at Haifa University during the late 1970s. More modern versions of their algorithm are referred to as Lempel-Ziv or LZ-based and differ in the method used to flush the dictionary, the number of pointers and size of the dictionary, and how pointers are coded in the compressed output.

One popular version of LZ coding is more commonly known as Lempel-Ziv-Welsh and is the method used in the CCITT V.42bis modem compression standard.

The LZW algorithm initially considers the character set as 256 individual string table entries whose codes range from 0 to 255. Then, the algorithm operates on the next character in the input string of characters as follows:

1. If the character is in the table, get the next character.
2. If the character is not in the table, output the last known string's encoding and add the new string to the table.

In the LZW algorithm, characters from the input data source are read and used to progressively form larger and larger strings until a string is formed that is not in the dictionary. When this occurs, the last known string's encoding is output and the new string is added to the table. The beauty of this technique is that the compressor and expander know that the initial string table consists of the 256 characters in the character set. Because the algorithm uses a numeric code as a token to indicate the position of a string in the dictionary's string table, this technique minimizes the token length as the dictionary begins to fill. To illustrate the simplicity of the operation of the LZW algorithm, let us view an example of its use.

Let us call the string previously read the *prefix* of the output string. Similarly, the last byte read becomes the *suffix*, where:

$$\text{prefix} + \text{suffix} = \text{new string}$$

Once a new string is formed, the suffix becomes the prefix (prefix = suffix).

Initially, each character in the character set is assigned a code value equivalent to its character code. Thus, in ASCII, "a" would have the code value 97, "b" would have the code value 98, etc.

Now assume that the input string is "ababc...." The first operation assumes that the prefix has a value of the null string, which we will indicate as the symbol "_." Thus, the first operation results in the addition of the null string to "a," which forms the new string "a." Because the "a" is in the dictionary, we do not output anything. However, because the suffix becomes the prefix, "a" now becomes the prefix for the next operation. This is illustrated in Table 13.1.

Processing the next character in the input string (b) results in the addition of the prefix (a) and the suffix (b) to form the new string (ab). Because this represents a new string that is not in the dictionary, we follow rule 2. That is, we output the last known string's encoding, which is 97 for the character "a" and then add the new string to the dictionary or string table. Concerning the latter, because codes 0 through 255 represent the individual

Table 13.1 Using LZW Compression for Encoding the String "ababc"

Prefix	Suffix	New String	Output
—	a	a	—
a	b	ab	97
b	a	ba	98
a	b	ab	—
ab	c	abc	256
c	—	c	99

characters in an 8-bit character set, we can use the code 256 to represent the string "ab." However, doing so obviously requires the token to be extended. Most LZW implementations use between 9 and 14 bits to represent a token whose length corresponds to the size of the dictionary. Next, "b," which was the suffix when generating the string "ab," becomes the prefix for the next operation, as indicated in row 3 in Table 13.1. Because the next character in the string to be encoded is "a," it functions as the suffix in creating the new string "ba." As that string is not presently in the string table, the last known string (b) is output using its ASCII code value of 98. Next, the string "ba" is added to the string table using the next available code, which is 256.

Because "a" was the suffix in creating the string "ab," it now becomes the prefix for the next string operation, as illustrated in row 4 in Table 13.1. The fourth character in the input string (b) is processed as the suffix to forming a new string. This results in the new string "ab," which was previously added to the string table. Because it is already in the string table, no output is generated and the string "ab" becomes the prefix for creating the next string.

Row 5 in Table 13.1 illustrates the creation of the next string. Here, the previously created string "ab" that was in the string table becomes the prefix for generating the next string, while the last character in the input data stream (c) becomes the suffix in forming the next string. The resulting string (abc) is not in the string table. Thus, the last known string "ab" has its code value output. Because "ab" was previously assigned the value 256, that value is output and the suffix (c) becomes the prefix for the creation of the next string. Because "c" was the last character in the input string, we simply output its code value of 99.

13.3.3 Performance Considerations

Although compression is standardized for use in modems, the same is not true for its use in remote bridges and routers. This means not only that vendor compression performing equipment will more likely than not fail to interoperate but, in addition, you may have to rely on vendor performance data. Unfortunately, some vendors have a tendency to place their equipment performance in the best possible light by transmitting files with a considerable degree of data redundancy and then claiming a high compression ratio, such as 4:1 or 5:1. If compression is an important equipment acquisition consideration, the author suggests that you create a set of files that are representative of your network traffic and have each vendor under consideration transfer those files and provide you with either their transmission time at a fixed WAN rate or their compression ratio.

13.4 Ethernet Frame Truncation

As noted in Chapter 2, Ethernet frames require a minimum length of 64 bytes, even when the frame carries just one information character. Thus, a query/response client/server communications session in which a work-station user on an Ethernet initiates queries by entering a few search characters results in the transmission of a frame with a large number of PAD characters to ensure that the minimum packet size of 64 bytes is reached.

13.4.1 Overhead

While the overhead associated with the use of PAD characters is relatively insignificant on a 10-Mbps 10BASE-T network, those PAD characters become more significant when frames are directed across a WAN transmission facility operating at a fraction of the LAN operating rate. Recognizing the effect of padded Ethernet frames on communications over WAN facilities, Advanced Computer Communications was among one of the first vendors to offer Ethernet frame truncation in its remote bridge and router products.

The use of frame truncation results in Ethernet padded frames having their PAD characters removed prior to transmission over a WAN. This results in the transmission of reduced-length frames that require less time to transmit. This technique also permits the remote bridge or router to strip PAD characters from minimum-length Ethernet frames as they are placed in memory, permitting more frames to be stored in memory as well as the faster servicing of frames when they are packetized and placed on the transmission line.

13.4.2 Utilization Example

As an example of the potential benefit obtained from the use of Ethernet frame truncation, consider a situation in which 20 stations on an Ethernet have users interactively working with a program located on a remote Token Ring network through remote bridges communicating at 19,200 bps. Let us assume a worst-case scenario in which each user simultaneously enters a query using a five-digit invoice number. Then, instead of five characters in the information field, each frame must contain 46 characters, including PAD characters to comply with the Ethernet minimum packet length standard. Without considering the overhead of the protocol used for transmitting frames from the Ethernet to the Token Ring network, this worst-case situation results in 20 * 46, or 920 bytes, presented to the remote bridge or router when only 20 * 5, or 100 bytes, actually require transmission. Then, the interactive traffic would use 920 * 8/19,200, or approximately 38 percent of the WAN bandwidth without Ethernet frame truncation. With Ethernet frame truncation, transmission would be reduced to 100 bytes, which would use 100 * 8/19,200, or approximately 4 percent of the WAN bandwidth.

13.5 Switched Network Use for Overcoming Congestion

One problem frequently encountered by network designers, managers, and analysts is determining the operating rate of a WAN transmission facility.

Almost all WAN transmission facilities are either leased analog or digital lines whose monthly cost is proportional to the data transmission rate they provide. Most organizations typically attempt to determine their busy-hour traffic and obtain a WAN transmission facility that provides an acceptable level of performance during the busy-hour. While this is a valid network design technique, it neither considers the use of a new class of equipment known as bandwidth-on-demand inverse multiplexers (BODIMs) nor the fact that in many organizations busy-hour transmission may considerably exceed normal transmission.

13.5.1 Using Bandwidth-on-Demand Inverse Multiplexers

To illustrate the use of bandwidth-on-demand inverse multiplexers (BODIMs), as well as a feature known as dial-on congestion incorporated into some remote bridges and routers, we need an example. Thus, let us assume that the network analysts determined that a fractional T1 line operating at 128 Kbps was required to interconnect two remote bridges at a cost of $4500 per month. Also assume that the cost of switched 56-Kbps transmission is $30 per hour. Further assume that during an eight-hour day, the WAN facility only requires 128 Kbps of bandwidth for 90 minutes, while the remainder of the workday, a bandwidth of 64 Kbps or less provides an acceptable level of performance.

Figure 13.6 illustrates the use of BODIMs that examine the flow of packets between remote bridges. As the flow of packets increases to the point where there is essentially no available bandwidth on the leased line for a pre-defined period of time, the multiplexer initiates a switched 56-Kbps call to the distant multiplexer. Based on our assumed cost of $30 per hour, switched 56-Kbps transmission for 90 minutes per day would result in a daily cost of $45, or $990 if there are 22 working days in the month. If a 64-Kbps fractional T1 line costs $2800 per month, the total cost of using a 64-Kbps leased line and supplementing its capacity via the use of switched 56-Kbps service would be $3790, not including the cost of the bandwidth-on-demand inverse multiplexers. Thus, in this example, the use of BODIM equipment would result in a monthly line cost reduction of $710.

13.5.2 Dial-On Congestion

To alleviate the cost of separate bandwidth-on-demand inverse multi-plexers, several vendors manufacturing remote bridges and routers have incorporated a dial-on-congestion capability into their products. This feature results in the use of a second port on a remote bridge or router for switched dial use during peak periods of activity

13.6 Network Interface Card

The network interface card (NIC) is a circuit board designed for insertion into the expansion slot of a specific type of computer, such as an IBM PC or

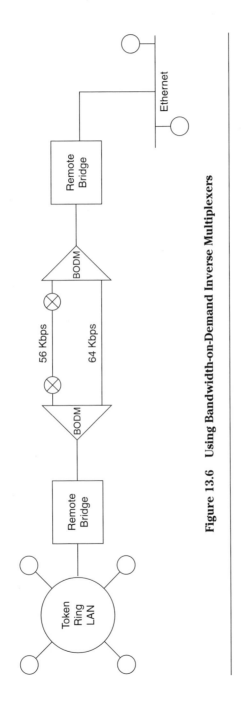

Figure 13.6   Using Bandwidth-on-Demand Inverse Multiplexers

compatible computer, a Micro Channel IBM PS/2 computer, or an Apple Macintosh. This card contains a series of chips or an integrated chip set that implements the network access protocol, as well as RAM memory, and other chips designed to perform specific functions. Both the hardware design and card functionality can have a considerable bearing on the ability of the adapter card to transfer data onto and receive data from the network.

13.6.1 Performance Considerations

The key to the ability of a NIC to transfer data onto and from a network is the method by which data transfer occurs between the adapter card and the computer in which it is inserted. Data transfer between the adapter card and the computer can be implemented in several ways, including direct memory access (DMA), I/O mapping, and shared memory.

13.6.1.1 DMA Interface. A direct memory access (DMA) interface is a data transfer technique in which the transfer of data between the adapter card and the computer's memory can occur simultaneously with other operations. To accomplish this, the DMA transfer is initiated by a board processor storing a starting and ending address and then initiating a DMA transfer operation, after which the processor can perform other operations during the time that data is transferred from the adapter card's memory to the workstation's memory. If the adapter card does not include an onboard processor, circuitry can be used to implement a DMA transfer. To accomplish this, an on-board buffer area on the adapter card receives data from the network. As the buffer fills, circuitry on the adapter recognizes this condition as a signal to generate a DMA transfer.

Although a DMA transfer permits the transfer of data from the NIC to the computer's memory to occur with other operations, it is generally slow in comparison to other methods of data transfer. The reason for this is due to the time required to set up and initiate a DMA transfer. A second factor that limits the capability of a DMA transfer is the fact that it requires contiguous memory in the host computer for its transfer operations. Because frames are often assembled from several different areas in memory, each DMA transfer may be limited to the amount of data that can be transferred.

13.6.1.2 I/O Mapping. I/O mapping is a data transfer mechanism based on the shared use of an I/O port between the adapter card and the host computer. This method of data transfer is faster than the use of a DMA transfer because it occurs at the I/O channel speed and eliminates the DMA transfer setup time.

13.6.1.3 Shared Memory. In a shared memory method of data transfer, a portion of the computer's memory is set up so that it can be used by both the adapter card and the computer. This results in a frame avoiding an actual transfer between the adapter and the computer, thus enhancing the data transfer between the computer and the network.

Most modern high-performance network adapter cards use some type of shared memory scheme to expedite the transfer of data from the computer to the network, and vice versa.

Typically, shared memory can be set up in increments of 16 Kbytes, from 16 to 64 Kbytes. Because the use of a LAN program and an application program will typically use a majority of conventional memory, many computers are limited to a setup in which only 16 Kbytes are used as shared memory. While this amount of memory will not adversely affect the operation of NICs connected to a 4-Mbps Token Ring or a 10-Mbps Ethernet network, the opposite can occur if you are connected to a 16-Mbps Token Ring network. This is because the 16-Mbps Token Ring network can have an information frame whose length can exceed 16 Kbytes.

In comparing the method used by the NIC (network interface card) for transferring data, performance can significantly differ based on the technique used. Although you may be tempted to simply select a vendor's adapter card based on their stated data transfer rate, there is one additional item you should consider prior to doing so. That additional item is the transfer rate of the hard disk of the computer in which you intend to install the NIC.

The transfer rate of the hard disk will vary based on the type of disk and disk controller used, as well as the bus interface of your computer. For example, antique PC XT computers have a disk I/O transfer capability under 1 Mbps. Thus, installing a shared memory network interface card with a 2-Mbps transfer capability would probably be extravagant because any sustained transfer of data to or from the computer's hard disk would be limited to 1 Mbps regardless of the type of NIC used. Thus, you should select a NIC in conjunction with the performance characteristics of the computer in which it is to be installed.

13.7 Change Network Routing and Advertising Protocols

The development of LANs can be traced to the 1970s, a period during which internetworking for many organizations consisted of linking together two networks in the same building. Protocols developed during that time period fall primarily into a category of protocols referred to as distance vector algorithms and have certain inefficiencies associated with their use that can adversely affect the level of performance when used with large networks. In this concluding section, we examine how changing your routing and advertising protocols can enhance the efficiency of your network. However, prior to doing so, let us discuss the difference between routing and advertising protocols so we have an understanding as to why they consume bandwidth and, under certain network topologies, can adversely affect communications between interconnected networks.

13.7.1 Routing Protocol

A routing protocol transfers information between network devices that provides them with the information necessary to route frames through a network. In a NetWare environment, the Routing Information Protocol (RIP) is an example of a routing protocol that facilitates the exchange of IPX packets.

The RIP can be classified as a distance vector algorithm in that it exchanges routing table information through periodic broadcasts to make network routers and servers aware of the current topology of the network. Distance vector algorithms use information stored and retrieved based on the distance in terms of the number of hops between networks, with each router considered to represent one hop.

The RIP used by Novell was based on the distance vector algorithm developed by Xerox and was originally designed for connecting small LANs together. Novell modified RIP to include a cost metric based on the original IBM PC's timer tick of about 1/18th of a second. When a RIP request is transmitted, the round-trip acknowledgment time is counted in terms of timer ticks and used as a decision criteria when two or more routes have the same hop count.

13.7.2 Advertising Protocol

In comparison to a routing protocol that seeks to find an optimum path through a network, an advertising protocol makes other devices aware of the presence of the device using the advertising protocol. One common example of an advertising protocol is NetWare's Service Advertisement Protocol (SAP).

In a NetWare environment, different types of servers advertise their presence by broadcasting a SAP every 60 seconds. While the bytes contained in a SAP packet have a minimal effect on network bandwidth, even when a network has 10, 20, or more servers, when two networks are interconnected by a wide area network, the effect of transmitting SAP packets becomes more pronounced and can considerably affect internetwork communications.

To illustrate how SAP packets can adversely affect inter-LAN communications that occur via WAN transmission facilities, consider Figure 13.7, which shows four LANs interconnected via three WAN circuits. In Figure 13.7, the arrows indicate the flow of SAP packets between networks, while squares with the letter S and a subscript numeric are used to identify a specific server. The table in the lower left portion of Figure 13.7 indicates the SAP flow by circuit. As indicated, the six-server internetwork will result in 12 SAP packets being transmitted every minute, or a total of 720 per hour, every hour.

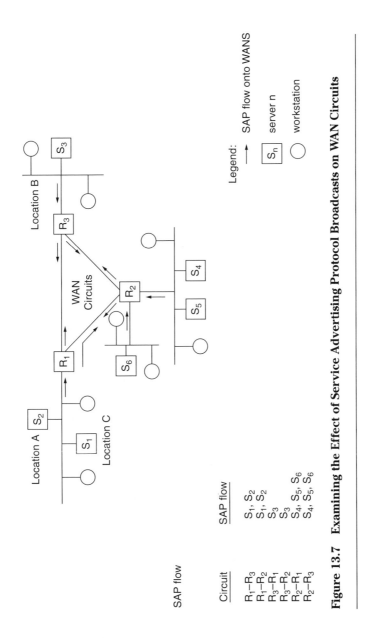

Figure 13.7   Examining the Effect of Service Advertising Protocol Broadcasts on WAN Circuits

SAP flow

Circuit	SAP flow
R_1–R_3	S_1, S_2
R_1–R_2	S_1, S_2
R_3–R_1	S_3
R_3–R_2	S_3
R_2–R_1	S_4, S_5, S_6
R_2–R_3	S_4, S_5, S_6

While the effect of a SAP on network users is negligible when transmission occurs on the LAN at an operating rate expressed in Mbps, when forwarding occurs across WAN circuits, the effect becomes more pronounced. For example, a 64-Kbps WAN represents approximately one 156th of the bandwidth of a 10-Mbps Ethernet LAN. Because NetWare's Service Advertisement Protocol is implemented as a distance vector algorithm, each server maintains a table of servers it knows and the routes to those servers. Thus, as an internetwork increases, the tables maintained by each server increases, resulting in longer data exchanges every 60 seconds or whenever there is a change in network topology.

13.7.3 NLSP

Recognizing the problems associated with distance vector protocols, several internetwork protocols were developed that result in the exchange of information by lengthening the interval between routing updates. In a NetWare environment, Novell developed a routing protocol called NetWare Link Services Protocol (NLSP) that significantly reduces bandwidth usage during router and server exchanges. To accomplish this, NLSP employs three databases: adjacency, link state, and forwarding.

The adjacency database keeps track of a router's immediate neighbors, to include servers and routers on the same LAN segment and the operational status of directly connected circuits. When a circuit becomes operational, the router periodically transmits "Hello" packets and listens for messages from its directly attached neighbors, with responses recorded in its adjacency databases.

Once neighbors are noted for each LAN segment, the NLSP selects a designated router. Here, the designated router represents all routers that provide traffic to a common circuit. Thus, a designated router can reduce traffic caused when two or more routers provide traffic onto a common circuit. In addition, the designated router maintains a link state database that includes portions of adjacency databases. Thus, the link state database can include information about other routers, which reduces the number of tables that must be exchanged. In addition, a link state database is only exchanged when changes to the database occur, further reducing overhead traffic.

The third database, the forwarding database, contains circuit costs based on an algorithm that identifies the shortest path between network nodes. Thus, this database that is created from information in the link state database governs how frames are forwarded.

In addition to significantly reducing the overhead required to perform routing on relatively low-capacity WAN circuits, the NLSP has several additional advantages. Those advantages include the use of IPX header compression, which further reduces overhead, as well as reduced router processing. The latter results from a decrease in routing table updates, which provides more CPU time for frame processing.

Because the NLSP eliminates both SAP and RIP traffic, it can provide additional bandwidth for low-speed WAN links that might otherwise require a costly upgrade. Due to its relative efficiency in comparison to RIP and SAP, those who operate NetWare should consider the use of this relatively new protocol.

Appendix A
Review Problems

The purpose of this appendix is twofold. First, the questions in this appendix provide readers with the ability to test their knowledge as they read each chapter. Second, questions in this appendix can be used by instructors as templates. Such templates provide the ability to develop homework assignments or examinations to test the knowledge of students or reinforce specific information covered in a course using this book.

Questions in this appendix are in chapter order, using the numbering system c.n, where c references the chapter and n simply references the question number for a specific chapter. Questions are included for Chapters 2 through 11, as the first chapter in this book primarily provides an overview of succeeding chapters and the last two chapters are oriented toward monitoring tools and optimization techniques.

Chapter 2: Ethernet, Token Ring, and ATM Frame and Cell Operations

2.1 Briefly describe how you could develop a program to discover the number of unique stations connected to an Ethernet or Token Ring LAN.

2.2 Define the functions of the following Ethernet fields:
Preamble
Start of frame delimiter
Destination address
Source address
Type/length
Frame check sequence

2.3 What does a destination address of all binary 1's indicate?

2.4 Briefly describe how you could develop a program to identify the manufacturer of the network adapter card that transmitted a LAN frame.

2.5 What is the purpose of the Gigabit Ethernet carrier extension field?

2.6 True or False: The efficiency of shared media Gigabit Ethernet is proportional to the length of the frames flowing on the network.

2.7 Explain how you could take advantage of the Ethernet frame overhead shown in Tables 2.1 and 2.2 when designing client/server applications.

2.8 What type of traffic adversely affects throughput obtainable on a Gigabit Ethernet LAN? Why does it adversely affect throughput?

2.9 Assume an Ethernet network's level of utilization begins to exceed 60 percent. List three options that you could use to reduce the level of network utilization.

2.10 What is the purpose of the Token Ring active monitor?

2.11 Describe the difference between a universally administrated address and a locally administrated address.

2.12 Given that an ATM cell has a 5-byte header and 48-byte payload, plot the percentage of overhead to total information bytes when your application needs to transfer 8, 16, 32, 64, 128, and 256 bytes of data.

2.13 How can ATM provide a Quality-of-Service capability?

Chapter 3: Estimating Network Traffic

3.1 True or False: When attempting to determine potential LAN activity, print jobs that flow to a remote printer may need to be considered as two separate data flows.

3.2 You were just hired by Mrs. Filberts Cookie Corporation as the network analyst. Your first job is to plan for the installation of an appropriate LAN. In interviewing personnel at Mrs. Filberts, you noted that all employees do the following work during the eight-hour workday:

a. Load a cookie sales program of 640K ten times per day.

b. Save the revised cookie sales program ten times per day.

c. Load a cookie design program of 640K ten times per day.

d. Print trial cookie designs of 10M twice per day.

3.3 Assume there are 200 employees at Mrs. Filberts. What, on average, is the expected data rate during an eight-hour workday, assuming an Ethernet LAN will be used?

Chapter 4: Understanding and Applying Waiting Line Analysis

4.1 Describe four types of waiting line systems with respect to channels and phases.

4.2 Assume your organization installed a router whose packet processing capability is 2000 per second. Based on the following packet arrival rate, draw the occupancy of the router's memory queue for times t_1 through t_{10}.

Time	Packet Arrival
t_1	0
t_2	1750
t_4	2250
t_5	2750
t_6	3000
t_7	3250
t_8	3500
t_9	1750
t_{10}	1500

4.3 Continuing your examination of the router service capacity and packet arrival rate described in Problem 4.2, describe what happens if the average length of a packet is 800 bytes and the router's buffer memory available for queuing packets is limited to 32,000 bytes of storage.

4.4 Assume constant arrival and service rates where the arrival rate is 10 frames/sec and the service rate is 12 frames/sec. At time (t) = 10 seconds, what is the size of the queue?

4.5 Assume the level of utilization of a service facility is 23.5 percent. What is the probability that the facility is empty?

4.6 Assume that the arrival rate of frames at a router varies as follows by seconds:

t = 0, 1,   t = 1, 3,   t = 2, 0,   t = 3, 6,   t = 4, 9

If the router service rate is fixed at 3 frames/sec, what is the router's queue length at t = 1, 2, 3, 4, and 5 seconds?

4.7 Under what conditions should you consider installing two circuits to interconnect distant locations, each operating at n/2 bps instead of one circuit operating at n bps?

4.8 *Waiting Line Analysis Practical Exercise:* Assume you were just hired by the industrial conglomerate McEars, Inc., as a senior network analyst. McEars has offices in Macon, Georgia, and Chicago, Illinois, and operates 100Base-T networks at each location. Currently, there is no connection between each local area network.

Your first project assignment at McEars is to determine an optimum line operating rate to interconnect the two isolated LANs. Based on an analysis of company-projected internetworking requirements, you determined the following information concerning the expected utilization of a leased line that would be installed to connect offices in Macon and Chicago:

The majority of inter-LAN communications will flow from corporate headquarters in Macon to Chicago, which enables you to select a line operating rate based on traffic flowing in that direction.

During the eight-hour workday, 600 e-mail messages can be expected to be transmitted from Macon to Chicago. The average length of an e-mail message is 1200 bytes, with 20 additional header bytes added when the message is transported on the expected wide area network (WAN) connection.

During the eight-hour workday, 20 files with an average file size of 2 Mbytes are expected to be transmitted from Macon to Chicago. Each frame transported on the WAN can be expected to have a header of 20 bytes added for the WAN protocol used to carry the frame between locations. Because the LAN frame preamble is stripped when the frame is encapsulated and transmitted on a WAN, assume that the maximum frame length on the WAN is 1538 bytes, to include the 20 bytes added by the WAN protocol.

Your assignment:

a. Compute the optimum line rate for a blended average of anticipated e-mail messages and file transfers during the eight-hour
workday. Explain the rationale behind your line operating rate
selection.

b. Assume you were able to determine that instead of transmission
occurring randomly but evenly over an eight-hour day a significant amount of traffic to include 300 e-mail messages and ten
files would be transmitted between 9 AM and 10 AM each day,
representing a busy-hour period. Does this change your line
operating rate selection? Explain.

Chapter 5: Sizing Communications Equipment and Line Facilities

Assume you located the following table of grades of service:

	Erlangs of Traffic		
Port	X	Y	Z
1	0.92	0.96	0.99
2	0.87	0.84	0.82
3	0.81	0.80	0.77
4	0.62	0.71	0.73
5	0.54	0.62	0.65
6	0.42	0.51	0.56
7	0.34	0.42	0.45
8	0.21	0.33	0.34
9	0.12	0.24	0.27
10	0.02	0.12	0.14
11	0.01	0.05	0.07

5.1 Assume the projected traffic is "Y" erlangs. How many ports will you
need to provide customers with a level of service such that only one
in eight calls encounters a busy signal?

5.2 Assuming traffic is now expected to be "X" erlangs, what number of
ports should be installed to provide customers with a 1 in 100
probability of encountering a busy signal?

5.3 Assume 5 erlangs of traffic are offered to a six-port access concentrator. Use the traffic analyzer program to determine the traffic carried
and traffic lost associated with each concentrator port.

Chapter 6: Using the Availability Level as a Decision Criterion

Assume your organization anticipates connecting LANs located in Macon,
Georgia, and Chicago, Illinois, via a 56-Kbps digital leased line using a pair

of data service units and two routers. Further assume that vandor literature suggests the following performance data concerning the equipment
you anticipate using:

	MTTF	MTTR
Data Service Unit	1 year	8 hours
Router	2 years	48 hours

When you contacted the telephone company, they told you that a typical 56-Kbps digital leased line can be expected to become inoperative six
times per year, with the average downtime being 30 minutes.

Assume you want to access a server in Chicago from a workstation in
Macon. According to Well Systems, which manufactured the servers
located in Chicago, its servers can be expected to fail once in a three-year
period and your organization's service contract provides for a maximum
downtime of 12 hours or Well Systems will replace the hardware. However,
if Well replaces the hardware, it will require an additional six hours to
restore data files onto the new computer.

Based on the preceding and not considering the performance level of
individual workstations on the Macon LAN, what level of availability do
you expect those stations to have when attempting to access the server in
Chicago, assuming:

6.1 A server failure in Chicago can be fixed without replacing hardware.
6.2 A server failure in Chicago that requires hardware to be replaced.

Chapter 7: Estimating Ethernet Network Performance

7.1 *LAN Throughput Practical Exercise:* Assume you are considering interconnecting 10-Mbps and 100-Mbps Ethernet networks that are
currently isolated networks. Let us assume from monitoring each
network you noted that LAN A, which operates at 10 Mbps, has an
average frame length of 640 bytes while LAN B, which operates at
100 Mbps, has an average frame length of 516 bytes. Further assume
than an average of four network users are on LAN A and three network
users are on LAN B. What is the expected throughput (in frames per
second) between networks? Note that you can use the LAN throughput predictor model or apply pen to paper to solve this problem.

7.2 In reviewing the specifications for shared media Gigabit Ethernet,
you noted that the minimum frame length is 520 bytes on a LAN.
a. Determine the frame rate for Gigabit Ethernet at 100 percent load for:
   i.   Minimum-length frames
   ii. Maximum-length frames

b. Compare Fast Ethernet's frame rate to shared Gigabit. Do so for both the frame rate and information transfer capacity.

Chapter 8: Estimating Token Ring Network Performance

8.1 Assume your organization operates a 50-station, 16-Mbps Token Ring network that is running at a high level of utilization and management is considering replacing the network. After examining the cable plant and putting a monitor on the network, you determined that 10,000 feet of existing cable could be reduced by 4000 feet. You also noted that the average frame length on the network is 128 bytes. Using Table 8.2, what could you tell management concerning the potential replacement of the network?

Chapter 9: ATM Performance

9.1 Discuss why the payload capacity of ATM operating at 155.520 Mbps can be as low as 113.0264 Mbps.

9.2 Discuss why LAN emulation reduces the throughput obtainable on an ATM network.

Chapter 10: Working with Images

10.1 Assume you anticipate placing a 3×5-inch photograph on your organization's Web site. You first use a 600-dot-per-inch scanner with a 24-bit color depth to scan the image onto a file. Determine the amount of storage required to store the image. Next, assuming a majority of customers access your Web site using 56-Kbps modems and the transmission overhead is 15 percent, how long will it take to download the image?

10.2 Assuming the image parameters described in Problem 10.1, and assuming you converted the image to JPEG and achieved a 30:1 data reduction, what would be the effect on modem downloads?

10.3 Jimmy just sent you a postcard of downtown Macon. It is so quaint that you decided to post it on your Web site. You decide to set your scanner to a resolution of 300 dots per inch vertical and horizontal. Assuming you scan the 3×5-inch postcard using a 24-bit color depth, what storage (in bytes) will be required if no compression occurs?

10.4 Assume your organization operates a popular Web server. That server has a JPEG picture on its home page that requires 200,000 bytes of storage while the text on the page requires 1000 bytes.

a. Assume your server receives 30,000 hits per day. Also assume that your organization's ISP bill for Internet access is $1200 per month plus $0.01 per Mbyte transmitted per month. What is the monthly cost for Internet access, assuming all hits are to the home page and there are 30 days in the month?

b. Assume you use a tool to compress and/or crop the JPEG to 50,000 bytes. What is the effect on the cost of monthly Internet access?

10.5 You just purchased a Bozo scanner that can be set to scan images at 150, 300, 450, and 600 dots per inch. Your just picked up the color photographs from your vacation in Tibliz and noted the monument to CVS was outstanding and would like to place it on your corporate Web page. You scanned the 3×5-inch photograph using a resolution of 300 lines per inch and a color depth of 30 bits per pixel. Your corporate Web home page is currently all text and has 1500 bytes of data. What is the storage (in bytes) required for placing the monument to CVS on your corporate Web page?

Chapter 11: Using Intelligent Switches

11.1 Assume you acquired a 64 port 10Base-T port switch. What is the maximum theoretical data transfer capacity of the switch?

11.2 Continuing Problem 11.1, assume you plan to connect 12 servers and 48 workstations to the switch. What is the maximum practical throughput through the switch you can expect when workstations operate in a client/server environment?

11.3 Suppose you looked at the vendor specification for the switch mentioned in Problem 11.2. If the specification indicates a backplane transfer rate of 100 Mbps, will this represent a problem? Why or why not?

11.4 Describe two methods of flow control supported by an Ethernet LAN switch.

11.5 Compute the delay associated with an Ethernet 10BASE-T store-and-forward switch on a per-frame basis for maximum and minimum length frames.

Index

393